OXFORD DATA PROTECTION AND PRIVACY LAW

Series Editors

CHRISTOPHER KUNER

Professor of Law, VUB Brussels

GRAHAM GREENLEAF

Professor of Law and Information Systems, University of New South Wales

The Risk-Based Approach to Data Protection

OXFORD DATA PROTECTION AND PRIVACY LAW

Series Editors

Christopher Kuner, Professor of Law, VUB Brussel
Graham Greenleaf, Professor of Law and Information Systems,
University of New South Wales

The aim of this series is to publish important and original books on legal issues of data protection and privacy. This includes many different areas of law, including comparative law, EU law, human rights law, international law, privacy on the Internet, and others.

Prospective authors are welcome to submit proposals for the series, as outlined on the series website: global.oup.com/academic/content/series/o/oxford-data-protection-and-privacy-law-odppl/

The Risk-Based Approach to Data Protection

RAPHAËL GELLERT
Radboud University

OXFORD
UNIVERSITY PRESS

OXFORD
UNIVERSITY PRESS

Great Clarendon Street, Oxford, OX2 6DP,
United Kingdom

Oxford University Press is a department of the University of Oxford.
It furthers the University's objective of excellence in research, scholarship,
and education by publishing worldwide. Oxford is a registered trade mark of
Oxford University Press in the UK and in certain other countries

First Edition published in 2020

Published in the United States of America by Oxford University Press
198 Madison Avenue, New York, NY 10016, United States of America

British Library Cataloguing in Publication Data

Data available

Library of Congress Control Number: 2020937905

ISBN 978–0–19–883771–8

Printed and bound by
CPI Group (UK) Ltd, Croydon, CR0 4YY

Series Editors' Preface

Data protection law has been undergoing a revolution in recent years. The laws enacted in the 1990s and early 2000s have generally been found inadequate to cope with the intensification of data processing by both the private and public sectors, which has led to the adoption of new data protection legislation in all regions of the world.

In the course of these legislative projects, questions have arisen about the approach that data protection law should take. One of the most frequent issues has concerned the significance that should be put on risks to data processing, which have been addressed under the general rubric of the "risk-based approach". This term seems to mean different things to different audiences, and has been the source of controversy: to some, it means focusing only on privacy "harm" (itself an elusive concept), which would seem to lead inevitably to a decrease in the level of protection; while to others, it indicates an approach to compliance that puts the greatest attention on the greatest data protection risks. At the same time, the increasing complexity of legislation has led data protection to become more and more of a risk-management exercise, which has made it imperative to clarify the relationship between the management of risks and the rights-based approach upon which most data protection laws are based.

This gap has now been filled by this important book by Raphaël Gellert. Untainted by any ideological agenda, the author provides a sober, scholarly examination of the legal and policy issues raised by the risk-based approach. The author goes beyond legal issues to also consider regulatory theory and demonstrates that a rights-based view of data protection and legal methods based on risk analysis need not necessarily be seen as antagonists. He also goes beyond legal analysis to consider how the responsibility for data protection operates in practice (or "on the ground"). The book displays a sovereign command not only of EU data protection law, but also of developments in other regions. As concepts based on risk analysis (such as data protection impact assessments) are increasingly incorporated into data protection law, the analysis provided in the book will become even more valuable.

This book makes a significant contribution to EU data protection law, regulatory theory, and the interface between the two. We are thus pleased to include it in our series.

Christopher Kuner and Graham Greenleaf

Preface

This book is a reworked version of my PhD thesis, which I defended at the Vrije Universiteit Brussel in June 2017. Its ambition is twofold. First, it provides an understanding of what exactly the risk-based approach to data protection actually means and how it translates in practice. Second, it seizes this encounter between data protection law, risk, and regulation, as an opportunity to provide an analysis of data protection in the light of regulation theory and risk literature. Dealing with various disciplines and literatures is a challenging exercise and I have strived to treat each discipline with the respect they deserve.

Writing this book has been a challenging journey, which I could not have accomplished on my own. There are too many persons to mention and thank, so I would like to limit myself to the following.

First, I would like to thank my two co-promoters: Prof Serge Gutwirth, whose commitment to slow science gave me the freedom and space to satiate my intellectual curiosity; Prof Paul De Hert for always being there for me and for providing me with great advice and support. Prof Veerle Heyvaert was the external member of my supervisory committee. Her attentive reading of my draft chapters and incisive remarks were tremendously helpful. I would also like to thank all the members of my jury: Prof Mireille Hildebrandt, Prof Gloria Gonzàlez-Fuster, Prof Christopher Kuner, Prof Ronald Leenes, and Prof Daniel Le Métayer. They all provided me with many valuable comments, which have been integrated in this book.

The research that led to the completion of the PhD would not have been possible without the following financial support. The European Union through its 7th Framework Programme (grant agreements no 244779 and no 261698), the Fonds Wetenschappelijk Onderzoek–Flanders (FWO) in the context of the research project no G046815N, and the Belgian American Education Foundation (BAEF) through its support of my year as a visiting researcher at the University of California, Berkeley.

I would like to thank the anonymous reviewers from Oxford University Press for their extremely helpful feedback and comments. I would also like to thank Oxford University Press for their editorial assistance, and in particular Natalie Patey and Brianne Bellio.

I would also like to thank my family for their continuous love and affection. Finally, I would like to express my love and gratitude to Maša for her love and support throughout this journey.

Raphaël Gellert

Table of Contents

Table of Authorities

CASES

European Court of Human Rights

Court of Justice of the EU

Germany

United Kingdom

United States

STATUTES

APEC

COUNCIL OF EUROPE

EUROPEAN UNION

Primary Law

Secondary Law

OECD

UNITED NATIONS

NATIONAL

Canada

List of Abbreviations

AI	Artificial intelligence
ALARA	As low as reasonably achievable
ALARP	As low as is reasonably possible
APEC	Asia-Pacific Economic Cooperation
Art 29 WP	Article 29 Working Party
BATNEEC	Best available technology not entailing excessive cost
BSI	German Federal Bureau for Data Security
CIPL	Centre for Information Policy Leadership
CJEU	Court of Justice of the European Union
CNIL	Commission nationale de l'informatique et des libertés
CoE	Council of Europe
CSA	Canadian Standards Association
DPA	Data Protection Authority
DPBD	Data Protection by Design
DPD	Data Protection Directive
DPIA	Data Protection Impact Assessment
DPO	Data Protection Officer
ECHR	European Convention on Human Rights
ECtHR	European Court of Human Rights
EDPB	European Data Protection Board
EDPS	European Data Protection Supervisor
EIA	Environmental Impact Assessments
EU	European Union
EUCFR	European Union Charter for Fundamental Rights
FCRA	US Fair Credit Reporting Act
FIPPS	fair information practice principles
FSA	Financial Services Authority
FTC	Federal Trade Commission
GDPR	General Data Protection Regulation
ICO	Information Commissioner's Office
IoT	Internet of Things
ISO	International Organization for Standardization
KDD	Knowledge discovery in databases
NIST	National Institute of Standards and Technology
NSA	National Security Agency
OECD	Organisation for Economic Co-operation and Development
PbD	Privacy by Design
PCAST	US President's Council of Advisors on Science and Technology
PETs	Privacy Enhancing Technologies

PIA	Privacy Impact Assessment
PIPEDA	Personal Information Protection and Electronic Documents Act
PMP	Privacy management program
QRA	Quantitative risk assessment
RFID	Radio frequency identification
STS	Science and technology studies
TA	Technology assessment
TFEU	Treaty on the Functioning of the European Union

Introduction

The risk-based approach as the opposite of the rights-based approach, or as an opportunity to analyse the links between law, regulation, and risk?

1. The risk-based approach: a contradiction in terms?

The goal of this book is to provide an understanding of what has been referred to as the risk-based approach to data protection.[1] Data protection can be defined as a set of "legal rules and instruments designed to protect the rights, freedoms, and interests of individuals whose personal data are stored, processed and disseminated by computers".[2] In turn, the risk-based approach refers to a trend that has emerged since the late 2000s/early 2010s, and which consists in enshrining risk management tools in data protection legal frameworks, in order to have better chances of achieving—or so it is contented—the protection of citizens' personal data. Even though the use of risk management tools is not limited to the EU, it should be mentioned from the outset, that the expression "risk-based approach" is a specificity of the EU debate insofar as it appeared during the reform process which led to the adoption of the so-called General Data Protection Regulation (GDPR),[3] replacing the 1995 EU Data Protection Directive (DPD).[4]

The introduction of risk tools in this legal framework might appear *prima facie* as startling. One can indeed argue that "rights and risks traditionally belong within different spheres of knowledge, practice, and social organisation. Rights typically belong to legal practices where they become articulated through legal concepts and procedures. Risks often belong to risk management practices, and are typically

[1] Art 29 WP, "Statement on the Role of a Risk-Based Approach in Data Protection Legal Frameworks" (2014).

[2] Frits W Hondius, *Emerging Data Protection in Europe* (North-Holland; American Elsevier 1975) 1.

[3] Regulation (EU) 2016/679 of the European Parliament and of the Council of 27 April 2016 on the protection of natural persons with regard to the processing of personal data and on the free movement of such data, and repealing Directive 95/46/EC (General Data Protection Regulation, [2016], *OJ L 119/1*.

[4] Directive 95/46/EC of the European Parliament and of the Council of 24 October 1995 on the protection of individuals with regard to the processing of personal data and on the free movement of such data *O J L 281*, 23/11/1995 pp 0031–0050.

The Risk-Based Approach to Data Protection. Raphaël Gellert, Oxford University Press (2020). © Raphaël Gellert.
DOI: 10.1093/oso/9780198837718.001.0001.

defined through scientific concepts of probability in dealing with the possibilities of futures events."[5]

In less conceptual terms, the topic of a risk-based approach has stirred quite some controversy, in particular during the adoption process of the GDPR (formally 2012–2016, but in practice more closely to 2009–2016). It has been portrayed as furthering the interests of the corporate agenda,[6] and more in general as a loosening of data protection provisions. In particular, the main fears and arguments against it argued that it would lead to a "US" harms-based type of protection, which goes directly counter the EU fundamental rights-based nature of data protection. In this sense, the discussions around the risk-based approach can also be seen as a forum opposing two radically opposing conceptions of what data protection is about and how it should be implemented. One that is EU flavoured and "rights-based",[7] and one that is US flavoured (or influenced to say the least) and is "risk/harm-based".

These two approaches can be contrasted in a number of ways.[8] First, one can point to a difference in their logic and *modus operandi*. The rights-based approach is a traditional legal approach, entailing that it follows a binary logic: a processing is either legal or illegal. Either it complies with the data protection core principles, or it does not. The risk-based approach displays a very different logic. Namely, the granular, scalable, logic of risk analysis: it is less a matter of whether the processing is too risky or not, than a matter of determining how much risk one can take (concerning a processing operation).

Second, these approaches might lead to a different type of protection. A rights-based framework applies the same rules to everyone irrespective of the level of risk or harm,[9] and therefore provides for a "minimum and non-negotiable level of protection for all individuals".[10] This is all the more so since the entry into force of the EU Charter of Fundamental Rights (EUCFR) which enshrines the right to personal data protection (Article 8), and which has therefore granted it the status

[5] Niels van Dijk, Raphaël Gellert, and Kjetil Rommetveit, "A Risk to a Right? Beyond Data Protection Risk Assessments" (2016) 32 Computer Law & Security Review 286, 289.

[6] See eg the support it gathered from Vodafone, "A Comprehensive Approach on Personal Data Protection in the European Union: Vodafone's Response" (2010) http://ec.europa.eu/justice/news/consulting_public/news_consulting_0006_en.htm, last accessed 06 February 2019; EUROFINAS, "Response to the European Commission's Consultation on the Commission's Comprehensive Approach on Personal Data Protection in the European Union" (2011); DigitalEurope, "Consultation on the Legal Framework for the Fundamental Right to Protection of Personal Data" (2009); DigitalEurope, "DIGITALEUROPE Comments on the Risk-Based Approach" 1.

[7] See eg Orla Lynskey, *The Foundations of EU Data Protection Law* (OUP 2015) 35–40.

[8] These arguments have been developed in Raphaël Gellert, "We Have Always Managed Risks in Data Protection Law: Understanding the Similarities and Differences Between the Rights-Based and Risk-Based Approaches to Data Protection" (2016) 4 European Data Protection Law Review 481.

[9] See Lynskey (n 7) 2 D. See also, *Amann v Switzerland* App No 27798/95 (ECtHR, 16 February 2000) §70: in order to determine whether a processing constitutes an interference, the fact that the data subject may "have been inconvenienced in any way" is irrelevant.

[10] Art 29 WP, "Opinion 1/98 Platform for Privacy Preferences (P3P) and the Open Profiling Standard (OPS)" (1998) 2.

of fundamental right of the EU.[11] Instead of applying the various data protection principles in an equal way, the risk-based approach first assesses the risks presented by a contemplated data processing operation, and second, decides on this basis whether to undertake operation at stake (ie it manages the risks). In this sense, it is the exact counterpart of the rights-based approach, since it is predicated upon the level of risk at stake and upon calculations in terms of harms and benefits. That is, the risk-based approach provides a protection that is by definition uneven insofar as it directly depends upon the level of risk at stake for each specific processing operation. Even more so, some have raised the concern that the risk-based approach would only apply to situations of high-risk,[12] and might, at the end of the day simply amount to a blank check for data controllers.[13]

At the height of the EU institutional debate surrounding the adoption of a risk-based approach in the GDPR (following the Council of the EU's adoption of a draft chapter IV under the Irish presidency),[14] the—then—Article 29 Working Party (Art 29 WP),[15] weighed in on the meaning of the risk-based approach. It made sure to sustain the distinction between risk- and rights-based approaches, and to emphasise that the EU data protection legal framework fundamentally pertains to a rights-based approach. As it put it, "the risk-based approach is being increasingly and wrongly presented as an alternative to well-established data protection rights and principles,"[16] entailing that it couldn't accept the point of view whereby "legal compliance should shift to (. . .) a strong harm-based approach".[17]

Instead of simply confirming this opposition and building upon it, one of the key objectives of the present book is precisely to (re)contextualise these debates and stark oppositions, and to see them in another light/through other lenses, namely, the analysis of the links between law, regulation, and risk. As a matter of fact, the introduction of risk management tools in legal frameworks is far from being a total novelty, with environmental law being a prime

[11] See Gloria González Fuster, *The Emergence of Personal Data Protection as a Fundamental Right of the EU* (Springer 2014).

[12] See eg the discussion in Christopher Kuner and others, "Risk Management in Data Protection" (2015) 5 International Data Privacy Law 95, 98.

[13] See Chris Jay Hoofnagle, "The Potemkinism of Privacy Pragmatism" *Slate* (2014) 1; Ann Cavoukian, "Evolving FIPPs: Proactive Approaches to Privacy, Not Privacy Paternalism" in Serge Gutwirth, Ronald Leenes, and Paul De Hert (eds), *Reforming European Data Protection Law* (Springer 2015).

[14] Council of the European Union, "Proposal for a Regulation of the European Parliament and of the Council on the Protection of Individuals with Regard to the Processing of Personal Data and on the Free Movement of Such Data (General Data Protection Regulation) - Key Issues of Chapters I-I" (2013).

[15] Now European Data Protection Board (EDPB). The present book still refers to the Art 29 WP where appropriate given that the EDPB has endorsed all Art 29 WP documents, but they remain authored by the Art 29 WP, see EDPB, "Endorsement 1/2018" (2018).

[16] Art 29 WP (n 1) 2.

[17] ibid 2–3.

example.[18,19] Since the early 2000s, financial law has also resorted to risk management as a specific duty for the financial institutions concerned. Among these, one can think of the pioneering US 2002 Sarbanes-Oxley Act,[20] and more recently, of the Third Basel Accord of 2011.[21] More recently even, the field of cybersecurity has witnessed the emergence of a risk-based approach, which also consists in bestowing risk management duties upon regulated organisations.[22] The main way in which the present book approaches this less than obvious merger between risk and law is through the notion of regulation. It has now long been acknowledged that risk can be used as a method of regulation, and this is particularly the case when risk management duties are enshrined in legal frameworks.[23]

To be clear, the reason why data protection is analysed from this standpoint is because the use of risk management tools now enshrined in the GDPR certainly does not come from *ex nihilo*. On the contrary, it is a regulatory model that has been used in other fields for quite some time now. Thus, instead of accepting the risk-based approach as a given, and as a starting point for an analysis, the present book tries to go back to its very rationale. In other words, if data protection is a fundamental right of the EU, how is it possible then to apply thereto a model of regulation, which itself is dependent upon risk management tools? If rights-based and risk-based versions of data protection law were as antithetical as the opposition purports, how come then that it has been possible to successfully adopt the GDPR with a risk-based approach at its core? Answering this question requires study of the links between data protection (law) and regulation, and between regulation and risk. Again, if the risk-based approach is simply the latest avatar of a series of regulation models, this must mean that data protection has *something* to do with regulation in the first place (thus, including in its rights-based version). In other words, the study of the risk-based approach from the perspective of risk, regulation, law, and their multiple entanglements might not only help us elucidate the meaning and scope of the risk-based approach per se. It might also tell us something about data protection law itself in the first place.

[18] Elizabeth Fisher, "Risk and Environmental Law: A Beginner's Guide" in Benjamin J Richardson and Stephan Wood (eds), *Environmental Law for Sustainability* (Hart Publishing 2006); see eg Nicolas de Sadeleer, *EU Environmental Law and the Internal Market* (OUP 2014).

[19] See also, EU Directive 2007/60/EC on the assessment and management of flood risks European Parliament and Council of the European Union, Directive 2007/60/EC of the European Parliament and of the Council of 23 October 2007 on the assessment and management of flood risks 2007 OJ L 288/27.

[20] United States Code, Sarbanes-Oxley Act of 2002, PL 107-204, 116 Stat 745, Codified in Sections 11, 15, 18, 28, and 29 USC, July 2002.

[21] Seehttp://www.bis.org/bcbs/basel3.htm.

[22] OECD, "Cybersecurity Policy Making at a Turning Point: Analysing a New Generation of National Cybersecurity Strategies for the Internet Economy" (2012).

[23] See eg Tanina Rostain, "Self-Regulatory Authority, Markets, and the Ideology of Professionalism", *The Oxford Handbook of Regulation* (OUP 2010).

2. On the links between law and regulation

The relationship between law and regulation is an uneasy one. At the most general, Black has likened the definition of regulation with Foucault's definition of the exercise of power in the context to what he has referred to as "governmentality", and which he has defined as "the conduct [of others'] conduct".[24] On this basis, Black has provided one of the most quintessential definitions of regulation as "the process involving the sustained and focused attempt to alter the behaviour of others according to defined standards or purposes with the intention of producing a broadly defined outcome or outcomes".[25]

As Black argues, at their broadest, definitions of regulation and law could simply be re-descriptions of one another, since both are concerned with "the set of norms which actors abstract from practice and invest with binding authority".[26]

Yet, the relationship between the two is an uneasy one. According to various scholars in the legal field, "regulation is less than law" insofar as it is just a subset of law, so-called "regulatory law" (which can be subsumed broadly speaking under public and administrative law),[27] and pertains to the achievement of social policy goals, or, as Black puts it, "regulatory law encodes the principles and instrumentality of the welfare state".[28] Similarly, it has been argued that the purely instrumental nature of regulation does not allow to take into account the broader concerns of law such as the values associated with the rule of law,[29] or with the practice of law itself.[30] Not to mention that, *prima facie*, regulation does not perform all the legal functions such as dispute resolution for instance.[31]

In an equal measure, the regulation community has also seen "law as less than regulation" insofar as it is just one of the regulatory instruments that have been mobilised in the pursuit of regulatory activity.[32] As regulatory activity has evolved,

[24] Julia Black, "Decentring Regulation: Understanding the Role Self-Regulation in a 'Post-Regulatory' World" (2001) 54 Current Legal Problems 103, 108. For Foucault's definition, see, "Governmentality" in James D Faubion (ed), *Power: Essential Work of Michel Foucault* (Penguin 2001).

[25] Black (n 24) 142.

[26] Julia Black, "Critical Reflections on Regulation" (2002) 27 Australian Journal of Legal Philosophy 1, 24.

[27] See eg William Twining, *Globalisation & Legal Theory* (Butterworths 2000).

[28] Black (n 26) 24.

[29] See eg Mireille Hildebrandt, "A Vision of Ambient Law" in Roger Brownsword and Karen Yeung (eds), *Regulating Technologies: Legal Futures, Regulatory Frames and Technological Fixes* (Hart Publishing 2008).

[30] Serge Gutwirth, Paul De Hert, and Laurent de Sutter, "The Trouble with Technology Regulation: Why Lessig's 'Optimal Mix' Will Not Work" in Roger Brownsword and Karen Yeung (eds), *Regulating Technologies: Legal Futures, Regulatory Frames and Technological Fixes* (Hart Publishing 2008); Serge Gutwirth, "Providing the Missing Link: Law after Latour's Passage" in Kyle McGee (ed), *Latour and the Passage of Law* (Edinburgh University Press 2015).

[31] See eg KN Llewellyn, "The Normative, the Legal, and the Law-Jobs: The Problem of Juristic Method" (1940) 49 The Yale Law Journal 1355.

[32] Black (n 26) 25. See eg Peter Goodrich, *Languages of Law: From Logics of Memory to Nomadic Masks* (Butterworths 1990).

so have definitions of regulation and its links with law. Initially, the canonical definition of regulation as "command and control" was equated to law. More in particular, regulation was thus seen as "the promulgation of rules accompanied by mechanisms for monitoring and enforcement".[33] Definitions have evolved in order to include additional "techniques" such as any form of state intervention, and beyond, "all mechanisms of social control or influence affecting behaviour from whatever source, whether intentional or not".[34] This has included, among others, the increasing role of a wide range of institutional actors in defining the regulatory process.[35] However, and more importantly, as Black observes, "the thing that is doing the regulating is increasingly broadened".[36] This is why for some, regulation can be effectuated by market forces (ie interaction of buyers and sellers, etc), whereas for others yet, regulation is the outcome of social forces such as cultural and social norms. Finally, technologies have been seen as one of the most important *loci* of regulatory activity.[37]

However, the relation between these various "tools"[38] (or more broadly forms of control) with regulation remain unclear, for the nature itself of regulation is unclear: is it a type of instrument, a process, an outcome, or even a property?[39] It is still unclear whether these various forms of controls (ie markets, social norms, etc) are constitutive of regulation itself, or whether "they are simply instruments that may or may not be employed in the activity of regulation".[40] These reflections are equally valid as far as the relationship between law and regulation are concerned, and are precisely encapsulated in the relationship between law and regulation, which are simultaneously more and less than one another.

Yet, and beyond these discussions, there are important links between law and regulation, which are clearly visible in the fact that classical command and control regulation has been equated to public, regulatory, law, or in the fact that for most scholars of regulation, the instrumental dimension of law makes little doubt.[41] As Black argues, there is clearly an overlap between the two, not least because they might be appraising the same set of social and political activities.[42]

As a matter of fact, the overlap is so important that a number of issues encapsulated under the regulation literature have been discussed for a long time in the legal

[33] Black (n 24) 129.

[34] ibid.

[35] See eg John Braithwaite and Peter Drahos, *Global Business Regulation* (Cambridge University Press 2008).

[36] Black (n 24) 132.

[37] ibid, and the references therein.

[38] See eg Lawrence Lessig, *Code 2.0* (Basic Books 2006).

[39] Black (n 24) 133.

[40] ibid 138.

[41] See eg Bronwen Morgan and Karen Yeung, *An Introduction to Law and Regulation: Text and Materials* (Cambridge University Press 2007); Karen Yeung, *Securing Compliance: A Principled Approach* (Hart Publishing 2004).

[42] Black, "Critical Reflections on Regulation" (n 26) 26.

theory literature. One can think of course about Hart's reflections on law and commands,[43] or Dworkin's distinctions between rules and principles.[44] These various analyses bear very close resemblance with regulation literature on the topics of standard setting, application of rules, etc. Similarly, many issues concerning the implementation of regulation models have an obvious kinship with the legal realism movement, which is probably best epitomised by Pound's century old distinction between "law in the books" and "law in action".[45] This book has made a conscious choice not to resort to legal theory literature *sensu latu*. Given the fact that the risk-based approach spurs a number of reflections situated at the crossroads of data protection, regulation, and risk, the present book resorts to three main bodies of literature: data protection law scholarship,[46] regulation literature,[47] and risk and risk management literature.[48]

3. On data protection as regulation

In line with these theoretical discussions on the overlapping scope and definitions of law and regulation, the understanding of data protection as pertaining to regulatory activity can in fact be traced back to its earliest days. For its emergence accompanied the development of a then novel technology—the computer. Data protection was indeed born in the context of "growing concern that automated personal data systems present a serious potential for harmful consequences, including infringement of basic liberties".[49] In other words, data protection law was seen since its inception as a legal framework, the goal of which was to tame technology, that is, to regulate it.

This appears quite clearly from Hondius' discussion of the characteristics of data protection statutes. He refers to the need to have legal instruments that can provide adequate protection against science and technology.[50] Burkert holds a similar reasoning when saying that "data protection regulations are thus part of a new type of regulations caused by technological changes", the function of which is therefore to

[43] HLA Hart, *The Concept of Law* (2nd edn, Clarendon Press 1994).

[44] Ronald Dworkin, "The Model of Rules" (1967) 35 The University of Chicago Law Review 14.

[45] Roscoe Pound, "Law in Books and Law in Action" (1910) 44 American Law Review 12. In a similar vein, one can also mention the institutionalist movement, see Neil MacCormick, *Institutions of Law: An Essay in Legal Theory* (OUP 2007).

[46] One can argue that the past decade and a half has seen the rise of a new field of academic inquiry dedicated to data protection law. It is probably best epitomised by the annual edited books, which stem from the Computers, Privacy, and Data Protection (CPDP) conference, see eg Ronald Leenes and others (eds), *Data Protection and Privacy: The Internet of Bodies* (Hart Publishing 2018).

[47] See eg Robert Baldwin, Collin Scott, and Christopher Hood (eds), *A Reader on Regulation* (OUP 1998).

[48] See eg Peter Taylor-Gooby and Jens Zinn (eds), *Risk in Social Science* (OUP 2006).

[49] US Department of Health Education & Welfare, *Records, Computers, and the Rights of Citizens* (The MIT Press 1973) viii.

[50] Hondius (n 2) 6.

reconcile basic values (ie fundamental rights) with technological change and development.[51] Interestingly, Burkert also argued that the role of data protection as a matter of taming the effects of technology onto society could be paralleled to exercises of technology assessment.[52]

Further, data protection's goal of taming technology was also explicitly framed as an issue of regulation. This is maybe best expressed by Miller who argues that "there is a strong similarity between the difficulties that gave rise to the complex and multifaceted regulation of the airlines, railroads, radio, and television and the problems that already are generating pressure for the regulation of computer transmissions and facilities in both the public and private sectors".[53] The so-called Ware Report also argued that processing of personal data "should be regulated by specific laws",[54] and Hondius saw data protection legislation as "the legal regulation of computers".[55] Some even already made the link with environmental protection and sustainable development, arguing that contrary to what had been done with the environment, there was a dire need not to leave the regulation of the computer to future generations.[56] As Bennett puts it, "data protection fairly rapidly became the rallying call for those seeking the regulation of information technology".[57]

One might counter-argue however that it is not uncommon to say that data protection law aims to regulate the processing of personal data, that as a matter of fact, it is a well-rehearsed trope. Be that as it may, the ambition of this book is to go beyond such tropes, and to take seriously the claim that data protection regulates. What does it mean to understand data protection as pertaining to regulatory activity? What can be learned therefrom, if anything? Further, what would be so different about data protection law, if it were conceived of in regulatory terms? One way to start this enquiry is by paying attention to the particular relation existing between regulation and risk.

[51] Herbert Burkert, "Institutions of Data Protection—An Attempt at a Functional Explanation of European National Data" (1981) 3 Computer Law Journal 167, 170, 173.

[52] Herbert Burkert, "Privacy—Data Protection: A German/European Perspective", *2nd Symposium of the Max Planck Project Group on the Law of Common Goods and the Computer Science and Telecommunications Board of the National Research Council* (1999) 56.

[53] Arthur R Miller, *The Assault on Privacy: Computers, Data Banks, and Dossiers* (The University of Michigan Press 1971) 8.

[54] US Department of Health Education & Welfare (n 49) 7.

[55] Frits W Hondius, "Data Law in Europe" (1980) 16 Stanford Journal of International Law 87. See also Mayer-Schönberger, for whom data protection law was to be seen as "an attempt to regulate technology", Viktor Mayer-Schönberger, "Generational Development of Data Protection in Europe" in Philip E Agre and Marc Rotenberg (eds), *Technology and Privacy: The New Landscape* (MIT Press 1997) 227.

[56] Which would otherwise "spawn new generations of computers or stockpile huge stores of personal data", Miller (n 53) 8.

[57] Colin J Bennett, *Regulating Privacy* (Cornell University Press 1992) 76.

4. The links between risk and regulation: the role of the proportionality principle

4.1 The proportionality principle as the missing link between law/regulation and risk

As Hutter has argued, "studies of regulation have long recognized that regulation and risk are inextricably connected; however, the relationship between the two was until recently assumed rather than explored".[58] The linkages between regulation and risk have naturally come to the fore with the advent of risk-based models of regulation.[59] However, even when the literature has reflected upon these linkages, it has tried to map out the various ways in which the two interact, but has refrained from providing an analysis on the conceptual commonalities between the two notions.[60] It is the following line of enquiry that the present book wishes to pursue.

Upon further analysis, it appears that the principle of proportionality is the link between data protection, regulation, and risk, since it is present in each case. In a nutshell, the main idea here is that one can find a proportionality test at the core of data protection law (and therefore regulation if one accepts the overlap between law and regulation), and at the core of risk. This will be discussed in extensive detail in Chapter 1 as far as regulation theory and risk are concerned. For the time being it suffices to say that as far as risk is concerned, the whole point of managing risks is to decide whether or not to take the risks at stake, which takes the form of a proportionality test involving the various harms and benefits associated to the risk.

Proportionality is also a standard legal technique of constitutional, administrative, and human/fundamental rights law, the role of which is hard to be disputed. It is at the heart of both the European Convention for Human Rights (ECHR) and the EUCFR.[61] And even though it is not a principle or a provision per se of data protection law, the links between data protection and proportionality have been underscored numerous times by the literature.[62] As Bygrave and Schartum put

[58] Bridget M Hutter, "Risk, Regulation, and Management" in Peter Taylor-Gooby and Jens Zinn (eds), *Risk in Social Science* (OUP 2006) 205.

[59] Among many, see eg Christine Parker, *The Open Corporation: Effective Self-Regulation and Democracy* (Cambridge University Press 2002); Neil Gunningham and Peter Grabosky (eds), *Smart Regulation: Designing Environmental Policy* (OUP 1998).

[60] See eg Fiona Haines, "Regulation and Risk" in Peter Drahos (ed), *Regulatory Theory: Foundations and Applications* (Australian National University Press 2017); Julia Black, "The Role of Risk in Regulatory Processes" in Robert Baldwin, Martin Cave, and Martin Lodge (eds), *The Oxford Handbook of Regulation* (OUP 2010).

[61] See eg Art 52(1) EUCFR.

[62] See eg Christopher Kuner, "Proportionality in European Data Protection Law And Its Importance for Data Processing Companies" (2008) 7 Privacy & Security Law Report 1615; Lee A Bygrave and Dag Wiese Schartum, "Consent, Proportionality and Collective Power" in Serge Gutwirth and others (eds), *Reinventing Data Protection?* (Springer 2009); Lee A Bygrave, *Data Protection Law—Approaching Its Rationale, Logic, and Its Limits* (Kluwer 2002). See also Recital 4 GPDR: "The right to the protection of personal data is not an absolute right; it must be considered in relation to its function in society and be balanced against other fundamental rights, in accordance with the principle of proportionality."

it, "the proportionality principle per se is not included as one of the classic 'Fair Information Practice' principles of data protection law, yet it underpins these and shines through in their interstices".[63]

This centrality of proportionality in law (and therefore in regulation) and in risk management is not new. Already in 2007, de Sadeleer observed that "the principle of proportionality is intertwined with risk management".[64] However, he did not push the reasoning further. Yet, one obvious conclusion one could infer therefrom is that when we do a legal proportionality test what we do is actually much closer to risk management than the current framing of the issue allows us to imagine and/or admit.[65]

In other words, if the rights-based approach is based on the proportionality principle, and if the risk-based approach is also based upon the proportionality principle, this seriously undermines the purported radical opposition and difference between them. Rather, and from this particular standpoint, these two supposedly incompatible approaches are much more similar than acknowledged. It is in this sense that the present book attempts to re-contextualise the debate between rights-based and risk-based approaches. Instead of radically different practices, the present perspective analyses the two approaches "merely" as different variations and takes on the proportionality principle. At their core, both the rights-based and the risk-based approaches to data protection are about assessing the proportionality of envisaged data processing operations. This finding, which may seem benign, or a mere truism, actually carries important consequences. For, if both approaches rely upon the principle of proportionality, this means they have something in common. This "something in common" is the principle of proportionality, and more in particular, the *modus operandi* of the latter, that is, the way it concretely functions and operates.

4.2 Defining the proportionality principle: two balancing tests associated with risk mitigation measures/safeguards

This then begs the question as to what the proportionality principle is, or at the very least, how it operates. The principle of proportionality can be defined as "a set of rules determining the necessary and sufficient conditions for a limitation of a constitutionally protected right to be constitutionally permissible".[66] Even though the

[63] Bygrave and Schartum (n 62) 162.

[64] Nicolas de Sadeleer, "The Precautionary Principle in European Community Health and Environment Law: Sword or Shield for the Nordic Countries?" in Nicolas de Sadeleer (ed), *Implementing the Precautionary Principle: Approaches from the Nordic Countries, EU and USA* (Earthscan 2007) 37.

[65] This is based on Raphaël Gellert, "Discussion · On Risk, Balancing, and Data Protection: A Response to van Der Sloot" (2017) 3 European Data Protection Law Review 180, 185.

[66] Ariel L Bendor and Tal Sela, "How Proportional Is Proportionality?" (2015) 13 International Journal of Constitutional Law 530.

proportionality principle continues to be an elusive concept, which is multi-folded, it has been widely accepted that the core of the notion of proportionality (or its most essential step) is the balancing of the various rights and interests at play. As de Sadeleer argues, "the balancing of the 'pros and cons', that is, the weighing of the different interests at play is the proportionality test *stricto sensu*".[67] Such a stance is in line with one of the most seminal authors on the principle of proportionality, Alexy. As he puts it, "the principle of proportionality in its narrow sense (. . .) is the requirement of balancing".[68] Even beyond Alexy, there is ample support in the literature.[69]

The emphasis upon the notion of balancing being at the heart of the proportionality principle is not benign. In order to uncover and show how proportionality is central to data protection law/regulation, and risk, the analysis relies upon the following understanding of proportionality: it can be conceptualised of terms of two balancing tests associated with risk mitigation measures.

4.2.1 Risk mitigation or safeguards?

Risk reduction (or mitigation) is a vocabulary that classically belongs to the field of risk, and which refers to measures taken in order to reduce the level of risk at stake. No trace of this expression can be found in a legal context, and in particular in the context of the proportionality test. However, there is an expression that comes across quite often, and which is that of "safeguards". The point made here is that risk mitigation measures and safeguards can be thought of as being equivalent, with safeguards referring to measures taken in order to reduce the extent of the interference with a fundamental right. This has been clear both in the context of the European Court of Human Rights (ECtHR),[70] as in the data protection context before the Court of Justice of the European Union (CJEU). In the *Digital Rights Ireland* case,[71] the CJEU argued that the obligation to retain communication data pursuant to Directive 2006/24/EC did not contain enough safeguards in accordance with Art 6 of the EU Data Protection Directive, such as those pertaining to the duration of the data storage,[72] or those pertaining to the limitation of purpose.[73]

[67] de Sadeleer (n 64) 38.

[68] Robert Alexy, *A Theory of Constitutional Rights* (English edn, OUP 2010) 67.

[69] See Matthias Klatt and Moritz Meister, *The Constitutional Structure of Proportionality* (OUP 2012) 1; Aharon Barak, *Proportionality: Constitutional Rights and Their Limitations* (Cambridge University Press 2012) 3. One can take note of debates surrounding the confusion, possible overlaps, and differences between balancing and proportionality, but careful analysis seems to conclude that they refer to the same principle, in line with the present text, see Moshem Cohen-Eliya and Iddo Porat, "American Balancing and German Proportionality: The Historical Origins" (2010) 8 International Journal of Constitutional Law 263.

[70] See for instance an earlier case such as *Kruslin v France*, 1990, where the Court explicitly refers to the supervision of secret surveillance measures by an investigative judge as a safeguard, (§34).

[71] Joined Cases C-293/12 and C-594/12 *Digital Rights Ireland Ltd v Minister for Communications, Marine and Natural Resources and Others* and *Kärtner Landesregierung and Others* [2014] ECLI:EU:C:2014:238 (here after *Digital Rights Ireland*).

[72] ibid §64.

[73] ibid §63.

It went on to say that the goal of these safeguards is to "ensure effective protection of the data retained against the risk of abuse and against any unlawful access and use of that data".[74] Similarly, the Art 29 WP argued that the goal of safeguards is to reduce the undue impact of processing operations on the data subjects "thereby changing the balance of rights and interests".[75] The literature has made a similar use of the notion.[76]

4.2.2 Proportionality as two balancing tests

Beyond that, the legal proportionality test can indeed be thought of in terms of two balancing tests in the following manner. The analysis examines the proportionality test as performed by the ECtHR, and more specifically, as performed in the case of Art 8 ECHR, enshrining the right to private and family life. It relies upon Opinion 1/2014 on "the application of necessity and proportionality concepts and data protection within the law enforcement sector" of the Art 29 WP.[77] This seems an adequate choice given that this opinion makes the link between the ECtHR's proportionality test and data protection law. However, it should be noted that such an analysis is grounded in case law,[78] and can find support with influential authors such as Van Gerven[79] or Gerards.[80]

The proportionality test contained in Art 8.2 ECHR concerns interferences with the right to private life. The interference is therefore the activity regulated/the risk managed. This proportionality test is composed of three requirements. An interference with the right will be legal if: it is in accordance with the law, it pursues one of the legitimate aims set out in Art 8.2 ECHR, and it is necessary in a democratic society.

The first criterion is of marginal importance for the discussion, as it requires a legal basis for the measure (which possesses certain qualities such as being accessible or providing rules governing the interference).[81]

74 ibid §66.

75 Art 29 WP, "Opinion 06/2014 on the Notion of Legitimate Interests of the Data Controller under Article 7 of Directive 95/46/EC" (2014) 31.

76 See eg Gabriela Zanfir, "Forgetting About Consent: Why The Focus Should Be On 'Suitable Safeguards' in Data Protection Law" in Serge Gutwirth, Ronald Leenes, and Paul De Hert (eds), *Reloading Data Protection—Multidisciplinary Insights and Contemporary Challenges* (Springer 2014); Lynskey (n 7).

77 "Opinion 01/2014 on the Application of Necessity and Proportionality Concepts and Data Protection within the Law Enforcement Sector" (2014).

78 See among others, ECtHR, *Sunday Times (I) v UK*, 1979 §62; ECtHR, *Dudgeon v United Kingdom*, 1981, §60; ECtHR, *Khelil v Switzerland*, 2011.

79 Walter Van Gerven, "Principe de Proportionnalité, Abus de Droit et Droits Fondamentaux" [1992] Journal des Tribunaux 305.

80 Janneke Gerards, "How to Improve the Necessity Test of the European Court of Human Rights" (2013) 11 International Journal of Constitutional Law 466.

81 Art 29 WP (n 77) 6.

The pursuit of one of the legitimate aims provided by the Convention itself is rather self-explanatory. However, the Art 29 WP indicates that it is directly instrumental in defining the pressing social need to be addressed (cf hereunder).

The last element—necessity in a democratic society—is probably the most important and complex one. Its content and meaning have long been characterised as unclear and subject to much discussion. Further, it has not always been applied in a consistent manner by the ECtHR.[82] However, the analysis of the Art 29 WP is particularly interesting because it breaks it down into two different tests: the "pressing social need" test, and the proportionality test.[83] Crucially, both of them can be analysed as balancing tests.

4.2.3 Test 1: pressing social need

Accordingly, the pressing social need test is the first balancing exercise. Its goal is to determine whether the aim pursued by the interference is legitimate in the first place. As seen, the ECtHR requires that a legitimate aim be pursued. According to Gerards, the pressing social need test therefore entails to determine whether this legitimate aim is "sufficiently legitimate". As she puts it, it "involves an element of weighing and balancing, since the social need served must be a 'pressing' one".[84]

Following the Working Party, "the notion of pressing social need will always involve identifying, within the broader sphere of the legitimate aim pursued, the specific societal need to be addressed".[85] This quote is important because it shows indeed that the pressing social need must always be determined *in concreto*, precisely through a balancing test. The Art 29 WP has indeed identified a number of criteria that are instrumental in determining whether such pressing social need exists.[86] It should be determined whether the issue at stake may result in harm to or have some detrimental effect upon society (or a section thereof) if left unaddressed. The higher the harm, the more legitimate the aim, and hence the existence of a pressing social need. This proves the point. The harm of not taking the interference must be balanced against the benefit of taking it. If the harm outweighs the benefit, then it means that the legitimate aim is "sufficiently legitimate to be pursued" and there is therefore a pressing social need at play.

[82] See eg Patricia Popelier and Catherine Van De Heyning, "Procedural Rationality: Giving Teeth to the Proportionality Analysis" (2014) 9 European Constitutional Law Review 230; Gerards (n 80); Alastair Mowbray, "A Study of the Principle of Fair Balance in the Jurisprudence of the European Court of Human Rights" (2010) 10 Human Rights Law Review 289; Janneke Gerards, "Margin of Appreciation and Incrementalism in the Case Law of the European Court of Human Rights" (2018) 18 Human Rights Law Review 495.

[83] The vocabulary used might be confusing insofar as "proportionality test" is used at times as a general expression, and at others as a specific element of the broader "necessary in a democracy test". Art 29 WP (n 77) 6–9.

[84] Gerards (n 80) 482.

[85] Art 29 WP (n 77) 7.

[86] ibid 8.

Once the legitimacy of the aim pursued has been established (first balancing test), it yet remains to be seen whether the interference can take place by determining whether it is proportionate to such pursued legitimate aim. This is the second balancing test.

4.2.4 Test 2: proportionality *stricto sensu*

The proportionality test *stricto sensu* (*ss*) embodies the second balancing exercise insofar as it requires that the interference does not go further than needed in order to address the pressing social need.[87] As evidenced by the Working Party, this is a matter of balancing, and more in particular, a balancing of the harms created by such interference against its benefits. As it puts it, "the proposed measure (...) must also be weigh[ed] up (...) above the rights and freedoms of the individuals".[88]

Such weighing up involves safeguards/risk mitigation measures, and the Art 29 WP does indeed divide the proportionality test into two distinct sub-steps. The first step concerns risk reduction measures/safeguards, while the second one concerns the balancing as such.

The first step is the so-called "necessity test" or examination of alternatives.[89] The idea is to compare the proposed measure with already existing measures. One way of doing this is to first review the effectiveness of existing measures over and above the proposed measure. Evidence must be provided that already existing measures are not being efficient, and thus, that the alternative is more efficient (ie necessary).[90] In other words, the comparison of alternatives intends to minimise the costs or harms of the interference. If it is decided to carry on with the proposed measure because no less harmful alternatives could be found, then a series of additional safeguards should be applied (again, to reduce the harms/costs). On the one hand, the scope of the interference should be limited as much as possible, for instance in terms of persons affected, fields to which it is applied, or the extent to which it is resorted to the measure. On the other hand, the Working Party indicates additional—more procedural—safeguards such as caveats determining how to undertake the measure, or rights of appeals afforded to the persons subjected to the measure.[91]

The second step is the weighing of interests *stricto sensu*. This entails comparing, weighing, the costs and benefits, respectively embodied in the interference and in

[87] ibid 9. See also, ECtHR, *Z v Finland*, 1997; ECtHR, *S & Marper v United Kingdom*, 2008.

[88] ibid 10. See also, Alexy (n 68) 102.

[89] Art 29 WP (n 77) 10.

[90] The Art 29 WP insists upon the importance of demonstrating that the proposed measure is more efficient than existing ones, and/or that existing measures are inefficient, ibid. Gerards agrees with such interpretation even though she argues that the case law of the ECtHR is not always clear cut on that matter, Gerards (n 80) 483. For an example of such test, see ECtHR *Ürper and Others v Turkey*, 2009, §43. See also, EDPS, "Assessing the Necessity of Measures That Limit the Fundamental Right to the Protection of Personal Data: A Toolkit" (2017).

[91] See the previous section on safeguards.

the pressing social need.[92] The Working Party argues that determining the costs of the interference is subjective and context bound. It must thus consider elements such as the activity being interfered with,[93] the type of data collected (in the case of data processing), the circumstances in which the measure was deployed, etc. On the one hand, one should evaluate the harmful effect upon society (or a section thereof) created by the interference. On the other hand, one should also evaluate the benefits resulting from the measure, that is, how necessary in a democratic society the measure is.[94]

Finally, it should be noted that the Art 29 WP identifies a third, additional test, that of providing relevant and sufficient reasons.[95] However, it is argued that there is no need to make it a third distinct test, since the Art 29 WP explicitly says that these reasons must be related to the first two tests.

As one can see, the legal proportionality test contains two balancing tests. One determining whether the legitimate aim is, in fact, sufficiently legitimate to be pursued. And another one determining whether the measures interfering with the fundamental right at stake are sufficiently tolerable or acceptable to be taken. Furthermore, a number of safeguards (including the so-called necessity test) must be taken, the goal of which is to diminish the impact of the adopted measures. The next chapters will build on this analysis in order to show that one can find balancing tests associated to safeguards at the core of risk, regulation theory, and data protection law.

5. Proportionality as the common root of law/regulation and risk: some first lessons

It follows from the previous that, rather than a stark opposition between a rights-based approach and a risk-based approach, one can re-contextualise the debate as a matter of variations around the concept of proportionality. As will be discussed, proportionality may be present both in law/regulation and risk, but that is not to say that both actualise and implement the principle in a similar way. On the contrary, there are differences. And it is maybe at these very counterpoints that the "real" debate between rights-based and risk-based approaches is, perhaps, better framed.

[92] Art 29 WP (n 77) 10–11.

[93] Note that the Art 29 WP explicitly refers not to the activity interfered with, but instead, to the "activity regulated", which points to the overlaps between law and regulation discussed *supra* ibid 10. See ECtHR, *Klass and Others v Germany*, 1978.

[94] As the Art 29 WP puts it: The more severe the issue and/or the greater or more severe or substantial the harm or detriment which society may be exposed to, the more an interference may be justified, Art 29 WP (n 77) 11.

[95] ibid. See also Alexy (n 68) 70.

Analysing the risk-based approach from the standpoint that there are conceptual commonalities between law, regulation, and risk, provides for a broad and (hopefully) rich picture. On the one hand, and as mentioned, it can help see data protection law from a different perspective. On the other hand, however, it can also tell us something on the way that risk and regulation relate to one another.

5.1 Proportionality at the core of regulation and risk: closely intertwined practices

On the basis of the proportionality principle being a common root, one can argue that regulation and risk are closely intertwined practices. On the one hand, one can argue that risk per definition regulates. In other words, managing a risk amounts to regulating it. This assertion can find some confirmation in the literature. Foucault, already, saw risk as a method of regulation.[96] This is probably the reason why Demortain argues that "a risk evaluation is thus always a regulatory evaluation".[97] The fact that the risk-based approach is precisely based on regulation models that resort to risk as their main tool only confirms this finding. On the other hand, and in perfect symmetry, this finding can also lead to the opposite conclusion, namely, that regulation per definition manages risks. That is, regulating an activity amounts to the management of the risks created by said activity. Or to put it differently, when an activity is regulated, the very way in which it is regulated is akin to a risk management operation. It is in this sense that data protection can be described as having always been about managing the risks stemming from the processing of personal data.

5.2 Proportionality as the hallmark of regulatory law: what consequences for data protection?

This reframing of the debate also tells us something about the links between law and regulation. As was discussed, the overlap between law and regulation even though real, is not a full one. More particularly, the overlap does not concern all types of law, but mainly concerns so-called regulatory law (more details in Chapter 1). The principle of proportionality appears in this sense as one of the defining features of such regulatory law.

Further, this reframing also tells us something about data protection law itself. If data protection is indeed constitutive of regulation, then this means that one can

[96] Michel Foucault, *Sécurité, Territoire, Population* (Gallimard, Seuil 2004).
[97] David Demortain, *Scientists and the Regulation of Risk—Standardising Control* (Edward Elgar Publishing 2011) 7.

apply regulation theory thereto from the very beginning, and in particular the constitutive elements of regulation (ie standard setting, monitoring, behaviour control).[98] And if the proportionality principle is the hallmark of regulatory law, then this also means that such constitutive elements can themselves be reframed as a matter of balancing tests associated to safeguards (this point will be extensively developed in Chapter 1). In other words, the whole of data protection framework can be understood as regulation, which simultaneously means that it can be understood as constituted of balancing exercises and safeguards. This re-understanding of data protection and its various mechanisms such as consent, data subject rights, data quality principles, etc as pertaining to regulatory activity is interesting for its own sake, but also because it can provide valuable insights on what data protection does, and how it does it. If data protection is first and foremost a matter of proportionality, this tells us something about the general meaning of compliance. Rather than the binary "yes/no" operation concerning the legality of data processing operations evoked earlier on, compliance can be understood as the answer to the following question: "what kind of processing should be allowed, and under what conditions?" It is probably in this sense that one should understand the Art 29 WP's assertion following which, "fundamental principles applicable to the controllers (ie legitimacy, data minimisation …) should remain the same, whatever the scope of processing and the risks for the data subjects. However, (…) they are inherently scalable."[99] Another good example is consent, which has most often been linked to the notion of privacy as informational control or self-determination.[100] Yet, an understanding of data protection as regulation demonstrates that consent can be "merely" seen as a regulatory mechanism. This can help better understand its functioning, its limitation, and its rationale in the whole data protection architecture.

Similarly, an understanding of data protection as regulation allows to better grasp what the object of data protection exactly is. Contrary to other fundamental rights, the substance of which is less contentious (eg private life and the respect for one's "private and family life, home and communications"), the content of data protection remains as elusive as ever,[101] in spite of recent contributions trying to find its essence.[102] The present author had previously argued that "the core content of the right to data protection amounts to a series of proportionality tests with

[98] On the constitutive elements of regulation, see eg Christopher Hood, Henry Rothstein, and Robert Baldwin, *The Government of Risk—Understanding Risk Regulation Regimes* (OUP 2001).

[99] Art 29 WP (n 1) 3.

[100] See eg the references in Art 29 WP, "Opinion 15/2011 on the Definition of Consent" (2011).

[101] For initial problematisations, see Gloria González Fuster and Serge Gutwirth, "Opening up Personal Data Protection: A Conceptual Controversy" (2013) 29 Computer Law & Security Review 531.

[102] See eg Maria Grazia Porcedda, "On Boundaries—Finding the Essence of the Right to the Protection of Personal Data" in Ronald Leenes and others (eds), *Data Protection and Privacy The Internet of Bodies* (Hart Publishing 2018); Maja Brkan, "The Concept of Essence of Fundamental Rights in the EU Legal Order: Peeling the Onion to Its Core" (2018) 14 European Constitutional Law Review 332.

regard to personal data processing operations, but to protect what exactly?".[103] A regulatory outlook might bring a more satisfactory response to this question, and conclude that the object of such proportionality tests are harms stemming from personal data processing operations. As will be demonstrated, the object of regulation can be thought of in terms of harms. That is, regulation is turned toward the achievement of socially desirable behaviours, precisely with the intention of avoiding the—social—harms stemming from behaviours that are "deviant, problematic, worrying, threatening, troublesome or undesirable in some way or another".[104]

It is in the same vein that the seminal "Ware Report" argued that the object of data protection were the "serious potential for harmful consequences [stemming from automated personal data processing systems], including infringement of basic liberties".[105] In this sense, the object of data protection are simply all the societal harms that can stem from the processing of personal data. And more particularly, these various harms can be said to be constitutive of the violation of fundamental rights (including privacy but also the right to a fair trial or not to be discriminated against), which in turn can themselves lead to material and moral harms. In this sense, one can argue that this regulatory perspective on data protection echoes, and reconnects with, some of the earlier works from the data protection founding fathers,[106] who purported what Bennett has qualified as an "instrumental" understanding of data protection.[107] That is, data protection is instrumental to safeguarding the other fundamental rights affected by the processing of personal data.

6. Approaching variations

Accepting the idea that law/regulation and risk are heavily underpinned by the proportionality principle, entails that the rights-based and risk-based approaches are "merely" variations around the concept of proportionality. However, what exactly are these variations? Again, this can only be answered by resorting to the findings on the links between law and regulation. And more particularly, the overlap existing between law and regulation, to the extent that data protection law can be conflated with regulation, and therefore qualifies as regulatory law. Even more so, nowhere has this overlap been fuller than with earlier forms of regulation,

[103] Raphaël Gellert, "Data Protection: A Risk Regulation? Between the Risk Management of Everything and the Precautionary Alternative" (2015) 5 International Data Privacy Law 3, 11.

[104] Hutter (n 58) 204.

[105] US Department of Health Education & Welfare (n 49) viii.

[106] Paul Sieghart, *Privacy and Computers* (Latimer 1976) 76; see eg James B Rule and others, *The Politics of Privacy: Planning for Personal Data Systems as Powerful Technologies* (Elsevier 1980) 22.

[107] Bennett (n 57) 33.

known as command and control. As seen, these are, one could say, the most legal forms of regulation since they do not rely on any other instruments (or regulatory tools) other than the adoption of legal rules backed by sanctions.[108] So, from this point of view, the rights-based approach to data protection can simply be equated with data protection as command and control regulation. As descends from its very definition, command and control regulation is characterised by rules.[109] As Black has demonstrated, in command and control regulation, rules seem to enjoy a dual status, which from the present perspective can directly be linked to the overlaps existing between regulation and (regulatory) law. On the one hand, rules are so-called "linguistic structures" in conformity with the most positivistic accounts of law.[110] Yet, on the other hand, rules are simultaneously regulatory commands, which means that they embody the very regulatory goals that underpin regulation, with a view of their implementation.[111] In this sense, rules are constitutive of regulatory activity, since they can be said to embody regulatory choices, and hence, to embody the standard setting function of regulation.[112] From this standpoint, it is possible to use rules and standards interchangeably. Given that they are defined by the legislator from the outset, rules/standards can be defined as "anticipatory, generalised abstractions".[113] Reframing this point from the perspective of the proportionality principles as the common root between rights-based and risk-based approaches, this means that data protection law embodies a number of balancing tests and safeguards from the very outset, which are enshrined in its various provisions.

However, the shortcomings associated with rules have long been documented.[114] With reference to Diver's seminal study on the optimal properties of rules,[115] one can argue that there are two main types of issues. The first one concerns the very types of outcomes that are achieved once rules are implemented (ie are these outcomes in line with the regulatory goals they are supposed to achieve?). In other words, the choice of adequate rules. The second one pertains to the difficulties associated with the implementation and the compliance with these rules. Rather than an obvious and straightforward task, implementing rules is riddled

[108] Black (n 24) 105.

[109] See also Julia Black, *Rules and Regulators* (OUP 1997) 5: "rules are associated with command and control regulation: a system of statutory rules backed by sanctions".

[110] ibid.

[111] ibid 9.

[112] For an additional confirmation that rules can be equated to the standard setting function, see Julia Black, "Risk-Based Regulation: Choices, Practices and Lessons Being Learnt" in OECD (ed), *Risk and Regulatory Policy: Improving the Governance of Risk* (OECD publishing 2010).

[113] Black (n 109) 5.

[114] See among many, Doreen McBarnet and Christopher Whelan, "The Elusive Spirit of the Law: Formalism and the Struggle for Legal Control" (1991) 54 The Modern Law Review 848; Robert Baldwin, "Why Rules Don't Work" (1990) 53 The Modern Law Review 321; Robert Baldwin, *Rules and Government* (OUP 1995).

[115] CS Diver, "The Optimal Precision of Administrative Rules" in Robert Baldwin, Collin Scott, and Christopher Hood (eds), *A Reader on Regulation* (OUP 1998).

with caveats.[116] As a matter of fact, an important part of the overhaul of the EU data protection framework, and more generally, the global shift towards the risk-based approach, can be seen as a response to these very shortcomings. In this sense, these debates are not unique to data protection but are simply the application of these various regulation debates and models to the data protection field.

And indeed, just like in other regulatory *fora*, the response to these command and control shortcomings has consisted in the adoption of new regulatory models, namely meta regulation. Meta regulation can be said to be part of a broader category of regulation models commonly known as "principles-based" regulation.[117,118] In contrast to command and control, which has sometimes been caricatured as a prescriptive regulation model, leaving little discretion to the regulatees, and focused on compliance with detailed provisions rather than on the achievement of the overall regulatory goals,[119] the family of principles-based regulations can be characterised by its collaborative nature and its focus on the achievement of regulatory goals.[120] This is achieved by relying on principles which impose outcomes to be achieved rather than relying upon strictly defined rules which would be described as "detailed processes for achieving [such goals]".[121] Because of their more general nature, these principles leave more discretion to the regulated entities (the regulatees) to determine how best to achieve the regulatory outcomes. However, with more discretion also comes greater responsibility.[122] To put it differently, principles-based regulation is inherently based upon the responsibilisation of the regulatee, which is the *sine qua non* condition for this collaboration to take place, and which in the data protection context is embodied through the principle of accountability. As Black puts it, "the rhetoric of principles-based regulation thus invoke[s], not deregulation, but a re-framing of the regulatory relationship from one of directing and controlling, [of telling and doing], to one based on responsibility, mutuality, and trust".[123] More in particular, such responsibility takes the form of so-called internal systems of management and controls (also known as internal controls) of firms and corporations. This is why principles-based regulation is also known as management-based regulation.[124] These firms' internal

[116] See also Julia Black, "The Rise, Fall and Fate of Principles-Based Regulation" in Kern Alexander and Niamh Moloney (eds), *Law Reform and Financial Markets* (Edward Elgar 2011) 10: "any regulatory regime requires firms to internalise the regulatory requirements into their own systems and processes for it to be complied with".

[117] See eg ibid 4.

[118] It should be pointed out that it is not so easy to clearly and analytically distinguish between regulatory regimes and models. As Black puts it, "principles based regulation is a moniker that is loosely applied to a number of regulatory regimes, however, and has no clear definition", ibid.

[119] ibid 5.

[120] ibid.

[121] ibid 13.

[122] ibid 10.

[123] ibid 14.

[124] See Parker (n 59).

management systems include a number of routines and practices such as internal policies, the assignment of roles and responsibilities, keeping of internal records, audit procedures, the existence of so-called chief risk officers, etc, and have been loosely translated in chapter IV GDPR (with such accountability-based provisions as DPO, records-keeping, etc). What is interesting to note, is that these systems of internal control are *per definition* risk-based. It has been demonstrated indeed that the adoption of these internal controls (also encapsulated in so-called enterprise-wide risk management systems) actually amount to broad and widespread exercises in risk management. And since they underpin all of the firms' activity, they have as an ultimate consequence to redefine and reframe the whole of corporate—and more generally organisational—activity as a matter of risk management.[125] PricewaterhouseCoopers for instance defines Enterprise-Wide Risk Management as "the overall management of risk that an organisation takes and holds to achieve its strategic aims".[126]

The fact that these collaborative regulation models are predicated upon the re-coding of the regulated organisations' activities as a matter of risk management brings us back to the contrast between rights-based and risk-based approaches. This does suggest that the risk-based approach to data protection entails that regulated organisations rely upon their internal risk management systems in order to achieve the regulatory outcomes and principles.[127] It is in this sense that risk becomes the method of regulation, and therefore embodies and signals the shift from one approach to the other.

From this perspective, the opposition between rights-based and risk-based approaches is embodied in the competition between diverging regulatory models. On the one hand, the command and control model sets standards (ie spells out the regulatory goals) and enshrines them into rules that are themselves set prior to any activity and for this reason are general and abstract. On the other hand, meta regulation (and the broader family of principles-based regulation), which relies upon the regulated firms' own risk management systems in order to achieve the regulatory goals on a case-by-case basis. Going back to the finding that both regulatory activity and risk management amount to the undertaking of a proportionality test (ie two balancing exercises with associated safeguards), this means that in one case such proportionality test is performed from the outset and the result thereof is enshrined into law, whereas in the other case this is done on a contextual, case-by-case basis through risk management tools. In other words, regulated firms perform their own balancing test and decide which safeguards are the most appropriate. In so doing, this addresses the two issues associated with rules underscored *supra*. Namely, the choice of adequate rules, and the adequate implementation thereof.

[125] See Michael Power, *Organized Uncertainty: Designing a World of Risk Management* (OUP 2007).
[126] https://www.pwc.com.au/risk-controls/enterprise-wide-risk-mgt.html, accessed 27 March 2019.
[127] See eg Black (n 116) 10.

However, such a solution ends up vindicating the critics of the risk-based approach since it precisely leads to a type of data protection where each regulated entity determines on a contextual basis what safeguards to apply and with how much intensity. In other words, a type of data protection which is based on the level of risk, and which is therefore contextual and uneven.

Yet, the risk-based approach has now been integrated into the GDPR (and a number of other legal frameworks), does this mean that it is this latter type of data protection that should be expected? In this regard, it is useful to refer again to the Art 29 WP's characterisation of the risk-based approach. As indicated *supra*, the Art 29 WP voiced clear opposition against framing the risk-based approach as an alternative to the data protection rules and principles.[128] As it put it, data controllers should "always be accountable for compliance with data protection obligations".[129] Thus, rather than an alternative to legally enshrined rules, the risk-based approach, and with it risk management tools, becomes a method to better comply with these very rules. As the Art 29 WP put it, the risk-based approach is "a scalable and proportionate approach to 'compliance' obligations".[130] In so doing, it only addresses the second issue associated with rules (ie how to implement them?), but leaves unaddressed the first one (how to determine the rules that best implement regulatory goals?). This however was the solution found in order to guarantee the unity and equal application of the data protection rules. It thus provides for a rights-based approach to the data protection principles combined with a risk-based approach relying upon risk management as the main means to achieve regulatory goals.

Does this mean to say that, quoting Candide in Voltaire's famous satirical novel, "all is for the best in the best of all possible worlds"[131]? Of course not. If the Art 29 WP's definition of the scope of the risk-based approach manages to provide for a coexistence of risk-based and rights-based approaches, it nonetheless has a number of consequences. The most important one being the notion of risk at the heart of the risk-based approach. Instead of a "data protection risk" which, it will be argued, also underpinned command and control iterations of data protection,[132] the shift towards the risk-based approach also entails a shift in the notion of risk that underpins the regulatory model, namely, a new notion of "compliance risk". What is gained, what is lost, when such a notion of risk is adopted?

Furthermore, the use of risk management tools as such is not neutral. As Black puts it, risk "imports particular conceptions of the problem at hand, and leads to the framing of a solution in a particular way".[133] Rights-based and risk-based

[128] Art 29 WP (n 1) 2.
[129] ibid 3.
[130] ibid 2.
[131] See Voltaire, *Candide* (Millennium Publications 2014) vi.
[132] Since as seen, the object of regulation are harms/risks. As a matter of fact, one can define data protection risk as certain properties or characteristics, which if displayed by processing operation, will lead to harms. These harms can be said to be constitutive of violations of fundamental rights, and lead themselves to moral or material harms. This will be discussed in detail in Chapter 6.
[133] Black (n 112) 188.

approaches might both be about compliance, but in the shift from one approach to another, the very meaning of compliance is transformed and redefined. This is probably best epitomised by discussions around data protection risk management methodologies, in particular as far as Data Protection Impact Assessments (DPIAs)—the main risk management tool enshrined in the GDPR—are concerned. Complying through risk-based instruments is simply not identical to complying from a "legal" viewpoint.

More generally, the turn towards risk-inspired regulatory frameworks entails a number of challenges of its own. To be sure, if the criticism against command and control/rules-based regulation is warranted,[134] meta regulation and principles-based regulations also come with their own set of caveats. Probably, the main one is linked to the collaborative nature of these models, that is the sharing of regulatory tasks between regulators and regulatees. It is predicated upon the responsibilisation of the latter, and further, upon a mutual trust that "each [will] fulfil their side of this new regulatory bargain".[135] This spurs a number of caveats concerning the attitude and strategies of the regulators and the way they apprehend their own role and this new relationship, in particular as far as the amount of discretion awarded to the regulatees is concerned (this is nowhere more obvious than in the discussions surrounding who gets to define the notion of high risk, which in turns triggers the DPIA obligation),[136] or as far as their enforcement strategy is concerned. Further, implementing risk-based frameworks at the organisational and institutional level is much more complicated than may seem to be the case *prima facie*. In particular, behind pretences of simplicity, cost-effectiveness, or consistency, risk management methodologies that are available to everyone are only "a piece of paper". In practice, their adequate implementation requires an institutional framework which can be resource intensive, very complex, and inconsistent.

Yet, and beyond, these "regulatory caveats", one can point to the deeper values underpinning meta regulation. As Power argues, these models of regulation embody a neoliberal regulatory ideal which could lead to the managerialisation of data protection. And with it, the danger that compliance with data protection law be emptied of all substance, and be instrumentalised as a mere self-legitimation exercise.[137] Similarly, Black argues that the collaboration between regulators and regulatees at the heart of the risk-based approach is powered by utopic visions.[138]

Ultimately, and not least because they are underpinned by powerful ideals and visions, the fact that in trying to address some of the command and control

[134] See Black (n 116) 4.

[135] ibid 14.

[136] On this issue, see Raphaël Gellert, "EDPB Opinion on the Draft Lists of Competent Supervisory Authorities Regarding the Processing Operations Subject to DPIAs" (2018) 4 European Data Protection Law Review 500; Raphaël Gellert, "The Article 29 Working Party's Provisional Guidelines on Data Protection Impact Assessment" (2017) 2 European Data Protection Law Review 1.

[137] See Gellert (n 103) 16.

[138] Black (n 116).

challenges, risk-based models of regulation create challenges of their own sheds a new light on the idea of regulation itself, which, at its core is about the steering of behaviour.[139] Is there such a thing as a perfect model of regulation that fully encapsulates and delivers on the regulatory ideals of behaviour control, and which can be seamlessly applied? Or are we bound to face regulatory hiccups and glitches, and, as a result, bound to engage in a never-ending tinkering process of regulatory models that can only deliver imperfect results at best? And if this is so, what does it mean for the future of data protection law?

7. Structure of the argument

Chapter 1 provides an in-depth analysis of risk and regulation. In each case it addresses a number of relevant caveats (eg what are the most prevalent ways of managing risks, what is the nature of regulation and its links with law). However, most importantly, it shows that both can be conceived of as a matter of two balancing exercises with associated safeguards.

Chapter 2 demonstrates that data protection can be understood as command and control regulation by applying the three constitutive elements of regulation (standard setting, monitoring, behaviour control) thereto.

Chapter 3 shows that a number of the issues that data protection has encountered can be understood from the regulatory viewpoint. More in particular, they amount to the traditional criticism addressed against command and control rulemaking, namely its “diagnosis-prescription” aspect, as well as sub-optimal enforcement practice.

Chapter 4 explains the rationale for changing regulatory models and in particular for shifting towards meta regulation from the standpoint of regulation theory. Particular emphasis is put on the responsibilisation of the regulatees. The latter is the necessary condition for any collaborative model of regulation. Among which meta regulation, which bestows regulatory tasks (ie standard setting, monitoring, and behaviour control) upon regulatees. Such responsibility however, also entails a re-coding of the regulatees activities as a matter of risk management.

Chapter 5 studies in depth the risk-based approach to data protection. It shows that it is only a partial implementation of meta regulation insofar as it focuses on a more consistent implementation of the framework. In so doing, and contrary to meta regulation, it refrains from delegating the regulatory function of standard setting to the regulatees. The chapter also addresses some policy proposals that feature a “full” implementation of meta regulation.

[139] See Black (n 24) 113.

Chapter 6 provides an in-depth study of the notion of compliance risk at the heart of the risk-based approach. Notably it also contrasts it with the "original" notion of data protection risk.

Chapter 7 discusses the various caveats associated to the risk-based approach in practice. They cover methodological, regulatory, and implementational issues.

Final conclusions follow. They contain a summary of the main findings. They also further reflect on the type of protection that can ensue from the risk-based approach in contrast to other regulatory models. These lead to final reflections on what can be expected from the idea of regulation itself, and hence, on what this means for the future of the protection of personal data.

1
Fundamental notions
Risk and regulation

> Risk has become an organising concept as never before (…) even though the concept remains elusive, contested, and inherently controversial[1]

> The Risk society is a regulatory society[2]

1. Introduction

The goal of this chapter is twofold. On the one hand it provides a solid overview of two key notions: risk and regulation. In the case of risk this includes the following. An explanation of risk and risk management, including an appraisal and description of the technical notion of risk as it appears in the International Organization for Standardization (ISO) Standards. It also provides for a discussion of some of the key methods for assessing and managing risks, including some of the main drawbacks and criticisms that have been raised against the use of risk management. In the case of regulation, it includes a more in-depth analysis of the notion, and of its constitutive elements; a discussion on the conflation between law and regulation; and a discussion on what exactly the object of regulation is. These discussions of key caveats pertaining to these two notions are useful to anyone willing to better understand them. However, they will also underpin many of the analyses carried out in later chapters (eg understanding data protection in the light of the constitutive elements of regulation, discussing various methods for data protection risk management, etc).

Finally, beyond these key caveats, this chapter also shows how both risk and regulation can be analysed as a matter of two balancing exercises with associated safeguards, and hence, as variations around the proportionality principle. A grid at the end of the chapter will summarise this by contrasting the way in which

[1] Michael Power, *The Risk Management of Everything—Rethinking the Politics of Uncertainty* (Demos 2004) 13–14.

[2] Richard V Ericson and Kevin D Haggerty, *Policing the Risk Society* (University of Toronto Press 1997) 48.

The Risk-Based Approach to Data Protection. Raphaël Gellert, Oxford University Press (2020). © Raphaël Gellert.
DOI: 10.1093/oso/9780198837718.001.0001.

balancing tests and safeguards are at play in the European Convention on Human Rights (ECHR)'s proportionality test, in risk, and in regulation.

2. Risk

2.1 Etymology and meaning of the concept

In everyday language, risk is often associated to the idea of potential future danger, that is, "an eventual danger that can be foreseen only to some extent".[3] The canonical technical definition of risk is that of "a combination of the probability of occurrence of a defined hazard and the magnitude of the consequences of the occurrence".[4] Whereas the focus of this definition on harms (ie negative consequences) can be criticised,[5] it remains nonetheless valid insofar as it points to a definition of a risk as an event of a certain magnitude (or severity) that has a number of chances of occurrence and which carries along with it a number of consequences, both positive and negative, which are themselves of a certain magnitude and have a probability of their own. Such a definition is confirmed by the Article 29 Working Party (Art 29 WP) for whom a risk is as "a scenario describing an event and its consequences, estimated in terms of severity and likelihood".[6]

Beyond this definition, risk can be considered foremost as a tool for decision-making, based on the prediction of events. In this sense, it is an anticipative decision-making tool. This duality is apparent in its origin. According to Ewald, the word risk comes from the Italian word "risico", which itself comes from the Latin "*resecum*", which refers to something that cuts. It appears during the 14th century. It was used to designate reefs, and more in general any sort of danger that threatened merchandises and the boats that were carrying them through the seas and oceans.[7] Peretti-Watel adds another origin to the word, that of the Roman "rixicare", which means brawl. This also evokes the idea of danger.[8] However, it would be wrong to equate the notion of risk solely with that of danger. As both authors observe, the notion is a neologism crafted by the first insurers, who precisely insured cargo ships against dangers at sea. Thus, rather than danger, risk can be equated to a will to undertake, to make decisions in situations that escape one's

3 Olivier Godard and others, *Traité Des Nouveaux Risques* (Gallimard 2002) 12.

4 Frederick Warner, "Introduction" in The Royal Society (ed), *Risk: Analysis, Perception and Management—A Report of a Royal Society Study Group* (The Royal Society 1992) 4.

5 See eg Douglas who argues that "whereas originally a risk meant a game in which a throw of the die had a probability of bringing gain or loss, now risk refers only to negative outcomes. The word has been pre-empted to mean bad risks." "Risk as a Forensic Resource" in Edward J Burger (ed), *Risk* (University of Michigan 1990) 3.

6 Art 29 WP, "Guidelines on Data Protection Impact Assessment (DPIA) and Determining Whether Processing Is 'Likely to Result in a High Risk' for the Purposes of Regulation 2016/679" (2017) 6.

7 "La Société Assurancielle" (1990) 1 Les cahiers de l'assurance 5, 6.

8 *La Société Du Risque* (Repères, La Découverte 2010) 7.

full mastery (which is the essence of dangers at sea).[9] Such a view is consistent with another etymology of the word. Accordingly, risk comes from the Italian "risicare", which means "to dare".[10] "In this sense, risk is a choice rather than a fate."[11]

These various origins point to the dual nature of risk. It is used for decision-making based on the measurement, or assessment, of future events. Its constitutive elements are two distinct yet joined operations: forecasting future events (both negative and positive) and making decisions on the basis thereof.[12] One can therefore argue that "any decision relating to risk involves two distinct and yet inseparable elements: the objective facts and a subjective view about the desirability of what is to be gained, or lost, by the decision".[13]

2.2 Risk and risk management

As a tool for decision making, risk remains a rather abstract notion in need of methodologies, templates, and processes that concretely implement it.[14] This is the whole point of risk management.

Hood *et al* point to the origin of the word, which comes from the Italian verb, *maneggiare*, which means to ride a horse with skill.[15] Following this metaphor, management is the process, taken as a whole, of handling risks. Risk management can thus be seen as the tools, processes, and methodologies that implement and actualise the otherwise abstract technique of risk (ie how to concretely assess and manage risks). Such a view is consistent with Jones and Hood's attempt to provide a broad and as general as possible definition of risk management following which it refers to "a range of related activities for coping with risks, including how risks are identified and assessed and how social interventions to deal with risk are monitored and evaluated".[16] In other words, risk management encompasses the measures intended to shape the development of risks and the responses thereto.[17]

However, risk management is also endowed with a stricter meaning. In the context of risk management, the measurement step is referred to as risk assessment, and the decision-making step is referred to as risk management *sensu stricto* (*ss*). It

[9] Peter L Bernstein, *Against The Gods—The Remarkable Story of Risk* (John Wiley & Sons, Inc 1996) ch 6.
[10] ibid 8.
[11] ibid.
[12] ibid 3.
[13] ibid 100. Note that the ISO defines risk as the "effect of uncertainty on objectives" "ISO: 31000 Risk Management—Principles and Guidelines" 1.
[14] Michael Power, *Organized Uncertainty: Designing a World of Risk Management* (OUP 2007) 12.
[15] "Risk Management" in The Royal Society (ed), *Risk: Analysis, Perception and Management—A Report of a Royal Society Study Group* (The Royal Society 1992) 135.
[16] David KC Jones and Christopher Hood, "Introduction" in Christopher Hood and David KC Jones (eds), *Accident and Design: Contemporary Debates in Risk Management* (UCL Press 1996) 7.
[17] That is, "who can take what risks and how", Hood and others (n 15) 136.

follows that risk management *ss* means "the process whereby decisions are made to accept a known or assessed risk and/or the implementation of actions to reduce the consequences or probability of occurrence" (ie the handling or control of risks).[18] In other words, to manage risks *ss*, is to take a decision as to whether or not to take a risk, and, if deemed necessary, to take measures to reduce the risk once it has been decided to take it.[19] Such measures can be referred to as risk reduction, risk control, risk response, or more generally, risk mitigation.[20,21]

It should be noted that risk management applies across a range of different disciplines such as economics, business, or finance, as well as public policy and governmental activity in general,[22] thus also including models of regulation such as those at stake in the present study.

2.3 The technique of risk and risk management

In addition to the general definition of risk the following lines aim to provide a technical definition of risk and of the various steps involved in the risk management process, based on the ISO 31000 risk management standard.[23]

First, one can provide some basic vocabulary used for the management of risk.

- The first element is risk. Risk is the event of a certain magnitude that may or may not happen, and which has a number of consequences both positive and negative. For this reason, the ISO refers to risk as "event",[24] and the *Commission nationale de l'informatique et des libertés* (CNIL) refers to risk as "feared event".[25]
- The second element are the risk factors. These determine whether and how the risk will materialise (ie probability), as well as the severity of the risk. They can also be referred to as threats.[26] The ISO defines them as "elements, which, alone or in combination have the intrinsic potential to give rise to risk".[27] It is to be noted that in order to provide a more fine-grained

[18] Warner (n 4) 5.

[19] See also, ibid 3: "risk management is the making of decisions concerning risk and their subsequent implementation".

[20] ISO (n 13) 6.

[21] One should also observe that sometimes there also exists a third step called risk communication. However, this is beyond the scope of the present analysis, see eg Olivier Laügt, *Discours d'expert et Democratie* (L'Harmattan 2000).

[22] Jones and Hood (n 16) 5; Hood and others (n 15) 136.

[23] ISO (n 13).

[24] ibid 4.

[25] "Methodology For Privacy Risk Management: How to Implement the Data Protection Act" CNIL (2012) 6.

[26] ibid.

[27] ISO (n 13) 4.

assessment, some distinguish risk sources from risk factors/threats. According to the CNIL, the risk source leads to risks because it is the source of risk factors.[28]
- The third element are the consequences,[29] or impacts of the risk.[30] When such impacts are negative they can be referred to as harms, and when they are positive they can be referred to as benefits. Like the event, there is a certain probability and magnitude attached to them.

Second, one can describe the different steps to be taken in order to manage a risk.

In a nutshell, the ISO makes the basic distinction between the assessment of risks and their management *ss.*[31]

However, and crucially, it divides the risk assessment step in a number of sub-steps: the risk criteria, the risk identification, and the proper risk assessment step.

- Risk assessment step:
  - The risk criteria step is the step containing the criteria for determining whether an event can be considered a risk, or in other words, the step that contains "the terms of reference against which the significance of a risk is evaluated".[32] These include the types of harms to be taken into account, harms to whom, how to measure the level of risk, what counts as a risk factor, etc.[33] Keeping in mind the distinction between epidemiology and toxicology, risk criteria thus contain elements of both. In the context of data protection, this would refer to the type of data processed, type of processing, etc (toxicology), and the types of harms, the people affected etc (epidemiology), (cf *infra*).
  - The risk identification step is closely linked to the risk criteria step. It can be defined as the "process of finding, recognizing and describing risks".[34] In other words, it consists in comparing the characteristics of the event at stake with those laid down in the risk criteria, and which will determine whether the event is sufficiently risky to be considered a risk.
  - Finally, if an event is considered a risk, it must undergo an assessment to determine its level in terms of likelihood and severity (or magnitude).[35]

28 CNIL (n 25) 7.
29 ISO (n 13) 5.
30 CNIL (n 25) 6.
31 ISO (n 13) 4.
32 ibid 5.
33 ibid 17; David Wright and others, "Surveillance Impact Assessment Manual" (2014) 28.
34 ISO (n 13) 5.
35 ibid 5–6, 18.

- Risk management step:
  - Balancing the harms/costs and the benefits: at its core, the managing *ss* of risks consists in the balancing of the costs and benefits associated thereto. A decision will ensue as to whether or not to take it.
  - Risk mitigation measures: Usually, the decision to take the risk is accompanied by a recourse to risk mitigation measures, which will help reduce the risk to a level deemed tolerable (ie sufficiently low).[36] Risk mitigation measures are critical to risk management, and have for instance been the object of a separate ISO Standard.[37]

2.4 Risk (management) as a matter of two balancing tests associated to risk mitigation measures

As one remembers from the introductory chapter, the link consists in the proportionality principle understood as a double balancing exercise associated to safeguards/risk mitigation measures. Can we also understand risk as a matter of balancing tests?

As confirmed by de Sadeleer,[38] the presence of the balancing of interests is most obvious at the risk management step. Determining whether or not to take a risk entails indeed to contrast the harms and benefits associated thereto. In other words, this is exactly what the balancing is about, namely, the weighing of the pros and cons of the different interests at play.[39] The issue of balancing can be encapsulated in discussions surrounding the tolerability or acceptability of the risk. The whole point of the balancing test is to determine whether, considering the harms and benefits at stake, it is acceptable to take the risk. In other words, it consists in determining what is a sufficiently acceptable risk.[40] Further, we have also seen that risk mitigation measures are an integral part of the risk management step.

However, another balancing test can also be found. This time, it consists in determining the existence of a risk in the first place, and therefore takes place at the risk criteria and risk identification steps. Contrary to the risk management step, which is concerned with whether the risk is sufficiently tolerable or acceptable,

[36] ibid 6.

[37] See ISO, "IEC 31010:2009: Risk Management—Risk Assessment Techniques" (2009).

[38] Nicolas de Sadeleer, "The Precautionary Principle in European Community Health and Environment Law: Sword or Shield for the Nordic Countries?" in Nicolas de Sadeleer (ed), *Implementing the Precautionary Principle: Approaches from the Nordic Countries, EU and USA* (Earthscan 2007) 37.

[39] ibid 38.

[40] See also, the EU Court of First Instance Case T-13/99, *Pfizer* [1999] ECLI:EU:T:2002:209 para 149 (hereafter *Pfizer*), which explicitly framed the risk management step as a matter of risk tolerance/acceptability: "(. . .) it is for the Community institutions to determine the level of protection which they deem appropriate for society. It is by reference to that level of protection that they must then (. . .) determine the level of the risk (. . .) which in their judgment is no longer acceptable for society *and above which it is necessary (. . .) to take preventive measures*", author's emphasis.

these two steps are meant to determine whether the risk at stake is sufficiently risky to be considered a risk in the first place (cf herein above). In other words, this amounts to contrasting the characteristics of the risk at play with those laid down in the risk criteria, that is, to balancing its degree of riskiness with that enshrined in the risk criteria.

One can conclude that risk can indeed be understood as composed of two balancing tests and a series of mitigation measures attached to the second test. As a reminder, the legal proportionality test contains two balancing tests. One determining whether the legitimate aim is, in fact, sufficiently legitimate to be pursued. And another one determining whether the measures interfering with the fundamental right at stake are sufficiently tolerable or acceptable to be taken. In the case of risk, the first balancing test determines what counts as sufficiently risky, and the second one determines what counts as sufficiently tolerable.

2.5 Different methods for assessing risks

One can distinguish between two main approaches to assessing risks.[41]

Toxicology is an approach that evaluates the qualities of a product, risk, or event, as such. The point is to predict and anticipate the hazardousness of the product.[42] It is predicated upon the idea of determining the severity and magnitude of the risk/event as such by determining at which dose it becomes harmful.[43]

Epidemiology on the contrary characterises the harm on an empirical basis.[44] It is not predicated upon a capacity to determine in advance whether the product is safe or not, but instead on the possible harmful effects it might create.[45]

The distinction between toxicology and epidemiology is of paramount importance to properly understanding risk assessment in practice. One can make the point that toxicology and epidemiology are the two sides of the same coin in understanding the level of risk. Whereas toxicology focuses upon the level of the risk itself, epidemiology focuses upon its effects (ie the harms it leads to). In other words, if a risk is considered as an event that has a certain number of consequences (in this case with a focus on negative consequences), in order to have a complete picture of such risk it is necessary to assess the level (severity and probability) of the event itself since it is the source of these negative consequences (ie toxicology), and to assess the level of the harms themselves, that is, as they occur on the "targets" of the risk, such as people, natural resources, economic resources, etc (ie epidemiology).

[41] See David Demortain, *Scientists and the Regulation of Risk—Standardising Control* (Edward Elgar Publishing 2011).

[42] ibid 37.

[43] Hood and others (n 15) 35.

[44] Demortain (n 41) 37.

[45] Hood and others (n 15) 69.

A practical example of the distinction can be given by having regard to the data protection field. As will be discussed *infra*, if a data processing operation is considered a risk, then such risk can be measured by resorting to toxicology and epidemiology. Toxicology will address the processing as risk as such (which is thus the source of harms), and will therefore include such elements as the nature and type of data, the type of processing operation, its scope, its context, the status of the controller and the data subject, etc.[46] Epidemiology will assess the harms in themselves and the way they affect data subjects (ie the risk targets). Such harms may include discrimination, defamation, loss of bargaining power, distress, irritation, fear, etc.[47]

2.6 Different ways to manage risks

As seen before, risk management *ss* refers to the decision-making aspect, which takes the form of a balancing of interest. To be clear, when one decides to take the risk, it means that they know that the risk and its negative consequences have a number of chances of occurring, but they nonetheless decide to go with it. The key then is to reduce the risk (both in terms of likelihood and probability) through risk mitigation measures. It has long been accepted that it is impossible to go for a "zero risk situation" (in other words to reduce the probabilities to zero).[48] This is why the whole point of risk management *ss* and risk mitigation is not to completely remove the risks, but rather, to be a "continuous striving" to reduce risk to a point where it becomes tolerable (or, it becomes tolerable to take it).[49,50]

In other words, risk management *ss* combines two elements: reducing risks (1), up to a point where they are deemed tolerable (2).

2.6.1 Risk management as an exercise in standard setting

Because risk management is concerned with reducing risks to a sufficiently low and tolerable level, it has been dubbed a standard setting practice, more in particular, setting standards, or specifications, of what is safe (enough). It is argued that the risk mitigation measures are the standards at stake.[51] Since the risk mitigation measures reduce the risk to a tolerable level, it is implicit that once the measure

[46] Art 29 WP, "Opinion 06/2014 on the Notion of Legitimate Interests of the Data Controller under Article 7 of Directive 95/46/EC" (2014) 36.

[47] ibid 37.

[48] Hood and others (n 15) 137.

[49] Jones and Hood (n 16) 7.

[50] In other words, what risk management—as a technique of risk—does, is to add the risk mitigation step to the balancing operation.

[51] Christopher Hood and David KC Jones, "Should Regulation Be Targeted on Physical Products or Institutional Processes?" in Christopher Hood and David KC Jones (eds), *Accident and Design: Contemporary Debates in Risk Management* (UCL Press 1996) 193. Hence technical standards adopted on the basis of the BATNEEC criteria for instance.

is adopted, the risk shall be taken. In this sense, the decision on tolerability (ie the balancing) is directly included in the standard. For these reasons, these standards are not about what is safe, but rather, about what is safe enough. Among many examples, such standards can concern the design of products or physical structures, but also be concerned with limits to maximum daily intake of certain products or daily maximum exposure to certain substances.[52]

2.6.2 How to balance the costs and benefits

As discussed, the management of risk takes the form of a balancing of the various harms/costs and benefits at stake. One salient question therefore concerns the way such balancing should be conducted. Historically, such balancing has taken the form of a cost-benefit analysis, that is, "an analytic technique for quantifying the estimated [aggregated] risks (...) and evaluating those risks against likely [aggregated] benefits".[53,54] Such a view is convenient because it provides decision makers with formalised, quasi scientific, and economic tools and methodologies for determining what a tolerable risk is. These include the well-known ALARA ("as low as reasonably achievable"), ALARP ("as low as is reasonably possible"), or BATNEEC ("best available technology not entailing excessive cost") criteria.

However, this sort of technique has been heavily criticised on the account that it does not address a number of relevant issues such as the use of distributional approaches instead of aggregate ones; the regular sole focus on economic costs and benefits, or the issue of how exactly and on the basis of whose view the decision maker comes to a decision on tolerability on the basis of the aggregated data.[55] One can therefore argue, that if cost-benefit analysis has been the predominant form of risk management for a number of years, it is not the only one. Of paramount importance, one should not amalgamate quantitative, aggregated, economic-oriented costs-benefit analysis with the notion of balancing as such. One can argue that this type of cost-benefit analysis is just a sub-set, or a very particular way of performing a balancing exercise.

2.6.3 The choice of the best risk mitigation measures

The crucial issue at the heart of the mitigation of risks is that of "what actions make what difference to risk outcomes".[56] In other words, what is the most efficient way to address and reduce risks?

Hood *et al.* make an important distinction between measures that target the source of risk (so called active or corrective measures), and measures that focus

[52] ibid.
[53] Hood and others (n 15) 137.
[54] See also Warner (n 4) 2. who notes the "use of risk-benefit analysis in the management of risk and allocation of resources".
[55] Jones and Hood (n 16) 7.
[56] ibid 6.

on the effects of risk (so called passive or preventative measures).[57] This distinction mirrors that between toxicology and epidemiology at the risk assessment level. Corrective measures will try to affect the probability and/or magnitude of the event, whereas passive measures will seek to diminish the effects eg through improved design, better protection, or insurance schemes that spread the losses. For example, is it better to modify a drug that benefits many but has harmful effects on few, or better to identify the high-risk individuals? Equally, in order to avoid road accidents, is it better to aim to directly influence human driving behaviour (eg speed bumps, radars, driving licence), or to adopt measures addressing the effects of such behaviour (eg crumple zones in cars, safety belts, compulsory insurance schemes)?[58] They insist that this distinction like all distinctions describes extreme positions for the sake of analytical clarity, but in reality, there are many intermediate steps and grey zones, and both approaches are followed.[59] One can also take examples from the data protection field. As will be discussed more in detail in later chapters, one can argue that the classical "core data protection principles" such as data minimisation or purpose limitation are corrective measures, whereas data subject rights are preventative measures.

Another series of caveats relate to the timing and cost (both in terms of resources and side effects) of risk mitigation measures. In terms of timing, Hood *et al.* distinguish between anticipationism ("looking forwards") and resilience ("bouncing back").[60] Anticipationists argue that action should be taken before a satisfactory risk assessment has been concluded. Such action includes both corrective measures (such as monitoring or warning systems in order to detect signs of risks, but also prohibition of specific substances) and passive measures (such as defensive structures).[61] The arguments for such an approach can be made in the context of the precautionary principle and our inability to assess contemporary, complex risks. The classical argument against being too anticipative is known as the risk *vs* risk trade-off, and relates to the cost and side effect of mitigation measures. By trying to avert a risk, one creates another risk.[62] A variant is known as the "Titanic effect", that is, too much anticipation may actually contribute to the very event it tries to avoid.[63] Proponents of these critiques therefore advocate for a resilient approach to risk management, the goal of which is to enhance the capacity to cope with risks through relief, emergency action, rescue, insurance, etc.[64] As one sees,

[57] Hood and others (n 15) 142.
[58] ibid 142–43.
[59] ibid 142.
[60] Christopher Hood and David KC Jones, "Anticipationism versus Resilience" in Christopher Hood and David KC Jones (eds), *Accident and Design: Contemporary Debates in Risk Management* (UCL Press 1996) 10.
[61] ibid 11.
[62] John D Graham and Jonathan Baert Wiener (eds), *Risk vs Risk—Tradeoffs in Protecting Health and the Environment* (Harvard University Press 1997).
[63] Hood and Jones (n 60) 12.
[64] ibid.

these measures are mainly passive, and don't aim at reducing the risks, but only mitigating their effect. A critique against this approach is that it is mainly suited for catastrophes and disasters, that is, risks with a very high impact but very low probability of outcome.[65] As one can see, the selection of the most adequate risk mitigation measure at a point in time is a delicate exercise, and the tolerance to risk that we ultimately opt for is tributary of these considerations, including the (economic) cost of such measures.[66]

Some argue that because risk reduction measures are not always effective, it is better to put the emphasis on the decisional process, that is on structuring the way decisions are taken.[67] This is often achieved through mechanisms of institutional design ensuring that decisions are taken in a way that is consistent enough to address risks (eg registers, training of employees ...).[68] As will be discussed later on, this approach has gained a lot of prevalence and is at the core of the risk-based approach.

Another caveat concerns the choices to be made between technical and human mitigation measures. The explicit recognition of risks as socio-technical issues has now been argued for a long time; entailing that reflective practice is to be preferred over pure technical instrumentality.[69] In other words, risks should be reduced through the use of science, technology, and engineering, but also through the reduction of human vulnerability.[70] Human vulnerability can be understood to refer to typical behaviours and cultures that contribute to the materialisation of risks. Among these, one can highlight the failure to learn from previous errors, over-reliance on risk management tools at the expense of personal judgement, but also conflicts of interests, secrecy, misallocations of resources, or lack of meaningful participation.[71,72] The human element can be seen for instance in the contractual obligations befalling upon data processors, and which include obligations not to share the data with third parties for instance.[73]

[65] In the context of the precautionary principle, some have argued that these approaches also embody the latter principle: in situations of uncertainties it is impossible to make prediction, and the focus should therefore be on resilience Poul Harremoës and others (eds), *The Precautionary Principle in the 20th Century: Late Lessons from Early Warnings* (Earthscan 2002).

[66] See Hood and others (n 15) 137.

[67] Hood and Jones (n 51) 194.

[68] ibid 111.

[69] Hood and others (n 15).

[70] Hood and Jones (n 51).

[71] Hood and Jones (n 60) 11–13.

[72] The classic example is Perrow's notion of "normal accident", Charles Perrow, *Normal Accidents: Living with High-Risk Technologies* (Basic Books 1984) 386. It argues that accidents are bound to happen because humans rely too much on their routines linked to existing procedures and mechanisms. Their lack of focus and attention is therefore the direct cause of accidents.

[73] See Art 28 General Data Protection Regulation (GDPR).

2.7 Challenges to risk management: beyond objectivity

2.7.1 Rise of risk analysis

It appears that in the 1970s and 1980s a method of risk management gained prevalence: risk analysis.[74] Risk analysis is a method of risk management which is based on quantitative risk assessment (QRA)[75] in combination with the use of economic, mathematical, and aggregated risk (or cost)-benefit analysis concerning the management step.[76] As its name indicates, quantitative risk assessment is an analytical technique for quantifying the estimates of a risk. It is grounded in the natural sciences.[77] It originated in the fields of natural hazards (fire, blood, earthquake), health, and safety, particularly in work context. For this reason, risk analysis flourished first in areas of technological failure and crisis management, and more in particular in so-called high-reliability organisations in such fields as nuclear, chemical, and transport.[78] Yet, it rapidly expanded,[79] and became the most prominent method of risk management, being used in such diverse fields as quality control, chemical toxicity levels, bureaucratic and administrative level, and for policy-making purposes more generally.[80] One can argue that it owes its success to its methodological plasticity, abstraction, and non-specificity,[81] but also to an expanding cultural trust in numbers as the basis for rational decision making.[82]

Notwithstanding these early successes, risk analysis underwent increasing criticisms in the 1970s and 1980s. The heart of the critique targeted risk analysis' pretences at objectivity.

Some of the criticisms emanating from the risk literature focused on issues of risk acceptability and tolerance—traditionally associated to the risk management step. They therefore contested the so-called rational methodologies used to aggregate the cost and benefits (cf *supra*, eg ALARA etc) that purportedly underpin "objective" risk management decisions.[83] In this sense, they emphasised cultural differences in framing risks, differences in responses to how risk is presented and communicated, etc.[84] This points to the fact that people value risk differently: some

[74] The emergence of risk analysis as a field and as a technical discipline owes a lot to Starr's 1969 seminal paper "Social Benefit versus Technological Risk" (1969) 165 Science 1232.

[75] Jones and Hood (n 16) 5.

[76] Warner (n 4) 2; Hood and others (n 15) 137.

[77] Jones and Hood (n 16) 6.

[78] Power (n 14) 12.

[79] Warner (n 4) 2.

[80] JK Mitchell, "Human Dimensions of Environmental Hazards" in Andrew Kirby (ed), *Nothing to Fear: Risks and Hazards in American Society* (University of Arizona Press 1990).

[81] Power (n 14) 13.

[82] Theodore M Porter, *Trust in Numbers: The Pursuit of Objectivity in Science and Public Life* (Princeton University Press 1995).

[83] Power (n 14) 14.

[84] Mary Douglas (ed), *Risk and Blame: Essays in Cultural Theory*, vol 22 (Routledge 1993); Daniel Kahneman and Amos Tversky, "Prospect Theory: An Analysis of Decision under Risk" (1979) 47 Economentrica: Journal of the Econometric Society 263.

are more risk averse, while others have a bigger appetite or tolerance. These attitudes to risks are very personal and not easily amenable to supposedly rational decision-making tools such as quantitative cost-benefit analyses. A specific argument is that those who manage risk should take into account public perceptions of risk as a way to determine risk tolerance, especially when the public has a stake and/or is affected by the risk at hand.[85]

In parallel, so-called science and technology studies (STS) also challenged the purported objectivity of the risk assessment step and the scientific authority it carried along. Authors like Wynne,[86] and Jasanoff,[87] challenged the divide between knowledgeable experts and ignorant laymen notably by demonstrating that "risks objects are more complex and ambivalent than risk analysis admits".[88] Within the ambit of this critique they focused upon the multiple methodological and value choices made during the assessment process. As Demortain puts it, "risks are in themselves evaluations and selections of dangers, cognitive operations that reflect particular frames through which social actors interpret the social and physical world".[89,90]

This last criticism of "objective risk assessment" points to the distinctions between risk and uncertainty, and more broadly, to the complexity of assessing and measuring risks.

Risk is intrinsically linked to numbers, and in particular, to the emergence of the first mathematical forecasting tool: the theory of probability, before really taking off with the advent of statistical sciences.[91,92] Because of the difficulty of reducing any type of potential future event in terms of probabilities, an important distinction found in the risk literature is that between a risk and an uncertainty, and further, between ignorance, and indeterminacy. Following the work of Keynes and Knight,[93] the key difference between risk and uncertainty is that it is not possible to numerically calculate uncertain events, to attach probabilities thereto.[94] Possibly because of the novelty of the activities concerned, or because of complexity or variability in their contexts.[95] Similarly, situations of ignorance are more acute because

[85] Power (n 14) 15.

[86] Brian Wynne, "Uncertainty and Environmental Learning—Reconceiving Science and Policy in the Preventive Paradigm" (1992) 2 Global Environmental Change 111.

[87] Sheila Jasanoff, "Technologies of Humility: Citizen Participation in Governing Science" (2003) 41 223.

[88] Power (n 14) 15.

[89] Demortain (n 41) 3.

[90] See also ibid and the references contained therein.

[91] Bernstein (n 9) 77.

[92] See also Alain Desrosières, *La Politique Des Grands Nombres: Histoire de La Raison Statistique* (Editions La Découverte 1993) 14: "*L'histoire du calcul des probabilités et des statistiques [est] liée successivement à la domestication du risque, à la gestion des Etats, à la maîtrise de la reproduction biologique ou économique des sociétés, ou au pilotage d'opérations militaires et administratives.*"

[93] Frank H Knight, *Risk, Uncertainty And Profit* (Century Press 1921); John Maynard Keynes, *A Treaties on Probability* (Macmillan 1921).

[94] See also Jenny Steele, *Risks and Legal Theory* (Hart Publishing 2004) 6–7.

[95] Harremoës and others (n 65) 188.

it is not only impossible to assign probabilities to the event, but also impossible to measure its magnitude. At the very end of the spectrum, situations of indeterminacy are characterised by an impossibility to even determine whether the event at stake should be valued positively or negatively.[96] It is in the context of the complex risk objects that the need for alternative assessment methods more qualitative in nature and more participatory emerged.

Yet, because of the need to resort to risk management and its convenience as a ready to use tool in the many contexts highlighted *supra* (and in general for decision-making processes be it at policy or organisational level both public and private), there has been a tendency to keep treating events as risks. This has been achieved by subsuming them under objective and scientific risk assessment and methodologies even though it is, strictly speaking, impossible to do so. This has been rendered possible through a number of hidden methodological choices such as framings and assumptions.[97] This is particularly true in the data protection context as far as the calculation of harms and risks to data subjects is concerned (cf Chapter 7).

As one can see, risk management is much less objective than it pretends at first sight. This can be traced back to the fact that even though it is grounded in the natural sciences, it is not, properly speaking, a science as such.[98] Rather, following Weinberg, it is concerned with answering policy questions that have been laid out in scientific language but which science can actually not answer. Weinberg therefore refers to is as "trans-science".[99] Similarly, Funtowicz and Ravetz speak of a "post-normal science",[100] or of a regulatory science.[101] This also points to the artificial nature of risk. One should keep in mind that risk is an artificial notion, there are no risks "out there". This is probably the meaning of Ewald's famous quote following which, "in itself, nothing is a risk, there are no risks in reality. Inversely, anything can be a risk; it all depends upon how one frames the danger, considers the event".[102] This last sentence should however not be understood as supporting a purely radical social constructivism. Risk management can work. As Bijker *et al.* argue, when an uncertainty is successfully characterised as a risk, it means that the risk can be described clearly, and it can be managed on the basis of "well-established routines that often will result in risk reduction".[103] This is possible they

[96] See Wiebe E Bijker, Roland Bal, and Ruud Hendriks, *The Paradox of Scientific Authority: The Role of Scientific Advice in Democracies* (The MIT Press 2009); Wynne (n 86).

[97] Andrew Stirling, "Risk at a Turning Point?" [1999] Journal of Environmental Medicine 119, 122.

[98] Demortain (n 41) 37.

[99] Alvin M Weinberg, "Science and Trans-Science" (1972) 10 Minerva 209, 209.

[100] Silvio Funtowicz and Jerome Ravetz, "Three Types of Risk Assessment and the Emergence of Post-Normal Science" in Sheldon Krimsky and Dominique Golding (eds), *Social Theories of Risk* (Praeger Publishers 1992) 252.

[101] Sheila Jasanoff, *The Fifth Branch: Science Advisers as Policymakers* (Harvard University Press 1990).

[102] François Ewald, "Insurance and Risk" in Graham Burchell, Colin Gordon, and Peter Miller (eds), *The Foucault Effect—Studies in Governmentality* (The University of Chicago Press 1991) 199.

[103] Bijker, Bal, and Hendriks (n 96) 159.

argue, because the risk has been "contained", that is, the knowledge for dealing with it has been stabilised and established.[104]

These remarks about the artificial nature of risk, and the inherently subjective dimension of risk management are deemed to be of crucial importance, since data protection now explicitly relies upon risk management tools.

2.8 Beyond risk analysis: sketching contemporary practices of risk management

These challenges to the risk analysis process will be the starting point for a new way to manage risk. One that is more corporate and managerial, and which directly results from dilemma concerning the best manner to address these issues.

A first type of response put the emphasis on better participation of lay public, along with a focus on improved risk communication.[105] However, in spite of the benefits in terms of risk identification and management, these enhanced processes also rendered the whole process more complicated and cumbersome, and also lead to a sort of consultative exhaustion.[106] Also, the science of risk analysis itself is complex, riddled with epistemological dilemmas, and does not lend itself easily to external verification.

A second type of response has been to put the emphasis upon the managerial process by which the analysis of risk is conducted. Institutions managing risks would start to put the emphasis upon risk communication and an instrumentalisation of democratic processes of public consultation, insofar as they would focus on the formal legitimacy of the process rather than on the content of risk analysis.[107] This was especially true in the wake of the public management reform prevalent in the 1980s, and further, reforms pertaining to corporate governance in the early 1990s whereby organisations started seeing the challenges to risk analysis increasingly as a challenge to their own legitimacy (as risk managers), and therefore as an "internal risk" to be managed.[108,109] This can be seen as the starting point of the shift from risk analysis to the managerialisation of risk analysis. As will be discussed in Chapter 4, it is argued that such a managerial conception of risk underpins meta regulation, and the use of risk for regulatory purposes.

104 ibid.
105 Power (n 14) 16.
106 ibid.
107 ibid 17–18.
108 ibid.
109 And would be framed as "reputational" or "institutional" risk, ibid 18; Henry Rothstein, Michael Huber, and George Caskell, "A Theory of Risk Colonization: The Spiralling Regulatory Logics of Societal and Institutional Risk" (2006) 35 Economy and Society 91.

3. Regulation

3.1 Defining regulation

Regulation is anything but a self-evident notion. As Ogus indicates, the expression "regulation" is not a term of art and has acquired a wide array of meaning.[110]

Part of the regulation literature links regulation to the notion of control understood as behaviour steering. This is the case of Hutter who refers to Cohen's definition of regulation as "the organized ways in which society responds to behaviour and people it regards as deviant, problematic, worrying, threatening, troublesome or undesirable in some way or another".[111] Following Freund, regulation "undertakes to control actions that would otherwise be free".[112] Parker *et al.* argue that regulation is concerned with behaviour control and intended to "shape the flow of events".[113] Black defines regulation as "a process involving the sustained and focused attempt to alter the behaviour of others with the intention of producing a broadly identified outcome or outcomes".[114] In other words, regulation is first and foremost concerned with the control of behaviour, and the modification thereof.

This previous definition is very similar to the much quoted one from Sleznick, which argues that regulation is the "sustained and focused control (…) over activities that are generally regarded as desirable to society".[115] It is generally inferred from this definition that the reference to socially desirable activities excludes criminal justice for instance from the scope of regulation,[116] although the scope of what is included under regulation has exponentially expanded over the past decades so that it is not clear whether any field escapes the broadly defined scope of "socially desirable activities".[117] Further and very importantly, the reference to sustained and focused control implies that regulation is not achieved simply by prescribing and/or prohibiting certain behaviours. On the contrary, it "requires detailed knowledge of, and intimate involvement with, the regulated activity".[118] This tends to suggest that a whole administrative apparatus of knowledge and involvement is intrinsic to the very meaning of behaviour control from a regulatory perspective.

[110] Anthony I Ogus, *Regulation: Legal Form and Economic Theory* (Hart Publishing 2004) 1.

[111] Bridget M Hutter, "Risk, Regulation, and Management" in Peter Taylor-Gooby and Jens Zinn (eds), *Risk in Social Science* (OUP 2006) 204.

[112] Ernst Freund, *Legislative Regulation: A Study of the Ways and Means of Written Law* (The Commonwealth Fund 1932) 104.

[113] Christine Parker and others, "Introduction", *Regulating Law* (OUP 2004) 2.

[114] Julia Black, "Critical Reflections on Regulation" (2002) 27 Australian Journal of Legal Philosophy 1, 20.

[115] Philip Selznick, "Focusing Organizational Research on Regulation" in Roger G Noll (ed), *Regulatory Policy and the Social Sciences* (The University of California Press 1985) 363–64.

[116] Giandomenico Majone, "Regulation and Its Modes" in Giandomenico Majone (ed), *Regulating Europe* (Routledge 1996) 9.

[117] Julia Black, "Decentring Regulation: Understanding the Role Self-Regulation in a "Post-Regulatory World" (2001) 54 Current Legal Problems 103, 132.

[118] Majone (n 116) 9.

Such observation is also sound from a historical point of view. Ideas of regulation can be traced back to the 15th century, a time whence the first embryos of what qualifies nowadays as administration appeared. During such time, regulatory activity was therefore already "administrativised", as it was entrusted to local administration.[119, 120]

Furthermore, such a perspective is consistent with the commonly shared view that regulation is composed of three constitutive elements, namely, standard setting, information gathering, and behaviour-modification.[121] These three elements correspond to the following processes: the setting of standards, processes for monitoring compliance with the standards, and mechanisms for enforcing the standards.[122] Black argues that these elements belong to the very definition of regulation.[123] As Baldwin *et al.* put it, the core task of regulation is: "detecting undesirable behaviour; developing responses and intervention tools to deal with errant behaviour; enforcing those tools on the ground".[124,125]

3.2 Regulation and law

3.2.1 Regulation, more than an economic concept

According to Ogus, regulation is fundamentally a politico-economic concept, which can best be understood by reference to different systems of economic organisation,[126] which is why it is traditionally framed in economic terms, and more in particular, in terms of market (in)efficiencies.[127,128] A well operating market brings about economic welfare, which is itself characterised by allocative efficiency, that is, a situation in which resources are put to their most valuable uses.[129] As Ogus indicates, the aim of regulation is to "direct or encourage behaviour which (it is

[119] Ogus (n 110) 6.

[120] Even though it was highly ineffective at the time, not least because of the lack of adequate administrative structures, ibid.

[121] Christopher Hood, Henry Rothstein, and Robert Baldwin, *The Government of Risk—Understanding Risk Regulation Regimes* (OUP 2001) 23.

[122] Parker and others (n 113) 1.

[123] See, Black, "Critical Reflections on Regulation" (n 114) 20: "Regulation is the sustained and focused attempt to alter the behaviour of others according to defined standards or purposes with the intention of producing a broadly identified outcome or outcomes, which may involve mechanisms of standard-setting, information-gathering and behaviour-modification."

[124] Robert Baldwin, Martin Cave, and Martin Lodge, *Understanding Regulation: Theory, Strategy, and Practice* (2nd edn, OUP 2012) 69.

[125] And also to assess and modify regulatory performance.

[126] Ogus (n 110) 1.

[127] ibid 15.

[128] See also Giandomenico Majone, "Introduction" in Giandomenico Majone (ed), *Deregulation or Re-regulation? Regulatory Reform in Europe and the United States* (Palgrave Macmillan 1990) 1–2. Furthermore, the present book is not concerned with so-called private interest theories, see Brownen Morgan and Karen Yeung, *An Introduction to Law and Regulation: Text and Materials* (Cambridge University Press 2007) ch 2.

[129] Ogus (n 110) 29.

assumed) would not occur without such intervention. The aim is to correct perceived deficiencies in the market system in meeting collective or public interest goals."[130]

Further, there is a traditional distinction between two types of—market—regulation: social and economic regulation.[131] The latter applies mostly to market situations characterised by monopolistic situations, which are constitutive of a specific type of market inefficiency. As Black argues, the archetypal regulators of the "regulatory state" identified by Majone,[132] are first and foremost economic ones, such as in the field of water, rail, telecommunication, competition, or energy.[133,134] Social regulation's ambit is broader as it addresses market failures more generally.[135] Its scope therefore encompasses issues such as health and safety, environmental protection, or consumer protection.[136] Unless specified otherwise, references to regulation refer to social regulation.[137]

However, Ogus also adds that there are legal forms that maintain such systems of economic organisation, and that the concept of regulation cannot be understood without reference thereto.[138] This last sentence is interesting because it shows well that in spite of regulation's blurred and open-ended definition, the reference to law is already present from the very beginning. Following Ogus, it seems indeed that law is one of its preferred vehicles. As he puts it "public law is not only about preventing the abuse of power; it is also about selecting legal forms which can best achieve the instrumental goals of collective choice".[139] Some legal cultures have a specific concept(s) to designate the legal instrument used for the purpose of regulatory activity. This is the case for the German "Wirtschaftsverwaltungsrechf" and the French "droit public économique", even though these instruments refer to economic regulation and not to regulation *sensu lato* (*sl*) (ie social regulation). There does not seem to be an equivalent concept in the Anglo-Saxon tradition, which therefore refers to regulation or regulatory law.[140]

130 ibid 1–2.

131 Morgan and Yeung (n 128) 2; see eg Keith Hawkins and Bridget M Hutter, "The Response of Business to Social Regulation in England and Wales: An Enforcement Perspective" (1993) 15 Law and Policy 199.

132 Giandomenico Majone, "From the Positive to the Regulatory State: Causes and Consequences of Changes in the Mode of Governance" (1997) 17 Journal of Public Policy 139.

133 Julia Black, "The Role of Risk in Regulatory Processes" in Robert Baldwin, Martin Cave, and Martin Lodge (eds), *The Oxford Handbook of Regulation* (OUP 2010) 305.

134 This should come as no surprise since the advent of Majone's "regulatory state" took place within a context of market liberalisation, Majone (n 132).

135 Even though Ogus argues that there is a more sustained focus on information needs and market externalities, which are specific types of market failures among a broader range of such failures Ogus (n 110) 4–5.

136 ibid.

137 This is even more so given that monopolistic situations are one type of market failure. Economic regulation is therefore a sub-category of social regulation, which receives specific emphasis given its importance and the variety of regulatory tools it uses, see ibid 3, 13–15.

138 ibid 1.

139 ibid v.

140 ibid 2.

The confusion, overlap, and conflation between regulation and law may stem from the fact that both are *in fine*, instruments of social policy.[141] One might add that conceiving of social policy in terms of market failures should not be so surprising in a context where political science, and more broadly the science of government understands society and markets as fundamentally entangled.[142] This observation is coherent with Black's remark that because it is possible to think of any social actor potentially as a market actor (either on the producing or consuming end), regulation has experienced a dramatic extension in scope, so as to include such fields as regulation of the family, health, reproduction, contracts, unemployment, even government itself.[143] As she puts it, "everything, it seems, is subject to regulation. What had simply been seen as 'law' before is now regulation: company law is re-described as 'regulation'; contract law is 'regulation' ".[144] This is also coherent with a number of theories that ground the rationale for regulation not in market terms, but rather, in broader political considerations pertaining to redistribution, participation, and more broadly, social justice.[145]

3.2.2 The characteristics of regulatory law

Regulatory law, which can also be referred to as legislative regulation—or regulative legislation,[146] can be pitted against private law, which differs from it in many respects.[147] Instead of being geared towards the achievement of socially desirable goals, private law has mainly a facilitative function (mainly through concepts such as property rights and contracts). It follows that the main distinction between regulation and private law lies in their respective *ex ante* and *ex post* mode of operation. The legal practice of private law operates mostly *ex post* insofar as courts have the jurisdiction to enforce rights only once an interference has -purportedly—taken place, with the content of the rights at stake specified by the court.[148] This stands in strong contrast with regulation and the whole *ex ante* administrative apparatus of monitoring and enforcement it presupposes

Freund distinguishes between regulative and declarative law. Accordingly, declarative law is mainly concerned with private, criminal, and procedural law, whereas, as stated, regulative legislation is concerned with public policy goals. Declarative law is largely the inherited product of Roman law and jurisprudence.[149]

[141] See again ibid 26, according to whom regulatory law is "designed instrumentally to achieve particular social goals".

[142] See Michel Foucault, *Sécurité, Territoire, Population* (Gallimard, Seuil 2004) 112.

[143] Black (n 117) 132.

[144] ibid.

[145] Morgan and Yeung (n 128) 2; see also Tony Prosser, *Nationalised Industries and Public Control: Legal, Constitutional, and Political Issues* (Willey Blackwell 1986).

[146] See Freund (n 112).

[147] Another similar seminal analysis of regulatory law has been performed by Teubner, see eg Gunther Teubner, *Dilemmas of Law in the Welfare State* (De Gruyter 1986).

[148] Ogus (n 110) 28.

[149] Freund (n 112) 10.

On the contrary, he defines regulative legislation as "the expression of government, in the nature of a rule of conduct, imposed upon (...) a situation, and generally operating with form requirements, precise quantities, or administrative arrangements".[150] This definition not only confirms that regulatory law is about behaviour control, but it also hints at the formal proprieties of such legislation: to some extent it is characteristic of regulatory law to be underpinned by administrative arrangements.[151,152] Ogus confirms this point by indicating that, during the Tudor and Stuart periods, regulation was implemented by what resembled the nucleus of an administration: justices of the peace, local officials, but also private individuals specially required for this matter. It is only in the 19th century that specific inspectorates were created, with the specific task of enforcing regulation (in this precise case, mainly health and safety measures).[153] This is also consistent with the definition of regulation stemming from the regulation literature, and which sees the three constitutive elements of regulation as partaking to its very definition (cf *supra*).[154]

As far as the relation between regulative and declarative legislation is concerned, it seems interesting to highlight two particular points. On the one hand, one should observe that declarative and regulative legislation are not mutually exclusive. On the contrary, Freund argues that much of declarative law "stands in need of supplementation by regulative devices". For instance, he points to the need for public records, or powers of sale.[155] Further, he argues that as most of contemporary legislative activity is concerned with regulative legislation, the latter goes so far as to transform declarative legislation. For instance, "accident liability is transformed into schemes of compensation and of social insurance, the labour law becomes a system of administration, and many commercial transactions are placed under some form of official supervision".[156] On the other hand, the role of jurisdictions should be highlighted. Freund argues that judicial practice is characteristic of declarative law inasmuch as its concepts must be interpreted and actualised as the case arises (and one could argue, to benefit from the *exequatur* of a judicial decision).[157] Regulative law he argues is to some extent alien to judicial practice insofar as it was born as an act (a command) of government, and it relies upon an administrative infrastructure. However, as regulation undergoes the process of juridification and "legification", courts and tribunals take on a renewed role, similar to that played in respect to declarative law.[158] These last observations tend

150 ibid 3.
151 ibid 10.
152 Among these diverse administrative arrangements, Freund underlines the following ones: notice requirements, public records, title registry, etc; ibid 9–10, 54.
153 Ogus (n 110) 81.
154 Ogus also characterises administrative structures as essential to regulatory law, cf ibid 6–8.
155 Freund (n 112) 9.
156 ibid 10.
157 ibid 12.
158 ibid 12–13.

to confirm some of the caveats mentioned in the introduction and pertaining to the relation between law and regulation, namely that regulation and law are more, and yet, also less than one another.

Finally, and as discussed in the introductory chapter, the conflation between law and regulation has arisen from the traditional model of regulation, known as "command-and-control". Following Ogus, "the great majority of regulatory forms adopted are coercive and hence are commonly styled "command-and-control".[159] Failure to comply may lead to the imposition of sanctions, if only as a last resort.[160] Command and control regulation can best be described as mirroring an "Austinian" understanding of law, that is, a set of standards of behaviour issued by the Sovereign, and associated to sanctions in case of non-respect.[161,162] This is confirmed by Ogus who evidences that "a prohibition combined with a sanction was the standard form used for the extensive regulation of the Tudor and Stuart periods".[163] It should be emphasised again that law is broader than such Austinian model. However, it might not be a coincidence if the conflation between law and regulation takes place around such a model of law, centred around commands and associated sanctions.

3.3 The object of regulation: harms

Just as the definition of regulation is not clear, so too is its object. It is posited that the object of regulation is risk understood in its vernacular acceptation, that is, as a potential future danger or harm (cf *supra*). Such point can be made from a variety of perspectives.

From the economic viewpoint, it was argued that regulation aims to address market failures. Economic theory itself frames the negative consequences for individuals—stemming from market externalities—in terms of harms.[164] This is confirmed by Gunningham who argues that "the purpose of regulation is indeed permeated by the economic logic of avoiding harms whilst at the same time fulfilling these obligations at the least cost for the duty holders".[165] Additionally, a number of these market externalities stemming from scientific and technological

[159] Although as will be seen, the role of command and control model of regulation is increasingly marginalised.

[160] Ogus (n 110) 79.

[161] Hutter (n 111).

[162] For a discussion and elegant critique of such Austinian understanding of law, see Victor Tadros, "Between Governance and Discipline: The Law and Michel Foucault" (1998) 18 Oxford Journal of Legal Studies 75.

[163] Ogus (n 110) 80–81.

[164] See ibid.

[165] Neil Gunningham, "Enforcement and Compliance Strategies" in Robert Baldwin, Martin Cave, and Martin Lodge (eds), *The Oxford Handbook of Regulation* (OUP 2010) 120.

evolutions as well as from industrial processes correspond to the vernacular understanding of risk and harm (eg environmental damage, consumer health issues, etc).[166] As Hutter argues, although these innovations created potential harms to consumer and citizens, the language of risk was seldom used. Instead, these harms were still framed within the logic of market failures.[167]

A specific type of regulation has, as its object, risk understood in its technical meaning: risk regulation. Risk regulation can be understood as a specific branch or iteration of regulatory activity that deals with such issues as chemicals, nanomaterials, food safety, etc. However, one should not confuse the very specific notion of risk regulation with the general notion of regulation.[168] This subtle and complex relationship between regulation and risk regulation has been eloquently commented by Demortain who argues that "although much work remains to be done in this area, it appears that [risk regulation] and [regulation] are sister disciplines, emerging together and producing similar sorts of tools".[169] Whereas the study of the linkages and articulation between regulation and risk regulation goes beyond the scope of the present book, it does tend to confirm that the object of regulation can be thought of in terms of risks. Either in the technical sense (risk regulation), or in the vernacular acceptation, ie harms (regulation).

The object of regulation can also be understood as harms with regard to the broader political rationales for regulation. This is the reason why Yeung qualifies regulation as "a system of social-harm reduction".[170] Beyond that, and having regard to the overall goal of regulation which is to achieve socially desirable outcomes, one can argue that regulation is geared towards the achievement of socially desirable activities insofar as it is instrumental to avoiding risks/harms to these objectives.[171] Black provides probably the most compelling argument since she argues that the aim of regulation can be understood either as "the goal which is sought to be achieved, or the harm which is sought to be avoided".[172]

In sum, the point of regulation is to achieve socially desirable outcomes or, symmetrically, to avoid the social harms stemming from adverse outcomes.

[166] Ogus (n 110) 13.

[167] Hutter (n 111) 205.

[168] For such a confusion, see Alessandro Spina, "A Regulatory Mariage de Figaro: Risk Regulation, Data Protection, and Data Ethics" (2017) 8 European Journal of Risk Regulation 88; for a similar point see Claudia Quelle, "The 'Risk Revolution' in EU Data Protection Law: We Can't Have Our Cake and Eat It, Too" in Ronald Leenes and others (eds), *Data Protection and Privacy: The Age of Intelligent Machines* (Hart Publishing 2017).

[169] Demortain (n 41) 1, fn 13.

[170] Karen Yeung, *Securing Compliance: A Principled Approach* (Hart Publishing 2004) 258.

[171] Fiona Haines, "Regulation and Risk" in Peter Drahos (ed), *Regulatory Theory: Foundations and Applications* (Australian National University Press 2017) 189.

[172] Julia Black, *Rules and Regulators* (OUP 1997) 7.

3.4 Studying the constitutive elements of regulation more in depth

The following lines study regulation more in depth and aim at showing that regulation can also be understood as a matter of two balancing tests associated to safeguards.

3.4.1 Standard setting

According to the regulation literature, standard setting is the first constitutive element of regulation. It entails the determination of a standard of behaviour, or rather, the quality of the activity that is deemed as safe.[173]

The literature identifies three types of standards: target standards, performance (or output) standards, and specification (or input) standards.[174]

Target standards do not contain requirements as to the quality of the activity, but rather prohibit certain harmful consequences arising from the activity.[175] Performance standards contain some requirements as to the quality of the activity, but leave the regulatee free to determine how to achieve them.[176] Finally, there are specification standards, which can exist in either positive or negative formulation. In either case they are the most prescriptive as they require to use or not to use specific production methods, materials, or processes.[177]

As will be seen more in detail in Chapter 2, the standard setting function embodies the two balancing tests, as well as safeguards. However, on top of that, the two other constitutive elements of regulation can also be seen as amounting to safeguards.

3.4.2 Monitoring and behaviour control

As indicated *supra*, monitoring refers to the processes for monitoring compliance with the standards, whereas behaviour modification embodies the tool for enforcing the standards. Activities of monitoring and behaviour control/modification can be seen as an issue of safeguards.

First, there is an obvious similarity with the risk mitigation at play in risk. The section dedicated thereto explained that some mitigation measures were concerned with the control of risks per se, whereas other mitigation measures were more concerned with the gathering of clues about the possible existence of risks and their extent, through monitoring or warning systems.

[173] Ogus (n 110) 150. This section refers mainly to Ogus, but it should be noted that similar points are made in Baldwin *et al.* (n 124) 14. Both Ogus and Baldwin *et al.*, link standards less to behaviour as such than to quality of the activity at stake (ie quality standards).

[174] Ogus (n 110) 151.

[175] ibid.

[176] ibid.

[177] ibid.

Second, in risk the distinction between the control *ss* of risks and their monitoring is not clear cut. And as a matter of fact, risk mitigation measures are not classified along it. Underlining the lack of clear-cut difference between the two, Demortain argues that "the evaluation of the chance of occurrence of a risk [amounts] to determining how to control the risk (…): evaluation is coextensive to intervention, i.e., control".[178] This is the reason why the chapter on risk has classified risk mitigation measures along different axes than the distinction monitoring/control (see *supra*, eg corrective *vs* preventative measures, or anticipationist *vs* resilient stances, and more generally, toxicology *vs* epidemiology). A similar lack of distinctiveness is at play in regulation. According to Hood *et al.* "it is well known that the mere gathering of information can sometimes alter behaviour—as with the placing of cameras to detect street crime or speeding on highways—such that the information-gathering and behaviour-modification elements of control are distinguishable only in an analytic, not physical or institutional, sense".[179] This is even more so if one follows Hood *et al.* for whom, ultimately, all the elements of regulation belong to the control function of regulation.[180]

Finally, one can also argue that monitoring and behaviour control can be understood as safeguards because just like risk mitigation measures, their goal is not simply to control risk or behaviours as such, but on the contrary to do so with a view of achieving a specific standard. Risk mitigation measures will reduce the level of risk to the level that has been deemed tolerable. Similarly, monitoring and behaviour control can be said to already incorporate a determination of the type of behaviour that is acceptable and desired. This is probably the reason why Hood *et al.* argue that behaviour control can be defined as "the ability to keep the state of a system within some preferred subset of all its possible states".[181] Similarly, Freund indicates that monitoring and behaviour control are always anticipative in nature, insofar as they focus on creating the conditions that should lead to the "proper" behaviour, that is, behaviour leading to achievement of the standards.[182]

3.4.3 Redefining the opposition between monitoring and behaviour control types of safeguards

If one accepts that monitoring and behaviour control are constitutive of safeguards, and that just like in the case of risk, the distinction between the control of risk per se and monitoring is a porous one, then this begs the question as to how should safeguards be distinguished and classified in the context of regulation. It is purported that it is possible to distinguish between substantive and formal safeguards.

[178] Demortain (n 41) 7.
[179] Hood, Rothstein, and Baldwin (n 121) 21. In a similar sense, see also Torin Monahan, *Surveillance in the Time of Insecurity* (Rutgers University Press 2010).
[180] Hood, Rothstein, and Baldwin (n 121) 23.
[181] ibid.
[182] Freund (n 112) 303.

Substantive safeguards partake per definition of behaviour modification because they directly address the content and modalities of what course of action is allowed or not under the standards set. Formal safeguards compel to the observance of prescribed modalities of action, which, allegedly, are not concerned with what is possible or not under the standards in place, and have more to do with classification, organisation, and procedure.[183] Freund lists the following examples: filing and report requirements; registries; logbooks; marks, labels, and certificates[184] All of these, he adds, are "generally supported by appropriate administrative powers of examination and inspection".[185] Contrary to substantive safeguards which are linked to behaviour modification, formal safeguards can partake either of monitoring or of behaviour modification; precisely because the difference between the two types of safeguards is such a fluid one. As Freund puts it, "there is hardly any conceivable formal requirement, which may not under circumstances become matter of substance".[186] He gives the example of the requirement that oleomargarine be coloured pink, which is tantamount to a direct prohibition since this formal requirement directly influences the properties of the product.[187]

Freund argues that formal safeguards are the most "popular", because they allow for the indirect standardisation of action.[188] In this sense they are underpinned by a discretionary power, because however undetermined the embodiment of the standard is, some determination needs to occur at some point (more on that in Chapter 2).

As one can see, monitoring and behaviour can also be thought of as safeguards, thereby further substantiating the claim of the kinship with risk because of a similar *modus operandi*. Even more so, and just like in the case of risk, the distinction between monitoring and control per se is a fuzzy and blurry one. It is suggested that the main distinction to be adopted here is that between substantive and formal safeguards (contrary to risk where the main distinction is between toxicology and epidemiology). The rest of the analysis will be carried out in Chapter 2. This chapter will confirm the analysis pertaining to which monitoring and behaviour control can be better understood as substantive and formal safeguards, by applying the three constitutive elements of regulation to data protection.

[183] ibid 63.
[184] ibid 65.
[185] ibid.
[186] ibid 63.
[187] Another useful example is the following: "an applicant for naturalisation must during the last preceding five years have *behaved* as a person attached to the constitution; the required oath contains *a declaration to the effect that he is attached* to the constitution", ibid 64.
[188] ibid 65.

3.4.4 The difference between enforcement and safeguards

Following Freund, regulation is always anticipative in nature, insofar as its proper way of controlling behaviour is undertaken through a focus on creating general and impersonal conditions leading to the desired behaviour.[189] As demonstrated, this is also the case for safeguards (ie monitoring and behaviour control, or rather, substantive and formal safeguards). In this sense, individual, specific, actions fall somewhat beyond the scope of regulation and safeguards.[190] In other words, the issue of enforcement and compliance, that is, of whether specific actors are behaving in a law-abiding way, is somewhat alien to safeguards, and to the notion of regulation in the general sense. Which is why it is the object of specific provisions especially dedicated to enforcement.

Enforcement deals specifically with instances of non-compliance, or resistance to safeguards. In such cases, compliance is achieved through punishment, sanctions, penalties, etc.[191] This approach to compliance through deterrence of a sanction is characteristic of so-called "command-and-control" regulatory models, which will be discussed more in-depth *infra* (even though all regulatory models rely upon sanctions and enforcement). Sanctions may include fines or imprisonment, forfeiture and the seizing of assets,[192] or liability as well as nullity clauses.[193]

Enforcement then is a limited type of provision; always secondary to the—primary—safeguards and to regulation more generally. Whereas safeguards are directly instrumental to achieving the desired standard(s), enforcement has only a punitive and deterrent dimension. Further, whereas safeguards are anticipative in nature because they are enacted in view of creating the conditions for achieving the desired standards, enforcement provisions have no relation with the standard at stake, which could explain why enforcement is per definition *ex post*.

That being said, the distinction between safeguards and their enforcement remains a subtle one since compulsion is at the heart of both. Freund gives the example of safeguards that are "self-enforceable", which are characterised by prescribing specific conditions and/or formal requirements that must be observed if the act is to be—legally—valid.[194] In such cases, no enforcement is required as the lack of legality of the act carries its own sanction.

[189] ibid 303.
[190] ibid.
[191] ibid 302–03.
[192] See also ibid 320: "In the nature of forfeiture is also the revocation of a license, the deportation of an alien, and any special disqualification imposed as the result of default or delinquency".
[193] ibid 317, 319, 336.
[194] ibid 54, 345. See also ibid 54: "This type of control is therefore concerned with the creation of powers, of disabilities, or of form requirements, or the three. In such cases, the behaviour will only be dependent upon compliance with prescribed conditions."

4. Risk and regulation as variations on the proportionality principle: a grid's eye view

This chapter has analysed in depth the notions of risk and regulation, in view of, among others, showing that both these notions can be thought of as exercises, and variations around the proportionality principle. As discussed in the introductory chapter, such proportionality takes the shape of two balancing tests with associated safeguards or risk reduction measures.

A grid is proposed herein below in order to make the point clearer.

	1st Balancing	2nd Balancing	Mitigation measures associated to 2nd balancing
ECtHR's necessity in a democratic society test	Pressing social need test: Is the legitimate aim legitimate enough?	Proportionality test *ss*: the measures addressing/achieving the pressing social need should not go further than needed	Safeguards: • Necessity test: are there alternative, less intrusive measures available or already existing? • Additional safeguards: scope (*ratione materiae*, *personae*, etc); transparency; oversight; right of appeal; etc
Risk	Risk assessment: is the risk sufficiently risky to be considered a risk?	Risk management (1): do we take the risk?	Risk management (2), risk mitigation: • Can we reduce the risk to an acceptable level, and how? • eg: Corrective measures (risk source) or passive measures (risk effects), anticipation or resilience? etc

	1st Balancing	2nd Balancing	Mitigation measures associated to 2nd balancing
Regulation	Standard setting function	Standard setting function	Monitoring and behaviour modification are actually reframed in the following terms: • Substantive safeguards • Formal safeguards

Bearing in mind the conflation between law and regulation, as well as the understanding of regulation as a variation around proportionality, the next chapter will show how the constitutive elements of regulation apply to data protection.

2
Data protection as command and control regulation

If, then, the term 'regulation' is used to denote the law which implements [it], what are its characteristics?[1]

1. Introduction: data protection as command and control regulation

As already suggested in the introduction, data protection, in its rights-based version, can be understood as command and control regulation. The present chapter will therefore provide an analysis of data protection as command and control regulation. If one wants to understand the *modus operandi* of newer models of regulation as applied to data protection (namely risk-based model of regulation), one must first understand the basis. That is, how data protection can be understood as regulation in the first place. This standpoint has another corollary. Since newer models of regulation are featured in contemporary statutes (with the General Data Protection Regulation—GDPR—as a prime example), an understanding of data protection as command and control regulation entails to study less contemporary statutes. The prime case study will therefore be the EU Data Protection Directive (DPD), which, even though not in force anymore is considered a suitable case for analysis as it embodies earlier models of regulation. Because this chapter is retrospective in scope (ie looking at previous data protection statutes in order to better understand the current ones), it often makes reference to historical sources of data protection (eg statutes and literature).

In terms of the regulatory analysis the chapter will proceed in two steps. The first step will demonstrate how the first constitutive element of regulation (standard setting) applies to data protection. This second step will continue the discussion by showing how the two other constitutive elements of regulation (monitoring and behaviour modification or control) apply to data protection. Chapter 1 on risk and regulation has shown that monitoring and behaviour control can be understood in

[1] Anthony I Ogus, *Regulation: Legal Form and Economic Theory* (Hart Publishing 2004) 2.

The Risk-Based Approach to Data Protection. Raphaël Gellert, Oxford University Press (2020). © Raphaël Gellert.
DOI: 10.1093/oso/9780198837718.001.0001.

terms of safeguards, and more specifically can be better understood as a matter of formal and substantive safeguards. In other words, regulation can be understood as a matter of "standard setting + safeguards". The first section of this chapter will show that the regulatory function of standard setting can be understood as "2 balancing tests + safeguards". Given that the following sections will discuss additional safeguards existing in data protection, one can understand regulation as the following variation on proportionality: "[(2 balancing tests + safeguards) + additional safeguards]".

2. Data protection and standard setting

The question this section wants to address is the following: how does data protection legislation fit with the first constitutive element of regulation: standard setting? It will proceed in the following way.[2]

First it will provide a more in-depth definition of standard setting from the regulation literature. It will also determine which data protection provisions correspond to this definition and how. It concludes that the data protection standard setting provisions are the so-called "core data protection principles",[3] also known as "data legitimacy" (Art 6 GDPR/7 DPD), and "data quality" (Art 5 GDPR/6 DPD).

Second, the remainder of the section will be dedicated to an in-depth analysis of the standard setting provisions in data protection. More in particular, it will be shown that they can indeed be analysed as constituted of two balancing tests associated with safeguards. In other words, data protection contains provisions on standard setting (first constitutive element of regulation), which can be thought of as a matter of two balancing tests and safeguards. The first balancing test is enshrined in the data legitimacy principle. In a similar fashion to the first balancing in risk, the goal of which is to determine whether an event is sufficiently risky to be considered a risk in the first place, the goal of data legitimacy is to determine whether the basis of the processing is sufficiently legitimate to be considered legitimate. The next step consists in mapping the second balancing test onto data protection. It is argued that such test is included in the data quality principle, and more in particular, in the requirement that the data processed should be "adequate, relevant and not excessive" with regards to the goal pursued. This means that the remainder of the data quality principle is composed of safeguards.

[2] Some of the arguments developed in this section were also considered in the following publications: Raphaël Gellert, "Data Protection: A Risk Regulation? Between the Risk Management of Everything and the Precautionary Alternative" (2015) 5 International Data Privacy Law 3; Raphaël Gellert, "We Have Always Managed Risks in Data Protection Law: Understanding the Similarities and Differences Between the Rights-Based and Risk-Based Approaches to Data Protection" (2016) 4 European Data Protection Law Review 481.

[3] cf Lee A Bygrave, *Data Protection Law—Approaching Its Rationale, Logic, and Its Limits* (Kluwer 2002) ch 3.

2.1 Data quality and legitimacy principles embody standard setting in data protection, and more in particular performance standards

As outlined in Chapter 1, standard setting is concerned with the quality of activities undertaken by individuals (and organisations), and one can distinguish between target, performance, and output standards. It is posited that Arts 6 and 7 DPD are the standard setting provisions.

It is maybe no coincidence that Art 6 of the Directive is the one relating to the quality of the data (data quality principle) since it is the only provision of Section I, which contains the "principles relating to data quality". Article 7 pertains to the legitimacy of the processing operation (data legitimacy principle) since it is the only provision of Section II, which contains the "criteria for making data processing legitimate".

The literature provides some evidence since it sometimes refers to the core principles as data management principles,[4] or proper data usage.[5] In effect, they determine under what conditions a given processing of data can be considered as safe, thereby echoing both notions of risk management and standard setting. Burkert provides further evidence by analysing the role and function of these principles in terms of *efficiency*—Art 6—and *legitimacy*—Art 7[6]—and by overtly placing them within what he refers to as "information management principles".[7]

One must then ask what type of standard is at stake. It is argued that the data quality principles are performance standards. On the one hand, they are more specific than mere generic interdictions of harmful outcomes, but not specific enough as to require specific processes, technical specificities, or even specific amounts of data. On the other hand, they prescribe certain qualities that the processing of data should feature, but fall short of prescribing how this should take place. This is exactly the definition of performance standards.

This is actually quite explicit: to be of a certain quality, the data must be processed in a fair and lawful (and transparent), non-excessive (both in terms of quantity and duration), specific and explicit, accurate way. The same holds true for Art 7: the processing must be necessary for a legitimate basis. If all these standards are met, then the processing is considered as safe. Yet, if these are undeniably qualities

[4] David H Flaherty, *Protecting Privacy in Surveillance Societies—The Federal Republic of Germany, Sweden, France, Canada, and the United States* (The University of North Carolina Press 1989) 4; Herbert Burkert, "Data-Protection Legislation and the Modernization of Public Administration" (1996) 62 International Review of Administrative Sciences 557.

[5] Alan Westin, "Entering the Era of Databank Regulation and How We Got There" in OECD (ed), *Policy Issues in Data Protection and Privacy—Principles and Perspectives* (OECD 1976) 99.

[6] Herbert Burkert, "Privacy—Data Protection: A German/European Perspective", *2nd Symposium of the Max Planck Project Group on the Law of Common Goods and the Computer Science and Telecommunications Board of the National Research Council* (1999) 57–58.

[7] Burkert (n 4) 558.

that the processing should possess, they nonetheless remain rather abstract requirements that need to be implemented in practice by the data controller who enjoys a margin of discretion for doing so. Such a take is confirmed by Hondius for instance, who argues that such requirements as relevance and non-excessiveness are very much a matter of "appreciation" for the data controller.[8]

The previous lines have demonstrated that the data protection core principles correspond to the standard setting function as it is explained in the regulation literature. The following lines will demonstrate that such standard setting is in line with the analysis carried out in the introductory chapter, namely, two balancing tests with risk reduction measures associated to the second one.

2.2 Article 7: data legitimacy as the first balancing test

Article 7 of the EU Data Protection Directive contains the criteria for making data processing legitimate, that is, whether a processing of data can take place at all. On the one hand, it is the only article of Section II Chapter II of the Directive, which concerns the criteria for making data processing legitimate. On the other hand, the provision starts with the following line: "personal data may be processed only if". In this sense, it encompasses the first standard setting operation (ie "sufficiently legitimate to be legitimate") insofar as it determines whether the goal pursued is sufficiently legitimate to begin with. This is a preliminary requirement that must be fulfilled before assessing the suitability of the contemplated measure (or in this case, the data processing operation).

According to Art 7, personal data can be processed only under the following conditions: the unambiguous consent of the data subject (7(a)); necessary to the pursuance of a contractual or legal obligation (7(b) and (c)); necessary to protect the vital interests of the data subject (7(d)); necessary to the exercise of public authority in the pursuit of the general interest (7(e)); or necessary to the interests of the data controller, which must not override the data subject's own interests (7(f)).

2.2.1 Data legitimacy is both about the legitimacy of the processing operation and its necessity

The question addressed here is how exactly such legitimacy of the processing is determined? It is purported that Art 7 contains two elements: the first balancing test, as well as what the European Court of Human Rights (ECtHR) refers to as the "necessity test" (the examination of less harmful alternatives), since all provisions of Art 7 (except consent) require that the processing be necessary in view of the legitimate basis chosen.

[8] Frits W Hondius, *Emerging Data Protection in Europe* (North-Holland; American Elsevier 1975) 116.

As an embodiment of the first balancing test, the whole point of the data legitimacy provision is to determine whether the basis of the processing is legitimate. This, as seen, entails to determine whether it is sufficiently legitimate. The condition of the necessity of the processing operation with regard to this goal embodies the necessity test also known as the examination of alternatives. As seen in the introductory chapter, according to ECtHR practice, safeguards are only concerned with the second balancing test. However, in an idiosyncratic way, data protection associates this safeguard to the first balancing test. It does make sense to join these two elements insofar as they both determine whether a data processing operation can take place or not in the very first place. Indeed, the first balancing test will determine whether the processing is worth being pursued at all, whereas the necessity test will determine whether the chosen means is appropriate or not. In both cases a negative answer entails the end of the process. It follows that Art 6 embodies the rest of the proportionality test *sensu stricto* (*ss*), that is, the second balancing exercise coupled with additional safeguards (cf *infra*).

2.2.2 Data legitimacy in practice (1): presumptions

It is argued that the first balancing test is contained in Art 7 of the Directive. But where should one start to demonstrate this? One obvious way forward is to look at Art 7(f), since it explicitly requires a balancing to be undertaken between the interests of the data controllers and those of the data subjects. In other words, the processing will have a legitimate ground if the data controller has a legitimate interest, which itself is the result of the balancing between two interests: those of the data controller and of the data subject. This proves the point: the legitimate basis of Art 7 is indeed the result of a balancing test. But if this is obvious for Art 7(f), what about the other articles of that same provision? It could be argued that, inversely, for these other provisions (Art 7(a)–(e)), the goal is presumed legitimate. Burkert supports such a view. According to him, Art 7 is at the heart of one of data protection's functions which is to perform a balancing of the different interests revolving around the processing of personal data. He distinguishes between two types of balancing: the implicit and the explicit one. The implicit has been done a priori as is the case with the legal obligation grounds, the public interest one, or the data subject's consent (consent is seen as a result of such balancing performed by the data subject).[9] Explicit balancing has yet to be done by the concerned actors, as is the case with Art 7(f) of the EU Directive, where it is up to the data controllers to determine whether or not their interest is legitimate enough.

It follows that Art 7 is structured around different presumptions (or implicit balancing tests). In the case of consent there is a double presumption: the basis is presumed legitimate, and the processing of data is presumed necessary to achieve its

[9] Herbert Burkert, "Institutions of Data Protection—An Attempt at a Functional Explanation of European National Data" (1981) 3 Computer Law Journal 167, 173–75.

aim (since indeed this is the only provision that does not explicitly require the processing of data to be necessary). Article 7(b) to (e) provide for a single presumption (or implicit balancing): these different grounds are presumed legitimate, but the data controller is yet to assess the necessity of the ensuing processing operations. Finally, Art 7(f) contains no presumption. The data controller must explicitly determine both the legitimacy of the chosen basis and the necessity of the data processing implementing the latter.[10]

The Art 29 WP has explicitly endorsed such an analysis, since it has argued that: "when processing is based on one of these five grounds, it is considered as a priori legitimate and therefore only subject to compliance with other applicable provisions of the law. There is in other words a presumption that the balance between the different rights and interests at stake—including those of the controller and the data subject is satisfied."[11]

However, these presumptions are not irreversible.[12] Very much like the list of goals provided by Art 8.2 European Convention on Human Rights (ECHR), these very broad bases are considered legitimate in principle, but it remains to be seen in each specific case whether it is true. In its case law, the Court of Justice of the European Union (CJEU) does indeed examine the legitimacy of the basis chosen (as well as the necessity of the data processing operations). The next sub-section will discuss in detail one such case to show that most of Art 7 DPD contains an implicit balancing test.

2.2.3 Data legitimacy in practice (2): *Heinz Huber*

An earlier yet very informative case is the 2008 *Heinz Huber* one.[13] This case concerns the AZR, a register of foreign EU nationals residing in Germany, which was

[10] Such a perspective is confirmed by the CJEU, at least concerning Art 7(f), (even though the present author does not necessarily agree with the vocabulary used). The ASNEF case, the CJEU made the following statement: "Art. 7(f) sets out two cumulative conditions that must be fulfilled in order for the processing of personal data to be lawful: firstly, the processing of the personal data must be necessary for the purposes of the legitimate interests pursued by the controller (…); and secondly, such interests must not be overridden by the fundamental rights and freedoms of the data subject", CJEU, Joined Cases C-368/10 and C-469/10, ASNEF, 2011, §38; see also §40 of the same case.

[11] Art 29 WP, "Opinion 06/2014 on the Notion of Legitimate Interests of the Data Controller under Article 7 of Directive 95/46/EC" (2014) 9.

[12] The following indications as to what exactly necessity means in the context of data protection can be gathered from Hans Peter Bull: "the necessity of a processing operation for the fulfilment of a task must be verified. If not verified it is not helpful: it keeps all doors open. Back doors in particular will never qualify as necessary", quoted in Hondius (n 8) 138.

[13] CJEU Case C-524/06, *Heinz Huber* [2008] ECLI:EU:C:2008:724 (hereafter *Heinz Huber*). There are other more recent cases dealing with the application of data legitimacy in practice, but a conscious choice has been made to focus on *Huber* since the reasoning is considered most relevant for the discussion at stake. See for instance, CJEU Case C-342/12, *Worten* [2013] ECLI:EU:C:2013:355 (hereafter *Worten*); CJEU Case C-291/12, *Schwarz* [2013] ECLI:EU:C:2013:670 (hereafter *Scwharz*); CJEU Case C-683/13, *Pharmacontinente* [2014] ECLI:EU:C:2014:2028 (hereafter *Pharmacontinente*); CJEU Case C-398/15, *Manni* [2017] ECLI:EU:C:2017:197 (hereafter *Manni*); CJEU Case C-13/16, *Rīgas satiksme* [2017] ECLI:EU:C:2017:336 (hereafter *Rīgas satiksme*); CJEU Case C73/16, *Puškár* [2017] ECLI:EU:C:2017:725 (hereafter *Puškár*).

used for purposes of application of the legislation concerning the establishment of foreign citizens on German soil, as well as for the purpose of fighting crime. The register was attacked before German courts for being discriminatory (§32).

In this reference for a preliminary ruling, the German court (*Oberverwaltungsgerich für das Land Nordrhein-Westfalen*) asked the CJEU precisely the question at stake in this discussion, that is, "whether the criterion of necessity imposed by Art. 7(e) of Directive 95/46 can be a criterion for assessing a system of general data processing such as the system put in place under the AZR".[14] The national court did in fact not discard the possibility that: "the directive may leave it open to the national legislature itself to define that requirement of necessity".[15] In the second part of its question, the court asks in substance how such assessment should be conducted.[16]

The CJEU responds positively to the first question. In essence the reasoning of the court is two-fold. It first bases itself upon the *Rundfunk* case, which states that both Arts 6 and 7 of the Directive should be complied with (§48).[17] Second, it rests its argumentation on the need for harmonisation in the application of the Directive (§§50–52). It therefore follows that Art 7(e) should be relied upon.

The Court then goes on to answer the second part of the question. As will be seen, and in accordance with the present analysis, assessing the necessity of the processing entails first to determine the legitimacy of the goal pursued. It distinguishes the two purposes.

Concerning the first purpose, the question referred to the Court is the following one: whether the use of a centralised database in order to provide support to the authorities responsible for the application of the legislation relating to the right of residence[18] is compatible with Art 7(e) of the Data Protection Directive as interpreted in the light of the requirements of the Treaty including in particular the prohibition of any discrimination on grounds of nationality under Art 12(1) EC (§46).

In the present case, the conflict at the heart of this first balancing test related to the right of free movement and establishment of an EU citizen in the territory of a Member State of which they are not a national, and the restrictions brought to that right by the said Member State (cf §54).[19] In order to determine the existence of such pressing social need, the Court immediately states that the right to free movement of EU citizens within the Union is not unlimited. Moreover, the limitations

[14] *Heinz Huber*, para 39.

[15] ibid.

[16] "However, should that not be the case, the question arises how that requirement is to be understood, and more particularly whether the objective of administrative simplification might justify data processing of the kind put in place by the AZRG" (§39).

[17] CJEU Joined Cases C-465/00, C-138/01, and C-139/01, Rundfunk [2003] ECLI:EU:C:2003:294 para 65 (hereafter *Rundfunk*).

[18] And to its use for statistical purposes, but this purpose is not addressed here.

[19] And such restriction should obviously be encompassed by a legitimate goal such as public order, national security, etc, although no mention is made of it in the case.

brought thereto should be foreseen by the Treaty[20] and the measures adopted to give it effect (§54). These lines can be seen as the exercise of a balancing test.

More in particular, the Court doesn't undertake the balancing itself, but refers to the balancing already performed in EU law, which it considers valid. Indeed, it goes on to describe the EU legislation and the measures that give effect to the balance operated by the Treaty on the Functioning of the European Union (TFEU). The court is quite deferring, as it does not question the restrictions provided by EU legislation and the balance that they struck (§§55–57).[21] Given that the goal is legitimate according to Art 7(e), the court then examines the necessity of the data processing. There is some confusion since it examines some criteria that typically belong to Art 6.[22] However it also addresses the necessity test, since—in typical fashion on the justification of the measure compared to alternatives—the Court states that it must be proven that the processing operations at stake contribute to the more effective application of the legislation. It leaves it up to the national court to determine this (§62).

The court is less deferential concerning the second aim of the AZR namely, the processing of non-national EU citizens for the purpose of crime fighting. In this case there is a legitimate aim (the protection of public order—§76), following which a more specific societal need is pursued, namely the specific targeting of non-national EU citizens residing on the territory of the Member State for the purpose of crime fighting. Hence, the heart of this balancing test opposes this societal need with the difference in treatment that it creates. The court therefore weighs the different interests at stake, and concludes that although the objective is a legitimate one it cannot be relied upon, since the fight against crime "necessarily involves the prosecution of crimes and offences committed, irrespective of the nationality of the perpetrators" (§§77–78). Thus, treating differently national and non-national EU citizens for the purpose of crime fighting is not sufficiently legitimate to be considerate a legitimate aim in the meaning of Art 7(e) of the Data Protection Directive. It follows that the examination of the necessity of the AZR with regards to this purpose is void of its object.

2.2.4 Comparison with other views that do not support the existence of the first balancing test within data protection legislations

The analysis provided of Art 7 contrasts with several views that have characterised data protection as a legal instrument that merely endorses already-made decisions

[20] Now Treaty on the Functioning of the European Union (TFEU); then Treaty of the European Community (TEC).

[21] In this case and in a nutshell, EU law grants this right only to certain categories of citizens. Furthermore, such right depends on the allocation of a residence permit, which itself is delivered on the condition that the citizens in question present specific documents to the authorities, and eventually register themselves.

[22] Such as not containing more information than necessary (data minimisation) or keeping the data up to date (data accuracy).

to undertake personal data processing. In such case, its function is that of limiting the impact of the processing. Such a view has explicitly been adopted by the Ware Report, which states that it was not "charged with developing criteria for determining when and for what purpose to establish personal data systems".[23] The fair information principles the report develops are only to be applied to already existing personal data processing systems.[24] Such a perspective is also popular as far as Directive 95/46 is concerned. For instance, Peter Hustinx, the first European Data Protection Supervisor, has argued that data protection "was not designed to prevent the processing of such information or to limit the use of information technology per se. Instead, it was designed to provide safeguards whenever information technology would be used for processing information relating to individuals."[25] Such a view can certainly find a base in Art 1(2) of the Directive, which provides that "Member States shall neither restrict nor prohibit the free flow of personal data between Member States for reasons connected with the protection" afforded to citizens with regards to the processing of their personal data. From this perspective, the Data Protection Directive is an instrument that aims foremost at removing barriers to the internal market concerning the processing of personal data.[26] Such stances echo critical views that have evidenced the potential of data protection legislations as a mere legitimising tool for data processing operations.[27]

However, it should be noted that both the Ware Report and Hustinx nuance their stance immediately thereafter. The authors of the Ware Report feel compelled to warn that even though their mandate does not go so far as to address the necessity and legitimacy of the purpose, persons who would want to establish automated personal data systems should be very cautious before doing so. These considerations reflect the balancing at play in the "pressing social need" test, and might result with averting the establishment of some data processing systems.[28] Equally, Hustinx adds that: "the real objective of [data protection] is therefore to protect individuals against *unjustified* [processing of their personal data]".[29] Both these last two sentences illustrate well the fact that data protection seems to be more than a mere instrument for mitigating the harmful effects of already existing data processing operations. It could actually be fit to address the legitimacy and broader social need to have data being processed at all, very much like Art 8.2 ECHR.

[23] US Department of Health Education & Welfare, *Records, Computers, and the Rights of Citizens* (The MIT Press 1973) 51.

[24] See also James B Rule, *Privacy in Peril: How We Are Sacrificing a Fundamental Right in Exchange for Security and Convenience* (OUP 2007) 22–24.

[25] Peter J Hustinx, "EU Data Protection Law: The Review of Directive 95/46/EC and the Proposed General Data Protection Regulation" (2014) 1.

[26] See Serge Gutwirth, *Privacy and the Information Age* (Rowman & Littlefield 2002) ch 5.

[27] B William and M Chiasson, "If Fair Information Principles Are the Answer, What Was the Question? An Actor-Network Theory Investigation of the Modern Constitution of Privacy" (2005) 15 Information and Organization 267, 271.

[28] US Department of Health Education & Welfare (n 23) 51.

[29] Hustinx (n 25) 5. Emphasis by the author.

A historical perspective on data protection statutes can also support such point of view. Just as it was the case for the Ware Report, early data protection statutes did not contain provisions on the purpose of the collection of data and its legitimacy. According to Hondius, the issue of purpose legitimacy "does not appear to have attracted much attention from the national legislators".[30] Purpose was presumed legitimate, or at least remained unquestioned both in Convention 108 of the Council of Europe,[31] and in most national statutes of the 1970s.[32] Interestingly, one of the reasons put forth to justify such a stance was the distinction then prevailing between those who collected and those who further processed data.[33] However, as the roles of controllers and further processors were increasingly merged, data protection statutes started to increasingly address purpose legitimacy. Thus, if historically data protection may have been more in line with analyses that frame it as a tool of legitimation (owing to specific and historically contingent assumptions concerning the life-cycle of data processing though), the existence of provisions on the legitimacy of processing grounds and their application by the CJEU tends to argue the opposite.

Further, it is to be noted that in several cases, even though commentators do not address the legitimacy of the processing ground as such, it seems that such discussion 'comes back through the backdoor'.[34] Bygrave discusses the legitimacy of the goal pursued as part of the purpose specification principle.[35] Hondius—following the explanatory report of Council of Europe (CoE) Resolution 74(29)[36]—argues that such discussion should take place as part of the fairness criterion.[37]

However, if in theory data protection allows for a questioning of the legitimacy and necessity of the processing, it remains to be seen what balance is struck in practice. It would seem that in many cases, such balance is lenient and rather permissive. This is the case for instance when a legislation serving as a processing ground

30 Hondius (n 8) 110.

31 Convention for the protection of individuals with regard to automatic processing of personal data (ETS No 108) 1981.

32 Hondius indicates the Austrian 1974 Data Protection Bill as an exception, as a specific statutory authorisation was required prior to the establishment of a data processing system, see Hondius (n 8) 110. See also Hustinx (n 25) 10: "The Directive also follows the basic principles for data protection set out in the Convention, but includes six criteria for the legitimacy of data processing which are not specified in the Convention." That was also the case in the first Data Protection Directive proposal of the Commission, see Eleni Kosta, *Consent in European Data Protection Law* (Martinus Nijhoff 2013) 89.

33 Hondius (n 8) 111.

34 In the case of Hondius, this may be due to the fact that as his book dates back to 1975, he comments on the two CoE Resolutions preceding Convention 108, and which did not contain such provision, see Hustinx (n 25) 10. The original OECD guidelines also lack such provision see, ibid 8. Indeed, the Data Protection Directive is the first—international—instrument to include a separate provision on legitimate grounds.

35 Bygrave (n 3) 61–62.

36 One of the two Council of Europe Resolutions that preceded the adoption of Convention 108 of 1981, Resolution (74)29 on the Protection of the Privacy of Individuals vis-a-vis Electronic Data Banks in the Public Sector 1974.

37 Hondius (n 8) 109–10.

strikes a balance that clearly favours the processing of data,[38] or when the CJEU simply refers to such legislation and the balance struck therein without further questioning it.[39]

2.3 Article 6: data quality

Article 6 is often referred to as containing the principles relating to data quality. These include—but are not limited to—the following: fair and lawful processing, purpose specification, data minimisation/minimality, data accuracy (including adequacy), storage limitation, security, etc. It should be noted that the naming of these principles vary according to different authors,[40] and that they are not present in a homogeneous manner in all data protection acts.[41]

Contrary to Art 7 that determines whether or not a processing can take place, Art 6 is based upon the premise that the processing can take place. Its function, then, is to spell out the modalities of the processing (keeping in mind that there is always a chance that the processing does not take place following the second balancing test).[42]

Pursuing the analysis, it is posited that since Art 7 embodied the first balancing as well as the safeguards pertaining to necessity/examination of alternatives, Art 6 comprises the second balancing exercise as well as a host of safeguards. Both of which concern the measures deployed to reach the—now—legitimate goal pursued.

2.3.1 Article 6(1)(c) as the embodiment of the second balancing test

Article 6(1)(c) DPD provided that data had to be "adequate, relevant and not excessive" (compare with Art 5(1)(c) GDPR, which provides that data should be "adequate, relevant and limited to what is necessary in relation to the purposes for which they are processed"). Given that, contrary to the Directive, the GDPR now refers to this provision as the data minimisation principle,[43] some clarification is warranted.

In the opinion of the author, from a purely conceptual and analytical point of view, conflating the requirement of adequacy, relevance, and necessity with that of

[38] See Rosemary Jay, *Data Protection Law and Practice* (Sweet & Maxwell 2007).
[39] cf *Worten*; *Pharmacontinente*; *Manni* (n 13).
[40] One can for instance compare Bygrave (n 3) 3, with Gutwirth (n 26).
[41] Flaherty has undertaken a—now dated—comparative overview of the various implementations of these principles in a number of legislations, see Flaherty (n 4).
[42] Accordingly, and contrary to Art 7, which provides that data "can only be processed if", Art 6 provides that "data processed must be [compliant with the following principles]".
[43] This is also the case for others such as Bygrave (n 3); Art 29 WP, "Opinion 01/2014 on the Application of Necessity and Proportionality Concepts and Data Protection within the Law Enforcement Sector" (2014).

minimisation of the data processed is unwarranted. Strictly speaking, data minimisation can be defined as the requirement to process as little data as possible.[44] This can be assimilated to a safeguard/risk reduction measure aiming to reduce the scope of the processing (cf below). Yet, and strictly speaking, this is quite different from the requirement to be relevant, adequate, and not excessive/limited to what is necessary. The latter can indeed be assimilated to a balancing test: one must have regard to the purpose, and on this basis, determine what constitutes an adequate and relevant processing operation.[45] There are many examples that support such interpretation. Bygrave for instance refers to Art 6(1)(c) as data minimisation, but nevertheless argues that it can be replaced by proportionality (or notions which he considers synonymous such as non-excessiveness, or even frugality).[46] Moerel and Tranberg also locate proportionality in Art 6(1)(c),[47] of the Art 29 WP.[48] So does Council of Europe Recommendation R (97) 18 on the Protection of Personal Data Collected and Processed for Statistical Purposes, which refers to the requirement of non-excessiveness as an obligation of proportionality,[49] or the Italian data protection authority.[50]

The author is aware that one of the objectives of the GDPR reform process was to strengthen then Art 6(1)(c) DPD on grounds that it was too lax, hence the slightly more stringent definition and the renaming of the principle as "data minimisation".[51] Yet, it is argued that Art 6(1)(c) DPD (or 5(1)(c) GDPR) embodies both requirements: a general requirement of proportionality, which is constitutive of the

[44] Art 29 WP, "Opinion 01/2014" (n 43) 18; Bygrave (n 3) 59.

[45] For evidence that relevance and non-excessiveness amount to a balancing exercise, see Section 21(2) of the original Federal German Data Protection Bill, which concerns the appropriateness in terms of duration (cf *infra*): "erasure may take place if it doesn't prejudice 'protection worthy interests' of the person concerned". Equally, Hondius argues that if the time of retention is *unreasonably* long, it will damage the data subject's privacy, see Hondius (n 8) 118. He also makes explicit that the interests of the data controllers and those of the data subject (consisting in harm avoidance) must be reconciled, Hondius (n 8) 120.

[46] Bygrave (n 3) 60. This last term is a reference to Section 3a of the German Federal Data Protection Act, which explicitly refers to data frugality ("*datensparsamkeit*"). See also ibid 59: "the amount of personal data collected should be limited to what is necessary to achieve the purposes(s) for which the data are gathered and further processed".

[47] Lokke Moerel, *Big Data Protection—How to Make the Draft EU Regulation on Data Protection Future Proof* (Tilburg University 2014); CB Tranberg, "Proportionality and Data Protection in the Case Law of the European Court of Justice" (2011) 1 International Data Privacy Law 239.

[48] Art 29 WP, "Opinion 01/2014 on the Application of Necessity and Proportionality Concepts and Data Protection within the Law Enforcement Sector" (n 43) 21. See also, Art 29 WP, "Opinion 15/2011 on the Definition of Consent" (2011) 34: "to comply with the *principle of proportionality under Article 6(1)(c)*". Author emphasis. Art 29 WP refers to the Data Protection Directive, hence the reference to Art 6.

[49] Recommendation NO R (97) 18 concerning the protection of personal data collected and processed for statistical purposes 1997 pt 4.7.

[50] Garante per la Protezioni dei Dati Personali, "Video Surveillance the General Provision Adopted by the Garante—Doc Web n 1003482" (2004).

[51] See European Commission, "Commission Staff Working Paper: Impact Assessment Accompanying the Document Regulation of the European Parliament and of the Council on the Protection of Individuals with Regard to the Processing of Personal Data and on the Free Movement of Such Data" (2012) 50.

second balancing test in the present analysis; and a requirement of minimisation, which can be assimilated to a safeguard (cf herein below).

Continuing the analysis, if the balancing test is embodied in Art 6(1)(c), this entails that the remainder of this provision is constituted by safeguards/risk reduction measures. It proceeds as follows. It lists the safeguards that are to be found in Art 6 DPD, with the corresponding legal provisions.

2.3.2 Safeguard 1 = Transparency: principle of lawfulness, fairness and transparency + principle of purpose limitation

Article 6(1)(a) provides that data should be processed lawfully, fairly, and in a transparent manner. The requirement of lawfulness will be examined as partaking of a different safeguard. The GDPR has now included an explicit obligation of transparency. That was not the case under the Directive, where the requirement of transparency was subsumed under the requirement of fairness (even though the latter's scope is broader and will be further examined below).[52] Transparency safeguards can also be found in the purpose limitation principle (Art 6(1)(b) DPD), in relation to the requirement for the purpose to be explicit.[53] Further, transparency also contributes to the fairness of the processing,[54] which leads to the next safeguard.

2.3.3 Safeguard 2 = Lawfulness, fairness, and legitimacy: principle of lawfulness, fairness and transparency + principle of purpose limitation

One can argue that the requirement of legitimacy enshrined in the purpose limitation principle encompasses and overlaps with the requirement of lawfulness and fairness embedded into Art 6(1)(a). According to the Art 29 WP, such legitimacy provides a link to Art 7 and the need to have a legitimate basis for the processing, but also goes further.[55] It requires indeed that the purpose be in accordance with law in the broadest sense. This includes data protection law as well as any other applicable law such as employment, contract law, etc. This also includes all forms of law, such as primary and secondary legislation, municipal decrees, constitutional principles and fundamental rights, jurisprudence, etc.[56] In this sense, it espouses

[52] See notably Recital 38 of the EU Data Protection Directive: "Whereas, if the processing of data is to be fair, the data subject must be in a position to learn of the existence of a processing operation."

[53] See Art 29 WP, "Opinion 03/2013 on Purpose Limitation" (2013) 13: "There is a strong connection between transparency and purpose specification. When the specified purpose is visible and shared with stakeholders such as data protection authorities and data subjects, safeguards can be fully effective. Transparency ensures predictability and enables user control." See also ibid: purpose limitation contributes to "transparency, legal certainty and predictability". See also, Hondius (n 8) 135: "The stated purpose of the data bank forms the standard for checking the conformity of data bank operations with the data protection rules. (. . .) It is absolutely essential that the purpose is firmly established and made known to the public."

[54] Art 29 WP (n 53) 11.

[55] ibid 12.

[56] ibid.

the content of the requirement of lawfulness enshrined in Art 6(1)(a), which is very similar if not identical.[57] However, legitimacy is also broader and goes on to overlap with the meaning of fairness insofar as it also includes other elements such as customs, codes of conducts, codes of ethics, and the general context of the case, which determines among others the reasonable expectations of the data subject as to the processing their data will undergo.[58] Fairness requires that data should not be collected in a surreptitious way as would be the case if the data controller abuses its power to force the data subject to provide additional personal data.[59,60] It is also linked to the data subject's—contextual—reasonable expectations.[61]

2.3.4 Safeguard 3 = reduction in scope: purpose limitation, data minimisation, storage limitation principles

The third safeguard one can identify is a reduction in the scope of the processing, either *ratione materiae* (eg amount and/or type of data) or *ratione temporae* (duration of processing).

With regards to the material scope, one can point again to the purpose limitation principle (Art 6(1)(b)). Such principle requires that data be processed for a specific purpose. Indeed, if the purpose is not specific enough, it can lead to processing operations that are not justified.[62] For instance, in the case of the defunct data retention Directive,[63] the Art 29 WP argued that the retention of all users' data for a period of two years with subsequent access granted to law enforcement authorities was too broad a purpose insofar as it lacked sufficient clarity.[64] Moreover,

[57] See Art 29 WP (n 43) 15. On lawfulness as a safeguard, see Hondius (n 8) 111: "Even though the [Austrian Data Protection] Bill was silent on the modalities of collection, the fact that such collection should be based on a statutory provision was in itself an important data protection safeguard." See also, ibid 117: "the criteria of relevance and appropriateness are closely connected with the principle of legality".

[58] Art 29 WP (n 53) 12, 20.

[59] Bygrave (n 3) 58, for a more recent account on fairness.

[60] See eg Principle N 3 of CoE Resolution 73(22), which states that "information should not be obtained by fraudulent or unfair means". In this case it appears quite clearly that fraudulence (or lawfulness) is a complement to fairness, Resolution (73)22 on the Protection of the Privacy of the Individuals vis-a-vis Electronic Data Banks in the Private Sector 1973 73. The point is to respect the broader legal environment. See also the reference to section 3(4) of the German Teleservice Data Protection Act of 1997, which forbids teleservice providers to force users to consent to the processing of their data for purposes other than the performance of the service.

[61] Bygrave (n 3) 59. It is also to be noted that such legitimacy/fairness can change over time, "depending on scientific and technological developments, and changes in society and cultural attitudes"—Art 29 WP (n 53) 20. Also, in this latter sense, fairness can be linked both to proportionality/non excessiveness, and to purpose specification. In a similar sense, see Damian Clifford and Jef Ausloos, "Data Protection and the Role of Fairness" (2018) 37 Yearbook of European Law 130.

[62] The Art 29 WP says that: "being clear about what [a measure] is trying to achieve should ensure that (. . .) any processing of personal data involved is the minimum amount required to fulfil its aim"—(n 43) 18.

[63] Directive 2006/24/EC on the retention of data generated or processed in connection with the provision of publicly available electronic communications services or of public communications networks and amending Directive 2002/58/EC.

[64] Art 29 WP (n 43) 12.

this principle requires that data should not be further processed in a manner that is incompatible with the initial purposes. This can also be seen as a safeguard reducing the amount of data that can be processed.[65]

Further, one can also point to the data minimisation (Art 6(1)(c)) principle understood as a requirement to process as little data as possible.[66] Even though not explicitly enshrined in Art 6 of the Directive (even though it is now part of the GDPR, cf herein above), Bygrave argues that it can also be read into the fairness and/or purpose limitation principles.[67]

Finally, Art 6(1)(e), known as the storage limitation principle requires that personal data be stored only for as long as necessary for the achievement of the purpose for which they were collected in the first place.[68] For the Group, the storage limitation principle is simply the continuation of the data minimisation principle at the specific level of data storage duration.[69] The Explanatory Report of Council of Europe (CoE) Resolutions 73(22) and 74(29) explicitly saw the erasure of data as a safeguard able to avoid potential harms to the data subject.[70]

2.3.5 Safeguard 4 = accuracy of the data: data accuracy principle

From a historical perspective, data accuracy was seen as a safeguard meant to address the harms stemming from the processing of erroneous data.[71] Thus by verifying the accuracy of the data processed, the risks of harms are diminished.[72] Article 6(1)(d) therefore provides that data must be accurate and up-to-date.[73] This

[65] Art 29 WP (n 53) 36.

[66] Bygrave (n 3) 59.

[67] ibid 60.

[68] The principle does not explicitly require that the data be erased, but rather, that they be kept in a form that no longer permits identification of the data subject, and which is, accordingly, a much less potent safeguard. On the pitfalls of anonymisation, see Paul Ohm, "Broken Promises of Privacy: Responding to the Surprising Failure of Anonymization" (2010) 57 UCLA Law Review 1701.

[69] Art 29 WP (n 43) 18. In a similar sense, see Bygrave (n 3) 60.

[70] See also, Hondius (n 8) 119. See also Point 21 of the Explanatory Report of the CoE Resolution 74(29) which puts forth that "individuals have a legitimate interest in seeing certain kinds of information about them, particularly that which is harmful to them, obliterated or rendered inoperative after a certain time has passed". Further, Hondius emphasises the link that has been made between erasure and the principle of lawfulness—Hondius (n 8) 116–17.

[71] See also Gloria González Fuster, "Inaccuracy as a Privacy-Enhancing Tool" (2010) 12 Ethics and Information Technology 87: "Behind such a principle stands the idea that the storing and the processing of inaccurate data can lead to unfair decisions being taken." See also CoE Resolution 73(22) on the protection of the privacy of individuals vis-a-vis electronic data banks in the private sector, which regarded accuracy as the prime principle applying to personal information stored in electronic databanks, justifying its importance by arguing that "mistakes may cause serious damage, because of the intensive use that can be made of the data". Furthermore, point 16 of the Explanatory Report of CoE Resolution 74(29) on the protection of the privacy of individuals vis-à-vis electronic data banks in the public sector argues that: "wrong or obsolete information can be particularly harmful when adverse administrative decisions have been taken on the basis of such data". Also, section 5 of the Norwegian Data Systems Bill used to require that the risk of error stemming from inaccurate data be taken into account when deciding to set up a new data processing facility.

[72] See section 9 of Swedish Data Act 1973: data should be completed, especially if the omission would cause "undue encroachment on privacy or a risk of loss of rights".

[73] Other formulations such as that of the OECD Guidelines (para 8) add that the data should be complete. These other formulations also see accuracy as a subset of a data quality principle that combines the

provision requires that personal data should be valid with respect to their processing purpose.[74] This qualification of the duty also gives weight to data accuracy being one of the safeguards complementing the balancing test.[75]

2.3.6 Safeguard 5 = security: principle of integrity and confidentiality

Finally, it is worth noting that Art 5(1)(f) GDPR provides for the security of the data, even though data protection and data security should not be conflated, data security can be seen as a precondition for the protection of personal data.[76] It is to be noted that in the system of the Directive, this is not a data quality principle per se, and is the object of a separate provision (Art 17).

2.4 Data protection, standard setting, and proportionality: conclusions

The previous lines have tried to show that the data protection core principles correspond to the standard setting function of regulation. On the one hand they correspond to so-called performance regulatory standards, whereby they prescribe certain qualities that the regulated activity should be endowed with, but leave it up to the regulatees (ie data controllers) to precisely determine how to do so. On the other hand, these lines have showed that the data protection core principles can be analysed as composed of two balancing operations as well as of a series of safeguards. Thereby also completing the demonstration that standard setting in regulation theory can also be analysed as a matter of two balancing tests and associated safeguards, just like the proportionality test (cf Introduction), and like risk (cf Chapter 1). Hondius' analysis of these principles echoes the present one insofar as he refers to them as "legal safeguards", following which, data controllers should be "allowed to derive maximum benefit from computer technology while enjoying fullest confidence of the community".[77] The latter echoes very much the idea of balancing at the heart of (regulatory) standard setting and data protection.

It should however be noted that data protection, through its core principles, implements the double balancing in a specific way, since it associates the "necessity

requirement of accuracy with that of non-excessiveness (which is a separate provision in the Directive) for instance the OECD Guidelines para 8; or Convention 108, Art 5—though in this case accuracy and non-excessiveness are separate provisions, but the explanatory report seems to link them together. See, González Fuster (n 71) 87.

74 Bygrave (n 3) 62.

75 Interestingly, Hondius has observed that at the time of the adoption of the first Austrian data protection statute, the opposition put forth an opposition bill, which provided that "the correction of the data is to be *safeguarded*" Hondius (n 8) 113. Author's emphasis.

76 See Bygrave (n 3).

77 Hondius (n 8) 135.

test" to the first balancing test, whereas, following the ECHR proportionality test, it should be associated to the second one. In this respect it can be argued that these different data protection embodiments of proportionality can be traced back to the origins of data protection and its purpose of regulating the computer. As Hondius has observed, "most data protection laws have laid down their provisions on the handling of personal information in the same sequence as that followed by computer operations".[78]

The next part of this chapter will analyse remaining provisions of the Data Protection Directive in the light of the remaining constitutive elements of regulation: monitoring and behaviour modification. In doing so, it will bring final confirmation that data protection does well amount to regulation.

3. Formal safeguards

The analysis will now examine formal safeguards as they are enshrined in the EU Data Protection Directive. It differentiates different types of formal safeguards. This section largely builds upon Freund's analysis of the various legal forms and means that regulatory law can adopt.[79] Even though the study is quite old, the author believes its relevance is still intact for the present analysis.

3.1 Formal safeguards (1): deferred control

3.1.1 Advance determination and corrective intervention

Freund defines deferred control as the vesting of discretionary administrative powers (usually to an administrative agency).[80] This sub-section therefore addresses the modality of exercise of this discretion.

Deferred control can operate in two ways: advance determination or corrective intervention. Advance determination takes the form of a—prior—approval granted upon the application of the individual, and without which he is forbidden to act. Such approval can take the form of several similar safeguards: licence, permit, or certificate. Corrective intervention takes the form of an administrative order that imposes upon the individual a duty of action, omission, or cessation, and thus includes powers of ban, interdiction, revocation of licences, restraining injunctions, etc.[81]

[78] ibid 107.
[79] Ernst Freund, *Legislative Regulation: A Study of the Ways and Means of Written Law* (The Commonwealth Fund 1932).
[80] ibid 74.
[81] ibid 75.

3.1.2 Advance determination in data protection: licence, notification/registration, and prior checking

As far as notification/registration is concerned, pursuant to Arts 18 and 19 DPD, controllers must notify the authority prior to undertaking the processing of data with the following information: identity of the controller, purposes of the processing, categories of data subjects, categories of recipient, etc (Art 19(1)). The point is solely to provide knowledge of data processing operations, independently of any prior approval. This system of notification is coupled to a public register accessible to the public (Art 21(1) and (2)).

Freund assimilates permits, licences, and certifications insofar as they constitute mechanisms of prior approval, and hence, of advance determination.[82]

Several early data protection statutes provided for a generalised system of licensing, the most famous one being the 1973 Swedish *Data Lag*. Most if not all of these have been abandoned to date.[83] The Directive featured a system of partial licensing, which applied in cases of data processing operations that are likely to pose specific risks to the rights and freedoms of data subjects because of their nature, scope, purpose, or because they rely upon the use of new technologies (Recital 53). Article 20(1) refers to such partial licensing as prior checking, and adds that the risks must be sufficiently important. When supervisory authorities are notified of such processing (Art 20(2)), they will check the level of risk thereof. Such checking may result with an authorisation, an opinion (Recital 54), or a refusal.[84] One can understand the possibility of giving an opinion as the power to impose a conditional approval. The possibility to approve with conditions is consistent with Freund's analysis according to which there are several gradations in the power of—prior—approval, with the power of annexing conditions constituting the broadest form of discretionary power.[85] It is certainly consistent with—early—data protection practice when licensing systems still existed. Hondius indicates that some early licensing systems restricted the licence to limited time periods; restricted the purpose, amount of data, the third parties to whom it could be communicated; and also provided explicit requirements in terms of security and technical equipment, information to be provided to the data subject, data conservation duration, etc.[86]

[82] ibid 75, 85. Hondius argues along the same lines since he says that "a licence is a special form of authorisation", insofar as it concerns a specific data processing system (as opposed to authorisations that may cover the whole type of processing operations regardless of individual cases), Hondius (n 8) 221.

[83] Colin J Bennett, *Regulating Privacy* (Cornell University Press 1992) 164–65.

[84] Even though the possibility for the DPA not to allow the processing is not explicitly foreseen in the Directive, Bygrave argues that it exists given the powers of blocking, erasure, ban, etc provided by Art 28(3)—Bygrave (n 3) 76.

[85] Freund (n 79) 77–78. Less discretionary powers include the so-called "veto-system" whereby the authority is given a certain time to forbid the action, past which the absence of reaction amounts to an authorisation; or the offer of an alternative which the individual is free to accept or not, ibid.

[86] Hondius (n 8) 223.

3.1.3 Advance determination as a good example as to why the distinction between monitoring and behaviour modification is of little relevance

In the system of the Directive, prior checking and notification/registration are the main formal safeguards of advance determination. This tends to show that the distinction between formal and substantive safeguards does not espouse that between monitoring and behaviour modification. Indeed, registration appears to be associated with monitoring, whereas prior checking, as a mechanism of prior approval is associated with behaviour modification. Yet, they are both formal safeguards. Further, the interplays between these two types of safeguards contribute to displaying the lack of clear distinction between monitoring and behaviour modification.[87] It is indeed possible to conceptualise both safeguards as partaking both of monitoring and behaviour modification.

The link between registration and monitoring is quite self-explanatory since it is a means to make the essential information pertaining to a data processing system available to authorities and to the public.[88] Yet, prior checking (or licensing) has also been analysed as a monitoring provision.[89] Hondius indicates that Norway used to enclose all licences into a publicly accessible register.[90,91] One can also add that in the system of the Directive a notification to the DPA underpins the functioning of both safeguards, and even though prior checking notifications do not have to be included in a register, the DPA still has the possibility to publish its opinion (Art 28(3)).

Equally, registration can also be analysed as partaking of behaviour modification. This is particularly explicit following Recital 48 of the Directive, which analyses registration simultaneously as a tool of publicity and control.[92] Freund makes the following point: "while mere registration, is neutral and respects private liberty, it may also be true that a mere registration requirement may tend to standardize private action".[93] As an example, he refers to the requirement of filing all policy forms used by companies, which indirectly compels the adoption of uniform contract provisions.[94] Prior checking is traditionally seen as modifying behaviour since it indeed directly conditions the possibility of undertaking the activity.

[87] See also Freund (n 79) 65 who refers to a case where "the principal method of controlling" are quinquennial reports, as well as other measures "mainly operating through publicity".

[88] Hondius (n 8) 224.

[89] See Bygrave (n 3) 75.

[90] Hondius (n 8) 225–26.

[91] Hondius also mentions a Dutch Interim Report (a governmental document preceding the Dutch Data Protection Act), which also foresaw a similar system, which it explicitly linked to the data subject's right to know—ibid 40–41. However, not every licensing system provided for a register, eg Sweden.

[92] "Whereas the procedures for notifying the supervisory authority are designed to ensure disclosure of the purposes and main features of any processing operation for the purpose of verification that the operation is in accordance with the national measures taken under this Directive."

[93] Freund (n 79) 85.

[94] ibid.

It is interesting to observe that what separates these two safeguards is, *in fine*, the amount of discretion awarded to the supervisory authority. In cases where the discretion is minimal to non-existing, the formal safeguard will amount to a tool of transparency and monitoring. In cases where on the contrary there is a substantial amount of discretion, the safeguard will partake to behaviour modification.

As indicated in Chapter 1, formal safeguards are so successful because they provide for a means of standardisation of action in cases where there is little agreement on substantive safeguards (ie it is difficult to specify the type of behaviour required in advance).[95] One can argue that for safeguards mainly concerned with publicity, transparency, and monitoring, such substantive discussion may even be bypassed. In other cases, however, the substantive discussion will be deferred to the supervisory authority (cf *supra*). This may be the reason why Freund argues that the distinction between publicity requirements, administrative checking powers, and administrative discretion exercised on a case-by-case basis is anything but clear.[96] It might account in any case as to why systems of registration and licensing are so closely connected.[97]

It is therefore interesting to see that the whole discussion on the distinction between monitoring and behaviour modification can ultimately be reframed either in terms of substantive *versus* formal safeguards, and further, in the case of formal safeguards, as a distinction hinging on the existence and/or extent of discretion awarded to the regulatory authority.

3.1.4 Corrective intervention: the data protection authorities' powers

Powers of corrective intervention entail that regulatory authorities are not simply agencies of enforcement, but, on the contrary, fully constitute safeguards, since their involvement is directly constitutive of the mode of operation of a number of them.[98] In this sense, powers of erasure or ban are not to be seen as enforcement capabilities, but as constitutive elements of—specific—safeguards. This is confirmed by Freund's observation that "prohibition can operate either by way of direct penalization, or by way of creating a power of administrative corrective intervention".[99]

The Data Protection Directive perfectly fits with Freund's analysis. Article 28(3) indeed contains provisions on both advance determination and corrective intervention. On the one hand, Data Protection Authorities (DPAs) are endowed with the power of authorising processing operation in the context of the prior checking

95 ibid 65.
96 ibid 84.
97 See Bygrave (n 3) 75–76, who indicates that several countries such as Hungary transformed their licensing schemes into registration ones. Sweden also rapidly transformed its system of licences into one of registration—Bennett (n 83) 165.
98 Freund (n 79) 73.
99 ibid 96.

mechanism (Art 28(3) does not include the mechanism of registration probably because it grants no discretion to the authority). On the other hand, they can "order the blocking, erasure, or destruction of data, [or] impose a temporary or definitive ban on [the] processing". Further, and in relation to this corrective intervention power, DPAs can also warn or admonish the controller.

3.2 Formal safeguards (2): regulation through organisation

To some extent, regulation through organisation constitutes a particular form of deferred control, that is, of delegation of discretionary authority.[100] Accordingly, instead of directly controlling regulatees, it provides for the setting-up of a "machinery of control by self-government".[101] More precisely, this is taken to equate the requirement that regulated organisations adopt a number of measures, in particular pertaining to their organisation if they are to be allowed to pursue their activities. It therefore constitutes a form of deferred control because some discretion is left to the regulated organisation in terms of self-organisation, but also to the regulatory authority, in determining whether such internal arrangements are adequate.

Regulation through organisation might entail the adoption of a number of formal requirements as in the case of compulsory planning, which requires the adoption of plans prior to the beginning of the activities. However, it can also extend to requiring the organisation to adopt a specific legal form, which has the specific authorisation to pursue the desired activity (eg corporation); or to specific substantial prescription such as quotas for the composition of boards.[102] This type of safeguard exists in data protection legislation. One can think of the obligation to have Data Protection Officers (DPOs), whose task is to ensure that the organisation of which they are a part respect the data protection principles. This obligation was already featured in several early statutes such as the German Data Protection Bill, but also in the 1973 Swedish Data Lag (*registeransvarig*—responsible keeper of the register). These built upon the UK Younger Report, which was the first to introduce the idea.[103,104] Hondius points to another example from the early days of data protection: functional separation within data controllers—ie separating the data collection units from those tasked with its further processing.[105,106]

[100] ibid 78.
[101] ibid 79.
[102] ibid.
[103] Kenneth Younger, *Report of the Committee on Privacy* (Stationery Office Books 1972).
[104] Which itself took inspiration from the Mines and Quarries Act 1954, which, for the purposes of the many safety requirements of the Act requires the owner of a mine to appoint a mine manager as "responsible person" charged with ensuring the safe operation of the mine in accordance with the Act's provisions.
[105] Hondius (n 8) 214.
[106] One can also mention accountability pursuant to Principle 14 of the 1980 OECD Guidelines.

3.3 Formal safeguards (3): beyond the Data Protection Directive

Freund provides additional types of safeguards. These are not necessarily be part of the Data Protection Directive, but some, at least, have been incorporated in the GDPR.

3.3.1 Facilities v requirements

This distinction points to the difference between compulsory and optional safeguards.[107] Freund argues that the distinction is of importance in particular in the field of marketed goods and professions.[108] A classic example is that of certification. Certification can be optional, in which case it will serve as *prima facie* evidence of quality. The quality at stake might simply indicate compliance with the standards, or it might indicate superior performance.[109,110] One should note that this is exactly the system put in place by Art 42 GDPR following which, the goal of certification mechanisms such as seals and marks is to demonstrate compliance with the Regulation. Another system is that of optional but privilege-carrying certification, which endows the bearer of the certification with additional capabilities as in the case of "registered nurses" who can perform more acts than unregistered ones.[111]

3.3.2 Regulation by classification

Classification is a type of safeguard used in combination with already existing publicity/transparency measures (eg certification, marks, labels), and is used to ends of comparison.[112] Its most common occurrence is through grades (eg A, B, C, D). The most important caveat with this safeguard is to make sure that it is possible to compare, grade, or classify the classes of products or practices at stake (if their properties are too alien, classification will not be possible).[113]

3.4 Formal safeguards (4): beyond Freund's classification: data subject rights

3.4.1 Data subject rights as safeguards: formal safeguards of deferred control

The last type of formal safeguards one can mention are the data subject rights. Even though they escape Freund's analysis because of their more contemporary nature,

[107] Freund (n 79) 91.
[108] ibid.
[109] ibid 93–94.
[110] See also ibid 92: "The optional system has the advantage from the point of view of legislative policy that it permits the setting of very much higher level of standards."
[111] ibid 91–92.
[112] ibid 66.
[113] ibid 66–67.

they can easily be linked to his classification. Data subject rights can indeed be conceived of as formal safeguards of deferred control (ie vesting of discretionary power to an entity, in this case the data subject). Those providing for *ex ante* obligations (eg transparency) can be assimilated to advance determination safeguards (ie preconditions of validity), whereas those providing for the *ex post* intervention of the data subject can be assimilated to corrective intervention safeguards (ie ex-post decision on the validity).

Evidence can be found in the data protection literature that data subjects rights are understood as safeguards, thereby sharply diverging from analyses in terms of informational control.[114] This is the case for instance in Art 2 of the explanatory memorandum of the original 1980 OECD Guidelines on the Protection of Privacy and Transborder Flows of Personal Data, which explicitly views data subject rights as safeguards.[115] Further evidence can be found in other documents such as the Art 12 of the Appendix of CoE Recommendation No R (99) 5 on the protection of privacy on the Internet,[116] or CoE Recommendation No R (95) 4 on the protection of personal data in the area of telecommunication services, with particular reference to telephone services.[117] Interestingly, Hondius also indicates that during the adoption of the first Austrian Data Protection Bill, the opposition explicitly viewed the right to rectification as a safeguard.[118]

3.4.2 Data subject's right to be informed (Arts 10 and 11): advance determination

Articles 10 and 11 of the Directive provide that at the time when the personal data are collected (either directly from the subject—Art 10, or from a third party—Art 11), a certain amount of information shall be given to the data subject, such as the identity of the controller, or the processing's purpose.[119] As measures of transparency, these data subject rights can therefore be linked to similar safeguards such as notification/ register obligations. In this sense, they qualify as formal safeguards of deferred control, and more particularly of advance determination.

3.4.3 Rights of access and to object: corrective intervention

Article 12 is divided into mainly two provisions.[120] The first one, Art 12(a), empowers the data subject to request information to the data controller pertaining

[114] Alan Westin, *Privacy and Freedom* (Atheneum 1967).

[115] OECD Guidelines on the Protection of Privacy and Transborder Flows of Personal Data 1980.

[116] Recommendation No R (99)5 for the Protection of Privacy on the Internet 1999.

[117] Recommendation No R(95)4 on the Protection of Personal Data in the Area of Telecommunication Services, with particular reference to Telephone Services 1995.

[118] Hondius (n 8) 113.

[119] Slight differences exist between Arts 10 and 11, such as an exception to the transmission of information in the case of Art 11 if it "would involve a disproportionate effort or if recording or disclosure is expressly laid down by law".

[120] The division of the right of access between access *ss* (ie simply accessing the data), and access *sensu lato* (*sl*) (requesting its rectification, erasure, or blocking), has been acknowledged in the CJEU

to the confirmation as to whether or not personal data are being processed as well as a series of information concerning the purpose of the processing, the categories of data, or the recipients, but also access to the data actually being processed (ie receiving a copy). Contrary to Arts 10 and 11, such access to information requires an active step from the data subject. This confirms that Art 12 is about corrective intervention and not about advance determination.

Article 12(b) on the contrary is concerned with the overall legality of the processing as it empowers the data subject not only to ask for the rectification of the data when they are not in conformity with the principle of data accuracy, but also to request their erasure or the blocking of the overall processing insofar as it does "not comply with the provisions of [the] Directive".[121] In this sense, Art 12(b) is about rectification, blocking, and erasure.

A few additional remarks are warranted concerning the right to erasure as an interesting *locus* to further reflect on the difference between safeguards and enforcement. As one recalls, the chapter on regulation argued that safeguards (within which behaviour control as a constitutive element of regulation is subsumed) are different from enforcement. More in particular, it was argued that regulation, (and thus safeguards), displays a focus on creating general and impersonal conditions leading to desired behaviour, (ie in a general fashion).[122] In opposition, enforcement has a punitive and deterrent function, and focuses upon individual instances of non-compliance. It was also pointed out that the distinction between the two, even though analytically sound, is a subtle one. The right to erasure is a good example insofar as it can be read both as a safeguard and as an enforcement provision.

Accordingly, the right to erasure's scope covers any unlawfulness that would taint the processing, even though it would appear that it is especially connected to the safeguards of minimisation and storage limitation. The link between erasure, data minimisation, and storage limitation should not come as a surprise since both are safeguards concerning the amount of data to be processed, either in quantity, either in duration (cf *supra*), and erasure can therefore be instrumental in this regard. From this perspective, erasure should not be seen as a tool of enforcement or compliance,[123] but rather as constitutive of the very safeguard itself.[124] From this

Rijkeboer case, and in particular, the ancillary role of access *ss* with respect to the other access rights. CJEU, *Rijkeboer*, Case C-553/07, [2009] ECLI:EU:C:2009:293 paras 51–52, 54 (hereafter *Rijkeboer*). See also, Antonella Galetta and Paul De Hert, "The Proceduralisation of Data Protection Remedies under EU Data Protection Law: Towards a More Effective and Data Subject-Oriented System?" (2015) 8 Review of European Administrative Law 123, 129; EDPS, "Guidelines on the Rights of Individuals with Regard to the Processing of Personal Data" (2014) 11.

[121] See also Hondius (n 8) 146, who refers to data subject rights as "the right to know", the purpose of which being nonetheless to "ascertain the legitimacy of data processing".

[122] Freund (n 79) 303.

[123] cf Galetta and De Hert (n 120).

[124] See also Hondius (n 8) 118, 120, who explicitly refers to data erasure as a safeguard.

perspective, erasure is both a substantive safeguard, the implementation of which is entrusted to the data controller through the principles of data minimisation and possibly storage limitation, and a formal safeguard of deferred control as corrective intervention falling within the remit of data subject rights.[125]

However, the opposite analysis can also be seen as valid. There could thus be some cases where the right of erasure is not seen as a safeguard, but rather, a sanction for illegal processing. This seems to be the case in EDPS case C 2009-0550,[126] where the European Data Protection Supervisor (EDPS) ordered the erasure of data once it was confirmed that the processing of the latter was illegal. As the EDPS itself argues, "under such circumstances, erasure represents a measure adopted in order to ensure compliance".[127] Hondius provided a similar analysis, seeing erasure as a specific sanction reinforcing the requirement of lawfulness.[128] However, as a further counter argument, one should not forget the fact that the right to erasure is not only linked to the principles of data minimisation and storage limitation, but to the overall lawfulness of the processing.[129] And in this sense, again, erasure is less of an enforcement mechanism, than a safeguard partaking of the overall lawfulness of the processing.

Similarly, Art 14 empowers the data subject to contest the balance struck by the data controller in the context of Art 7(e) and (f). From this vantage point Art 14 is a formal safeguard of deferred control as corrective intervention insofar as it empowers the data subject to participate—and contest—the explicit balancing undertaken by the controller.

4. Substantive safeguards

Some substantive safeguards have already been discussed in the context of Art 6, and standard setting. This section discusses the concept of substantive safeguard more in detail and provides additional examples.

One can argue that prohibitions—and use restrictions in general—are provisions that best embody behaviour modification, since they explicitly preclude the performance of specific acts, or require specific modalities in that respect.

According to Freund, the two main types of substantive safeguards are prohibitions and requirements.

[125] The same holds true for the German Federal Data Protection Act: "erasure may take place if it doesn't prejudice 'protection worthy interests' of the person concerned".

[126] Full reference not available.

[127] EDPS (n 120) 22. Even though it is not clear from this case which principle exactly was violated. In case it were the data minimisation one, the example would not be a valid one.

[128] Hondius (n 8) 109.

[129] eg, Principle 7 of CoE Resolution 73(22) on access rights provides for a right of erasure, and is directly connected to Principle 3 on lawfulness. See also EDPS (n 120) 22, and CJEU, *Vinci v BCE*, Case F-130/07 [2009] ECLI:EU:F:2009:114 para 67 (hereafter *Vinci*).

Whereas a prohibition entails that one should refrain from acting (it thus creates a disability), a requirement attaches conditions to an act. To give an example, speed regulation belongs to prohibition, but traffic light regulation belongs to requirements. In both cases, the goal is to avoid—some of—the effects and consequences that stem from an action.[130] In some cases, it will be difficult to distinguish between requirements and prohibitions, since a prohibition may resemble a requirement if the avoidance of the forbidden action entails special precautions or duties.[131] Article 16 of the Directive illustrates the possible confusion between a prohibition and a requirement. On the one hand it is phrased as a duty or requirement of confidentiality for data processors, and it can be read as the requirement to process data only when asked by the controller or if required by law. On the other hand, it can also be read as a prohibition to process data, except in the cases stipulated by the provision.

Even though prohibitions are formulated as disabilities, in most cases such disabilities will be enacted through so-called qualified enabling provisions, in which cases there is an incapacity in the first place, which the law lifts in parts through a series of qualifications. These can include restrictions such as limitations on duration or object, etc, as well as various other requirements.[132] It is thus a combination of a prohibition and requirements. This is exactly the *modus operandi* of the data quality principle (eg data minimisation or purpose limitation principles).

A prime example in the Directive is the prohibition to process so-called sensitive data (or now special categories of data).[133] The processing of the latter is prohibited in principle (Art 8(1)). However, Art 8(2)–(5) provide for a series of exceptions to the general prohibition, subject to various qualifications. For instance, Art 8(2)(a) contains a requirement, namely the explicit consent of the data subject. Article 8(2)(b) provides for a restriction (data can be processed insofar as necessary for the purposes of employment relations). Finally, Art 8(2)(d) contains both restrictions and requirements, since the data can be processed by religious, philosophical, political, organisations, insofar as necessary for their purposes and as long as the data are not communicated to third parties.

5. Safeguards and data legitimacy

At this point of the reasoning, the analysis has covered all the safeguards that underpin data protection law. However, as a way to conclude the understanding

[130] Freund (n 79) 87–88.
[131] ibid 88.
[132] ibid 57–58.
[133] These data concerned are those relating to: "racial or ethnic origin, political opinions, religious or philosophical beliefs, trade-union membership, and the processing of data concerning health or sex life".

of data protection as command and control regulation, it is deemed useful to revisit the principle of data legitimacy (Art 7 DPD) in view of Freund's analysis and classification of safeguards. A previous section had underscored an idiosyncrasy of data protection. Namely, that Art 7 DPD, which correspond to the first balancing test contains the "necessity" safeguard, whereas following the proportionality principle safeguards should only be associated to the second balancing test. Following Freund's conceptualisation of safeguards, it is shown that the data legitimacy principle actually contains additional safeguards. This can be considered an additional idiosyncrasy of data protection.

5.1 Presumption: the main safeguard

As indicated *supra*, the data legitimacy principle is permeated by a presumption of legitimacy, except for the "legitimate interests" ground (and a double presumption in the case of consent). This presumption is considered a safeguard, and more in particular a formal safeguard of deferred control, and even more specifically, of advance determination. One can argue that presumptions are similar to prior approval, except that in this case the advance determination is not made by the supervisory authority (as in licensing schemes or prior checking). In the case of consent, it is granted by the data subjects themselves, whereas in the case of the other grounds it is granted by virtue of the ground itself (eg contractual obligation, exercise of public authority, etc), ie the law. Only Art 7(f) (legitimate interests of the data controller) is void of safeguards, which is the reason why it is the only ground that requires that a balancing be undertaken. However, and paradoxically, because it is void of any safeguards, its actual application might lead to the implementation of additional safeguards—both formal and substantive (cf herein below).

The following lines will examine two grounds more in-depth: consent and the legitimate interests of the data controller.

5.2 Consent

5.2.1 Consent as a safeguard in data protection

The data subject's consent has often if not always been retraced to the notion of informational control, which purportedly underpins the logic of data protection. In this sense it can be argued that consent embodies more than any other principle the link between privacy and data protection.[134] However, following the present analysis, consent is simply a formal safeguard.

[134] And indeed, as Viktor Mayer-Schönberger, "Generational Development of Data Protection in Europe" in Philip E Agre and Marc Rotenberg (eds), *Technology and Privacy: The New Landscape*

Such differing view on consent is at least historically justified. In her genealogy of regulation in the United States, Jasanoff recalls the emergence in the 20th century of a whole new lot of provisions and mechanisms (ie safeguards) aiming at better protecting citizens in the face of new industrial processes. Among these new rights, she clearly identifies informed consent within the broader ambit of provisions on consumer protection, which was one of the areas receiving most attention at the time.[135]

The view of consent as presumption of safety (and thus as a safeguard) also finds some echo in the legislative work that led to the adoption of the DPD. More in particular, the first Commission proposal for the Data Protection Directive contained no Article 7. Consent was then one among the data subject rights (Article 12 of the proposal), which as we have seen are safeguards. Furthermore, in the private sector it was a necessary requirement for all processing operations except for a number of limited exceptions which were considered safe enough.[136] The industry response to the Commission's first proposal for the Data Protection Directive also highlights this understanding of consent.[137] It distinguished between potentially harmful, and generally trivial uses. The latter (which included direct marketing) were seen as safe per definition and therefore did not require consent (at least no explicit one). The former required an explicit consent by the data subject.[138]

Burkert also confirms this analysis of consent as a safeguard by arguing that individual consent is one mode of legitimising data processing operations, which derives from the contractual model.[139] Rather than privacy considerations, what is at play according to him, is the negotiation of what is permitted under the model of private law, and more in particular, consumer protection.[140]

(MIT Press 1997), retraces, this principle appeared in data protection acts as a consequence of the 1983 Census decision enshrining the right to informational self-determination. See also, Art 29 WP (n 48) 8–9.

[135] Sheila Jasanoff, "Beni Incalcolabili. Reimmaginare Il Nostro Futuro Technologico" in Sheila Jasanoff, Alice Benessia, and Silvio Funtowicz (eds), *L'innovazione tra utopia e storia* (Codice edizioni 2013) 17.

[136] However, notably after industry lobbying, which saw the systematic collection of consent too stringent and burdensome, Art 7 was adopted, and the consent of the data subject then became only one of the possible grounds for collection—not to mention the scope of the Directive applying both to public and private sector. See Kosta (n 32) 86–96.

[137] Proposal for a Council Directive concerning the protection of individuals in relation to the processing of personal data COM(90) 314 final—SYN 287, [1990] OJ C277/3.

[138] Kosta (n 32) 90.

[139] Burkert (n 4) 560: "Individual consent seems to borrow its legitimizing effect from the private law model."

[140] Recital 32 of the Proposal for a Data Protection Regulation as adopted by the European Parliament in March 2014 supports such analysis to the extent that it refers to the protection afforded by Directive 93/13/EEC of 5 April 1993 on unfair terms in consumer contracts in order to protect consent as legitimate basis, Legislative Resolution of 12 March 2014 on the Proposal for a Regulation of the European

The Art 29 WP has also explicitly stated that consent should be seen as a safeguard, be it in a general sense,[141] or in the context of the purpose limitation principle where it is considered as one of the safeguards that might render a further processing compatible with the original purpose.[142] Consent has also been explicitly dubbed a safeguard in the case of specific processing operation, as is the case with Art 6 Convention 108, which allows the processing of so-called sensitive data provided some safeguards have been implemented, and among which the consent of the data subject.[143] Also, the fact that the Art 29 WP has underscored that consent has often been used as a device to limit the controller's liability is more than probably linked to its nature as a presumption, and hence, as a safeguard.[144]

5.2.2 Consent as a safeguard in other fields

Consent has also been dubbed a safeguard in other fields. Consent—and more particularly prior informed consent (PIC)—has been used in the regulation of the international trade of hazardous chemicals and pesticides,[145] where it has been qualified as a "regulatory device".[146] Ross refers to prior informed consent as a regulatory device for the following reason. First, "[PIC] attempts to promote safe and efficient use".[147] This appraisal comes quite close to the understanding of consent as a presumption of safety.[148] Second, and as will be discussed herein below for consent under data protection, PIC relies upon transparency, ie the production and exchange of information. In a nutshell, national and international databases are created, which contain information on the hazardousness of the chemical potentially subject to trade. The information contained therein should be transmitted to the importing country.[149]

Parliament and of the Council on the Protection of Individuals with regard to the Processing of their Personal Data and on the Free Movement of such Data 2014.

141 See Art 29 WP (n 48) 7: "As a principle, consent should not be seen as an exemption from the other data protection principles, but as a safeguard."

142 Art 29 WP (n 53) 26–27.

143 But several authors have also made the same point, eg Bygrave (n 3) 66. This is also the case for Art 8 Directive, which even provides for a stronger safeguard since consent must be explicit.

144 Art 29 WP (n 48) 9.

145 See Text of the Convention on the Prior Informed Consent Procedure for Certain Hazardous Chemicals and Pesticides in International Trade, as Agreed by the Intergovernmental Negotiating Committee at Its Fifth Session, UN Doc. UNEP/FAO/PIC/CONF/2 (1998) [hereinafter Rotterdam Convention]. The Convention was last updated in 2013, see <http://www.pic.int/TheConvention/Overview/TextoftheConvention/tabid/1048/language/en-US/Default.aspx> accessed 15 January 2019.

146 Jenifer Ross, "Legally Binding Prior Informed Consent" (1999) 10 Colorado Journal of International Law and Policy 499, 500 518 ff.

147 ibid 512.

148 See also ibid 513–14: "[PIC] allows countries to take some responsibility and control over the importation of hazardous chemicals and pesticides while simultaneously maintaining a lucrative trade". This shows well that at the heart of consent there is a balancing exercise at the heart of consent procedures.

149 ibid 512–14.

5.2.3 Consent as advance determination: prior approval, and transparency

It was argued that consent is a formal safeguard of deferred control of advance determination (as opposed to corrective intervention), which Freund links mainly to prior approval. This seems sensible, since the use of consent is precisely about gaining the data subject's prior approval. The fact that consent operates as a prior approval mechanism appears clearly from the fact that it should be gathered at the latest at the moment of collection, or from the reference to the German notion of "*Einwilligung*", which translates as "prior acceptance".[150]

As discussed *supra*, advance determination also includes measures pertaining to transparency such as registers and notification mechanisms. Valid consent does require the provision of information to the data subject, ie the consent must be informed.[151]

In sum, consent as a formal safeguard of deferred control as advance determination can be linked to prior approval and transparency.[152]

5.3 The legitimate interests of the data controller

As discussed, Art 7(f) of the EU Directive requires the data controller to undertake an explicit balancing between their legitimate interests and the interests of the data subject. In this sense, it embodies the core of the first standard setting operation. The Art 29 WP has provided guidance as how to weigh the conflicting interests. Of importance for the present discussion, it argues that when it results from the weighing of interests that the processing of data would unduly impact the data subject, it is nonetheless possible to proceed to such processing provided that additional safeguards, both formal and substantive (thereby going beyond existing law), are implemented.[153] They include technical and organisational measures to ensure functional separation, or the possibility to opt-out of the processing.[154] As one can see, the use of safeguards at the level of the first balancing test is an idiosyncrasy of data protection, which is not to be found in risk nor in the proportionality test pursuant to the ECHR.

150 Art 29 WP (n 48) 9.

151 Art 29 WP emphasises that transparency is instrumental for consent to be informed, ibid 9, 19.

152 Additionally, one can also link it to the notion of data subject participation. As a matter of fact, the Ware report already contemplated public participation as a safeguard, US Department of Health Education & Welfare (n 23).

153 As the Working Group puts it, "After analysing and weighing the two sides against each other, a provisional 'balance' may be established. Where the outcome of the assessment still leaves doubts, the next step will be to assess whether additional safeguards, bringing more protection to the data subject, may tip the balance in a way that would legitimise the processing." Art 29 WP (n 11) 34.

154 ibid 31. If these safeguards do not sufficiently mitigate the harms on the data subjects, this means that the data controller should resort to another legitimation ground.

6. Enforcement

As discussed, the classical scheme of enforcement is based upon sanctions, fines, and liability. This often goes with DPA's powers of supervision and inspection.

According to Art 28(3)(1) of the Directive, DPAs must be endowed with investigative powers allowing them to access specific data sets *in situ*, and to collect all the data necessary to the performance of their tasks. The Directive was silent as to whether DPAs have the power to impose fines and/or compensation for damages, and as to whether they can issue legally binding orders.[155] The GDPR is now very clear on the topic (see in particular Art 58(2)).

The liability regime of the Directive is enshrined in Art 23, according to which data controllers are presumed liable in case of breach of the Directive unless they prove otherwise, and Art 24 simply states that suitable sanctions should be adopted. Several statutes such as the Swedish and the Danish Private Bill used to contain a—now—defunct provision on strict liability.[156] The GDPR now contains provisions on joint liability between controllers and/or processors (Art 82(4–5)).

7. Conclusions: data protection as command and control regulation and the proportionality principle

This chapter has endeavoured to show that data protection amounts (or used to) to command and control regulation. This has been proven by mapping onto it the different constitutive elements of regulation. Given the conclusive analysis, one can safely refer to data protection as regulation.

Understanding data protection as regulation also sheds a better light on the links between proportionality and regulation, since it shows more in detail how the various balancing tests and safeguards can be mapped onto the three constitutive elements of regulation. In this sense, it is also a confirmation of the earlier findings.

The following table helps clarify the findings, and the various takes on proportionality at stake:

[155] However, see CJEU Case C-230/14, *Weltimmo* [2015] ECLI:EU:C:2015:639 para 49 (hereafter *Weltimmo*). See also Bygrave (n 3) 72.

[156] See Hondius (n 8).

	1st Balancing	2nd Balancing	Mitigation measures associated to 2nd Balancing
ECtHR's necessity in a democratic society test	Pressing social need test: Is the legitimate aim legitimate enough?	Proportionality test *ss*: the measures addressing/ achieving the pressing social need should not go further than needed	Safeguards: • Necessity test: are there alternative, less intrusive measures available or already existing? • Additional safeguards: scope (*ratione materiae, personae*, etc); transparency; oversight; right of appeal; etc
Risk	Risk assessment: • Is the risk sufficiently risky to be considered a risk?	Risk management (1): • Do we take the risk?	Risk management (2), risk mitigation: • Can we reduce the risk to an acceptable level, and how? • eg Corrective measures (risk source) or passive measures (risk effects), anticipation or resilience? etc
Regulation: constitutive elements	Standard setting function	Standard setting function	• Monitoring • Behaviour modification
Regulation: data protection	Data legitimacy: • Is the basis sufficiently legitimate to be legitimate? • Also includes the necessity test • Operates through a number of presumptions (except for the legitimate interests ground)	Data quality (1): • The processing must not be excessive in relation to its purpose	Data quality (2): • The rest of the provision contains only safeguards/mitigation measures: • Transparency = Fairness • Scope = PSP, Data min, Data retention • Data accuracy +

	1st Balancing	2nd Balancing	Mitigation measures associated to 2nd Balancing
	• Consent: a formal safeguard of deferred control of advance determination • Legitimate interest ground: can lead to additional safeguards		Other safeguards: • Formal safeguards (notification, data subject rights, etc) • Substantive safeguards (sensitive data, etc)

When looking at things from this perspective the links between data protection, regulation, and risk, as variations on the proportionality principle appear quite clearly.

3

Issues with data protection as command and control regulation

> The debate usually operates at the level of deciding whether an activity should be regulated or not: in setting standards, should regulators err on the side of protecting consumers or favouring producers[1]

1. Introduction: data protection and issues with command and control regulation

As discussed, command and control is the traditional model of regulation. It was argued that command and control regulation mirrors an "Austinian" understanding of law, that is, a set of standards of behaviour issued by the Sovereign, and associated to sanctions in case of non-respect.[2] In other words, command and control is a regulatory model whereby both standards and safeguards are determined from the start "by the Sovereign". Such Sovereign ensures that they are abided by, by resorting to sanctions, which operate as threats.

On the basis of this definition it is possible to argue that the command and control model of regulation is based upon two assumptions. First, enforcement is operated through sanctions or the threat thereof—what is referred to as deterrence,[3] and it is assumed that such deterrence always works.[4] Second, it is assumed that the regulatory goals (and the standards they lead to) are somewhat unproblematic. The unproblematic nature of regulatory goals can be read in the light of the links between regulation, and economics and market logic (cf avoidance of externalities), but more fundamentally in its framing as a "diagnosis-response" tool. Following

[1] Julia Black, "Risk-Based Regulation: Choices, Practices and Lessons Being Learnt" in OECD (ed), *Risk and Regulatory Policy: Improving the Governance of Risk* (OECD Publishing 2010) 188.

[2] Bridget M Hutter, "Risk, Regulation, and Management" in Peter Taylor-Gooby and Jens Zinn (eds), *Risk in Social Science* (OUP 2006); Julia Black, *Rules and Regulators* (OUP 1997); Julia Black, "Decentring Regulation: Understanding the Role Self-Regulation in a 'Post- Regulatory' World" (2001) 54 Current Legal Problems 103.

[3] Neil Gunningham, "Enforcement and Compliance Strategies" in Robert Baldwin, Martin Cave, and Martin Lodge (eds), *The Oxford Handbook of Regulation* (OUP 2010) 120–21.

[4] Julia Black, "The Role of Risk in Regulatory Processes" in Robert Baldwin, Martin Cave, and Martin Lodge (eds), *The Oxford Handbook of Regulation* (OUP 2010) 308.

The Risk-Based Approach to Data Protection. Raphaël Gellert, Oxford University Press (2020). © Raphaël Gellert.
DOI: 10.1093/oso/9780198837718.001.0001.

Black, regulation is seen as a linear process of "diagnosis-prescription" insofar as its aim is to detect "wrong" behaviours and to modify them according to the functioning of the market, which, if allowed to function properly, will "naturally" bring about all public goods and interests.[5] This type of thinking points towards the analytic logic underlying command and control regulation, which assumes direct causality links between actions and reactions, between responses brought to purportedly "bad behaviours" and the appropriate modification of the latter. In this case, it is assumed to know what is good and what is bad behaviour, and how to fix the latter.[6] It is argued that the evolution of data protection, and more specifically, its shift from the command and control model towards the use of risk management tools, echoes some of the issues encountered by command and control regulation, which directly follow from the assumptions described herein above.

A first set of issues are linked to the purported unproblematic, as well as linear nature of regulatory goals and responses. They affect both the process of standard setting and the efficiency of safeguards. This set of issues is multi-dimensional insofar as it affects the determination of what counts as an adequate safeguard. But it also affects the implementation in practice of these safeguards. Just as determining what is the behaviour that will lead to the achievement of regulators is less than obvious, so is the concrete implementation and compliance with the various safeguards that are meant to lead to such behaviour. The second set of issues are linked to enforcement practice, which as indicated, is predicated upon a—purportedly—linear and all-encompassing application of deterrence. Finally, one should pay proper attention to technological developments that have occurred in the past decades, and which have led to new types of processing practices. These developments should not be seen as a turning point signalling a sort of "new technological epoch" that would, as such, render the existing data protection legal framework obsolete. However, it indubitably paves the way to new data processing practices that put an additional strain on the existing framework in many respects. The chapter will show how these challenges apply at the data protection level. It should be kept in mind that some of these challenges might sometimes seem to be a little "outdated". This is so because the debates surrounding command and control regulation, and further, the adoption of the risk-based approach started more than a decade ago.[7] Yet, it is crucial to go back to them in order to understand the transformations of the regulation models that have taken place in the data protection field.

[5] ibid 307–08.

[6] With an ancillary role for enforcement to nudge recalcitrant actors into adopting required behaviours.

[7] See eg Art 29 WP and Working Party on Police and Justice, "The Future of Privacy: Joint Contribution to the Consultation of the European Commission on the Legal Framework for the Fundamental Right to the Protection of Personal Data" (2009).

2. Issues resulting from the "diagnosis-prescription" aspect of command and control regulation

It should be borne in mind that the issues discussed hereunder apply to all the constitutive elements of regulation, ie standards and safeguards (monitoring and behaviour modification, or rather, substantive and formal safeguards).

Command and control regulation is based upon the setting of standards in advance, that is, to enshrine them in legislation from the outset. One of the reasons for shifting from a traditional command-and-control to a risk-based model of regulation lies in the difficulty of determining appropriate standards in advance, and is therefore closely linked to the "diagnosis-prescription" aspect of command and control regulation (which assumes to know what is good and what is bad behaviour). Ogus argues that the rise of self-regulation notably in the financial industry during the 1960s and the 1970s can be directly linked to disappointments with the results of such *ex ante* approach.[8] He recounts that around that time it became quite obvious that command and control regulation was unable to adequately achieve the public interest goals it pursued. According to him, it either did not succeed at all in addressing the market failures at stake, or it did so in an inefficient way insofar as it gave rise to a misallocation of resources in other fields, and/or the corrective measures taken pursuant to this type of legislation were redhibitory.[9] For the purpose of this discussion, he points to one important set of explanation, which pertains to so-called "technical failures": insufficient expertise and forethought were gathered in determining the best method of achieving the regulatory goals.[10] In other words, this line of argumentation points to inadequate expertise, and information in order to determine the standards that are most adequate in order to reach the regulatory goals. It also points to failure to anticipate important side effects of the use of these standards, including avoidance behaviour.[11]

One can argue that this analysis touches upon the core of the merits of the traditional approach to setting standards, and in particular, the direct causality it entails between the formulation of standards and the ensuing modification of behaviours. In this regard, Hayek has formulated what remains the foundation of the seminal criticisms addressed towards command and control regulation. Following Hayek, the very idea of setting standards is flawed by an intrinsic synoptic delusion, that is, "the fiction that all the relevant facts are known to someone's mind, and that it is possible to construct from this knowledge of the particulars a desirable social

[8] Anthony I Ogus, *Regulation: Legal Form and Economic Theory* (Hart Publishing 2004)</IBT> ch 55.

[9] ibid 56.

[10] See Ross Cranston, *Regulating Business: Law and Consumer Agencies*, vol 53 (Macmillan 1979).

[11] Concerning more in particular the linear dimensions of standard setting, he argues that it has been sometimes referred to as a "polycentric problem": "issues cannot be resolved independently and sequentially; they are, rather, interdependent, and a choice from one set of alternatives has implications for preferences within other sets of alternatives". Ogus (n 8) 117.

order".[12] In other words, the amount of information regulators rely upon in order to edict standards of behaviour can never cover all the reasons and motives behind individuals' behaviours. Therefore, one could never adequately anticipate the entirety of circumstances to which regulation must apply, and further, whether a standard determined in advance can indeed adequately apply to all the future activities within its scope.[13]

These critiques against standard setting echo important discussions in the literature around the limitations of rules.[14] Among this broad literature,[15] one can point to the work of Diver according to whom, standards (or rules) should possess the following three properties: transparency, congruence, and simplicity or accessibility,[16] or Yeung's analytical framework following which regulation must be efficient, clear and predictable, and flexible, responsive, and timely.[17]

Congruence can be understood as the success of the standard in ensuring that the regulatory goals pursued are achieved.[18] Issues in terms of congruence are perfectly epitomised by Hayek's critique, given that the application of standards (and safeguards) sometimes leads to incoherent, counter-productive, and contradictory solutions, as has been the case with complex situations where many factors are to be addressed in order to achieve regulatory objectives.[19]

However, there are other issues associated with standards, and which are linked to their implementation (and therefore with the compliance thereof). In this sense, they are indirectly linked to the achievement of regulatory goals. That is, Hayek's critique points to the difficulty of achieving regulatory goals with standards set in advance in legislation, whereas these ulterior critiques point to difficulties in implementing those very standards, regardless of whether their adequate implementation would in fact lead to the achievement of regulatory goals.

As Hutter notes it, "compliance with laws, rules, and regulations is assumed to be a straightforward and uncomplicated matter which simply denotes whether or not individuals and organisations have fulfilled the demands of the law. In practice,

[12] Friedrich A Hayek, *Law, Legislation and Liberty: A New Statement of the Liberal Principles of Justice and Political Economy* (Routledge 1982) 14.

[13] Ogus (n 8) 57; Hayek (n 12).

[14] Which as seen in the introduction can be said to embody standard setting —Black, *Rules and Regulators* (n 2) 1.

[15] See eg Robert Baldwin, "Why Rules Don't Work" (1990) 53 The Modern Law Review 321; Robert Baldwin, *Rules and Government* (OUP 1995); Karen Yeung, *Securing Compliance: A Principled Approach* (Hart Publishing 2004); Black, *Rules and Regulators* (n 2); Robert Baldwin, Collin Scott, and Christopher Hood (eds), *A Reader on Regulation* (OUP 1998).

[16] CS Diver, "The Optimal Precision of Administrative Rules" in Robert Baldwin, Collin Scott, and Christopher Hood (eds), *A Reader on Regulation* (OUP 1998).

[17] Yeung (n 15). But see also Black, *Rules and Regulators* (n 2) 21–23, for a similar analytical framework, and the references to Baldwin therein.

[18] See Black, *Rules and Regulators* (n 2) 9, 21.

[19] Susan Sturm, "Second Generation Employment Discrimination: A Structural Approach" (2001) 101 Columbia Law Review 458, 461. This critique can also be related to Black's analysis of rules as being either over or under-inclusive Black, *Rules and Regulators* (n 2) 7 ff. Yeung provides a similar analysis in terms of effectiveness, namely, "the realisation of [regulatory] goals", Yeung (n 15) 31.

things are not so simple."[20] Such observation is valid both from the perspective of regulatees and from the perspective of standard setting.

Indeed, quite some uncertainty surrounds the application of these standards and safeguards, which can be linked to Diver's notion of transparency,[21] or Yeung's notions of clarity and predictability, and flexibility and responsiveness.[22] Following Offe, legal provisions assume by definition a level of generality that sits uneasily with the particularities of each case, and yet the ambition is precisely this one.[23] As Black puts it, "[standards] are inherently indeterminate. Their indeterminacy arises in part from the nature of language, in part from their anticipatory nature, and in part because they rely on others for their application."[24] Attempts to address indeterminacy have often lead to the following tension between a style of rule-making that is either too detailed and narrow, and not adapted to the variety of possible and changing situations,[25] and one that is formulated in terms that are too general in order to receive any sort of concrete application.[26] Further, when standards and/or safeguards are too detailed the discretion left to the regulatee is reduced to a minimal level.[27] In this sense, the regulator is given a central role as it is entrusted with the task of fixing and interpreting the meaning of regulatory mandates,[28] which relies mainly upon "in house" expertise.[29] However, this goes against inclusiveness, or flexibility,[30] which implies "a willingness to adopt a more purposive approach to the interpretation and application of rules, in order to give effect to their underlying purpose or spirit".[31] Yet, such inclusiveness can also lead to abuses from regulatees who might abuse the discretion at their disposal.[32] Symmetrically, curbing such discretion with more detailed standards is also not a panacea. Critics have noted that when standards and safeguards are too detailed they also lead to a process of bureaucratisation which has perverse side effects insofar as it skews the behaviour

[20] Bridget M Hutter, *Compliance: Regulation and Environment* (OUP 1997) ix.

[21] See Black, *Rules and Regulators* (n 2) 22–23.

[22] Yeung (n 15) 33–34.

[23] Claus Offe, *Contradictions of the Welfare State* (John Keane ed, Hutchinson & Co 1984) ch 1.

[24] Black, *Rules and Regulators* (n 2) 10.

[25] See also Alfred A Marcus, "Implementing Externally Induced Innovations: A Comparison of Rule-Bound and Autonomous Approaches" (1988) 31 Academy of Management Journal 235, 250–51.

[26] Graham K Wilson, "Social Regulation and Explanations of Regulatory Failure" (1984) 32 Political Studies 203. See also Black, *Rules and Regulators* (n 2) 28: "there are inevitable tensions involved in the choice of rule type. The most obvious tension (. . .) is that between flexibility and certainty."

[27] Gary Coglianese and Evan Mendelson, "Meta-Regulation and Self-Regulation" in Robert Baldwin, Martin Cave, and Martin Lodge (eds), *The Oxford Handbook of Regulation* (OUP 2010) 152.

[28] See Kenneth A Bamberger and Deirdre K Mulligan, "Privacy in Europe: Initial Data on Governance Choices and Corporate Practices" (2013) 81 The George Washington Law Review 1529, 1645: "the French regulator built the largest regulatory infrastructure, and thus focuses on providing even more detailed and refined guidance to firms regarding specific registration requirements with which they must comply".

[29] Kenneth A Bamberger, "Regulation as Delegation: Private Firms, Decisionmaking, and Accountability in the Administrative State" (2006) 56 Duke Law Journal 377, 458–67.

[30] Black, *Rules and Regulators* (n 2) 32.

[31] Yeung (n 15) 34.

[32] Black, *Rules and Regulators* (n 2) 28 et seq.

of regulatees towards seeking compliance with standards and safeguards as an end in itself rather than as a means of achieving the—broader—regulatory goals.[33] This has also been referred to as "creative compliance".[34,35] It consists in "creating legal techniques that make it look like companies are complying, while making as little real change as possible".[36]

Finally, the last issue can be linked to Diver's simplicity and accessibility or Yeung's efficiency. This last caveat is mostly prevalent from the regulatee's perspective and pertains to the steps required by the standard in view of its achievement,[37] or to the deployment of resources in the realisation of regulatory goals.[38] Referring to Hutter again, compliance could be defined as conformity with the law, but even assuming that the law's requirements are clear, predictable, and transparent, it is precisely what is meant by such conformity that is not self-evident.[39] Rather than an event, compliance should be regarded as a process, and more in particular, the complex process of defining responses to mandates.[40]

3. Issues revolving around enforcement

As indicated *supra*, command and control regulation is predicated upon the assumption that deterrence "always works", that is, that every infraction can be sanctioned, and that every sanction or the threat thereof produces a deterrent effect (ie will prevent the regulatee from adopting the incriminated behaviour in the future).

However, as Ogus notes, the enforcement of regulation became a concern for scholars in the early 1970s. The general perception that emerged at the time was that regulation had "failed". Some of the explanations put forth concerned the pusillanimity of agencies in dealing with offenders, which was particularly reflected

[33] See eg Robert K Merton, *Social Theory and Social Structure* (The Free Press 1968).

[34] See eg Julia Black, "Learning from Failures: 'New Governance' Techniques and the Financial Crisis" (2012) 75 Modern Law Review 1037; Julia Black and Robert Baldwin, "Really Responsive Risk-Based Regulation" (2010) 32 Law & Policy 181.

[35] The term "creative compliance" has been coined by Doreen McBarnet and Christopher Whelan, "The Elusive Spirit of the Law: Formalism and the Struggle for Legal Control" (1991) 54 The Modern Law Review 848.

[36] Christine Parker and Adrian Evans, *Inside Lawyers' Ethics* (Cambridge University Press 2006) 218. In other words, the point is to "devise legal techniques that abuse the law by achieving corporate goals regardless of the real purpose of the law involved", ibid. See also the EDPS' opinion 7/2015 concerning challenges associated to big data: "These assessments often raise challenging questions of business ethics and fairness, and cannot be reduced to a simple and mechanical exercise of ticking off compliance boxes." EDPS, "Opinion 7/2015: Meeting the Challenges of Big Data: A Call for Transparency, User Control, Data Protection by Design and Accountability" (2015) 16.

[37] Black, *Rules and Regulators* (n 2) 21.

[38] Yeung (n 15) 31.

[39] Hutter (n 20) 12.

[40] ibid 13. There are of course additional issues associated to rules and standards such as their over or under inclusiveness see, Black, *Rules and Regulators* (n 2), but these fall out of the scope of the present discussion.

in their reluctance to initiate formal prosecutions.[41] At the time, many people blamed the supposed complacency of the regulator and the—purported—vested interests.[42] However, Ogus puts forth another set of explanation. He reminds that at the heart of regulators' enforcement practice there is also a balancing exercise taking place: one between their limited resources and the benefits associated to an enforcement action.[43] As he puts it, "perfect [deterrence] is neither practicable nor desirable, given that the costs of achieving it will invariably outweigh the benefits".[44] It follows that the appropriate target is optimal deterrence. In other words, it should be clear that the goal of a regulator with regards to enforcement is to minimise the harm resulting from violations of regulatory provisions at the lowest administrative cost.[45] In other words, even enforcement, which is ancillary to regulation *ss*, is actually also a matter of balancing. As Ogus argues, a policy of systematic and linear enforcement (ie no balancing) would simply be "irrational".[46] The model of optimal deterrence therefore suggests that regulators should make certain choices in their enforcement activities, such as choosing between occasional monitoring of all regulated firms and intensive monitoring of firms suspected of contraventions, or choosing between systematically prosecuting all known offenders and merely cautioning all but the most recalcitrant.[47] Moreover, Power also argues that there is also an issue of timeliness associated with enforcement actions (ie by the time violations are detected and action is taken it is too late in many cases).[48] Furthermore, even when regulators do decide to prosecute regulatory violations, it is not guaranteed that the sanction will have its deterrent role for the simple reason that not all regulatees react in the same manner to a sanction and it is therefore not possible to predict the exact behaviour of the sanctioned organisation.[49] In the same vein, there are also issues concerning the efficiency of sanctions. Sanctions are often smaller than what they ought to be in order to produce the desired deterrent effect. However, this leads to another issue coined as "deterrence trap": sanctions must be high enough but not too high either, otherwise this would lead to the bankruptcy of the regulatee, which is not the effect sought.[50]

[41] Ogus (n 8) 90.

[42] What is referred to as private interest theories of regulation, see ibid 4.

[43] Among the costs related to enforcement actions, one can list: the monitoring of behaviour (ie on the spot visits and inspections), conducting prosecutions, and administering sanctions, ibid 91. See also Power who argues that direct surveillance is an impossible ideal of pure transparency *Organized Uncertainty: Designing a World of Risk Management* (OUP 2007) 40.

[44] See Ogus (n 8) 92, where he describes some of the regulators' strategies to maximise their resources.

[45] ibid 90.

[46] ibid 95. On the high costs of enforcement actions, see Cento G Veljanovski, "Regulatory Enforcement: An Economic Study of the British Factory Inspectorate" (1983) 5 Law and Policy Quarterly 75.

[47] Ogus (n 8) 91.

[48] Power (n 43) 40.

[49] Ogus (n 8) 91–92. In some cases it can even produce counter-productive solutions Gunningham (n 3) 124.

[50] Ogus (n 8) 93.

4. List of challenges related to evolutions in data processing practices

There are three factors surrounding contemporary practices of personal data processing that might account for the changes—and the trigger thereof—to the data protection legal framework.

The first factor relates to a surge in processing power coupled to ever cheaper computer memory, which lead to "improved capacities for storing, organising, and retrieving great quantities of [data]".[51] Early data protection statutes were mainly targeting large, centralised databases, the cost of which could only be afforded by large organisations or administrations.[52] However, the democratisation and increasing power of data processing technology has meant that although large organisations have remained the major players, smaller organisations as well as individuals have now also become involved with the processing of personal data. It has also meant that an increasing number of activities are now undertaken with the help of automated data processing systems, such as "vital records, welfare records, estate property, holdings and transactions, mortgages, insurance premiums, but also records taken from search engine logs, retail purchasers records, etc.".[53] As far as individuals are concerned this is particularly true in the context of the so-called web 2.0,[54] in the context of the so-called "appification of society",[55] and further, in a context of the so-called "internet of things" and/or smart environments.[56] All of which rely upon user-generated input.

The second factor is related to advances in the fields of science and engineering of digital electronic networks, and in particular the internet and the world wide web, as well as related wireless technologies.[57] Additional factors include easy and inexpensive storage, or standardised database formats.[58] This has meant that large

[51] Helen Nissenbaum, *Privacy in Context: Technology, Policy, and the Integrity of Social Life* (Stanford University Press 2010) 36.

[52] See eg David H Flaherty, *Protecting Privacy in Surveillance Societies—The Federal Republic of Germany, Sweden, France, Canada, and the United States* (The University of North Carolina Press 1989).

[53] Nissenbaum (n 51) 39–40; European Commission, "Commission Staff Working Paper: Impact Assessment Accompanying the Document Regulation of the European Parliament and of the Council on the Protection of Individuals with Regard to the Processing of Personal Data and on the Free Movement of Such Data" (2012) 12.

[54] Yves Poullet, "EU Data Protection Policy. The Directive 95/46/EC: Ten Years After" (2006) 22 Computer Law & Security Review 206; Luiz Costa and Yves Poullet, "Privacy and the Regulation of 2012" (2012) 28 Computer Law & Security Review 254. See also CJEU, Case C-101/01, *Bodil Lindqvist* [2003] ECLI:EU:C:2003:596 (hereafter *Bodil Lindqvist*).

[55] 35th International Conference of Data Protection and Privacy Commissioners, "Warsaw Declaration on the 'Appification' of Society" (2013). See also Pavan Duggal, *Appification of Society and the Law* (Saakshar Law Publications 2013).

[56] Art 29 WP and Working Party on Police and Justice (n 7) 12; Mireille Hildebrandt, *Smart Technologies and the End(s) of Law* (Edward Elgar Publishing 2015).

[57] Nissenbaum (n 51) 36–37.

[58] ibid 40.

quantities of information can be moved around the globe at great speed, and conversely, can also be accessed from any available location (cf cloud computing).[59] Nissenbaum argues that one can treat the web as a virtual warehouse insofar as it can be conceived of as "a huge distributed data repository, with search engines making it possible for people to retrieve targeted information from it".[60] In the context of the reform of the EU Directive, these issues were referred to as pertaining to "the globalisation of data flows".[61]

Finally, the third factor is linked to new uses of data, and more in particular, advances in the analysis of the latter. These are made possible by advances in computer and information science and management, or statistical analysis. One should specifically mention profiling, and data mining. In a nutshell, profiling, and data mining, (also known as data analytics or knowledge discovery in databases—KDD) can be assimilated to big data, and more recently to machine learning or artificial intelligence (AI). Even though the heyday of big data is long gone at the time of writing,[62] the present book resorts mostly to the notion of "big data analytics" as a way to connect to the buzzword that was dominant at the time of the General Data Protection Regulation (GDPR) reform process, and the shift of regulatory models. Very briefly, it amounts to utilising very large—aggregated- data sets to draw inferences about individuals, that is, to generate more information about the individuals at stake than is actually given in the data set, and to make predictions on this basis.[63]

As mentioned in the previous paragraphs, the GDPR process reform was predicated upon a need to address then novel technological evolutions. Interestingly and ironically, issues associated to big data analytics did not seem to feature among the technology-related challenges. For instance, data mining or profiling were barely mentioned if at all in the various institutional documents that accompanied the reform process of the Data Protection Directive (DPD), and were not associated to any proposals for change.[64]

The following lines will show how these different command and control challenges apply at the data protection level.

[59] ibid; Art 29 WP and Working Party on Police and Justice (n 7).

[60] Nissenbaum (n 51) 42.

[61] European Commission, "Communication from the Commission to the European Parliament, the Council, the Economic and Social Committee and the Committee of the Regions: A Comprehensive Approach on Personal Data Protection in the European Union" (2010) 4.

[62] March 2019.

[63] Nissenbaum (n 51) 43; see also Mireille Hildebrandt and Serge Gutwirth (eds), *Profiling the European Citizen: Cross-Disciplinary Perspectives* (Springer 2008).

[64] See eg European Commission (n 53) 12, 23; Art 29 WP and Working Party on Police and Justice (n 7) 16, 26.

5. Command and control issues at the data protection level

5.1 Inefficiency of the data protection core principles/congruence

One should not be lured into thinking that evolutions in technology and data processing practices have the natural tendency to render the core data protection principles obsolete, as opposed to a situation in which these principles would always be valid and applicable because of the lower level of technology. These principles are often hailed as constitutive of strong data protection, that is, if applied correctly it is assumed that strong protection of personal data would ensue automatically. Such a vantage point echoes the "diagnosis-prescription" aspect of command and control regulation. However, if one is to be consistent with the critique of Hayek *et al.*, it would mean that inconsistencies in the application of the data protection core principles have existed since their inception. The literature has underlined a few of these.

Gonzalez Fuster has underscored the tensions underpinning the data accuracy principle.[65] As indicated in a previous chapter, the principle of data accuracy came about in the context of the emergence of databases starting to process important amounts of data. In this context it appeared that many of the data processed were inaccurate or out of date thus harming the data subjects (eg letters never received because of a change of address, confusing two different persons, etc). However, Gonzalez Fuster insists that providing inaccurate data to data controllers might be a worthwhile way of protecting one's privacy in the context of online behavioural advertising, spamming, data mining, etc.[66] In other words, this shows that the strict and linear application of the data accuracy principle does not systematically lead to adequate protection.

Another principle the application of which might lead to contrasting results is that of data minimisation. Dwork *et al.* have made this argument by arguing that minimising the amount of data processed runs directly counter to the possibility of preventing discrimination when making decision on the basis of a classification built on the basis of a data set.[67] They argue that in order for such decision to be fair (ie non-discriminatory),[68] it might be necessary to process more data rather

[65] Gloria González Fuster, "Inaccuracy as a Privacy-Enhancing Tool" (2010) 12 Ethics and Information Technology 87.

[66] ibid. Brunton and Nissenbaum have made the exact same argument in Finn Brunton and Helen Nissenbaum, *Obfuscation: A User's Guide for Privacy and Protest* (The MIT Press 2015).

[67] Cynthia Dwork and others, "Fairness Through Awareness", *Proceedings of the third ICTS* (ACM 2012).

[68] Dwork *et al.* come to equate fairness to non-discrimination understood in its multiple acceptations. Fairness therefore means treating differently people in different situations, treating them similarly when they are in similar situations. It also requires to pay attention to so-called indirect discrimination, ibid.

than less, and in particular sensitive data. Indeed, in order to be able to take a fair decision, one needs a minimum of information. In other words, minimising the amount of data processed might have discriminatory consequences.

Van der Sloot has made a similar argument concerning the application of the data minimisation principle in the context of data mining and profiling. Following him, the loss of contextuality in profiling and data mining leads to privacy and discrimination issues. Rather than making things better, the implementation of the data minimisation principle often leads to a further loss of context.[69] Therefore, whereas data minimisation can be seen as an effective safeguard regarding issues such as data misuses (including putting limits on the use of particularly compromising data) or data leakages, it should not be seen as a silver bullet, the linear application of which to any data processing situation would automatically lead to adequate protection.[70] He gives the example of police surveillance mostly taking place in particular neighbourhoods with a lot of ethnic minorities. In such a case, the data gathered about criminal activities would be heavily biased towards these groups. It is therefore important, he argues, to include contextual data so as to avoid discrimination and stigmatisation towards these minorities.[71] On this basis, van der Sloot argues in a slightly provocative—yet quite enjoyable—fashion for a data minimumisation principle: instead of collecting data to a minimum, a minimum set of data should always be collected.[72] Interestingly he shows that such a minimumisation principle can be supported through the data accuracy principle (since it requires to take positive action, including the processing of data in order to keep the latter accurate). This leads to an additional issue with the data minimisation principle: at times there is a conflict between data accuracy and data minimisation. This supports the point previously made on the limits of the data accuracy principle, and about the limits of the core data protection principles more in general.[73]

In the context of big data discussions, a number of actors sympathetic to the corporate agenda have argued that the data protection core principles were inadequate

[69] "From Data Minimization to Data Minimummization" in Bart Custers and others (eds), *Discrimination and Privacy in the Information Society: Data Mining and Profiling in Large Databases* (Springer-Verlag 2013) 282. For a discussion on the limits of data minimisation, see also Seda Gürses, Carmela Troncoso, and Claudia Diaz, "Engineering. Privacy by Design", *Computers, Privacy and Data Protection Conference (CPDP)* (2011), http://www.ncbi.nlm.nih.gov/pubmed/17761870, last accessed 22 February 2019.

[70] See van der Sloot (n 69) 281: "data minimization is not always able to exclude privacy violating or discriminatory results given the redlining effect. Data minimization not only offers no adequate solution in this respect, it might also make it difficult to assess whether a rule is indirectly discriminating or privacy violating."

[71] ibid.

[72] ibid 282.

[73] For a reflexion on the tensions, conflicts, and limitations of such principles, see Joris Van Hoboken, "From Collection to Use in Privacy Regulation? A Forward-Looking Comparison of European and US Frameworks for Personal Data Processing" in Bart Van Der Sloot, Dennis Broeders, and Erik Schrijvers (eds), *Exploring the Boundaries of Big Data* (Amsterdam University Press 2016).

insofar as they would prevent from reaping the benefits of technological advances.[74] However, the criticisms put forth have less to do with the issue of congruence than with an appetite for risk (cf risk tolerance), and further, with the implementation of standards (cf the third regulatory issue of transparency and accessibility). Issues of congruence, however, have also come to the fore in recent years, postdating the GDPR reform, with the debates surrounding machine learning (and associated issues such as profiling). Faced with a number of novel issues for data protection law to address, several scholars have argued that the traditional standard setting provisions such as data minimisation or purpose limitation can regulate the machine learning process only in a sub-optimal way. This is because the type of protection embodied in these standards misses out on several key aspects of machine learning algorithms.[75] To paraphrase de Vries, is data protection able to "encounter a profiling algorithm as a profiling algorithm"?[76]

Interestingly, these types of regulatory issues were not addressed during the EU data protection overhaul process. On the contrary, the European Commission was very clear that the preparatory work and studies leading up to the overhaul process "confirmed that the core principles of the [Data Protection] Directive are still valid".[77] The emphasis should rather be put on "making the implementation of existing principles by Member States more effective and their application more cost efficient".[78] These latter objectives correspond to the two other regulatory issues at play, which will be examined more in detail hereinbelow. It is interesting to observe already at this stage of the analysis that the fact that these issues which are most probably the most fundamental ones associated with standard setting from a command and control perspective have been left out of the scope of the GDPR reform process are not without incidence on the risk-based approach. As will be seen later, the risk-based approach builds on regulatory models that include at their heart the regulatory standard setting function (the issue being precisely to transform it as a risk management exercise). This will have a number of consequences that will be examined in detail.

5.2 Uncertainty/lack of clarity, predictability, transparency

As indicated, one of the reasons for shifting to risk-based models of regulation is the uncertainty surrounding the application of—legal-based—standards.

[74] Fred H Cate and Viktor Mayer-Schönberger, "Data Use and Impact Global Workshop" (2013).

[75] Katja de Vries, "Machine Learning/Informational Fundamental Rights: Makings of Sameness and Difference" (2016) 422; Seda Gürses and Joris van Hoboken, "Privacy After the Agile Turn", *Cambridge Handbook of Consumer Privacy* (2017) 21.

[76] de Vries (n 75) 422.

[77] European Commission (n 61) 3.

[78] European Commission (n 53) 38.

Koops points to the complexity of data protection law as one of the factors leading to uncertainty in its application. In the case of the former Dutch Data Protection Act,[79] this complexity stemmed from the length of the Statute (83 articles). Part of this complexity can also be imputed on the grounds of the key terms and concepts, which are supposed to be applied with little to no discretion, but which have received very little clarification and substantiation through guidelines, case law, etc. As a matter of fact, earlier data protections scholarship has lamented the lack of case-law.[80] Koops and the source he quotes therefore see—Dutch—data protection as containing a series of very broad norms, the application of which in practice is uneven, uneasy, and highly uncertain.[81] This therefore points to some issues associated with abuses of discretion. Koops does claim that "in reality, controllers do not intend to restrict data processing to the bare minimum".[82] And the uncertain and open-ended applicability of data protection provisions enables them to "easily argue that what they do is "necessary" for the purposes they define themselves with usually less than razor-sharp precision, until, in rare cases, some supervisory authority stops them".[83] In a similar way, Determann seems to point to issues of creative compliance that allow companies to get away with a number of "dubious" processing operations.[84]

Other countries on the contrary have opted for curbing the regulatees' discretion as much as possible. This is the case in France for instance, where the national data protection authority (DPA), the *Commission nationale de l'informatique et des libertés* (CNIL), which has one of the largest number of employees in the world leaves very little flexibility and goes on to produce exhaustive guidance for all the possible processing operations, not only for categories of processing, but also on a case-by-case basis.[85] As an example, an interviewed practitioner recounted the following: "the CNIL would like to give precise instructions ... for example, when

[79] Wet bescherming persoonsgegevens [Data Protection Act], *Staatsblad* 2000, 302.

[80] See Lee A Bygrave, "Where Have All the Judges Gone?: Reflections on Judicial Involvement in Developing Data Protection Law Judicial Involvement" in P Wahlgren (ed), *IT och juristutbildning. Nordisk årsbok i rättsinformatik*, vol 7 (Jure AB 2000). However, it would seem that there has been an increase in case-law and judicial activity in the past six to seven years, not least because of the increased relevance of data protection as a policy issue, and because of the work of the CJEU. Already rebutting Bygrave's claim, see Paul De Hert and Serge Gutwirth, "Data Protection in the Case Law of Strasbourg and Luxemburg: Constitutionalisation in Action" in Serge Gutwirth and others (eds), *Reinventing Data Protection?* (Springer 2009).

[81] "The Trouble with European Data Protection Law" (2014) 4 International Data Privacy Law 250, 254. Further, Koops notes that the same observations had already been made as far back as the 1980s and 1990s, see JEJ Prins *et al.*, *In Het Licht van de Wet Persoonsregistraties: Zon, Maan of Ster?* (Samsom 1995).

[82] Koops (n 81) 254.

[83] ibid 254–55.

[84] See Lothar Determann, "Social Media Privacy: A Dozen Myths and Facts" (2012) 7 Stanford Technology Law Review 1, 4: "there is still a wide gap between assertions by European data protection authorities and legal commentaries as to what is allowed and forbidden and what companies and government authorities are actually doing and getting away with".

[85] Bamberger and Mulligan (n 28) 1620.

there's an authorization, they'd like to list the type of data one by one. You're allowed to use the last name, the first name, gender;" and also: "it goes to the details, you have to put these sentences [in] a consent form. You have to give access only to the people who do accounting and not to the people who do reporting."[86]

Kuner points out that some obligations are never complied with in practice not owing to the bad faith of the controllers, but simply because it is genuinely difficult for them to determining—parts of—their legal obligations.[87] Thus, pointing the criticism pendulum back to issues associated with overly complex mandates. For instance, it has been observed that in France and Spain, safeguards and standards have reached such a high level of complexity that firms know in advance that they won't be in a position to fully comply, and have therefore a budget specifically dedicated to compliance fines.[88] One reason he alludes to in this regard are the DPAs' lacunae in terms of publicising and explaining the applicable rules, at least insofar as a number of data processing operations are concerned.[89] Similarly, addressing the complexity of data protection provisions was also at the heart of the GDPR reform process.[90] And it was directly associated to some elements of the reform process that are at the core of the risk-based approach.[91]

The challenges posed by the development of new technologies and the processing practices they allow for were maybe best expressed by Kuner: "data processing has become so complex in recent years that it is becoming impossible for the law to provide rules for all the new processing situations that are developing, so that data controllers, [and] data processors are frequently placed in the position of having to determine their rights and obligations for situations that are not contemplated under the law".[92] This is the case for instance with online processing, which takes place in a networked and globalised context. In such cases, the processing is very often distributed among a large number of computers, many of which will be located in separate jurisdictions. This distributed nature of data processing greatly complicates data controllers' ability to determine what exactly their obligations pursuant to data protection law are, since it multiplies the number of rules applicable to their operations.[93] Another difficulty is linked to some of the trends

[86] ibid 1619.

[87] Christopher Kuner, "The 'Internal Morality' of European Data Protection Law" (2008) 5.

[88] Bamberger and Mulligan (n 28) 1600.

[89] Kuner (n 87) 10–12.

[90] European Commission (n 53) 20. See also eg Recital 102, of the EU Commission's proposal for a General Data Protection Regulation, following which, one of the aims of the reform is to "simplify the regulatory environment, thus eliminating unnecessary costs and reducing the administrative burdens".

[91] Internal mechanisms pertaining to the risk-based approach were explicitly framed as a response to the goal of ensuring a more consistent EU data protection legal framework, and further, to enhance the internal market dimension of data protection law, ibid 43.

[92] Kuner (n 87) 11–12. With the processing of data for a different purpose being one of the prime cases, see eg Bart Custers and Helena Uršič, "Big Data and Data Reuse: A Taxonomy of Data Reuse for Balancing Big Data Benefits and Personal Data Protection" (2016) 6 International Data Privacy Law 4.

[93] Kuner (n 87) 7; see also Christopher Kuner, *Transborder Data Flows and Data Privacy Law* (OUP 2013).

described herein above (eg big data, aggregated—virtual—databases, profiling, and data mining), all of which involve multiple data controllers and processors, the processing of data for a very high number of different purposes and often in an automated way, and most importantly, in a very opaque way so that even the data controllers asking for consent do not fully understand the details of the processing operations they are—purportedly—responsible for.[94]

5.3 Simplicity and accessibility

Among data protection safeguards, systems of licensing and registration appear as the oldest ones since they had been adopted by pioneering data protection statutes such as the 1973 Swedish *Datalag*.[95] The shortcomings of such systems were identified early on. Accordingly, the main reason for criticism lied in the overly bureaucratic and cumbersome nature of the system.[96] In Sweden, licensing was required for all automated personal data systems, and not least because of the important development of data processing-based activities, the amount of work it lead to, was much greater than anticipated. As a result, licensing became so routinised that it transformed into a mere formality resulting with the automatic granting of the licence.[97] The result was a modification of the original system into a standardised approach for routine processing (mainly a registration system) and a special one for more dangerous processing operations (this is analogous in the EU Directive).[98] As analysed *supra*, licensing and registration differ by little (the discretion afforded to the regulator is non-existent in this latter case). The system of registration underpinned the 1984 UK Data Protection Act. It is also at the basis of the protection afforded by the EU Directive.[99] In addition to these systems being bureaucratic, authors also underlined their failure in bringing about a stronger protection of personal data. Korff for instance argued that in addition to being burdensome, the information provided in notices was too abstract so as to provide any kind of added value.[100] Along the same lines, Burkert has argued that these routinised processes have failed in bringing about public attention and debate,

[94] Koops (n 81) 252.

[95] (Sweden) Data Act given in the Palace of Stockholm, May 11 1973, SFS 1973: 289.

[96] Colin J Bennett, *Regulating Privacy* (Cornell University Press 1992) 159. See also Flaherty (n 52) 395.

[97] Bennett (n 96) 164–65.

[98] ibid 165. See also Flaherty (n 52) 116.

[99] Even though in this case it is not explicitly labelled as such, but results from the combination of the obligations to notify DPAs of new data processing operations and to publish these notifications (Arts 18, 19, and 21).

[100] Douwe Korff, "EC Study on Implementation of Data Protection Directive—Annex 3: Report on the Findings of the Study" (2002) 156 ff. See also Art 29 WP and Working Party on Police and Justice (n 7).

and have therefore lead to the bureaucratisation of data protection.[101] Buitelaar goes along the same lines, arguing that if the original goal of notification obligations was to provide transparency to data subjects, in practice however, notification is mainly seen as part of a due diligence duty in order to make sure that the data controller is fully compliant,[102] and so did the European Commission in its Communication on the reform of the EU Data Protection Directive.[103] More in particular, the Article 29 Working Party (Art 29 WP) argues that "the information provided relates to broad categories of data and is quite vague, whereas regulators need context-specific information where there are risks to individuals".[104] One of the consequences of the inadequacy of the information provided, is that in many cases DPAs have to request additional information from the concerned data controllers. A process which is very cumbersome and impractical.[105] Licensing and notification are particularly ill-adapted to the fact that contemporary processing relies upon a number of trivial processings, which often take place at internal level (of the data controller) and are necessary in order to conduct the data processing operations. This is the case with the internet and the World Wide Web. In order to be operational from a purely technical perspective, any website must process a number of data that can be considered personal such as IP addresses.[106] This theoretically means that a huge number of notifications should be made on a daily basis, which is simply impossible.

Similarly, the European Commission was also quite critical of the rules concerning the transfer of personal data to third countries, which it subjected to the same "red tape"/administrative burden/box ticking criticism as the notification obligation. In particular, it argued that none of those mechanisms were ensuring effective protection of personal data.[107]

[101] He also argued that German data protection agencies shifted "uneasily between the image of data protection bureaucratization and an ombudsman role", Herbert Burkert, "Privacy—Data Protection: A German/European Perspective" *2nd Symposium of the Max Planck Project Group on the Law of Common Goods and the Computer Science and Telecommunications Board of the National Research Council* (1999) 63.

[102] JC Buitelaar, "Privacy: Back to the Roots" (2012) 13 German Law Journal 171, 179.

[103] European Commission (n 61). More in particular, the current obligation to notify all data processing operations to the DPAs is considered a cumbersome obligation which does not in itself provide "any real added value for the protection of individuals' personal data", ibid 10.

[104] Art 29 WP, "Advice Paper on Notification" (2011) 6. It also adds that "while this may have been the case when the Directive was introduced, a public register is no longer the best and most appropriate way for individuals to understand what an organisation is doing with their personal data, and who to contact when things go wrong". ibid.

[105] ibid 7. Interestingly, the Working Party underlines that whereas the data processing-related information may appear somewhat useless for any practical purpose, the notification system continues to play a useful role insofar as it provides regulators with all of the controller's contact details. This is important since regulators "need to know who they regulate and how to contact them". In this wake, the Art 29WP had suggested to reform the notification system, but to keep the systematic notification of controllers' contact details ibid 9. This proposal was not considered in the reform package however.

[106] See Art 29 WP, "Opinion 4/2007 on the Concept of Personal Data" (2007); Art 29 WP, "Working Document Privacy on the Internet—An Integrated EU Approach to On-Line Data Protection" (2000).

[107] European Commission (n 53) 40.

In 2008, Bennett wrote that: "the privacy advocacy community has generally not made extensive use of the complaints investigation and resolution process under data protection law", despite the fact that doing so "cost[s] no money and very little time".[108] Accordingly, this resulted from the fact that data protection authorities are relatively "under-resourced and legally constrained," and that some "do not have enforcement powers" or simply have not used them.[109] Beyond the practical difficulties existing for exercising such rights (in terms of financial resources, knowledge, time, etc),[110] one can argue that data subject rights have suffered from flaws since their inceptions. Following Mayer-Schönberger, data subject rights were not always part of data protection legislations, but became standard data protection provisions with the advent of what he refers to as the second generation of data protection statutes.[111] These saw data subject rights as safeguards of paramount importance in the wake of the German 1983 census decision, which established the right to informational self-determination as a fundamental freedom.[112] Interestingly, Mayer-Schönberger hailed the emergence of these mechanisms and their potential for stronger protection, and simultaneously criticised their lack of efficiency. According to him, the exercise of these rights often leads to a style of data protection based on formal legitimacy but not bringing any concrete protection, leading him to describe data protection statutes as mere "paper tigers".[113] Koops argued that the exercise of data subject rights is highly theoretical. Current data practices are simply too complex for the data subject to be able to understand what exactly is going on with their personal data, and whom to address. He further argued that the scope of these rights was often limited to the accuracy of the data.[114] Moreover, even if they manage to contact the data controller, it is not even certain that the latter understands better what exactly is taking place.[115] During the

[108] Colin J Bennett, *The Privacy Advocates: Resisting the Spread of Surveillance* (The MIT Press 2008) 118.

[109] ibid; see also Bamberger and Mulligan (n 28) 1550; Determann (n 84).

[110] For a critical overview, see Antonella Galetta and Paul De Hert, "The Proceduralisation of Data Protection Remedies under EU Data Protection Law: Towards a More Effective and Data Subject-Oriented System?" (2015) 8 Review of European Administrative Law 123; Xavier Duncan L'Hoiry and Clive Norris, "The Honest Data Protection Officer's Guide to Enable Citizens to Exercise Their Subject Access Rights: Lessons from a Ten-Country European Study" (2015) 5 International Data Privacy Law 190.

[111] Viktor Mayer-Schönberger, "Generational Development of Data Protection in Europe" in Philip E Agre and Marc Rotenberg (eds), *Technology and Privacy: The New Landscape* (MIT Press 1997).

[112] *Urteil des BVerfG v 15.12.1983 zum VZG 83* (1 BVerfGE 65).

[113] Mayer-Schönberger (n 111).

[114] Koops (n 81) 253. The European Commission provided for a similar assessment, emphasising the difficulties associated with the exercise of access rights see, European Commission (n 53) 27.

[115] Koops (n 81) 252. Of course, much has changed since then in the wake of the *Schrems* case, CJEU C-362/14, *Schrems* [2015] ECLI:EU:C:2015:650 (hereafter *Schrems*). See for instance, René LP Mahieu, Hadi Asghari, and Michel Van Eeten, "Collectively Exercising the Right of Access: Individual Effort, Societal Effect" (2018) 7 Internet Policy Review 1. Even though Koops would probably still remain sceptical of these developments: "Your average Internet user simply is not Max Schrems, and your average data controller does not neatly send you a 1222-pages cd with all the data they process about you." (n 81) 252.

reform process of the GDPR, the European Commission held similar views on data subject rights.[116]

The difficulties associated with simplicity and accessibility also concern the data protection standard setting provisions. Discussing the reform process of the EU Directive, Koops argued that there is a fundamental disconnection between data protection law "in the books" and data processing practices "on the ground".[117] He refers to "all the databases in which [our] personal data are stored", and to big data practices predicated upon massive data collections (1.2 zettabytes in 2010 with an estimate growth rate of 60 per cent a year). He then wonders "who in his right mind can look at the world out there and claim that a principle of data minimisation exists?".[118] He holds a similar reasoning as far as the purpose specification and data retention principles are concerned. A number of scholars have developed this criticism further, by pointing to the purportedly conflicting logics existing between big data analytics and some of the core data protection principles, in particular as far as the requirement of having a unified purpose is concerned. A common trope that accompanied "big data" as a "hype" and "hot topic" of data protection debates at the time suggested that big data is purposeless (ie it doesn't collect data to answer pre-existing question, but instead collects data to find answers to questions that were not yet envisaged), which in turns has been used as a justification by companies to collect large troves of data in an attempt to make sense out of it at "a later stage".[119] Even though the purposelessness of big data (and further, machine learning) has been dispelled by any serious study and analysis of the practice,[120] these authors nonetheless point to a number of caveats. As far as consent is concerned, one of the requirements indeed is that it be specific to each separate processing purpose (and therefore be collected at the beginning of each new processing).[121] In order to accommodate consent's purpose specificity with big data practices, many controllers rely upon overbroad information notices, which in practice allow for any processing operation.[122] Conversely, when controllers try

[116] See European Commission (n 53) 27.

[117] Koops (n 81) 256.

[118] ibid.

[119] See eg Centre for Information Policy Leadership, "Big Data and Analytics: Seeking Foundations for Effective Privacy Guidance" (2013) 1.

[120] See eg Mireille Hildebrandt, "Privacy As Protection of the Incomputable Self: From Agnostic to Agonistic Machine Learning" (2019) 20 Theoretical Inquiries in Law 83, 102; John D Kelleher and Brendan Tierney, *Data Science* (The MIT Press 2018). Even the Art 29 WP has acknowledged that even "exploratory research is never operated at total random in practice" Art 29 WP, "Opinion 8/2014 on the Recent Developments on the Internet of Things" (2014) 16.

[121] See Art 29 WP, "Opinion 15/2011 on the Definition of Consent" (2011) 9, 17–19. See also Art 4(11) GDPR, and Art 29 WP, "Article 29 Working Party Guidelines on Consent under Regulation 2016/679" (2018).

[122] Cate and Mayer-Schönberger (n 74) 7. Even though such notices are in principle illegal, see Art 29 WP, "Opinion 15/2011 on the Definition of Consent" (n 121) 17–19, or Art 29 WP, "Article 29 Working Party Guidelines on Consent under Regulation 2016/679" (n 121), the fact remains that this is what current practice looks like.

to provide sufficiently granular information they are faced with the challenge that information notices are static, since a number of traditional big data operations (eg re-use or third party sharing) are difficult to foresee.[123] But even when such operations are included in notices, it remains to be determined whether they fall within the data subject reasonable expectations,[124] since such expectations are context-dependent, ie. subjects might think that certain re-uses and third party sharing might fall within their expectations in certain contexts but not in others. Again, the static dimension of information notices does not allow to take such context into consideration.[125] Given these shortcomings, it is very likely that a new consent is required for a number of further processing operations. But this last option appears as impractical as it would overburden the data subject with a huge number of consents to be provided on a continuous basis.[126] Another instance is that of the purpose specification and limitation principle, which requires that purposes be specified at the time of collection, and data should not be further processed for incompatible purposes. This is probably the principle that best embodies the requirement to process data for a given purpose and to relate all the processing life cycle to the initial purpose. Many controllers involved in so-called big data processing operations therefore often provide purposes defined in such broad terms that they become meaningless.[127] Just like in the case of consent, the only alternative is to consider these further uses as new operations requiring a legitimate ground of their own, thus facing the same issues.[128]

Furthermore, the use of consent as a legitimate ground has also been often reduced to a mere "box ticking" exercise, what US scholars have referred to as the "consent fallacy".[129] Scholars have argued that in such a context, consent is largely theoretical and has no practical meaning. People will often simply tick consent boxes without reading and/or understanding privacy notices, and some service providers sometimes just assume that visiting their website is equivalent to valid

[123] Because consent must be specific, the information provided must be granular enough Art 29 WP, "Opinion 15/2011 on the Definition of Consent" (n 121) 17.

[124] Following the Art 29 WP, it is simply impossible to exhaustively describe all the operations with their every detail that take place under one purpose (eg all data or just a part, at what time, for which compatible purposes, etc). Therefore a consent is specific enough when it encompasses the future operations that fall within the data subject's reasonable expectations ibid.

[125] Cate and Mayer-Schönberger (n 74) 8. This may also be the reason why Cate and Mayer-Schönberger argue that data subjects often prioritise short term gains over long term risks, ibid 7.

[126] ibid 8–9.

[127] Centre for Information Policy Leadership (n 119) 13.

[128] Cate and Mayer-Schönberger (n 74) 9–10.

[129] Paul M Schwartz, "Privacy, Participation, and Cyberspace: An American Perspective" in Bruno Baeriswyl and Beat Rudin (eds), *Perspektive Datenschutz: Praxis und Entwicklungen in Recht und Technik* (Schutless Juristiche Medien AG 2002). See also Daniel J Solove, "Privacy Self-Management and the Consent Dilemma" (2013) 126 Harvard Law Review 1880. See also, Bart Custers and others, "Informed Consent in Social Media Use—The Gap between User Expectations and EU Personal Data Protection Law" (2013) 10 SCRIPTed 435; Paula J Bruening, "Data Privacy Day 2014: Today Has Been a Day to Rethink Privacy" (2014) <http://blogs.intel.com/policy/2014/01/28/today-day-rethink-privacy)/> accessed 29 January 2019.

consent.[130] The European Commission was also aware of similar difficulties in the context of the reform process.[131] Further, in the context of big data analytics, and internet of things, some scholars have argued that implementing consent becomes very difficult in practice. According to them, it is becoming increasingly difficult to trace data subjects in order to ask them for consent since it many cases data is collected from a variety of sources not involving the data subject (eg sensors or inferred from existing data).[132] In this regard, efforts to make consent more practical for instance by resorting to multi-layered notices,[133] or by using short texts and icons appear as illusory.[134]

Again, it should be emphasised that these various objections do not reflect the views of the author. They are simply put forth as a way to show that regulatory issues associated with simplicity and accessibility have also existed at data protection level, thereby illustrating the fact that compliance is a much more complex process than is sometimes acknowledged. In any case, this has led some authors to lament the bureaucratic and ineffective nature of data protection law, the latter being a mere "paper tiger". Following Koops, again, "current data protection law, with its many *ex ante* requirements, can hardly be said to have demonstrably led to preventing unnecessary data processing in practice".[135] Similarly, addressing the inefficiency of the data protection framework, stemming in part from "red tape" and costly administrative burdens was at the heart of the GDPR reform process, and further, the risk-based approach.[136]

5.4 Enforcement

5.4.1 Under enforcement

Enforcement has always been an issue regarding the application of the EU Data Protection Directive. In the first report on the implementation of the Directive, the EU Commission notably underlined that the low priority granted to enforcement

[130] Solon Barocas and Helen Nissenbaum, "On Notice: The Trouble with Notice and Consent", *Proceedings of the Engaging Data Forum: The First International Forum on the Application and Management of Personal Electronic Information* (Cambridge, Massachusetts 2009); Solon Barocas and Helen Nissenbaum, "Big Data's End Run around Anonymity and Consent" in Julia Lane and others (eds), *Privacy, Big Data, and the Public Good* (Cambridge University Press 2014).

[131] See European Commission (n 53) 30, 37.

[132] See eg Cate and Mayer-Schönberger (n 74) 9.

[133] Art 29 WP, "Opinion 15/2011 on the Definition of Consent" (n 121).

[134] Koops (n 81) 252. For a critical perspective on these efforts, see Wendy Grossman, "Licensed to be confusing, restrictive and obtuse", The Guardian, 24 April 2008, http://www.theguardian.com/technology/2008/apr/24/law.software; last accessed 24 March 2019. Among much research on the topic, one can also look at the project of Solon Barocas, Nicholas Doty, and Ashkan Soltani, who did an inventory of the various efforts towards better policies, http://solon.barocas.org/?page_id=200, last accessed 24 March 2019.

[135] Koops (n 81) 254.

[136] European Commission (n 53) 43.

action by the DPAs would be the consequence of under-resourced enforcement departments.[137]

In the years following this report, Kuner observed a ratchetting-up of enforcement actions, yet he argues that the amount of enforcement actions is quite small in proportion to the number of data processing taking place. Therefore, the chances of an enforcement action being brought for a violation are still relatively low in most cases.[138] Kuner also argues that there is a gap between the complexity of the rules that govern the processing of data and the low risk of enforcement coupled to the—relative—mildness of the sanctions.[139] A notable area of under-enforcement has traditionally pertained to consent. In most cases major online services frame their consent policies in a "take it or leave it" sort of way. Even though such consent policies are not in compliance with the interpretation of consent given by the Art 29 WP,[140] they have been widespread. In 2010, the EU Fundamental Rights Agency issued a report on data protection authorities which garnered a lot of attention. This report pointed to a generalised lack of enforcement, arguing that "in some Member States, prosecutions and sanctions for violations of data protection law are limited or non-existing".[141] Very critically, the Agency pointed to lacks of resources (including understaffing), limited powers, but also sometimes, a willingness to adopt softer methods of dialogue and guidance when "harder" sanctions were clearly more adequate.[142] The GDPR reform process did take these concerns into account.[143]

5.4.2 Issues with advances in technology

Ogus argues that technological evolutions have a role to play in the difficulties associated with enforcement on the deterrence mode. He observes that the development of technology goes towards ever-increasing complexity. This entails that the regulators' monitoring task is also becoming increasingly complex to the extent that "it is often very difficult to predict where and when violations will occur".[144]

Kuner suggest a similar influence of technology in the context of enforcement related to international transfers of data. Following him, the biggest problem in this regard is probably "the increasing flood of personal data now being transferred

[137] Douwe Korff, "EC Study on Implementation of Data Protection Directive: Comparative Summary of National Laws" (2002); Korff (n 100). See also Lawrence Speer, "Variable Funding of EU Privacy Law Means Uneven Enforcement Across European Union" (2007) 7 Privacy & Security Law Report 49.

[138] Kuner (n 87) 6, 9.

[139] ibid 9. Even though the enforcement of data protection has significantly improved since then, see eg David Wright and Paul De Hert (eds), *Enforcing Privacy: Regulatory, Legal and Technological Approaches* (Springer 2016).

[140] Art 29 WP, "Opinion 15/2011 on the Definition of Consent" (n 121).

[141] EU Fundamental Rights Agency, "Data Protection in the European Union : The Role of National Data Protection Authorities Strengthening the Fundamental Rights Architecture in the EU II" (2010) 6.

[142] ibid.

[143] See eg European Commission (n 53) 30.

[144] Ogus (n 8) 95.

online, and the limited possibility of enforcing transborder data flow regulation by traditional means".[145] Indeed, networked and globalised data practices not only hamper the determination of the applicable law, they also threaten the DPAs enforcement competences insofar as the number of entities performing processing operations is higher, and some of them might be out of their jurisdictions.[146] Furthermore, "the definition of transborder data flows is so broad that it can cover most acts of data processing on the internet, and no national regulation could ever be consistently enforced with regard to such a vast amount of data processing on a global scale".[147]

The transborder-related challenges to enforcement are not directly related to the regulatory changes accompanying the risk-based approach, even though it predicated upon a promise of increased consistency. Further, and in the case of the GDPR, these issues can also be seen as instrumental in leading to a more general trend towards stronger enforcement powers of regulatory authorities.[148]

[145] Kuner (n 93) 154–55.
[146] Kuner (n 87) 7–8.
[147] Kuner (n 93) 155.
[148] See Art 58 and Art 83 GDPR, not to mention the consistency and one-stop-shop mechanisms Arts 60–67 GDPR, or the extended territorial scope, Art 3 GDPR.

4
Changes of regulatory models
From command and control to meta regulation

> Corporate Social Responsibility is about changing not merely corporate behaviour but the very concept of the corporate entity, and in particular, the concept of its role in society, or what is loosely called 'the licence to operate'.[1]

1. Introduction

As one remembers, the issues associated to command and control regulation stem from two of its characteristics: its "diagnosis-prescription" aspect, and its reliance upon deterrence. In other words, regulators assume that they know what is a "good" and a "bad" behaviour (which is embedded in the standards they set), and how to best implement the standards that address such behaviour. The only reason why regulatory goals are not achieved then is because of avoidance behaviour, which is itself remedied through a sanction or threat thereof. However, and as shown, the picture is more complicated than that. First the effectiveness of deterrence strategies has often been deceiving. Second, linear processes of standard setting and the safeguards associated thereto have not always managed to properly address the harms stemming from data processing practices. In other words, the standards themselves might not lead to satisfactory regulatory outcomes, and/or their adequate implementation is trickier than envisaged.

Therefore, evolutions in regulatory models have sought to address these two issues: how to devise and better implement more adequate standards (and associated safeguards), and how to achieve better enforcement results. As will be described, the two go hand in hand. Enforcement will cease to be sought through punishment, but rather, through collaboration and dialogue between the regulator and the regulatee; the object of such dialogue being a problematisation of how best to achieve regulatory goals. Simultaneously, in terms of standard setting and safeguards, new regulatory models will consist in endowing regulatees with regulatory

[1] Michael Power, "Risk Management and the Responsible Organisation" in Richard V Ericson and Aaron Doyle (eds), *Risk and Morality* (University of Toronto Press 2003) 146.

The Risk-Based Approach to Data Protection. Raphaël Gellert, Oxford University Press (2020). © Raphaël Gellert.
DOI: 10.1093/oso/9780198837718.001.0001.

responsibility (in terms of implementing or even devising standards and safeguards), and enabling regulators to assess their performance. It is interesting to observe that the notion of risk will play an increasingly important role in these different models of regulation, insofar as such regulatory responsibility entails a recoding of the regulatees activities as a matter of risk management. In particular, the latest model, known as meta regulation, is completely predicated upon the use of risk management tools.

2. The plinth of meta regulation: the "risk management agenda"

In order to fully grasp the meaning of meta regulation, it is necessary to go back to the notion of risk that was studied in Chapter 1. As a reminder, that chapter ended with the insight that in spite of its successes, risk analysis as a specific iteration of risk management became very much contested during the 1980s, and in particular the various subjective methodological choices that permeate it. Whereas early responses to these challenges focused on improving the quality of risk management, subsequent evolutions will rather rely upon a transformation of risk management as a managerial process.

One should observe that the author refers to risk analysis as the process of both assessing and managing risks. Even though one could also refer to it as "risk management" (since risk analysis is a specific iteration of risk management understood as the whole process of assessing and managing risks), the "risk analysis" expression is sometimes used in the following lines in order to clearly distinguish it from what will be referred to as the "risk management agenda". The latter is specific iteration of risk management which includes mechanisms of organisational design, and of which the actual process of assessing and managing risks is only a part.

2.1 The rise of corporate governance

The transformation of risk management as a managerial process owes a lot to the notion of corporate governance, which came about in the 1990s after a number of organisations were found to be in situations of non-compliance in high profile cases, and in the wake of reforms in the public sector pertaining to the so-called new public management.[2] In this sense, it affects both the private and public sectors. As a matter of fact, the present book often refers to organisations and regulatees as interchangeable words. Even though regulatees can in theory be natural persons as

[2] Michael Power, *Organized Uncertainty: Designing a World of Risk Management* (OUP 2007) 34.

is the case in the General Data Protection Regulation (GDPR) for instance, which provides that a data controller can be a natural or legal person,[3] in practice they will often be legal persons. This is even more so the case with meta regulation, since it is predicated upon the sharing of regulatory tasks between regulators and regulatees explicitly conceived as organisations.[4] Further, and as Black argues, the regulatory literature usually equates an organisation to a firm or a business, although analytically it could be any type of organisations such as school, prison, university, etc.[5] Beyond that, and as Power notes, the word "governance" has acquired policy and scholarly momentum since the mid-1990s.[6] It is, however, a contestable concept, not least because of its lack of definitional clarity. As Drori argues, governance is a hybrid concept, which encompasses both logics of democratic engagement and of managerial process, and within which, both are in constant tension—tough to varying degrees.[7] Whereas the first logic is in line with democratic ideals of responsiveness and engagement, the second one is inward-looking with a focus on technical efficiency, organisational design, and on managerial practices, all of which pertain to organisational activity and logic.[8] That is not to say that the increasing prevalence of ideals of managerialism over those of democratic participation evacuates aspirations for openness and engagement. Rather, the latter are subsumed and recoded within a logic of good—corporate—governance of the risk management practice. In other words, instead of addressing issues per se, governance is about making organisational activity more legitimate (by transforming it along the ideals of managerial practice, that is, making more it transparent, accountable, auditable, and assessable).[9]

2.2 The role of corporate governance in the transformation of risk and risk management: emphasis on process

The rise of corporate governance will directly affect the way that risk management is conducted. Whereas up until the 1980s, the bulk of efforts had been

[3] Art 4(1)(7) GDPR.

[4] See egChristine Parker, *The Open Corporation: Effective Self-Regulation and Democracy* (Cambridge University Press 2002). See also Julia Black, "Decentring Regulation: Understanding the Role Self-Regulation in a 'Post- Regulatory' World" (2001) 54 Current Legal Problems 103, 120: "the defining feature is that an individual organisation is responsible for exercising a regulatory function".

[5] Black (n 4) 120.

[6] Power (n 2) 18. See eg David Levi-Faur, "From 'Big Government' to 'Big Governance'?" in David Levi-Faur (ed), *The Oxford Handbook of Governance* (OUP 2012); Christopher Torfing and Jacob Ansell (eds), *Handbook on Theories of Governance* (Edward Elgar 2016).

[7] Gili S Drori, "Governed by Governance: The New Prism for Organizational Change" in Gili S Drori, John M Meyer, and Hyoku Hwang (eds), *Globalization and Organization: World Society and Organizational Change* (OUP 2006).

[8] Power (n 2) 19.

[9] ibid 35.

directed towards improving the "science" of risk analysis, the widespread adoption of governance will lead to a new type of risk management (one could call it risk governance), which, in line with the ideals of governance, is foremost concerned with the—external—legitimacy of the process. In other words, the—corporate—governance of risk puts the focus upon the organisational design—and its management—within which risk analysis is conducted.[10] By "organisational design" one should understand the institutional context, that is, the institutional mechanisms that are in place and used in order to conduct the risk analysis exercise such as the quality of senior management, or internal and external accountability.[11] In short, the shift from risk analysis to risk governance can be understood as a shift towards a form of governance of the risk analysis process which is more corporate in form insofar as it focuses upon the managerial—and thus organisational—process within which risk analysis is undertaken.[12] One can therefore contrast the situation that prevailed in the 1960s, which was characterised by an expansion of risk analysis towards an increasing number of new "risk objects", and the situation since the 1990s which is still prevailing up to this date, and which has put the focus on the management process within which risk analysis is undertaken.[13]

The advent of this hybrid notion of governance has two corollaries: a new notion of risk turned towards risk taking, and the transformation of organisational activity as a matter of risk taking/risk analysis.

2.3 Governance and the neoliberal logic of risk: responsibilisation and risk taking

The rise of the notion of governance as a strategy to perform risk analysis and management can be put in parallel with the concomitant rise of a so-called "neoliberal" modality of risk. The advent of so-called neoliberalism in the past decades has led to a new modality of risk that puts the emphasis on individual responsibility and risk taking (as opposed to, say, conventional risk analysis, which was traditionally concerned with risk avoidance).[14] Following a neoliberal framing of things, individuals are transformed into market actors responsible for their own risks (ie ill-fortune),[15] but also for maximising risk taking (what Baker and Simon refer to as "embracing risk").[16]

[10] ibid 19.

[11] ibid 19–20.

[12] ibid.

[13] ibid 20.

[14] See eg Manfred B Steger and Ravi K Roy, *Neoliberalism: A Very Short Introduction* (OUP 2010); Michel Foucault, *The Birth of Biopolitics: Lectures at the Collège de France, 1978–1979* (Michel Senellart ed, Palgrave Macmillan 2008).

[15] Mitchell Dean, *Governmentality—Power and Rule in Modern Society* (Sage 2010) 214.

[16] Tom Baker and Jonathan Simon (eds), *Embracing Risk: The Changing Culture of Insurance and Responsibility* (The University of Chicago Press 2002); Tom Baker and Jonathan Simon, "Embracing Risk" in Tom Baker and Jonathan Simon (eds), *Embracing Risk: The Changing Culture of Insurance and Responsibility* (The University of Chicago Press 2002).

Power argues that these analyses concerning individuals are also valid as far as organisations are concerned.[17] He refers to a new conception of organisations, which are complex, confident, and responsible actors, expected to manage uncertainties in a rational way, not least because they are self-reflective and self-improving.[18] This is epitomised by the widespread adoption of what is known as enterprise-wide risk management programmes.[19] In other words, what one can see here is that the notion of governance as an approach to risk management emphasising the legitimacy of its process can only take place under a neoliberal conception of risk. That is, one that simultaneously relies upon the responsibilisation of the concerned entity, and which is turned predominantly towards the creation of value; which in the case of organisations translates into the achievement of organisational objectives and goals.[20]

2.4 Governance and the transformation of organisational activity as risk taking: from risk governance to the risk management agenda (or risk management 2.0): the turning inside out of organisations

The second crucial corollary of the move to governance is the transformation of organisations' activities as a matter of risk taking, ie as a matter of risk management.

The notion of governance is indeed predicated upon a notion of neoliberal risk, which itself implies a responsibilisation and an *ethos* of risk taking. It is argued here that such responsibilisation is possible only insofar as one's activities are recoded in terms of risk management. In other words, an important aspect of governance is the "turning inside out of organisations", meaning that the design of organisations and managerial practices (that form the heart of organisational practice, ie what it is that people do when they work within an organisation) become a matter of risk management/risk taking.[21]

In this sense, there is a two-folded transformation process of organisations at stake. Governance first redefines risk analysis into a matter of management, that is, as a managerial practice endowed with the corporate ideals discussed herein above

[17] Power (n 2) 22.

[18] ibid 23.

[19] ibid 22. As seen in the introduction, Enterprise-Wide Risk Management can be defined as "the overall management of risk that an organisation takes and holds to achieve its strategic aims", https://www.pwc.com.au/risk-controls/enterprise-wide-risk-mgt.html, last accessed 27 March 2019.

[20] See John Meyer, "Globalization and the Expansion and Standardization of Management" in Kerstin Sahlin-Andersson and Lars Engwall (eds), *The Expansion of Management Knowledge: Carriers, Flows and Sources* (Stanford University Press 2002).

[21] Power (n 2) 28–29.

(in particular a focus on process and legitimacy). Second, this logic of governance and the redefinition of risk analysis it entails is only possible insofar as it relies upon a neoliberal modality of risk. As a result, organisations not only manage a notion of risk favouring first and foremost opportunity and value creation (ie organisational objectives). They also come to embody values and ideas of efficiency, opportunity, accountability, good governance, and very importantly, responsibility.[22] In other words, corporate governance can only take place in combination with a modality of risk which is turned towards the achievement of organisational goals, and which itself entails that organisations become "responsible entities". Crucially, this responsibilisation is made possible through a reframing of their activities as a matter of risk taking/risk management. This has the direct consequence of transforming existing management (ie managerial) structures, processes, and tools as a matter of risk.

Demortain has described these changes as partaking of what he has coined as "*the risk management agenda*".[23] We retain this concept as it aptly captures the transformation that risk analysis and management has undergone. Namely the transformation of risk analysis as a managerial practice, and, symmetrically, the transformation of managerial practice as risk analysis, but a specific form of risk analysis, conceived on a managerial mode.

Power sees this re-organisation and reconceptualisation of management activity in the name of risk as a form of administrative innovation, which reframes the pre-existing managerial instruments as risk tools, and more specifically, these risk analysis tools must themselves be viewed as "new concepts of risk and its management".[24] In sum, the turn towards the risk management agenda reflects "neoliberal ambitions for the constitution of a new kind of organizational self".[25]

3. The risk management agenda in practice

This section engages further in the analysis of the "risk management agenda" (that is, what does it "concretely" mean for an organisation), since it is at the core of meta regulation, and hence, the risk-based approach.

[22] ibid.

[23] David Demortain, *Scientists and the Regulation of Risk—Standardising Control* (Edward Elgar Publishing 2011) 78–79.

[24] Power (n 2) 28.

[25] ibid 29. Or, as Power puts it, "a 'managerial' concept of risk management" embedded into specific logics and values, ibid 3, which is both attuned to the concerns of risk governance and to the neoliberal logic of risk taking.

3.1 Role of internal controls

3.1.1 Original meaning of internal controls

In order to understand what it means for an organisation to conceive of its activities as a matter of risk management, one must pay attention to the backbone thereof: internal controls. Internal controls, also sometimes referred to as internal management controls,[26] are simply a number of routines and procedures partaking of managerial activity. Until then, they were little formalised and had received little attention. They include for instance the obligation to keep proper books and records, monitor capital adequacy, segregation of duties, due exercise of authority, etc.[27]

3.1.2 The transformation of internal controls as risk management: the role of audit and quality control

Power argues that the instrumental factor in this transformation is what he refers to as the audit implosion.[28] Audit is primarily a financial tool which covers organisations' financial statements and, as a consequence, provides tokens of integrity and legitimacy.[29] However, throughout the 1980s and 1990s, audit will be reinvented in the name of corporate governance.[30] For this reason, its scope will expand to include the organisation in a holistic way. The way to do this is to expand the focus from financial integrity towards the measurement of the whole business process, something known as business strategy.[31] The way to make business strategy auditable is to adopt a business risk approach to audit and transform it into business risk analysis, that is, into an assessment of the risks that the organisation will not meet its strategic objectives.[32] The object of this renewed audit as a risk assessment exercise is internal controls. Instead of assessing transactions, audit now focuses upon internal controls because the latter are seen as a window on the organisation and its strategy, and are therefore seen as the best way to identify the different risks.[33]

Another factor to consider is what is known as "quality control".[34] The latter aims at ensuring the engineering and technical quality of industrial processes.[35]

[26] See Julia Black, "The Rise, Fall and Fate of Principles-Based Regulation" in Kern Alexander and Niamh Moloney (eds), *Law Reform and Financial Markets.* (Edward Elgar 2011) 4.

[27] Power (n 2) 48–49, 61, 78.

[28] Michael Power, *The Audit Society: Rituals of Verification* (OUP 1997); Michael Power, "The Audit Implosion: Regulating Risk from the Inside" (1999).

[29] Michael Power, "Auditing and the Production of Legitimacy" (2003) 28 Accounting, Organizations and Society 379.

[30] Power (n 2) 42.

[31] ibid 44.

[32] ibid 45, 47.

[33] See, WM Lemon, KW Tatum, and S Turley, *Developments in the Audit Methodologies of Large Accounting Firms* (Auditing Practices Board 2000).

[34] Power (n 2) 50.

[35] See Christopher Hood and others, "Risk Management" in The Royal Society (ed), *Risk: Analysis, Perception and Management—A Report of a Royal Society Study Group* (The Royal Society 1992).

Arguably, there are many conceptual similarities between quality control and risk analysis.[36] For this reason, quality control has been used as a template for the design of internal controls as risk management. In this regard, it is particularly interesting to observe that quality control is conceptualised as relying upon the following elements: statement of function, monitoring and feedback, and audit.[37] These elements are at the very core of modern risk management standards, and in particular the 2018 version of the International Organisation for Standardization (ISO) 31000 risk management standard, which puts a renewed emphasis on them.[38]

In 1995, following these developments in quality control and auditing, as well as a number of influential reports such as the 1991 COSO report,[39] the first standard of risk management was jointly published by the Australian and New-Zealand standards organisations (AS/NZS 4360 Risk Management).[40] In this Standard as in all the following ones, the very core of organisational activity is defined as risk management. This is achieved by integrating all internal controls within risk management exercises.

In other words, internal controls are the organisational design. They are the processes and tools through which organisational activity takes place. As they are redefined as a matter of risk management, so will the very essence of engaging in organisational activity. The whole organisational life, can be thought of as an exercise in risk management. More in particular, and as will be discussed more in detail, internal controls can be understood in terms of risk mitigation measures (or safeguards) insofar as they constitute the very tools and processes through which risk is managed. This helps better understand their inherent link with risk management. As safeguards, they are by definition dependent on the balancing exercises that characterise risk management, and can only be grafted onto them.

3.2 The risk management agenda's methodologies

In addition to internal controls constituting the tools and processes through which organisational activity is carried, and hence, risks are managed, there is a need for risk management methodologies. The methodologies at play will come from the field of financial economics and financial risk management. Risk metrics for

[36] Brian Wynne, "Uncertainty and Environmental Learning—Reconceiving Science and Policy in the Preventive Paradigm" (1992) 2 Global Environmental Change 111; Power (n 2) 52.

[37] Christopher Hood, "Control Over Bureaucracy: Cultural Theory and Institutional Variety" (1995) 15 Journal of Public Policy 207.

[38] ISO, "ISO 31000:2018-02 Risk Management—Guidelines" (2018).

[39] See http://www.coso.org/documents/internal%20control-integrated%20framework.pdf, last accessed 2 March 2019.

[40] See https://www.standards.govt.nz/search-and-buy-standards/standards-information/risk-managment/, last accessed 2 March 2019.

organisational risks will directly be modelled upon financial risk, ie volatility in financial returns.[41] This is quite significant because it means that risk management performed by organisations is modelled upon a methodology that encourages risk taking rather than avoiding it. In this sense, this is consistent with the concept of risk at play, which is a neoliberal one, aimed foremost at the achievement of organisational goals.[42]

Crucially, one can also see how governance's focus upon process legitimacy transforms risk management from the inside. Within this ambit, the point is not to directly address the substance of risks through analysis and ensuing mitigation. Rather, it is to address them through internal controls and processes, ie organisational design. The idea being that if all the controls preached by organisational design have been implemented (ie if the organisation is designed in a certain way and a number of specific tools and processes have been abided by), the risk should be controlled. Traditional risk analysis issues such as those concerning the efficiency of mitigation measures are bypassed and managerialised as a matter of whether organisational design is in place.[43] Very importantly, first order (or primary risks) are indeed internalised as internal control risks (or secondary risks).[44] One can conclude that the risk management agenda "displaces the 'technological fix' of risk analysis with something more powerful and far reaching: an 'organisational fix' ".[45]

3.3 The values of the risk management agenda: responsibility as a "social licence" to operate

As was argued, the risk management agenda is closely intertwined with the values of corporate governance such as legitimacy, transparency, accountability, the achievement of organisational goals, etc. Furthermore, it was also argued that this whole project hinges upon a self-understanding of organisations as responsible entities. As will now be seen, such responsibility is embedded in a number of values, and notably can be said to have an internal and an external dimension.

The internal dimension of responsibility is easy to understand. If organisations are going to be legitimate actors, they must be made responsible for their risks. This entails heightened internal responsibilisation for risk within organisations and thus, an articulation of the roles and responsibilities. Senior managers must routinely consider risks to business objectives and risk owners' must be indicated.[46] This is a matter of efficiency for achieving results.

[41] Power (n 2) 69–70.
[42] See Baker and Simon (n 16).
[43] See, Hood and others (n 35), for whom risk management is equated to management.
[44] Power (n 2) 62.
[45] ibid 98.
[46] ibid 93.

This internal responsibility also has an external dimension. For, if organisations are to achieve their organisational goals, external actors upon whom they depend in this regard must also see the organisation as responsible. This is the reason why responsibility is closely associated to the values of corporate governance highlighted beforehand. This is the reason why Power argues that risk management is a signal of good governance that has always been intended to be certifiable and auditable,[47] and "is coextensive with the language of accountability".[48] This is the reason why being a good organisation has come to be strongly identified with establishing, and being able to demonstrate conformity with, the principles of the risk management agenda.[49]

However, this external dimension of responsibility has another aspect to it, which is only indirectly instrumental to the efficiency of the organisational process, and further, the achievement of goals. This external responsibility has indeed led to the development of so-called ethics programmes, or programmes of corporate social responsibility. The idea behind these programmes is that heightened corporate responsibility is not only about organisational virtue, ie the legitimacy and efficiency of the organisational process, but rather, that such efficiency comes also to encompass the social consequences of organisational activity.[50] In this sense, organisations are made responsible both at level of their profit making and strategy objectives, and at the broader level of the social consequences of their activities (ie this is corporate social responsibility). Organisational efficiency relies upon a "social licence" to operate.[51] However, very much like strategy objectives, these "ethical concerns" are internalised and recoded as a matter of internal controls, the latter being a managerial process aimed first and foremost at achieving organisational objectives.[52]

One can therefore argue that the risk management agenda is an embodiment of (corporate) governance. In this sense, it is based on the legitimacy of organisations and the associated values such as efficiency, transparency, accountability, the achievement of organisational goals, etc. The enactment of these values is possible only insofar as these organisations are responsible (internally and externally) both

[47] ibid 52.

[48] ibid 98. From this vantage point, governance and risk management partake of "a neoliberal logic which draws heavily on the intellectual resources of economics, and principal-agent theory"; ibid 60.

[49] ibid 94.

[50] John Boli, "The Rationalization of Virtue and Virtuosity in World Society" in Marie-Laure Djelic and Kerstin Sahlin-Andersson (eds), *Transnational Governance: Institutional Dynamics of Regulation* (Cambridge University Press 2006). See also Judith Freedman, "Defining Taxpayer Responsibility: In Support of a General Anti-Avoidance Principle" (2004) 4 British Tax Review 332.

[51] See John W Meyer and Brian Rowan, "Institutionalized Organizations: Formal Structure as Myth and Ceremony" (1977) 83 American Journal of Sociology 340.

[52] Power (n 2) 96. For instance, this is typically the case with public participation exercises, which bear the promise of a different science and practice of risk analysis, and which have been recoded as "stakeholders participation", which is a specific occurrence of "reputational risks" (ie risks to the organisations themselves), see eg Lee Clarke, *Using Fantasy Documents to Tame Disaster* (University of Chicago Press 2001).

concerning the organisational process and concerning social (or ethical) responsibility issues, which in turns entails to recode their activities as a matter of risk management. Finally, this concept of risk management is predicated upon a "neoliberal notion of risk", that is, one which is turned towards risk taking.

4. The ISO 31000 Standard as an embodiment of the risk management agenda

The goal of this section is to highlight and illustrate the conceptual points made herein above concerning the risk management agenda through a description of the ISO 31000 Risk Management Standard, which, it is argued, embodies such risk management agenda. As has been alluded to earlier in this chapter, the latest version of the standard is the 2018 one.[53] However, this later version does not bring many changes to the original, 2009, standard, except for an increased focus on monitoring and review, and associated feedback loops mechanisms.[54] In view of the concrete understanding of the risk management agenda and the various internal controls that constitute it, the present description will therefore focus on the 2009 iteration, except where otherwise indicated.

The ISO 31000 Standard can be broken down into three elements: principles, framework, and process.[55] The section on principles contains general principles about the values put forth by risk management. The section on framework addresses the organisational design aspect (that is, the internal controls), whereas the process section addresses risk analysis, that is how to assess and manage risks.

4.1 Risk management principles

Eleven principles are listed as reflecting the values and commitment of risk management.[56] Among them, one can underline a few. The creation and protection of value; risk management as an integral part of the management process, as facilitating continual improvement of the organisation, and as critical to transparency and inclusiveness.

[53] See ISO (n 38).
[54] Among the changes compared to the previous version of the Standard, the ISO notes "greater emphasis on the iterative nature of risk management", or "the integration of risk management, starting with the governance of the organization", see ibid iv.
[55] ISO, "ISO: 31000 Risk Management—Principles and Guidelines" vi.
[56] ibid 7–8.

4.2 Risk management framework

The ISO confirms that organisational design is modelled after the cybernetic model of constant monitoring and feedback, since it defines the framework step as a "set of components that provide the foundations and organizational arrangements for designing, implementing, monitoring, reviewing and continually improving risk management throughout the organization".[57]

The ISO divides the risk management framework (or organisational design) in five steps (with the second step itself being divided into six sub-steps).

The first step, entitled mandate and commitment, requires support for the risk management framework from the upper management. As its name suggests, this is a preliminary step where commitments are made and general principles are established.

This is the step where upper management defines and endorses the risk management policy—a statement of the overall intentions and direction of an organisation related to risk management;[58] ensures that the organisation's objective and goals are aligned with the risk management programme, which entails to determine risk management performance indicators that are aligned with the performance indicators concerning the organisation's objectives. This is also the point where internal accountabilities and responsibilities are assigned; resources are allocated. Emphasis is put on ensuring that the design continues to remain appropriate.[59]

The second step is the actual design of the framework (or mechanisms for organisational design). The framework design is based upon a number of sub-steps.

The first sub-step is about understanding the organisation and its context, that is, evaluating and determining the level of risk generated by the organisation's activities by taking into account the following factors. First the external context, which is constituted by the external environment, that is, the social and cultural, political, legal, regulatory, financial, technological, economic, natural and competitive environment. Second, the internal context, which is constituted among others by the governance structure and the organisation's culture, the organisation's objectives and strategy, information flows, both human and material assets.[60] The level of risk will determine the intensity of the risk management framework.

The second sub-step concerns the establishment of the risk management policy. Typically, the latter is about stating the organisation's objectives and rationale for pursuing risk management as well as clear commitments towards the latter approach. The policy should therefore state the links between organisational goals and risk management results, define accountabilities and responsibilities, state the

[57] ibid 2.
[58] ibid.
[59] ibid 9–10.
[60] ibid 10.

commitments in terms of resources, link the organisation's objectives with risk management and provide indicators for performance assessment, as well as a commitment to the iterative nature of risk management by providing for periodical yet continuous processes of monitoring and revision of the framework.[61]

The third sub-step concerns the accountability structure. The ISO refers here to the internal accountability of the organisation, that is, to its governance structure, in other words who bears risk ownership within the organisation. This entails to identify the responsible and competent persons in charge of the different steps constituting risk management at organisational level, but also the process of risk analysis as such. In addition to identifying these responsible persons, their tasks and competences should be spelled out, and standards for performance measurement should be established. These should be in service of internal audit, and external audits too if deemed appropriate.[62] Curiously the ISO does not go into greater detail concerning the role of the person in charge of implementing the framework (sometimes referred to as compliance officer, quality control officer, or chief risk officer).

The fourth sub-step is about concretely embedding risk management into the organisational structure and activities. This is to be done through a so-called risk management plan, which is a document that summarises the concrete efforts and measure taken to implement the framework (eg what is the risk management policy, who is the chief risk officer, how many resources are allocated, what is the methodology for risk analysis and to which activities it is applied, etc).[63] The purpose of such a risk management plan is to integrate the risk management policy and commitments within the business policy, strategy, plans, commitments, etc, thus effectively recoding organisational activity as risk management.[64] In particular, it should provide for an application of risk analysis to all organisational activities (cf *infra*).

The fifth step is dedicated to the allocation of resources in terms of people, training, material, etc.[65]

The sixth and final sub-step is about communication and reporting, both internal and external. Internal communication is used as a means of ensuring internal accountability and risk ownership, that is, proper allocation of responsibilities for the different tasks and ensuring that the latter are properly undertaken. This internal transparency relies upon communication between the different involved actors; internal reporting concerning the effectiveness of the organisational design, and making the information gathered available to all; but also, consultation with internal stakeholders (that is, those who are implementing the framework). The

61 ibid 10–11.
62 ibid 11.
63 ibid 2.
64 ibid 11.
65 ibid.

overall aim is to consolidate the available risk management knowledge.[66] External communication aims at rendering the organisation transparent with regards to external stakeholders, and therefore to build confidence in the organisation and strengthen its legitimacy. The first step consists in determining appropriate external stakeholders, including members of the public affected by the organisation's activities, or institutional stakeholders such as legislators and regulators. With regards to regulators, the emphasis is put on—external—reporting, the goal of which is to foster compliance with "legal, regulatory, and governance requirements". This can be seen as an embodiment of the kind of collaboration partaking of meta regulation. In terms of other stakeholders, the emphasis is put on communication as a way to build confidence. Further, communication (with all stakeholders) is seen as particularly important in the event of a crisis or contingency. Finally, external communication is also seen as a means to consolidate the organisation's risk knowledge.[67]

The third risk management framework step is about implementing the latter framework in practice.[68] In other words, it provides practical steps that are essential to the successful implementation of risk management. Such practical steps include the need to define appropriate timing and strategy for implementation of the organisational mechanisms; the application of the risk management policy to every organisational activity; the need to hold information and training sessions; or the importance of consolidating risk knowledge through stakeholder communication. Particular emphasis is put upon the risk management process, ie risk analysis per se. Risk analysis must be included in the risk management plan, through which it is applied to all of the organisation's activities, decisions, and goal setting.[69] This is crucial because it shows well that the risk management agenda is about transforming all of organisational activity as risk analysis, and subsuming the latter in a broader governance structure. Furthermore, it also provides additional light on the articulation between the process of risk analysis and the governance mechanisms. One can argue that the purpose of these mechanisms is two folded. On the one hand, it is about ensuring that risk analysis is integrated within every activity, process, decision-making, etc of the organisation. On the other hand, these mechanisms of organisational design are about ensuring that such risk analysis is efficient and legitimate. In this sense, risk analysis and organisational design should not be seen as two different moments of organisational life, but rather, as coextensive to one another (organisational design is void of object without risk analysis, and risk analysis cannot be implemented within the organisation without design). Crucially this proves the point about internal control mechanisms as being safeguards.

[66] ibid 12.
[67] ibid. One can think here about data breach notification provisions, cf *infra*.
[68] ibid 13.
[69] ibid 12–13.

The fourth and fifth steps are about the constant monitoring, reviewing, and improvement of the framework. The performance of risk management should be regularly reviewed against the performance indicators, which should themselves be reviewed. Organisational activity should be measured against the risk management policy and plan, and the appropriateness of the latter should also be reviewed in the light of potentially changing risk context. On this basis, decisions should be made towards the improvement of the overall framework.[70]

4.3 Risk management process

As indicated, what the ISO coins as risk management process is actually risk analysis (ie risk assessment and management), and is the last element of the Standard. At this point, the ISO has already evidenced the place occupied by risk analysis within the ecology of its Standard, and the section dedicated to risk analysis therefore addresses the methodology, ie how to concretely undertake a risk analysis.

The ISO provides a quite comprehensive methodology which has, arguably, served as template for a number of methodologies in the privacy field, including European research projects.[71] It is interesting to note, however, that the ISO scarcely addresses how the process should be conducted from an organisational point of view (ie who should conduct it, when should it be conducted, etc).[72] The only implicit piece of guidance in this regard is the obligation to regularly review and monitor the process in order to detect new harms, new risks factors, etc, and which implicitly argues that a new risk management process should be conducted in such cases.[73]

5. Addressing the command and control issues

5.1 Command and control shortcomings: lack of expertise and resources

Now that the meaning of risk management and the risk management agenda has been discussed in detail, the analysis can turn its focus to the role it plays in new regulatory models. As alluded, evolutions in regulatory models have sought to address these two issues: how to better set standards (and associated safeguards), and

[70] ibid 13.
[71] See eg CNIL, "Methodology For Privacy Risk Management: How to Implement the Data Protection Act" (2012); David Wright and others, "Surveillance Impact Assessment Manual" (2014).
[72] ISO (n 55) 5.
[73] ibid 20.

how to achieve better compliance with the latter (in terms of implementation of standards and of their enforcement).

Several shortcomings of the model were underscored *supra*. They can be reframed as issues of expertise and resources (ie not enough resources to enforce all regulatory violations and to implement standards and safeguards, not enough resources and expertise to determine the adequacy of standards, compliance strategies, and enforcement strategies). This directly stems from the fact that command and control regulation is predicated upon the role of the state and its various agencies, which centralise the regulatory functions. This lack of resources and expertise will be the starting point for new regulatory models that draw on the resources of regulated organisations and on collaboration with the latter.[74]

5.2 Command and control as responsive regulation: deterrence and compliance

For a start, one can argue that the command and control regulatory model is more aspirational than descriptive,[75] and that somehow command and control regulation is permeated by a "legalistic illusion" (cf *supra*, *Austinian* model of law) of being a linear process of commands backed up by sanction. However, regulatory scholarship has long observed that in reality command and control and enforcement are more of a negotiated and variable nature.[76]

For many years, the debate on enforcement has indeed been dominated by the dichotomy between deterrence and compliance.[77] Whereas the deterrence strategy is based upon the detection and ensuing punishment of inadequate behaviours (with the goal that as a result the guilty will modify their behaviour according to the issued standard), compliance aims at "preventing harm rather than punishing evil".[78] Its conception of enforcement relies upon the attainment of regulatory standards rather than sanctioning their violations.[79] Compliance is thus based upon "negotiation and bargaining" with the regulated firms in order to advise and persuade them to take positive accomplishments, that is, to put in place the mechanisms that are themselves supposed to achieve the public interest goal the regulation pursues.[80]

[74] Power (n 2) 93.

[75] Robert Baldwin, Martin Cave, and Martin Lodge, *Understanding Regulation: Theory, Strategy, and Practice* (2nd edn, OUP 2012).

[76] Bridget M Hutter, *Compliance: Regulation and Environment* (OUP 1997); Keith Hawkins, *Law as Last Resort: Prosecution Decision-Making in a Regulatory Agency* (OUP 2003).

[77] Neil Gunningham, "Enforcement and Compliance Strategies" in Robert Baldwin, Martin Cave, and Martin Lodge (eds), *The Oxford Handbook of Regulation* (OUP 2010) 120–21.

[78] ibid 121.

[79] ibid.

[80] ibid 122–24.

In practice, regulators always resort to a mix of both deterrence and compliance, along a so-called pyramid of enforcement,[81] following what is referred to as responsive regulation.[82] Responsive regulation thus blends deterrence and compliance along a pyramid of enforcement that starts with compliance-style measures, and ends with deterrence-style measures (eg prohibitions, court cases). Its aim is to use tools of compliance and/or deterrence when they are most useful. The responsive nature of this type of regulation lays in its dialogic nature: information and dialogue with the regulatee are heavily relied upon in order to determine which enforcement tool is the most adequate in a given situation. This information gathering process covers both the negotiating aspect of compliance as that of deterrence, eg either convincing the firm of engaging in specific regulatory mechanisms and safeguards, or about learning about the firm's practices, its motivation, good or bad faith, etc.[83]

Gunningham argues that deterrence and compliance are the two sides of a uniform practice of enforcement, which pertains to a command and control model of regulation.[84] This is true given that it remains a centralised model of regulation that problematises little the efficiency of standards, and which remains enforcement-based. Yet it also reveals the negotiated and collaborative nature of regulation from its inception one might argue.

Ensuing regulatory models will build upon and formalise this sort of "street level pragmatic" collaboration,[85] by resorting to models of regulation that build upon the self-regulation of the regulatees. These models should not be equated to "pure" self-regulation. Rather, they have been referred to as "enforced self-regulation" since they are predicated upon a legally enforced collaboration between regulators and regulatees.[86]

6. Smart regulation

6.1 Defining smart regulation

A first shift away from the command and control model has been dubbed smart regulation. The key idea of this model is to delegate (or decentralise) the production

[81] ibid 126.

[82] See Ian Ayres and John Braithwaite, *Responsive Regulation: Transcending the Deregulation Debate* (OUP 1992).

[83] And which requires frequent on-site inspections, Gunningham (n 77) 129.

[84] ibid 125–26.

[85] Power (n 2) 36.

[86] See John Braithwaite, "Enforced Self-Regulation: A New Strategy for Corporate Crime Control" (1982) 80 Michigan Law Review 1466.

of standards, and the operationalisation of safeguards and their enforcement (insofar as both are conflated under this model, cf hereunder) to third parties.[87]

Smart regulation can therefore be defined as "an emerging form of regulatory pluralism that embraces flexible, imaginative, and innovative forms of social control which seek to harness not just governments but also businesses and third parties".[88] In other words, smart regulation is about diminishing the hands-on role of the regulators and delegating parts of their tasks to non-state actors such as profit or non-profit entities,[89] who would perform this task through more informal devices such as audits, certificates, standards, marks, labels, seals, codes of conduct, etc.[90]

In terms of standard setting, regulators edict standards but leave their fine tuning and specific determination, that is, their implementation, to third parties, who arguably possess finer grained expertise. This is explicitly the case with codes of conducts for instance, but also holds true for other, formal, safeguards such as audits, marks, labels etc.[91] Such informal, decentralised regulatory model is possible on the condition that the safeguards operated by third parties benefit form a certain homogeneity. For this reason, one can argue that smart regulation is based upon a standardisation of safeguards and hence of performance (which is being assessed by such safeguards).[92] Contrary to command and control regulation, predicated upon informal dialogue and collaboration, smart regulation relies upon formalised assessment tools and methodologies. Formalised assessment methodologies often take the form of self-assessment tools, best practices documents, codes of conduct, etc. Institutes of standardisation have an important role to play as well, since many of these standards are crafted under their auspices.[93]

Safeguards operationalised by third parties typically include audits, certificates, marks, labels, seals, etc. One should also keep in mind the distinction between substantive and formal safeguards. Contrary to substantive safeguards, which directly address the standard (eg prohibition), formal safeguards are more procedural in nature and are articulated with the discretionary power of the regulator (eg licensing depends upon a notification obligation and a discretionary decision by the regulator). By definition, substantive safeguards cannot be operationalised by third

[87] Neil Gunningham and Peter Grabosky (eds), *Smart Regulation: Designing Environmental Policy* (OUP 1998); Black (n 4); Gunningham (n 77).

[88] Gunningham (n 77) 131.

[89] Such list includes the following actors: international standard organisations, trading partners, commercial institutions and financial markets, peer-pressure and self-regulation (through industry associations), internal environmental management systems and culture, and civil society *senso latu*, but also certification bodies, institutes of standardisation, etc. See ibid 132.

[90] ibid 131. Power notes that smart regulation is part of a family of related concepts of regulation models that includes enforced self-regulation, mutual regulation, de-centred regulation, or even the notion of soft law, Power (n 2) 37.

[91] cf *supra*, a control always entails the setting of a standard, and the twos are ultimately blurred.

[92] Christine Parker, "Compliance-Oriented Regulatory Innovation" (2000) 32 Administration and Society 529.

[93] Gunningham (n 77).

parties insofar as they apply directly to the regulatee. Formal safeguards in contrast can be delegated to third parties, which means that they are in charge of the formalities and/or the discretionary power is being delegated to them.

As far as enforcement is concerned, we have underlined the partial overlap between safeguards and proper enforcement mechanisms. In the case of smart regulation, it appears that when safeguards are operationalised by third parties they also play a role in terms of enforcement. The idea(l) is that, since safeguards are built through performance standards, regulatory failures become more explicit and apparent under the form of technical failures during the operationalisation of the safeguards.[94] In this sense, smart regulation purports a model of "natural compliance" or "self-enforced compliance" insofar as regulatory deviance can be addressed by the regulated entity or the third party in charge of safeguards. Self-discovery and reporting as well as organisational learning and responsibility are therefore ideals underpinning smart models of regulation. Furthermore, the fact that detailed standard setting capacity is delegated to third parties as well as directly concerned regulatees, who have, arguably, better and finer grained expertise is also seen as a driver towards better compliance.[95]

So, what is the role of regulators under this collaborative model? In terms of formal safeguards, even though the discretionary power has shifted, they still play a role (eg accreditation of certification bodies). In terms of enforcement, it is part of a ladder of response, very much like in the case of responsive regulation (cf *supra*). Whereas organisations develop and enforce their own standards, the regulator will periodically inspect. In case of violation, the regulator has at its disposal a number of sanctions with ever more serious consequences.[96]

The shift from command and control to smart regulation signals a change in regulatory practice moving from the *ex post* discovery and sanction of rule violations to *ex ante* anticipation, which is itself based upon prevention and self-discovery via internalised and third party-based systems of compliance.[97] Overall smart regulation tries to make a virtue out of a necessity insofar as it combines the benefits of the enforcement of sanctions with the benefits of cooperation.[98]

6.2 Smart regulation and data protection

One can argue that the application of smart regulation to the data protection field really started to develop as of the mid-1990s and early 2000s. As seen in Chapter 3,

[94] Parker (n 4); Hutter (n 76).
[95] See Parker (n 4); Parker (n 92).
[96] Gunningham (n 77) 125.
[97] See Leigh Hancher and Michael Moran, "Organizing Regulatory Space" in Leigh Hancher and Michael Moran (eds), *Capitalism, Culture and Economic Regulation* (OUP 1989).
[98] Power (n 2) 37.

the 1990s marked the end of the centralised databases and led the way to world wide web and the Internet. As discussed, this signalled a technological shift from limited and localised databases, towards a context characterised by the increasing pervasiveness of our everyday life by micro-computers connected to a decentralised global network, operated by data carriers whose business models relies upon the—unhindered—processing of personal data.

From the smart regulation perspective, this technological shift created the following challenges: the need for harmonised rules applying throughout all the network (irrespective of jurisdictional status), the difficulty of enforcing data protection statutes, and the inadequacy of a number of safeguards (cf *supra*). This situation whereby the application of data protection was uncertain, and in many cases simply disregarded by a number of data controllers, spurred a number of initiatives characteristic of smart regulation.

One can point to the emergence of data protection standards as a first way to address these issues.[99] The first data protection standard is the Canadian standard, the CSA model code, developed in 1996 by the Canadian Standards Association (CSA), and which consist of ten basic principles.[100] It has inspired other such codes in Japan and Australia.[101] Resorting to Standards is a way to provide harmonisation, but also to provide for new safeguards operated by third parties, insofar as standards are normally bundled with such mechanisms as audits and certification.[102] This is also the case for the CSA model code which includes mechanisms of certification and audit.[103] The European Committee of Standardization also initiated standardisation initiatives in the late 1990s,[104] but they do not seem to have resulted with long-lasting outcomes. In a similar vein, one can also mention TrustArc, which is a well-known certification scheme for providers of online content among others.[105] Finally, as part of this smart regulation move, one can

[99] According to Dumortier and Goemans, standardisation is simply the process of finding an agreement on a standard, of a technical nature, or concerning the characteristics of activities and products Jos Dumortier and Caroline Goemans, "Data Privacy and Standardization: Discussion Paper Prepared for the CEN/ISSS Open Seminar on Data Protection" (2000) 26.

[100] The Model Code for the Protection of Personal Information (CAN/CSA-Q830-96). The CSA has also published a handbook in order to put them into practice, entitled: "Making the CSA Privacy Code Work for You" (PLUS 8300).

[101] As well as the Canadian federal data protection law for the private sector itself, PIPEDA, which has enshrined this very standard. Colin J Bennett, "Convergence Revisited: Toward a Global Policy for the Protection of Personal Data" in Philip E Agre and Marc Rotenberg (eds), *Technology and Privacy: The New Landscape* (The MIT Press 1997).

[102] Dumortier and Goemans (n 99) 30–31, 32.

[103] Bennett (n 101) 115. One can also mention Standards like the ICX Code of Conduct, or the BSI DISC PD0012:1999 and BS 10012:2009 Standards (http://searchsecurity.techtarget.co.uk/definition/BS-100122009), which provide guidance on how to comply with the EU Directive and/or the UK Data Protection Act. Last accessed 14 March 2019.

[104] See Dumortier and Goemans (n 99).

[105] See eg BBBOnLine, http://www.bbb.org/online/business/relbusapp.aspx; or CPA Web Trust, see https://www.trustarc.com/, last accessed 14 March 2019.

also mention the emergence of technical standards for data protection: Privacy Enhancing Technologies (PETs), which would, later on, become known as Data protection by Default under the GDPR (cf *infra*).[106] As discussed in Chapter 1 on risk management, different types of safeguards/risk mitigation measures can be mobilised to reduce harms, among which, certain focus on licensing or insurance schemes requirements, whereas others concern the design of products and/or of physical structures. This new[107] focus on the design and technical capacities of data processing systems can therefore be seen as an attempt to compensate for the failures of more traditional data protection safeguards in this technological context, in addition to providing standardised technical design for data processing.[108]

Following this evolution, a number of data protection statutes have started integrating elements of smart regulation. The most famous one is probably the German Telecommunication law of 1997,[109] which integrated an obligation to enact the principle of data minimisation through PETs. Such obligation would also be upheld in the Federal Data Protection Act (a provision known as data frugality "*datensparsamkeit*"), which provided for the possibility of Audits.[110] The French Data Protection Act was also amended to provide for labels and certificate to be delivered by the *Commission nationale de l'informatique et des libertés* (CNIL)—French Data Protection Authority—DPA—(Art 11 (3° c)). At the same period Canada also issued the QMI program, which is a three-tiered audit/certification programme.[111]

[106] For a discussion and demonstration that PETs/data protection by default is an application of technical standardisation to the data protection field, see Matthias Pocs, "Will the European Commission Be Able to Standardise Legal Technology Design without a Legal Method?" (2012) 28 Computer Law & Security Review 641. See also Lee A Bygrave, "Data Protection by Design and by Default: Deciphering the EU's Legislative Requirements" (2017) 4 Oslo Law Review 105.

[107] Even though the need to focus upon the technical capacities of data processing systems is not really a new topic, insofar as it has existed since the inception of the first data protection statutes Herbert Burkert, "Privacy-Enhancing Technologies: Typology, Critique, Vision" in Philip E Agre and Marc Rotenberg (eds), *Technology and Privacy: The New Landscape* (The MIT Press 1997). However, it had received little to no attention until this period (ibid).

[108] And, of course, one should also mention the potential of technology for issues of enforcement, which has spurred a broad literature on so-called techno-regulation, see: Lyria Bennett Moses, "How to Think about Law, Regulation and Technology: Problems with 'Technology' as a Regulatory Target" (2013) 1 Law Innovation and Technology 1; Roger Brownsword and Karen Yeung (eds), *Regulating Technologies: Legal Futures, Regulatory Frames and Technological Fixes* (Hart Publishing 2008); Roger Brownsword, *Rights, Regulation and the Technological Revolution* (OUP 2008); Bert-Jaap Koops, "The (In)Flexibility of Techno-Regulation and the Case of Purpose-Binding" (2011) 5 Legisprudence 171. As discussed *supra*, this dissertation does not share the premises of this literature since it has carefully avoided to conflate control as a constitutive element of regulation with the ancillary function of enforcement, even though overlaps have been acknowledged and in particular in the context of smart regulation.

[109] Telecommunication Act (TKG) of 17 December 1997, Federal Law Gazette I p 3108.

[110] Federal Data Protection Act (BDSG) of 30 June 2017 (Federal Law Gazette I p 2097).

[111] Which includes, declaration, verification, and registration, see http://www.qmi-saiglobal.com/Default.asp?language=english, last accessed 14 March 2019.

7. From smart regulation to meta regulation

7.1 Defining meta regulation

A further evolution of regulatory models is that from smart to meta regulation. Rather than endowing third parties with competences in terms of standard settings and safeguards, meta regulation consists in placing the operational substance of standards and safeguards within regulated organisations themselves.[112]

As Gunningham puts it, "under such an approach the role of regulation ceases to be primarily about government inspectors checking compliance with rules, and becomes more about encouraging the industry to put in place its own systems of management which are then scrutinised by regulators".[113] In other words, "a regulator would identify a problem and command the [regulatee] to develop plans aimed at solving that problem and then the [regulatee] would respond by developing its own internal regulations".[114] At this point, regulators do not set standards anymore (which are indicative of adequate behaviour insofar as they are deemed to lead to the achievement of regulatory goals), but rather, formulate the general regulatory goal(s). It is then the task of regulated organisations to determine whether and how these regulatory goals can be achieved. They do so with risk tools and methodologies, thereby redefining regulatory goals through the language of risk.[115] As Hilgartner argues, constructing a risk object consists in defining an object (in this case the regulatory goal) and linking it to a—series of—harm(s).[116] Such a move is seen as the best response to the issues associated with the "diagnosis-prescription" aspect of regulation, and it is undertaken through risk analysis. In other words, it is up to organisations to assess the harmfulness of their activities (if at all), and to determine what the most adequate safeguards are. On this basis, organisations can determine whether the activity can be pursued or whether it is too risky given the regulatory goals. Thus, regulatees become competent for the setting of standards reframed as a risk analysis exercise, but also for determining safeguards (which also follow directly from risk analysis), as well as for determining how to implement the latter. This concerns both substantive safeguards, which they can directly integrate within their operations (eg prohibition, limitations, etc), as well as the

[112] Joanna Gray and Jenny Hamilton, *Implementing Financial Regulation: Theory and Practice* (John Wiley & Sons, Ltd 2006); Parker (n 4).

[113] Gunningham (n 77) 135.

[114] Gary Coglianese and Evan Mendelson, "Meta-Regulation and Self-Regulation" in Robert Baldwin, Martin Cave, and Martin Lodge (eds), *The Oxford Handbook of Regulation* (OUP 2010) 150.

[115] Gunningham (n 77) 136.

[116] Stephen Hilgartner, "The Social Construction of Risk Objects: Or, How to Pry Open Networks of Risk" in James F Short Jr and Lee Clarke (eds), *Organizations, Uncertainties, and Risk* (Westview Press 1992) 46.

determination and operationalisation of formal safeguards (and the shift of discretionary power that goes with it). As will be discussed in the next section, the way to implement such formal safeguards is through the organisational design aspect of the risk management agenda, ie internal controls. In other words, these internal controls that are a means to carry out organisational activity are simultaneously transformed as a regulatory resource for developing and implementing these new formal safeguards. As in the case of smart regulation, formal safeguards may rely upon a collaboration with regulators, even though the extent of their collaboration may vary (cf Chapter 5).

In terms of enforcement, meta regulation also relies upon collaborating with, and incentivising regulatees. The point is not so much to develop intelligence on the extent to which compliance falls short of standards.[117] Rather, the latter is marginalised with respect to the very determination of these standards (and safeguards), and hence, to the assessment of the regulatees' performance. Regulatees must report on their performance in order for the regulator to assess such performance, that is, to actively challenge regulatees to demonstrate that their risk analysis and management measures work in practice and meet their regulatory obligations.[118] In this sense, and just like with smart regulation, meta regulation is underpinned by ideals of improved and "natural compliance", self-discovery, and reporting, as well as organisational learning and responsibility. Equally, meta regulation should not be seen as a departure from, but rather, an evolution of smart regulation. This means that is also relies upon the operationalisation of safeguards by third parties (eg audit, certification, codes of conducts, etc). Hence, the core of meta regulation is not enforcement but—regulatory—performance and the assessment thereof, for it is the latter that determines whether "plans have been implemented and key objectives achieved".[119] Consequently, risk analysis—and more broadly the risk management agenda—is at the core of meta regulation.[120] All in all, meta regulation entails the placing of regulatory responsibility upon the regulated firms with the approval of the regulators whose role is "to risk-manage the[ir] risk management".[121]

[117] Baldwin, Cave, and Lodge (n 75) 272.

[118] Gunningham (n 77) 135. This also includes the assessment as to whether it possesses adequate leadership, staff, systems, and procedures, ibid.

[119] ibid 136.

[120] ibid 138.

[121] ibid 136, 140. He gives the example of the regulation of major hazard facilities, such as the Seveso II Directive (now replaced by the Seveso III Directive 2012/18/UE of 4 July 2012), which places the responsibility upon the operators to submit their safety plans for prior authorisation. These plans should include a systematic risk analysis in conjunction with controls and a safety management system (which itself entails to provide adequate documentation to the regulator).

8. The role of internal controls and the risk management agenda in collaborative models of regulation

8.1 Risk management at the heart of collaborative models of regulation

As already indicated, internal controls play a crucial role in these models of collaborative regulation, and in this sense illustrate why the risk management agenda is crucial for these collaborative models of regulation.

Collaboration between regulators and regulatees is seen as the plinth for addressing the issues of expertise and resource that plague command and control regulation. Because it is impossible to constantly monitor regulatees (which would otherwise lead to the same issues encountered by command and control regulation), regulators decide to collaborate only with regulatees who are trustworthy. It is here that internal controls play a crucial role, insofar as they are considered as the material representation, or proxy, for organisational trust. Instead of directly monitoring organisations, regulators pay heed to their managerial commitments embodied in internal controls.[122]

Just as with governance, the way for internal controls to address the whole spectrum of organisational activity, including the uptaking of regulatory tasks, is to have them undergo a risk-based transformation. For this reason, one can argue that "risk-based internal control [and more broadly, the risk management agenda] has become a resource for regulation".[123] In other words, internal controls are used for the carrying out of organisational activity as a matter of risk management. And they are simultaneously used for the uptaking of a number of regulatory tasks that have also been framed as risk management.

From this perspective, it is interesting to observe that there is a simultaneous double push for the transformation of internal controls—and further, organisational activity—as risk management. On the one hand—corporate—governance seeks to make organisations more legitimate and responsible in the wake of regulatory failures. On the other hand, these regulatory failures are seen as an impetus for regulators to develop new models of regulation that rely upon collaboration with organisations, which is itself only possible provided that the latter are trustworthy and hence, legitimate and responsible.[124]

This last point also warrants the shedding of additional light on the role and significance of internal controls in the context of regulation, namely, their role as an interface between regulatory, and business values and objectives.[125] It

[122] Power (n 2) 39–40.
[123] ibid 61.
[124] See ibid 42: "Internal controls are at the heart of a process by which organisations are being turned into responsible actors."
[125] ibid.

has been discussed that new regulatory models are more efficient through the pooling of resources and expertise, which contribute to the determination of better standards, better implementation thereof, and more efficient enforcement strategies. However, such collaboration is only possible because it relies upon a transformation of regulated organisations as trustworthy and responsible. Such being responsible it is argued, is very similar to the two-folded notion of responsibility purported by governance. On the one hand, such responsibility is in line with increased—regulatory and organisational—efficiency. For an organisation, to be responsible is to make commitments to organisational goals (which is carried out through internal controls).[126] On the other hand, such responsibility is also endowed with an external and ethical meaning, namely to be committed to the regulatory goals at stake, and hence to collaboration. As regulatees become responsible for the implementation of regulatory goals, they come to transform their activities by incorporating these very regulatory goals within their own business goals. In doing so, organisations can therefore simultaneously be compliant and nurture their business strategy. Following Power, this is a neoliberal regulatory ideal whereby "the traditional 'problem of compliance' no longer exists because regulatory and business goals are perfectly aligned".[127] Further, the blurring of the lines between managerial and regulatory activity at the level of organisations also leads to a managerialisation of regulation itself which, rather than devoting attention and resources to traditional regulatory activity (ie determination of standards, operationalisation of safeguards, and enforcement), puts the emphasis upon the different elements of the risk management agenda as proxies of organisational trustworthiness.[128] In this sense the increasing centrality of internal controls not only contributes to improving the efficiency of regulation, it also pervades it with a specific neoliberal logic of governance.[129]

8.2 Summarising the collaborative shifts taking place

Summarising the interactions between regulators and regulatees under these collaborative models of regulation, one can state the following.

The responsibilisation of the regulatee is at the heart of these models. It is the *sine qua non* condition for enrolling the regulatees and benefiting from their

[126] One can therefore see the placing of responsibility as a way to address avoidance-behaviour.

[127] Power (n 2) 41.

[128] ibid 41–42. See also Parker (n 4); Carl Macrae, "Regulating Resilience? Regulatory Work in High-Risk Arenas" in Bridget M Hutter (ed), *Anticipating Risks and Organising Risk Regulation* (Cambridge University Press 2010).

[129] Power (n 2) 63; Michael Huber, "Colonised by Risk—The Emergence of Academic Risks in British Higher Education" in Bridget M Hutter (ed), *Anticipating Risks and Organising Risk Regulation* (Cambridge University Press 2010).

resources and expertise. Being responsible (and hence, trustworthy and legitimate) signals a commitment to both the organisational and the regulatory goals pursued. Regulatees become responsible by being turned inside out through the risk management agenda. Once this is the case, they are transformed into naturally compliant entities since, as responsible entities, they are committed to pursuing and implementing the regulatory goals (ie alignment of organisational and regulatory goals); meaning that traditional *ex post* enforcement ceases to be an issue.

Once regulatees are made responsible, they can start collaborating with regulators and taking up some of their tasks, namely standard setting and safeguards, and the implementation thereof. In terms of safeguards a distinction must be made between substantive and formal safeguards. Substantive safeguards are to be applied directly by the regulatee, therefore the regulator's role is less about operationalising them than determining their substance. Formal safeguards, however, can also be operationalised by regulators in cases where they are in charge of the formalities required, and/or their discretionary power is needed.

Smart regulation is therefore about entrusting third parties to further define standards (eg for specific sectors of activity), and to operationalise formal safeguards. Under a meta regulation model, most of the regulatory activity is delegated to the regulatee. The standard setting function is internalised as a matter of risk analysis. The latter is also used for determining substantive and formal safeguards. Safeguards are operationalised through the organisational design aspect of risk management (and might entail some collaboration with the regulator). Further, risk management is itself a regulatory resource: internal controls are both a way to implement risk management in view of the achievement of organisational goals, and a way to implement the regulatory goals to which organisations are now committed. Finally, even though *ex post* enforcement is theoretically superfluous within these models, one can see that it nonetheless still plays a role. In the case of smart regulation, it proceeds along the so-called "ladder of enforcement", whereas in the case of meta regulation it becomes a matter of assessing the regulatee's performance (with sanctions also following the ladder of enforcement). Equally, regulators are not entirely absent from the operationalisation of—formal—safeguards. The latter usually require some collaboration between regulatees and regulators (eg accreditation of certification bodies). Nonetheless, their role is strongly diminished.

In this sense, the risk management agenda and the risk transformation of regulatees that goes with it is a resource for these models of regulation because it allows for making regulatees responsible, while simultaneously giving them the tools to uptake—part of—the regulatory activity.

9. Conclusion: meta regulation and data protection, towards the risk-based approach

One can summarise the various findings on meta regulation and its articulation with risk management, into three main dimensions.

First, it entails to transform regulatees into responsible, naturally compliant entities, that is, their "turning inside out" through the risk management agenda—ie transforming their activities as a matter of risk taking (first dimension). Responsibility can also be constructed as a two-folded notion, with an internal and an external dimension. Being responsible internally entails a commitment to the organisation's goals (ie business objectives). External responsibility entails a commitment to broader societal goals, in this case regulatory goals. Both these goals are aligned. Once made responsible, regulatees can start collaborating with regulators, and thus be entrusted with some of their tasks, namely setting standards (second dimension) and operationalising safeguards (third dimension).

As one can sense, the risk-based approach to data protection basically amounts to the implementation of meta regulation at the data protection level, and the use of risk as a regulatory tool. A crucial observation must nonetheless be made. In theory, meta regulation delegates the whole standard setting process to the regulatees, and thus addresses all the issues associated with the "diagnosis-prescription" flaw associated with command and control. Namely, both the selection of standards that will lead to satisfactory regulatory outcomes, and the adequate implementation (or compliance with) the latter. However, as was observed in Chapter 3, the reform process leading to the GDPR did not address the first issue, and instead concentrated the reform on how to best implement data protection rules. This focus on (better) compliance is not without consequences for the risk-based approach at the heart of the GDPR (but this is also true for the other statutes that have uptaken it), since it signals that it is only a partial implementation of meta regulation. This is the topic of the next chapter.

5
Meta regulation in data protection law: the risk-based approach

Yet we think embracing risk also encompasses a broader idea of governing through risk[1]

1. Introduction

Chapter 3 has underlined a number of regulatory challenges for data protection, with reference to the reform process at the EU level. The present chapter will explore the way the risk-based approach has been uptaken in data protection statutes. Specific emphasis is put upon the EU level, but as shown, the insights are valid as far as other legal frameworks are concerned.

As one remembers, and summarising the findings on meta regulation from Chapter 4, it is possible to boil down meta regulation to three dimensions. First, it entails to transform regulatees into responsible, naturally compliant entities, that is, their "turning inside out" through the risk management agenda—ie transforming their activities as a matter of risk taking (first dimension). Responsibility can also be constructed as two-folded notion, with an internal and an external dimension. Being responsible internally entails a commitment to the organisation's goals (ie business objectives). External responsibility entails a commitment to broader societal goals, in this case regulatory goals. Both these goals are aligned. Once made responsible, regulatees can start collaborating with regulators, and thus be entrusted with some of their tasks, namely setting standards (second dimension) and operationalising safeguards (third dimension).

As alluded at the end of Chapter 4, the risk-based approach to data protection is only a partial implementation of meta regulation, insofar as it doesn't fully delegate the standard setting function to the regulatees. Instead of addressing all of the issues associated with the "diagnosis-prescription" flaw associated with command and control (ie the selection of standards that will lead to satisfactory regulatory

[1] Tom Baker and Jonathan Simon, "Embracing Risk" in Tom Baker and Jonathan Simon (eds), *Embracing Risk: The Changing Culture of Insurance and Responsibility* (The University of Chicago Press 2002) 11.

The Risk-Based Approach to Data Protection. Raphaël Gellert, Oxford University Press (2020). © Raphaël Gellert.
DOI: 10.1093/oso/9780198837718.001.0001.

outcomes, and the adequate implementation or compliance with the latter), it only focuses on the better implementation of the data protection provisions. In this sense, one can make a distinction between two main approaches to the risk-based approach. Those that focus on the regulatory dimension (ie better implementation of the framework), and those that focus on the standard setting function. Both of them are in any case predicated upon the risk transformation of data controllers through the risk management agenda.

As far as the first approach is concerned, it is referred to as being "regulatory oriented" insofar as it is concerned with the role regulatees play in the operationalisation of safeguards, that is, the use of internal controls as regulatory resources. Indeed, if, as demonstrated in the introduction and in Chapter 1, regulatory rules amount to standards and safeguards, then one can argue that their implementation amounts to their operationalisation. One can see that this approach is the most popular and most developed one as it is prevalent in all legislations that have turned towards meta regulation, including the General Data Protection Regulation (GDPR). These legal frameworks are indeed predicated upon the responsibilisation of data controllers through accountability obligations as a way of better complying. And they also entrust regulatees to varying degrees with the operationalisation of safeguards that previously fell within the regulators' remit, and which are now based upon the regulatees' internal controls.

The second approach is mainly concerned with the standard setting function of meta regulation, and thus seeks to replace the traditional command and control regulation way of setting standards with a risk management exercise. This approach, which is referred to as the "standard setting oriented risk-based approach" has, to date, not found expression in statutes. Rather, it was put forward mainly in the US, and in particular, by actors close to Microsoft, and other technology companies, and was notably explained in a number of reports endorsed by the US White House. Some EU stakeholders also made some proposals in the same direction but with less impact.

2. The risk-based approach to data protection: meta regulation with a regulatory focus

2.1 Introduction

This section will proceed to analyse the risk-based approach in the GDPR and in other statutes with the following steps.

First, it will confirm its regulatory focus, targeting the better implementation of the existing legal framework.

Second, it will look at the responsibilisation aspect of meta regulation. It is argued that the regulatees' responsibilisation is to be found in the modern principle of accountability. An in-depth discussion of the accountability principle will therefore show that it does correspond to the notion of responsibilisation featured in the risk management agenda and in meta regulation, both because it provides for a risk-based transformation of the regulatees activities, and because of its internal and external dimensions (ie nurturing of organisational and regulatory goals). On this basis, and given that the notion of a "risk-based approach" is completely absent from the GDPR, one can argue that it is actually embodied in the accountability principle (and possibly in the principle of data protection by design although this is more ancillary). The section then reflects on what it means to understand the principle of accountability as reframing all of the data controllers' activities as a matter of risk management. In particular, this means that the whole of the GDPR becomes risk-based, and not simply chapter IV (concerning accountability). Given the risk-based approach's focus on the implementation of the legal framework, this should simply be taken to mean that all of the framework should be implemented pursuant a risk-management exercise. The potential incongruence between the data controllers' risk-based transformation and the rights-based nature of a number of provisions is solved through a specific notion of "compliance risk".

Third, this section will discuss the way the risk-based approach has been upheld in a number of statuses such as the GDPR, Canada's PIPEDA (Personal Information Protection and Electronic Documents Act), Council of Europe (CoE) Convention 108+, etc. Key to the discussion are issues such as the safeguards and type of regulatory collaboration these statutes provide for, or how the risk management obligations fare in comparison to the International Organization for Standardization (ISO 31000) risk management Standard, which can be considered the canon in this matter.

2.2 The regulatory oriented approach's goal: making the regulatory architecture more efficient

Among many of the GDPR reform's objectives, one of the major goals was to render the existing legal framework more efficient, in particular by offering improved implementation of existing principles, as well as to provide safeguards that were more efficient.[2] As was clear in the reform process, the data protection principles were regarded as sound, especially in view of them being technology neutral.[3] In

[2] Two out of three policy objectives of the reform pertained to such efficiency. Policy objective 1 (enhancing the internal market dimension of data protection) and Policy objective 2 (increasing the effectiveness of the fundamental right to data protection). See European Commission, "Commission Staff Working Paper: Impact Assessment Accompanying the Document Regulation of the European Parliament and of the Council on the Protection of Individuals with Regard to the Processing of Personal Data and on the Free Movement of Such Data" (2012) 43.

[3] See eg European Commission, "Communication from the Commission to the European Parliament, the Council, the Economic and Social Committee and the Committee of the Regions: A Comprehensive Approach on Personal Data Protection in the European Union" (2010) paras 2–3.

other words, one of the main objectives of the EU data protection overhaul was to build upon existing principles and strengthening them, notably through a reform of the "regulatory architecture".[4] As was aptly captured by the Rand Corporation in its famous review of the Data Protection Directive (DPD), "while the widely applauded principles of the Directive will remain as a useful front-end, they will need to be supported by a harms-based back-end in order to cope with the growing challenge of globalisation and international data flows".[5] In what amounts perhaps the closest to an official definition of the risk-based approach, the European Commission confirmed that the latter's scope would be limited to the better implementation and compliance with rules, by arguing that the goal of the future data protection instrument should be to "mak[e] the implementation of existing principles (. . .) more effective and their application more cost efficient".[6]

2.3 Responsibilisation of the data controller through accountability

As indicated, the first element of meta regulation consists in the responsibilisation of the regulatee, which is a preliminary step in view of regulatory collaboration and the uptaking by the regulatee of the various regulatory tasks. As will be demonstrated, the way for data controllers to become responsible entities is through the principle of accountability.

The role of regulatees' responsibility in the improved implementation of the data protection regulatory architecture appears quite clearly from the reform process. For the European Commission, an increased responsibility/accountability is the solution to the issues surrounding the notification and registration safeguards.[7] Similarly, such increased responsibility/accountability is seen as a crucial for the better implementation of the data protection principles.[8]

2.3.1 Risk-based approach, responsibility or accountability?

It seems that the European institutions are not very clear on their choice of terms. Sometimes they refer to accountability, and sometimes they refer to responsibility. This is particularly clear in the GDPR itself. Article 5(2) enshrines the principle of accountability. However, this principle is further developed in Art 24, which is

[4] See Neil Robinson and others, "Review of the European Data Protection Directive" 1 para x.

[5] ibid vii.

[6] European Commission (n 2) 38.

[7] ibid 14; see eg European Commission (n 3) 10.

[8] European Commission (n 2) 39; European Commission (n 3) 10–11; EDPS, "Opinion of the EDPS on the Data Protection Reform Package" (2012) paras 9, 166; see eg Art 29 WP, "Opinion 01/2012 on the Data Protection Reform Proposals" (2012) 25.

entitled "responsibility of the controller".[9] In the eye of the present author it leaves no doubt that the principle of accountability and responsibility are one and the same principle. This is particularly obvious for instance when looking at the Article 29 Working Party (Art 29 WP)'s opinion on the accountability principle,[10] or looking at Art 24 of the European Parliament's GDPR proposal, entitled "responsibility and accountability of the controller".[11]

The question remains whether such accountability/responsibility principle corresponds to the logic of responsibility at play in the risk management agenda and in meta regulation. A historical analysis of the development of the accountability principle allows to give a positive answer to this question.

2.3.2 History of the accountability principle: The—data protection—principle of accountability: origins

In the data protection field, the first formulation of the principle of accountability can be found in Principles 14 of the OECD Guidelines.[12]

Alhadeff *et al.* note the specific context surrounding the adoption of the principle. As they put it, "the OECD Guidelines are rooted in the then emerging reality of transborder data flows. While the accountability principle is not specifically addressed or limited to transborder data flows, it is used to give effect to all of the principles both domestically and upon transfer."[13] As one recalls, the OECD Guidelines were adopted in a context of internationalisation of data flows (with the goal of the Guidelines to protect privacy and facilitate data flows).[14] In this context, the goal of the accountability principle was to make sure that all the OECD principles were still given effect in practice in cases of data transfer. In order to ensure such continued application, the principle of accountability vests primary responsibility for compliance within the data controller. And such responsibility

[9] The same can be argued as far as the policy documents surrounding the overhaul process are concerned. See among many instances, European Commission (n 2) 39: "the reform leaves space to actors to implement appropriate measures to achieve the purpose of the instruments, e.g. by strengthening **accountability and responsibility** of data controllers", author's emphasis.

[10] Art 29 WP, "Opinion 3/2010 on the Principle of Accountability" (2010).

[11] European Parliament, Legislative Resolution of 12 March 2014 on the proposal for a regulation of the European Parliament and of the Council on the protection of individuals with regard to the processing of their personal data and on the free movement of such data 2014.

[12] OECD Guidelines on the Protection of Privacy and Transborder Flows of Personal Data 1980. Principle 14 states that: "A data controller should be accountable for complying with measures which give effect to the principles stated above."

[13] Joseph Alhadeff, Brendan van Alsenoy, and Jos Dumortier, "The Accountability Principle in Data Protection Regulation: Origin, Development and Future Directions" in Daniel Guagnin and others (eds), *Managing Privacy Through Accountability* (Palgrave Macmillan 2012) 55.

[14] See OECD Guidelines governing the protection of privacy and transborder flows of personal data [C(80)58/FINAL] 2013. Following these, the principle of accountability was introduced in a number of statutes, including the Canadian PIPEDA, or the APEC Privacy Framework, cf *infra*.

does not end once the data are transferred to another party or jurisdiction (where there are strong chances that a third party will be involved in the processing).[15]

It is to be noted that even though the original accountability principle can be seen as a formal/organisational safeguard addressing the effects of technological developments and endowing the data controller with new responsibilities to that end, it should not necessarily be equated with the contemporary version of the principle. The latter amounts to a transformation of the regulatee's activity as risk management. The former does indeed allocate primary responsibility for ensuring compliance within controllers, but does not require any such risk transformation. Instead, it simply requires that states provide adequate sanctions in cases where controllers do not uphold their obligations.[16]

2.3.3 The modern accountability principle: responsibility following the risk management agenda

Whereas this first embodiment of the principle was somewhat remote from risk management, subsequent versions can indeed be characterised as embodiments of the risk management agenda.

The origins of this risk management-based accountability principle can be traced back to a number of different, yet concomitant sources. The first such source has been known as "the Accountability Projects". The Centre for Information Policy Leadership (CIPL, or "the Centre"), a Hunton & Williams based think tank,[17] launched in collaboration with a number of EU stakeholders (such as representatives from data protection authorities, governments, industry, and academia), a series of projects collectively known as "the Accountability Projects".[18] The impetus for these projects were the success of the accountability principle within the APEC (Asia-Pacific Economic Cooperation) context, and its prominent place during the International Conference of Data Protection and Privacy Commissioners.[19] Another driver of accountability as risk management was the Spanish data protection authority, which, in February 2009, put forth a Joint Proposal for an International Privacy Standard, including an accountability

[15] Alhadeff, Van Alsenoy, and Dumortier (n 13) 53–54. In particular, see para 62 of the Explanatory Memorandum of the Guidelines, which suggests that a data controller should remain responsible with regards to a processing carried out by a third party on its behalf. Note that this does not preclude responsibility of any third party involved, see ibid 54.

[16] Para 62 of Explanatory Memorandum; Alhadeff, Van Alsenoy, and Dumortier (n 13) 53.

[17] See https://www.informationpolicycentre.com/, last accessed 24 February 2019.

[18] See https://www.informationpolicycentre.com/organizational-accountability.html, last accessed 24 February 2019. It is to be observed that the accountability project, adopted a number of documents, each corresponding to a phase of the project: the Galway Project (2009), the Paris Project (2010), and the Madrid Project (2011).

[19] International Conference of Data Protection and Privacy Commissioners, "Resolution on the Urgent Need for Protecting Privacy in a Borderless World, and for Reaching a Joint Proposal for Setting International Standards on Privacy and Personal Data Protection" (2008); Alhadeff, Van Alsenoy, and Dumortier (n 13).

principle, which was later upheld by the 2009 International Conference of Data Protection and Privacy Commissioners, which included it in its so-called Madrid Resolution.[20] There was a similar push at the EU level, coming from the Art 29 WP. In its famous 2009 "future of privacy" document (jointly drafted with the Working Party on Police and Justice), the Working Party sketched some of the main themes that would define the overhaul process of the EU data protection legal framework, among which the principle of accountability.[21] In 2010, the Art 29 WP followed-up on its 2009 contribution and published an opinion dedicated to the principle of accountability wherein it explained the rationale for adopting such principle, and also sketched potential constitutive elements of the principle.[22] Contrary to the OECD (Organisation for Economic Co-operation and Development) version of the principle, this version is fully in line with the risk management agenda and its use within the regulatory context.

Accountability is explicitly framed as a response to a number of compliance challenges linked to the inefficiency of existing centralised regulatory mechanisms, with a particular emphasis on evolutions in data processing technologies and business models.[23] The accountability project does acknowledge from the outset that even though the principle of accountability was first devised as a means to address the increasing internationalisation of data flows, it should be conceived as a mechanism of "privacy governance" (in the text) not limited to these sole issues.[24] Thus, if contemporary challenges certainly encompass the global nature of data flows,[25] they also include additional issues such as the increasing scope of data collections, and advances in data analytics.[26] The Accountability project argues that in the face of these changing processing practices, a number of regulatory mechanisms are of limited effect and "may burden organisations without yielding commensurate benefits".[27] The Art 29 adopts similar arguments.[28,29]

[20] International Conference of Data Protection and Privacy Commissioners, "International Standards on the Protection of Personal Data and Privacy: The Madrid Resolution" (2009).

[21] Art 29 WP and Working Party on Police and Justice, "The Future of Privacy: Joint Contribution to the Consultation of the European Commission on the Legal Framework for the Fundamental Right to the Protection of Personal Data" (2009) 20.

[22] Art 29 WP (n 10).

[23] Alhadeff, Van Alsenoy, and Dumortier (n 13) 59.

[24] The Centre for Information Policy Leadership, "Data Protection Accountability: The Essential Elements" (2009) 2–3.

[25] One can note that challenges related to transborder data flows have been given renewed acuteness with challenges stemming from cloud computing see eg Christopher Millard (ed), *Cloud Computing Law* (OUP 2013).

[26] The Centre for Information Policy Leadership (n 24) 2, 4.

[27] ibid 9.

[28] Art 29 WP and Working Party on Police and Justice (n 21); Art 29 WP (n 10).

[29] See also The Centre for Information Policy Leadership (n 24) 17: "In the face of such complexity and rapid change, data protection must be robust, yet flexible. Privacy can no longer be guaranteed either through privacy notices and consent opportunities for individuals, or through direct regulatory oversight."

It should come as little surprise that all the regulatory issues plaguing data protection are addressed in terms of accountability. This just confirms that accountability as the data protection-oriented embodiment of responsibility is indeed the plinth and keystone of any collaborative model of regulation.[30] The following lines will briefly evocate the content of the principle. They will show that accountability can indeed be seen as the keystone for the adoption of meta regulation in the data protection context insofar as it is predicated upon the responsibilisation of the controller, which is itself achieved by recoding the latter's activities as risk management.

According to the Art 29 WP, accountability is a requirement that "data controllers put in place appropriate and effective measures to ensure that the principles and obligations set out in the Directive are complied with and to demonstrate so to supervisory authorities upon request".[31] A similar definition is at play in the GDPR,[32] as well as in various institutional documents pertaining to the reform process.[33] Such a definition does indeed embody the idea of responsibilisation of the regulatee, that is, to transform it into a naturally and self-complying entity, coupled with the possibility for the regulator to assess the regulatees' performance (which can eventually lead to enforcement actions). The accountability project offers a similar perspective, arguing that accountability is an "approach to data governance characterised by its focus on setting privacy-protection goals for organisations (…) and allowing organisations discretion in determining appropriate measures to reach these goals".[34]

Data controllers are therefore put in a position whereby they can determine the safeguards that are most adapted to the specificities of each data processing operation, and which can be adapted where needed, thus providing maximum flexibility.[35] In this sense, accountability and the discretion to regulatees it offers is the counterpoint to the "rigid", centralised safeguards provided by command and control regulation. As seen, in addition to phagocytising resources, these often offer scant protection, and have been criticised as mere "box-ticking" exercises.

[30] See also Vodafone's response to the European Commission 2009 consultation: "Vodafone believes that *accountability as the outward assumption of responsibility*, has a very important role to play in *engendering the internal governance* and assurance processes that will deliver better privacy outcomes in practice." Vodafone, "A Comprehensive Approach on Personal Data Protection in the European Union: Vodafone's Response" (2010) 6, http://ec.europa.eu/justice/news/consulting_public/news_consulting_0006_en.htm, last accessed 06 February 2019, author's emphasis.

[31] Art 29 WP (n 10) 3. See also The Centre for Information Policy Leadership (n 24) 17: "An accountability approach shifts the focus of privacy governance to an organization's ability to achieve fundamental data protection goals and to demonstrate that capability."

[32] See Art 24(1) GDPR: the data controller "shall implement appropriate technical and organizational measures to ensure and to be able to demonstrate that processing is performed in accordance with this Regulation."

[33] EDPS (n 8) 170; Art 29 WP (n 8) 22.

[34] The Centre for Information Policy Leadership (n 24) 8.

[35] ibid.

In contrast, safeguards directly determined by controllers supposedly afford "substantive privacy outcomes" that are directly integrated into business processes, and that can be measured and demonstrated, thus proving much more efficient insofar as they "move data protection from theory to practice".[36,37]

Therefore, when data controllers are accountable, they should be relieved from centralised safeguards such as notification or registration.[38] Further, accountability makes substantive room for third party operationalised safeguards such as certification, seals, or third-party audits,[39] thereby confirming the ideals of auditability and certifiability at the heart of the risk management agenda. Finally, it also paves the way for a transformation of the regulator's role, which is less about operationalising all safeguards, than about collaborating with data controllers and enforcing the cases that present the highest risks.[40] This is precisely the reason why data controllers must be able to demonstrate adequate accountability upon request.[41]

Furthermore, the accountability principle is predicated upon (one could say is coextensive to) a number of provisions that have been analysed as internal controls in the context of the analysis of the risk management agenda, and which as a matter of fact the European Commission explicitly recognises as such.[42] According to the accountability project, data controllers must adopt privacy policies that must receive approval from senior management. Second, they must put in place mechanisms that give effect to these policies. These include decision-making tools like data protection impact assessments (DPIAs), or staff training and education. Such mechanisms must be built into all business processes that collect or process

[36] ibid 8, 12, 17; Art 29 WP (n 10) 3.

[37] The following definition of accountability is also interesting because it combines the idea of responsibilisation with that of efficient protection following from the alignment of organisation and regulatory goals, and the integration of the latter into organisational processes: accountability is "a concept that has governance and ethical dimensions. It envisages an infrastructure that fosters responsible decision-making, engenders answerability, enhances transparency and considers liability. It encompasses expectations that organisations will report, explain and be answerable for the consequences of decisions about the protection of data. Accountability promotes implementation of practical mechanisms whereby legal requirements and guidance are translated into effective protection for data." The Centre for Information Policy Leadership, "Demonstrating and Measuring Accountability A Discussion Document Accountability Phase II—The Paris Project October 2010" (2010) 2.

[38] ibid 4.

[39] The Centre for Information Policy Leadership, "Implementing Accountability in the Marketplace A Discussion Document Accountability Phase III— The Madrid Project November 2011" (2011); Art 29 WP (n 10); The Centre for Information Policy Leadership (n 37).

[40] The Centre for Information Policy Leadership (n 37) 4; The Centre for Information Policy Leadership (n 39) 3.

[41] According to the accountability project, such demonstration can occur in a number of situations, such as when the data controllers wants to have its accountability validated by the regulator, as part of a random check from the regulator, as part of an investigation concerning suspected or actual regulatory violations, or as a follow up to an enforcement action, The Centre for Information Policy Leadership (n 39). See also, The Centre for Information Policy Leadership, (n 24) 10: "accountability does not wait for a system failure; rather it requires that organisations be prepared to demonstrate upon request by the proper authorities that it is securing and protecting data in accordance with the essential elements".

[42] It mentions "internal control mechanisms", European Commission (n 3) 12.

data. Third, controllers must have systems of ongoing internal oversight, the role of which is to assess whether privacy policies are adequate and whether they are satisfactorily implemented (this can be done through internal audit). Sometimes, external verification might also be warranted. Fourth, controllers should provide as much transparency as possible regarding their data practices. And fifth, data controllers should provide remedies in case of infringements.[43] As one can see, this is exactly the same logic as that of the ISO 31000 Standard.[44] Equally, the Art 29 WP has provided a list of ten possible accountability measures that are very similar.[45] These measures form the bulk of chapter IV of the GDPR, and have been presented as constitutive of the responsibility/accountability principle (or at least closely articulating therewith insofar as it contains the measures to be taken pursuant to the accountability principle) since the very beginning of the GDPR overhaul process, both at the European institutional level,[46] and at an external policy level.[47] This confirms that the accountability principle, understood as "establishing safeguards and mechanisms which make data protection compliance more effective while at the same time reducing and simplifying certain administrative formalities",[48] espouses the notion of responsibility underpinning meta regulation insofar as it is explicitly predicated upon the use of internal controls as regulatory resources.

2.4 Internal and external responsibility: the value dimension of responsibilisation

2.4.1 The alignment of regulatory goals

One element is still missing from the analysis of accountability as responsibility. As one remembers, the risk management agenda is predicated upon a number of values that pertain in equal measure to democratic engagement and business efficiency (eg transparency, accountability), and which can be connected to the notion of responsibility at play. The latter is attuned both to the organisation's needs, and

[43] The Centre for Information Policy Leadership (n 24) 13–14.

[44] The fact that the contemporary data protection accountability principle very much espouses the responsibilisation of the regulatees following from the risk management agenda is made quite explicit in the following quote. Accordingly, "companies seek to design, implement, and demonstrate accountability through corporate privacy management programmes and an ethical approach, often through programmes of corporate and social responsibility" Centre for Information Policy Leadership, "A Risk-Based Approach to Privacy: Improving Effectiveness in Practice" (2014) 2.

[45] These include among other, the establishment of privacy policies, the mapping of procedures, staff training and education, the establishment of internal complaints mechanisms, or the ongoing review and monitoring, Art 29 WP (n 10) 11–12.

[46] See eg European Commission (n 2) 52; Art 29 WP and Working Party on Police and Justice (n 21) 20; European Commission (n 3) 12.

[47] See eg Robinson and others (n 4) xiii.

[48] European Commission (n 3) 12.

to the social needs (in this case, the regulatory needs). Hence the alignment of organisational and regulatory goals, and the ideal of "natural compliance".

When looking for the origins of the risk-based approach in the GDPR, it is very common to go back to the study carried out in 2009 by the RAND Corporation on behalf of the ICO (Information Commissioner's Office), not least because it is probably the first document that introduced the "risk-based approach" expression.[49] What has been less underscored however is that the so-called "RAND Report",[50] is only one of a series of documents that the ICO produced in the years preceding the official start of the overhaul process of Directive 95/46/EC.[51] Among these reports, two are worth mentioning. The first one is the 2008 "Privacy by Design" report, which was commissioned to the Enterprise Privacy Group.[52] In a nutshell, this report argued that the lack of concern from enterprises for data protection issues stemmed from a lacking "business case".[53] This latter point was elaborated further in detail in the second report, entitled "The Privacy Dividend".[54]

This report is considered crucial because "making the business case" in fact amounts to aligning regulatory goals with organisational goals (in line with the meta regulation logic). Contrary to the RAND Report, which focuses on the regulatory dimension of the risk-based approach and lays the ground for the regulatory responsibility through the accountability principle, "the privacy dividend" can even be considered more fundamental insofar as it lays the very values that underpin such regulatory architecture, such as accountability, efficiency, opportunity, good governance, transparency, responsiveness, etc.

It elaborates on the fact that organisations and businesses are responsible entities, since they need to acknowledge that their operations can "affect people's lives".[55] It also shows that organisations are indeed responsible since they integrate these social values insofar as they have a strong desire to " 'do the right thing' with regard to privacy, ie be trustworthy, transparent and respectful of people's privacy".[56] On this basis, it goes on to show that organisations' concern for being

[49] For such accounts, see eg Milda Macenaite, "The 'Riskification' of European Data Protection Law through a Two-Fold Shift" (2017) 8 European Journal of Risk Regulation 506; Claudia Quelle, "The 'Risk Revolution' in EU Data Protection Law: We Can't Have Our Cake and Eat It, Too" in Ronald Leenes and others (eds), *Data Protection and Privacy: The Age of Intelligent Machines* (Hart Publishing 2017).

[50] Robinson and others (n 4).

[51] The ICO used to have a website containing all the policy documents commissioned for the GDPR overhaul process, but it does not seem to exist anymore.

[52] At the time of writing (8 January 2019), the report was not accessible online. Following e-mail correspondence with the ICO, it appears that it is not possible to have access to the report.

[53] ICO, "The Privacy Dividend: The Business Case for Investing in Proactive Privacy Protection. Volume 1—The Business Case" (2010), foreword.

[54] ibid; ICO, "The Privacy Dividend: The Business Case for Investing in Proactive Privacy Protection. Volume 2—Supporting Material" (2010).

[55] ICO (n 53) 9.

[56] ibid 11.

responsible (wishing to do the right thing as far as processing of personal data is concerned), is not antithetical to their business objectives. On the contrary, both are perfectly aligned (or so they claim). As they put it "protecting people's privacy can bring substantial benefits to the organisation. These are real benefits in that they help the organisation to succeed and to achieve its business objectives".[57] Interestingly, the report also spells out more in detail what these benefits are. Some are mission-enhancing benefits such as "increased take up of services, revenue up-lifts or cost-reductions".[58] Others are risk-reducing benefits such as "improvements in resilience or the reduction of assurance or compliance risks".[59] In other words, organisations are responsible also concerning social values, which pertain to the democratic-oriented values of corporate governance.[60] Yet, as just explained, these values are aligned with corporate values and objectives of value creation.

The report also confirms the analysis of risk management and meta regulation, which is predicated upon the alignment of democratic and corporate values (characteristic of governance and of the risk management agenda), and further the alignment between business and regulatory goals. This is clearly expressed in statements arguing that the social value of privacy can be grasped through organisations' desire to "do the right thing" and through "the concerns expressed by regulators and legislators".[61] This confirms the finding that the responsibilisation of organisations signals a commitment to regulatory goals, thereby transforming them into naturally compliant entities.

In the language of the report, the alignment of business and data protection regulatory goals is referred to as privacy by design (which under the GDPR will become data protection by design). Among others, it is predicated upon the uptake of data protection-oriented enterprise-wide management programmes.[62]

Finally, it should be pointed that, again confirming the theoretical analysis, the goals are more than simply aligned. Rather, the social concerns around the protection of people's right to data protection are subsumed under business objectives. They are recoded as a matter of internal risks to the business objectives (either the positive ones such as increased take up of services, revenue up-lifts, or the negative ones such as reputational risks or loss of trustworthiness.[63]

[57] ibid 12.
[58] ibid.
[59] ibid.
[60] See also BEUC, "Response to the European Commission's Consultation on the Commission's Comprehensive Approach on Personal Data Protection in the European Union" (2011) 12: "the social value of personal information places an imperative on the organization to protect privacy".
[61] ICO (n 53) 12.
[62] Which, as seen *supra*, are foundational to governance, ibid 16.
[63] ibid 3.

2.4.2 The dual dimension of the risk management agenda's values: democratic ethos and business efficiency, and their recoding as a matter of business goals

Further, the dual dimension of responsibility (ie nurturing public interest goals as well as business goals), and the alignment of goals can also be witnessed by observing the reactions to the accountability principles. Support for these measures not only came from the corporate or institutional world, but also from civil society, and academics.

This is for instance the case of BEUC's (the European Consumers' Organisation) response to the European Commission's first public consultation of 2009 which was carried in view of the overhaul of the EU framework. In its response, BEUC clearly supports the principle of accountability.[64] It also provides support to the alignment of regulatory and business goals through the data protection by design principle.[65] It also clearly supports risk management tools such as data protection impact assessments coupled to audit procedures, data protection officers, or certification schemes.[66] Similarly, several scholars have also hailed the potential beneficial dimension of data protection impact assessments, the main risk management tool in the data protection context (cf *infra*).[67]

At the other end of the spectrum, these very same principles and tools have been hailed as beneficial to the corporate/data controllers' agenda. In their response to the same European Commission consultation, DigitalEurope welcomes more responsible organisations uptaking regulatory tasks following the accountability principle. While this increased responsibilisation is obviously beneficial to data subjects and for regulatory purposes, it is also seen as directly instrumental to the nurturing of business objectives, and in particular the fostering of trust and reputation.[68]

At the institutional level, similar remarks are echoed through a number of important policy documents. This is the case for the European Commission's impact assessment accompanying the Commission's Regulation proposal, which sees data

[64] BEUC (n 60) 16.
[65] ibid 14.
[66] ibid 16.
[67] See Colin J Bennett and others, "Privacy Impact Assessments: International Study of Their Application and Effects" (2007); David Wright, "The State of the Art in Privacy Impact Assessment" (2012) 28 Computer Law & Security Review 54; David Wright and Paul De Hert (eds), *Privacy Impact Assessment* (Springer 2012).
[68] DigitalEurope, "Consultation on the Legal Framework for the Fundamental Right to Protection of Personal Data" (2009) 3. This is also the case for additional responses to the European Commission's consultation, see eg Vodafone (n 30).

controllers' accountability and increased regulatory responsibility as beneficial to both said controllers and data subjects.[69]

2.5 The risk-based approach as accountability and, possibly, data protection by design

Following the previous lines, one could argue that the risk-based approach to data protection is embodied through the principles of accountability and data protection by design.[70] Accountability is the main principle since it enshrines the regulatees' regulatory responsibility and risk-based transformation. Data protection by design is ancillary but equally important insofar as it embodies the values characteristic of meta regulation and governance, and in particular the alignment of social and business values, as well as the recoding of social values as a matter of business values (though the latter part is not explicit to the principle).

One could nonetheless argue that the main provision of the risk-based approach remains the accountability principle since the risk-based responsibilisation it provides for entails *ipso facto* the alignment of values described herein above. Similarly, the Irish Presidency of the Council of the EU explicitly enshrined the risk-based approach in the accountability principle.[71] In this sense, data protection by design, as a specific provision providing for the alignment of values, can be seen as just another internal control, ancillary to the main accountability provision. This lack of clear analytical distinction between the provisions is also visible in the "privacy dividend" document, which we have flagged as best representing the alignment of values under data protection by design. It also contains numerous references to responsibilisation and risk-based transformation of data controllers' activities, so that neatly distinguishing between what elements of meta regulation fall under accountability and/or data protection by design is sometimes difficult. Furthermore, and as will be seen below, a number of statutes that implement the risk-based approach solely rely upon the accountability principle leaving data protection by design out of the equation.

[69] European Commission (n 2), 42. In a similar sense, see the EDPS's opinion on the data protection reform package seeing increased data controller's responsibility as beneficial from a regulatory viewpoint, EDPS (n 8) 166. Equally, the Art 29 WP in its own opinion saw the increased responsibility as beneficial to data controllers ("simplification and greater consistency"), and beneficial from a regulatory viewpoint Art 29 WP (n 8) 6.

[70] For a similar reasoning, see Quelle (n 49).

[71] Council of the European Union, "Proposal for a Regulation of the European Parliament and of the Council on the Protection of Individuals with Regard to the Processing of Personal Data and on the Free Movement of Such Data (General Data Protection Regulation)—Key Issues of Chapters I-I" (2013) para 21.

2.6 Accountability, or the risk-based approach? And beyond

The issue this section addresses is the following: so far (EU) debates surrounding the application of meta regulation to data protection seem more concerned with the principle of accountability than with a "risk-based approach".

As a matter of fact, the expression risk-based approach was not part of the overhaul debate until mid-2013. In all the policy documents surrounding the Commission's initial proposal (such as the Commission's 2010 Communication or its impact assessment, the European Data Protection Supervisor (EDPS)'s and Art 29 WP's reaction to the initial proposal, the European Parliament's own proposal...) the notion of a risk-based approach is nowhere to be found.[72]

The earliest trace of the expression risk-based approach can probably be found in the RAND's review of the DPD.[73] What is interesting is that the way they define the risk-based approach is similar in all points to the way that the accountability and responsibility principle is defined in the EU institutions' policy document surrounding the GDPR reform. Namely the endowing of responsibility for compliance (and demonstration thereof) to the data controller.[74]

The term risk-based approach came to the fore of the debate in 2013 with the issuing by the Council of the European Union—under Irish Presidency—of Chapters 1 and 4 of its first draft GDPR proposal.[75] As a matter of fact, the Commission's initial GDPR proposal contained no reference to risk in its accountability provision, which simply restated the data controllers' regulatory responsibility to implement appropriate measures in view of ensuring compliance.[76] Similarly, the principle of accountability was not associated to the notion of risk in any of the EU institutional policy documents adopted in the early stages of the reform.[77]

One can therefore speculate that the introduction of the notion of a risk-based approach follows from worries that the lack of references to risk in the legislative proposals obfuscated the intrinsic risk-based nature of the accountability principle.[78] Indeed, if the principle of accountability embodies the meta regulation/risk management agenda's notion of responsibility it is risk-based per definition. The

[72] Except very marginally in the Commission's impact assessment, which mentions a "risk-based model of accountability" in the context of data transfers to third countries, European Commission (n 2) 86.

[73] Robinson and others (n 4) xii.

[74] ibid; see eg European Commission (n 3) 11.

[75] Council of the European Union (n 71).

[76] European Commission, "Proposal for a Regulation of the European Parliament and of the Council on the Protection of Individuals with Regard to the Processing of Personal Data and on the Free Movement of Such Data (General Data Protection Regulation)", vol COM(2012) (2012) pt 22.

[77] European Commission (n 2); eg Art 29 WP and Working Party on Police and Justice (n 21); European Commission (n 3).

[78] This is for instance very clear in the comments of Digital Europe following the Council's draft, see DigitalEurope, "DIGITALEUROPE Comments on the Risk-Based Approach" 1.

risk-based nature of the accountability principle, even if implicit until the issuing by the Council of the European Union of its first draft Chapters 1 and 4 of its GDPR proposal, can nonetheless be uncovered in previous policy documents. This stems from the Commission's impact assessment relating to its initial GDPR proposal for instance. The latter explicitly refers to accountability as the principle that allows for the data controllers (and data processors at that stage of the process reform) to implement measures that will achieve the goals and purposes of the envisaged instruments; with such measures consisting in the assessment and mitigation of "data protection risks".[79] Further evidence is given by the fact that both this document,[80] and the Art 29 WP,[81] refer to implementation measures taken in the name of accountability as "internal controls", and see their implementation as risk-based per definition. This is the case for the data protection officers obligation, limited to "risky processing",[82] but also for the documentation obligation which originally did not apply to data controllers "employing fewer than 250 persons that is processing personal data only as an activity ancillary to its main activities" (ie low risk situation) among many examples.[83] The RAND Report also argued that the choice and implementation of these internal controls should be determined based on the level of risk.[84]

One can therefore argue that in establishing a risk-based approach, the Council of the European Union simply made the risk-based nature of the accountability principle explicit, and enshrined it in the GDPR. It follows that the accountability/responsibility principle is a horizontal provision, which should be risk-based. Similarly, all the measures to be taken pursuant to the latter (such as data protection officers, data breach notifications . . .) would also be redrafted so as to be risk-based.[85] This risk-based redrafting of the responsibility/accountability principle and accompanying measures has made its way in the final text of the GDPR.[86]

Yet, and in spite of the anchoring of various GDPR provisions into risk, the expression risk-based approach remains completely absent from the GDPR. One can therefore argue that it can be equated to the accountability principle. This is actually confirmed by the Irish delegation's input to the Council of the EU's GDPR proposal, whereby it professes support for "the risk-based approach set out in article

[79] European Commission (n 2) 39.

[80] European Commission (n 3) 11.

[81] Art 29 WP and Working Party on Police and Justice (n 21) 3.

[82] For the example of data protection impact assessments, and data protection officers, see European Commission (n 2) 69.

[83] European Commission (n 76) 28(4)(b).

[84] Robinson and others (n 4) xii.

[85] See Council of the European Union (n 71) 22.

[86] It is to be noted that the accountability provision of the European Parliament was drafted in a similar way insofar as it was also risk-based, even though the "risk-based approach" as such had not made its way into the proposal.

22" (ie accountability principle).[87] At its core, and whether one frames it as a matter of accountability or as a matter of a "risk-based approach", the points is to transform the regulatee (in the case of GDPR, only the data controller) into a responsible entity. The latter responsibilisation entails a transformation of the regulatee's activities as a matter of risk management. It has both an internal and an external dimension. Further, it is a necessary condition in order to endow regulatees with regulatory functions along the logic of collaborative models of regulation.

2.7 Risk-based accountability and the risk-based transformation of the data controller

The previous lines have shown that the principle of accountability is the key principle concerning the risk-based approach, notably because it features the responsibilisation of the regulatee (in the case of the GDPR, the data controller). Such responsibilisation is risk-based and is predicated upon the adoption of internal controls—ie mechanisms of organisational design, which are also risk-based by definition. It should therefore follow that risk management is at the heart of the accountability principle and of the risk-based approach. This is so because once organisations are made responsible their activities are also transformed as a matter of risk management, which simultaneously allows them to fulfil the whole spectrum of their role under meta regulation.

Yet, the risk-transformation at the heart of the risk management agenda and meta regulation has left many uneasy in the data protection context. For many, this risk retransformation of the whole of organisational activity has been something difficult to grasp. A common misunderstanding has been to consider the risk management exercise as an additional obligation, coming on top of the general duty to fully comply with the GDPR in any case. This misunderstanding fails to perceive that the introduction of the accountability principle entails a full recoding of data controllers' activities—including compliance—with data protection law as a matter of risk-taking. Crucially, if all of the data controller's activities are recoded as a matter of risk taking, and if compliance also becomes a matter of risk taking, this means that the whole data protection legal framework is affected by such risk-based transformation and not only chapter IV. In other words, arguing that it is possible to separate a general, "non-risk-based" compliance, from risk-based measures stemming from chapter IV GDPR does not hold.

[87] Council of the European Union, "Proposal for a Regulation of the European Parliament and of the Council on the Protection of Individuals with Regard to the Processing of Personal Data and on the Free Movement of Such Data—Risk Based Approach" (2014) 79.

This uneasiness is visible for instance in discussions among Member States in the Council of the European Union relating to the adoption by the latter of the risk-based approach. The Austrian delegation argued that Art 22 (on accountability) should include an obligation to carry out a "preliminary risk assessment/ rough check/simple test". The object of such test would be to establish the type of risk the envisaged processing operation presents ("low or moderate-to-high").[88] In the opinion of the present author this type of reasoning embodies the misunderstanding at play, precisely because the whole point of the accountability principle is for the data controller to carry out a risk analysis by definition. Similar positions have been adopted in the context of data protection impact assessments, which only apply in cases of high risk (cf *infra*). Several actors have argued that the assessment of the impact of a high-risk situation is simply an additional compliance measure coming on top of regular, full compliance, thereby failing to perceive that such compliance is already risk-based.[89]

However, the previous lines have shown that accountability is risk-based per definition. The risk-based nature of the accountability principles has also not escaped the attention of the CIPL. In a further paper on the role of risk management in data protection, the CIPL argues that risk management (or risk analysis) "is an integral component of organizational accountability".[90] Similarly, in a discussion paper used to kick start its work on the risk-based approach to data protection, the Centre argued that the risk-based approach directly flows from the accountability principle, and that "the accountability principle calls upon organizations to assess and mitigate the privacy risks to individuals raised by data use".[91]

2.8 The risk-based approach as a contradictory implementation of meta regulation?

The previous section highlighted the fact that the full risk-transformation of the regulatees is an intrinsic feature of the accountability principle which has not

[88] ibid 113.

[89] See Felix Bieker and others, "A Process for Data Protection Impact Assessment Under the European General Data Protection Regulation", *Privacy Technologies and Policy: 4th Annual Privacy Forum, APF 2016 Frankfurt/Main, Germany, September 7–8, 2016, Proceedings*, vol 3 (2016); Art 29 WP, "Statement on the Role of a Risk-Based Approach in Data Protection Legal Frameworks" (2014). Implicitly adopting a similar position, see Art 29 WP, "Guidelines on Data Protection Impact Assessment (DPIA) and Determining Whether Processing Is 'Likely to Result in a High Risk' for the Purposes of Regulation 2016/679" (2017). For an overview of these debates, see Raphaël Gellert, "Understanding the Notion of Risk in the General Data Protection Regulation" (2018) 34 Computer Law and Security Review 279.

[90] Centre for Information Policy Leadership, "The Role of Risk Management in Data Protection" (2014) 14.

[91] Centre for Information Policy Leadership, "'A Risk-Based Approach to Privacy?' An Initial Issues Paper for Privacy Risk Framework and Risk-Based Approach to Privacy Project" (2014) 2.

always been clearly understood. The present section points to another caveat. It directly follows from the previous, and concerns the notion of risk at play.

Following meta regulation theory, once organisations are transformed through the risk management agenda, so are their activities, which become a matter of risk analysis. In this sense, organisations do not have to comply with pre-determined regulatory standards, since they determine these standards themselves. Yet, the risk-based approach is not concerned with standard setting. As seen, its goal consists in relying upon the risk transformation of the regulatee and the internal controls that go along with it as a regulatory resource in view of a more efficient implementation of the data protection principles.

Such a stance has been evidenced in relation to the reform process of the GDPR. It was also confirmed by a strong statement from the Art 29 WP on the role and meaning of the risk-based approach where it explicitly rejected a risk-based approach that would also encompass the standard setting function. It argued that "the risk-based approach is being increasingly and wrongly presented as an alternative to well-established data protection rights and principles",[92] entailing that it could not accept the point of view whereby "legal compliance should shift to the framing of data use [and to] a strong harm-based approach [that] can help to promote responsible data use based on risk management".[93] Thus, the Art 29 WP explicitly rejects a conception of the risk-based approach that encompasses the standard setting function (ie defining regulatory goals and linking them to harms, cf Chapter 4). Instead, its vision of the risk-based approach is one that is limited to compliance. As it puts it, the risk-based approach is "a scalable and proportionate approach to compliance".[94]

The paradox is therefore the following. Most of the GDPR (including the core principles) remains "rights-based", whereas the only risk-based provisions can be found in chapter IV. Yet, this coexistence of rights-based and risk-based approaches overlooks the risk transformation of regulatees, which entails that their activities are a matter of risk, which is coextensive to standard setting. In other words, the risk transformation following from meta regulation entails per definition that regulatees perform the regulatory activity of standard setting since, by definition, meta regulation relies upon risk management as the main regulatory tool. And because of their responsibilisation, their very activity is a matter of risk. Or to put it even differently, the risk management exercise that regulatees perform in order to carry out their activities becomes conflated with the regulatory function of standard setting. In this sense, the pursuit of organisational activity amounts to the management of data protection risks (understood as the chances that the

[92] Art 29 WP (n 89) 2.
[93] ibid 2–3.
[94] ibid 2.

properties of a processing operation will harm the data subject),[95] which amounts to the regulatory task of standard setting. However, this is impossible under the risk-based approach in the GDPR, since it does not allow data controllers to set standards, and instead limits their task to improving their compliance with the existing standards. Yet, data controllers remain-risk based, hence the paradox.

Another way of looking at it, however, is to argue that this paradox paves the way for a new concept of data protection risk, which is aimed primarily at compliance. Therefore, rather than paving the way for a shift between standard setting through command and control and standard setting through risk management, the risk-based approach provides us with a new notion of data protection risk. Instead of assessing the chances that the properties of a processing operation will harm the data subject, the data controllers will assess their chances of complying with the data protection provisions, and on this basis adopt the safeguards (ie internal controls) that best address this risk.[96]

Both the notions of data protection risk and compliance risk will be studied in Chapter 6. Yet, it is to be noted that the "compliance risk" is the only one able to reconcile the risk-based approach's regulatory focus (ie better implementing "rights-based" principles) with the risk transformation of the regulatees' activities it entails. The next section confirms the present finding by looking at the extent of the risk-based approach's scope.

2.9 The scope of the risk-based approach: a focus on safeguards

Several positions seem to have been competing concerning the scope of the risk-based approach.

First, one can point to the position that is most in line with meta regulation theory. As one remembers, following the canon of meta regulation, regulated organisations are entrusted with the setting of regulatory rules or standards (ie the data protection core principles), following which they devise the most adequate safeguards, which they also operationalise. They do so with risk tools and methodologies, thereby redefining regulatory goals through the language of risk.[97] This was initially the case of the CIPL, which later changed position on the matter. In its discussion paper kick starting its project on the risk-based approach the Centre argued that "calls for a risk-based approach extend beyond the focus on

[95] See Chapter 6.

[96] Note that such lack of compliance can itself also result with harms for the data subject since data protection provisions are safeguards in the first place.

[97] Neil Gunningham, "Enforcement and Compliance Strategies" in Robert Baldwin, Martin Cave, and Martin Lodge (eds), *The Oxford Handbook of Regulation* (OUP 2010) 136.

Accountability".[98] Among the reasons why it argues so, the Centre refers to the shortcomings concerning standard setting discussed in Chapter 3.[99] It therefore concludes that one of the aims of the risk-based approach is to "address regulatory limitations or uncertainties".[100] Yet, such standard setting dimension of the risk-based approach will be abandoned in the subsequent papers.

The approach retained in the GDPR is a different one. As indicated *supra*, the goal of the EU data protection overhaul has never been to modify the data protection core principles. On the contrary, these have been considered still valid.[101] The whole point of the reform therefore consisted in complementing these principles with measures that would enable for a more effective implementation thereof.[102] As seen, this was also the approach advocated by the RAND Report, which distinguished between the "front-end" principles (ie the core principles), and the "back-end" implementation measures of these very principles. Only the latter are to be risk-based.[103] In a series of subsequent white papers, the CIPL shifted its understanding of the risk-based approach to mirror the one at play in the GDPR. It is useful to recount these papers because they provide for various eloquent descriptions of what the risk-based approach is about. Accordingly, the primary role of risk analysis is to determine the scope and extent of accountability-based measures (ie organisational design measures), that is, to calibrate accountability.[104] Because the scope of accountability depends upon the risks presented by the processing operations, risk analysis determines the extent of mechanisms of organisational design to be taken pursuant to the principle of accountability.[105] From this perspective, risk management is not concerned with standard setting activities, but solely with organisational design, that is, the internal controls organisations deploy in their transformation as responsible entities in order to manage risks, and which can be used as regulatory resources. That is the reason why it is argued that accountability "does not redefine privacy, nor does it replace existing law or regulation. Accountable organizations must comply with existing applicable law";[106] and "risk management does not alter rights or obligations", and is simply a tool for calibrating compliance.[107] In other words, "organisations are accountable for

[98] Centre for Information Policy Leadership (n 91) 3.

[99] ibid 3–4.

[100] ibid 5.

[101] Though in need of strengthening and uniform interpretation, such as the notion of personal data or the data minimisation principle, see European Commission (n 2).

[102] see eg Art 29 WP and Working Party on Police and Justice (n 21) 15.

[103] Robinson and others (n 4) 41.

[104] Centre for Information Policy Leadership (n 90) 13.

[105] ibid 14.

[106] Centre for Information Policy Leadership (n 24) 9. See also: Robinson and others (n 4) 10: "the accountable organisation complies with applicable law and then takes the further step to implement a program that ensures the privacy and protection of data based on an assessment of the risks to individuals raised by its use".

[107] Centre for Information Policy Leadership (n 90) 1. See also Centre for Information Policy Leadership (n 44) 4: "the risk-based approach is not meant to replace or negate existing privacy

complying with applicable law and regulations", and must simultaneously perform "ongoing risk assessment and mitigation" that is strictly limited to their measures of organisational design.[108] Such ongoing risk assessment and mitigation "in no way change or affect the substantive principles of data protection, instead they are designed to make them work better".[109,110]

Finally, one can also mention a third approach, which is a hybrid version of the two previous ones. Even though it does not go as far as replacing all of data protection provisions with risk management tools, it nonetheless introduces risk considerations for some of the data protection provisions going beyond accountability-based measures. This has been the case of authors such as Hintze who argued that pseudonymisation of data reduced the overall risk of the process and should therefore result in reduced data subject rights, among others.[111] The same can be said of the views purported by DIGITALEUROPE who argued for a definition of personal data depending upon the level of risk at stake,[112] or even the Estonian delegation during the drafting of the Council of the EU's GDPR proposal, who also argued for a calibration of the data subject rights pursuant to the level of risk.[113] These views however, have not prevailed.

In other words, even though compliance with the whole of the GDPR becomes risk-based, the object of such risk is only concerned with issues of compliance. That is, risk management tools can only help determine "how to comply" with the whole GDPR, but not "what to comply with". This is consistent with the present analysis, which frames the risk-based approach as only a partial implementation of meta regulation.

2.10 Summarising the risk-based approach in the GDPR and its rationale

As indicated, the risk-based approach in the GDPR consists in implementing a risk-based accountability principle. There are various reasons for adopting such a

regulation and data protection principles", and "while the risk-based approach may be used to calibrate obligations and compliance of organisations, it should not be seen as a dilution of individual rights, nor as a means of avoiding legal obligations".

108 Centre for Information Policy Leadership (n 37) 5.

109 Art 29 WP (n 10) 5.

110 The Rand Report argued along similar lines: "A risk-based approach should thus not be interpreted as arguing for the application of regulations only when there is a sufficient risk of harm" Robinson and others (n 4) xii. Rather, risk considerations should be at play in "determining in what way the fundamental right to the protection of personal data as specified in the European Charter of Fundamental Rights may be best safeguarded" ibid.

111 Mike Hintze, "Viewing the GDPR Through a De-Identification Lens: A Tool for Clarification and Compliance" 1, <https://fpf.org/wp-content/uploads/2016/11/M-Hintze-GDPR-Through-the-De-Identification-Lens-31-Oct-2016-002.pdf> last accessed 14 March 2019.

112 DigitalEurope (n 78) 6.

113 Council of the European Union (n 87) 63.

risk management-based accountability principle. Some of them have already been spelled out, but they will now be summarised and systematised.

The first reason pertains to the fact that, as already discussed, it can provide for "real protection on the ground", as opposed to a "protection on paper", which is often reduced to box-ticking exercises.[114] This is the whole argument following which accountability is meant to provide for an "effective implementation of the substantive [data protection] obligations and principles".[115] In order to understand the difference, one can pay heed to Bamberger and Mulligan's empirical study on the role of risk management for data protection in practice.[116] They argue that traditional verification of compliance, is undertaken by a lone, dedicated employee, often at the end of projects, when their features have already been decided upon.[117] Pursuing to the accountability principle, on the contrary, regulatory goals are integrated within business processes from the start, precisely through internal controls.[118] Following this integration into internal controls, regulatory goals are therefore coextensive with organisational activity, hence the "protection on the ground".[119] A similar argument can be made concerning the scant level of protection offered by a number of formal safeguards, chief amongst which, the now defunct notification obligation (cf Chapter 3).[120] The latter might offer protection on paper but the respect thereof might have very little to do with whether data subjects are harmed or not as a result of their data being processed.[121]

A protection on the ground also means a contextual application of compliance obligations. By affording data controllers some responsibility and discretion, which follows from the alignment and integration of regulatory goals with business processes, accountability enables them to implement requirements in a flexible, context-specific way, as opposed to their linear application in all situations.[122]

[114] See also, Centre for Information Policy Leadership (n 44) 3: the point of accountability is "to improve the effectiveness of privacy protection in practice", and "to facilitate the application of existing data protection principles in practice", ibid 4.

[115] Art 29 WP and Working Party on Police and Justice (n 21) 79. See also European Commission (n 2) 50; EDPS (n 8) 173.

[116] Kenneth A Bamberger and Deirdre K Mulligan, *Privacy on the Ground: Driving Corporate Behavior in the United States and Europe* (The MIT Press 2015).

[117] Confirming that so-called compliance checks are performed "at the end of the line", see David Tancock, Siani Pearson, and Andrew Charlesworth, "Analysis of Privacy Impact Assessments within Major Jurisdictions" [2010] 8th International Conference on Privacy, Security and Trust 118, 119; Bennett and others (n 67).

[118] Adam Barth and others, "Privacy and Utility in Business Processes" [2007] Proceedings—IEEE Computer Security Foundations Symposium 279.

[119] Centre for Information Policy Leadership (n 44) 4: accountability enables data controllers to "interpret, elaborate, and make meaningful requirements and fundamental data protection principles, which inevitably are often cast in general terms."

[120] See eg European Commission (n 2) 14.

[121] As the Rand Report puts it: "when is privacy affected by personal data processing and when is it not, and how strong should the link between data protection regulations and privacy protection be?" Robinson and others (n 4) viii.

[122] See eg Art 29 WP (n 8) 15.

The contextual application of obligations is directly related to the possibility for data controllers to calibrate their obligations, and mobilise resources where it matters most, ie to avoid so-called "red tape". As the Centre puts it, the point of calibrating data controllers' obligations is "to avoid wasting scarce resources on less important or bureaucratic requirements that neither benefit individuals nor better protect their information".[123,124]

Finally, the CIPL also points to the harmonisation potential of a risk management-based accountability principle.[125] It is therefore argued that a common approach and understanding of accountability tools and mechanisms "would create harmonised practices and outcomes",[126] and would "improve prospects for global interoperability".[127] Such harmonisation would also sway currency with regards to the relation between data controllers and DPAs, since it would help regulators to better fix and communicate their priorities in terms of enforcement, and notably where data controllers should focus their compliance resources.[128] It would also provide regulators with a "common language" in order to assess the data controllers' activities.[129] This is also in line with the EU data protection reform's objectives of improved enforcement, which sought to address the lack of resources as well as the lack of prioritisation (and the related need for closer cooperation).[130]

These various "selling points" for the risk-based approach are all consistent with the theory of meta regulation. They can be related to the implementation of rules and safeguards, which becomes more efficient through the regulatees' risk management strategies. In this sense, they can be seen as addressing the various issues poising command and control regulation discussed in Chapter 3. They can also be related to the fact that enforcement is predicated upon the so-called "ladder of enforcement" as well as upon the prioritisation of enforcement activities according to the level of risk. Equally, such enforcement is based upon internal controls as windows (or proxies) on the activities of the regulatee. This is also consistent with the fact that accountability entails both the taking of implementation measures as well as the capacity to demonstrate it.[131]

123 Centre for Information Policy Leadership (n 44) 4; see also European Commission (n 3) 10.
124 The point is therefore to "implement and calibrate existing legal requirements and compliance in practice, to make them more effective". Centre for Information Policy Leadership (n 44) 11.
125 ibid 4.
126 ibid.
127 ibid.
128 ibid 10.
129 ibid.
130 European Commission (n 2) 17. This is in line with Kuner *et al.*'s remark according to which the risk-based approach is an effective means for prioritising regulators' enforcement actions "Risk Management in Data Protection" (2015) 5 International Data Privacy Law 95, 2.
131 See eg EDPS (n 8) 166; European Commission (n 2) 26.

2.11 The "regulatory focus" of the risk-based approach in the GDPR, and beyond

As mentioned, the risk-based debate is, as such, very EU-centric. However, one can observe that the regulatory oriented approach to meta regulation that the risk-based approach embodies is not alien to other legal tradition.[132] As a matter of fact, it has been uptaken in other statutes and instruments. The absence of the "risk-based label" does not change the fact that they equally rely upon a mix of accountability and data protection by design provisions in view of a more efficient implementation of existing principles.

2.11.1 The GDPR

Following Art 24 GDPR, the data controller shall implement measures to ensure compliance with the GDPR, having regard to the "risks of varying severity and likelihood".

Article 25(1) GDPR contains the principle of data protection by design. It is also risk-based, and provides that regulatees shall integrate regulatory goals directly into their processing operations. This is exactly the logic of the alignment of goals.

2.11.2 Council of Europe, Convention 108+

The Council of Europe's Convention 108 on the protection of individuals with regard to the processing of personal data was recently modernised by Protocol (CETS No 223), following which it has become Convention 108+.[133]

As far as the risk-based approach is concerned, one can argue that Convention 108+ has adopted a similar position. It follows from the Explanatory Report that the challenges and goals of the reform are quasi identical to that of the GDPR. Namely, challenges stemming from increased use of digital technology including the globalisation of data flows associated to the need for a more efficient implementation of the principles of the convention,[134] which are technology neutral and should be maintained since they remain valid.[135]

There is no mention of a risk-based approach or accountability/responsibility principle.[136] Yet Art 10, simply entitled "additional obligations" is precisely

[132] The seminal study in this regard remains that of Bamberger and Mulligan (n 116).

[133] Convention 108 + Convention for the protection of individuals with regard to the processing of personal data (CETS No. 223) 2018. At the time of writing the protocol has not entered into force yet due to insufficient ratifications, see https://www.coe.int/en/web/conventions/full-list/-/conventions/treaty/223/signatures (last accessed 1 March 2019).

[134] Council of Europe, Explanatory Report—Modernised Convention for the Protection of Individuals with Regard to the Processing of Personal Data 2018 paras 1, 7.

[135] ibid para 2.

[136] Except in ibid para 85 of Explanatory Report: "to ensure adequate data protection is linked to the responsibility to verify and be in a position to demonstrate that data processing is in compliance with the applicable law".

about that. Article 10(1) provides that controllers (and processors, contrary to the GDPR), shall "take all appropriate measures to comply with the obligations of this Convention and be able to demonstrate (…) that the data processing under their control is in compliance with the provisions of this Convention". Such responsibility to comply with the Convention, is risk-based since it must have "regard to the risks arising for the interests, rights and fundamental freedoms of the data subjects" (Art 10(4)). One can also pay heed to Art 10(2), the meaning of which is not entirely clear to the author. On the one hand, it requires regulatees to assess the impact of the envisaged data processing operations on the data subject's rights and fundamental freedoms before being carried out, and in this sense can be seen as an additional confirmation of the risk-based dimension of the responsibility to comply. On the other hand, it can be seen as a provision akin to the GDPR's data protection by design provision insofar as it states that regulatees "shall design the data processing in such a manner as to prevent or minimise the risk of interference with those rights", thereby signalling the alignment of goals at the heart of the latter.[137]

2.11.3 Canada: PIPEDA and the Privacy Management Program

Another interesting statute to explore is Canada's private sector legislation, PIPEDA (Personal Information Protection and Electronic Documents Act).[138] According to PIPEDA Art 5(1), the obligations contained in Schedule 1 are compulsory. Schedule 1 is the 1996 CSA Standard referred to in Chapter 4.[139] Its principle 1 is the accountability principle according to which, organisations are responsible for implementing measures and policies giving effect to the Act. Following the Privacy Commissioner of Canada, the manner of doing so is by implementing a privacy management program.[140] The privacy management program (PMP) is a guidance document that has been jointly developed by the Privacy Commissioners of Canada, Alberta, and British Columbia in 2012.[141] Here, the link between the data protection accountability principle and the risk management agenda is maybe the most explicit: being accountable entails implementing a "management program".

[137] And therefore, what the convention refers to as data protection by design is actually data protection by default.

[138] See, Privacy legislation in Canada: Factsheet, https://www.priv.gc.ca/resource/fs-fi/02_05_d_15_e.asp, last accessed 1 March 2019).

[139] Personal Information Protection and Electronic Documents Act 2000 (SC 2000, c 5).

[140] Office to the Privacy Commissioner of Canada, *A Guide for Businesses and Organisations: Privacy Toolkit* (2014) 8. See also Office of the Information and Privacy Commissioner of Alberta, Office of the Privacy Commissioner of Canada and Office of the Information & Privacy Commissioner for British Columbia, "Getting Accountability Right with a Privacy Management Program" (2012) 1: "an accountable organisation must have in place appropriate policies and procedures that promote good practice which, taken as a whole, constitute a privacy management program".

[141] Office of the Information and Privacy Commissioner of Alberta, Office of the Privacy Commissioner of Canada and Office of the Information & Privacy Commissioner for British Columbia (n 140).

Furthermore, "accountability as PMP" is explicitly conceptualised as an exercise in risk management.[142] Finally, contrary to the GDPR, the alignment of business and regulatory goals is inherent to the accountability principle and is not subject to a specific data protection by design provision, thereby confirming the—somewhat—artificial distinction between the two.[143]

2.11.4 A similar regulatory oriented approach in Canada: Cavoukian's Privacy by Design

A similar approach has also been promoted by former Ontario Privacy Commissioner Ann Cavoukian. Cavoukian is known for having put forth on the front of the scene her own take on the risk management agenda, which she named privacy by design.[144] Her version of privacy by design is different than the one studied in the EU context. Cavoukian's privacy by design (PbD) is a sort of policy agenda on how to apply risk management at the data protection level. The fact that such PbD is constitutive of risk management has been made explicit in one document where she argues that the ISO 31000 standard for risk management should be used to implement her notion of PbD.[145] It is constituted of seven foundational principles.[146] In a nutshell it can be boiled down to a combination of accountability and the risk transformation that goes with it (Principles 1, 3, 4, 6) with the use of PETs and/or data protection by default (Principle 2).

2.11.5 The Revised OECD Guidelines

The original 1980 OECD "Guidelines on the Protection of Privacy and Transborder Flows of Personal Data" were revised in 2013, with risk management at their core.[147]

The way in which risk management is incorporated through the Guidelines is also through the principle of accountability. Whereas the accountability principle of the original Guidelines (Art 14) was alien to the risk management agenda (cf *supra*), the new Guidelines transform this accountability principle into "a means to promote and define organisational responsibility for privacy protection",[148] ie

142 ibid 1.

143 ibid 3.

144 See eg Ann Cavoukian, "Privacy by Design: The 7 Foundation Principles" (2009).

145 Information and Privacy Commissioner Ontario Canada, "Privacy Risk Management: Building Privacy Protection into a Risk Management Framework to Ensure That Privacy Risks Are Managed, by Default" (2010) 3.

146 Namely they are: Proactive not Reactive (Preventative not Remedial); Privacy as the Default Setting; Privacy Embedded into Design; Full Functionality—Positive-Sum, not Zero-Sum; End-to-End Security—Full Lifecycle Protection; Visibility and Transparency—Keep it Open Privacy; Respect for User Privacy—Keep it User-Centric; see Cavoukian (n 144) 2.

147 Recommendation of the Council concerning Guidelines governing the Protection of Privacy and Transborder Flows of Personal Data 2013.

148 OECD, Supplementary explanatory memorandum to the revised recommendation of the council concerning guidelines governing the protection of privacy and transborder flows of personal data 2013, 19, 23.

into risk management. Such transformation is undertaken by using privacy management programs (PMP) as an implementation of accountability (Art 15(a)). It is also quite clear that such accountability and PMP are risk-based. Article 15(a)(ii) provides that the intensity of the PMP is dependent upon the level of risk at stake, and safeguards should be adopted following a privacy risk assessment (Art 15(a)(iii)). The alignment of goals is inherent to the notion of accountability since Art 15(a)(iv) indicates that the PMP should be integrated into the controller's governance structure.

2.11.6 The APEC Privacy Framework: a more risk-prone risk-based approach?

The APEC adopted a Privacy Framework in 2005,[149] and updated it in 2015.[150]

The 2005 version has often been qualified as risk-based,[151] mainly because of two of its principles. Principle I is explicitly entitled "Preventing Harm". It acknowledges that the misuse of personal information can be harmful to data subjects, and should therefore be prevented, following a risk calculation. Whereas Principle I signals the presence of risk analysis as the technical-analytical component of the risk management agenda, Principle IX enshrines the principle of accountability as its organisational aspect. It states that data controllers should be accountable for complying with the framework. This latter provision can quite certainly be endowed with the organisational meaning and dimension of the risk management agenda. This is very clear in the 2015 overhaul of the Guidelines, which links accountability to privacy management programs.[152]

Furthermore, one can argue that the 2005 APEC is slightly different from the previous approaches. Whereas the GDPR and all the other frameworks limit the scope of risk issues of compliance, the APEC features a "riskier" iteration since some of the actual substantive provisions are also subject to a risk calculation.[153] In this sense it echoes the interpretation of the risk-based approach that certain lobbies and countries like Estonia (in the Council of the EU) had defended (cf *supra*). The 2015 version however, has been aligned with the regulatory focus of the risk-based approach from the GDPR.[154]

149 APEC Privacy Framework 2005.

150 APEC Privacy Framework 2015.

151 See Centre for Information Policy Leadership (n 90) 9.

152 APEC Privacy Framework 2015 (n 150).

153 Graham Greenleaf, "Five Years of the APEC Privacy Framework: Failure or Promise?" (2009) 25 Computer Law & Security Review 28, 30. Such an observation is without prejudice as to the actual level of protection afforded by the safeguards, which, accordingly, is rather shallow. See Graham Greenleaf, "APEC's Privacy Framework Sets a New Low Standard for the Asia-Pacific" in Andrew T Kenyon and Megan Richardson (eds), *New Dimensions in Privacy Law: International and Comparative Perspectives* (Cambridge University Press 2006).

154 APEC Privacy Framework 2015 (n 150).

2.12 Beyond the responsibilisation of the regulatees: internal controls, regulatory resources, and enforcement

The previous section has reviewed the meaning given to the risk-based approach across a number of statutes. Even if only the EU explicitly refers to it as the risk-based approach, these various statutes all provide for a risk transformation of the regulatees along the lines of the risk management agenda in order to endow them with regulatory responsibility, in view of a more effective implementation of existing principles. Such risk-based transformation of the regulatees activity is also predicated upon the notion of internal control, which were analysed more in detail through the ISO 31000 risk management Standard. In this sense, internal controls are crucial insofar as they constitute the concrete safeguards through which organisational activity is carried out as a matter of risk management. Simultaneously, these internal controls are also regulatory resources insofar as they are also used as safeguards to the ends of carrying out the regulatory tasks befalling upon the regulatees. However, the role of internal controls is not identical in all frameworks.

First, and taking the ISO 31000 Standard as a bottom line, one can observe that there are notable differences between the latter and data protection statutes. Canada's PMP is closest to the Standard, whereas the GDPR consists in a freer implementation thereof.

Second, the use of internal controls as a regulatory resource varies significantly amongst statutes. If, according to the articulation between meta regulation and the risk management agenda these internal controls are indeed recoded as regulatory resources (ie safeguards), these safeguards are not operationalised in an equal manner. In some cases, they are turned into fully-fledged collaborative safeguards between regulatees and regulators. In most cases however, they are purely internal to the regulatee, with the exception of data breach notification.

Finally, the role of the regulator should also be mentioned insofar as meta regulation is not antithetical to enforcement, and builds upon the so-called ladder of enforcement.

2.12.1 Internal controls: regulatory resource only—or most exclusively—at the internal level

Most of the data protection statutes only envisage internal controls as purely internal measures, simply geared towards the individual responsibility of accountable regulatees, at the exception of data breach notification.

This is the case for CoE 108+, the Revised OECD Guidelines, or Canada's PIPEDA. They all rely upon similar measures, which are essentially purely internal controls. They include employees training, or "setting up internal procedures to enable the verification and demonstration of compliance";[155] support from senior management, internal oversight mechanisms, ongoing monitoring, and improvement;[156] or designating one individual internally responsible for compliance matters.[157]

As one can see these are purely internal measures. They can be said to be regulatory resources insofar as they are instruments of improved compliance. Yet, they involve no interaction or joint operationalisation with the regulator. In all these cases, the only exception is the provision on data breach notification. Each of these instruments provide that in case of data breach, the data controller shall notify the regulator, provided the risk is high.[158]

It is fair to say that this iteration of the risk-based approach provides for only minimal collaboration—in the form of joint operationalisation of safeguards—between regulatees and regulators and one can therefore doubt its overall efficiency.

2.12.2 The GDPR: a much more collaborative iteration of the risk-based approach

In stark contrast to these statutes, and in addition to the purely internal controls which it provides for (which will be discussed more in detail *infra*), the GDPR provides for what is probably the most advanced collaboration between regulators and regulatees in the data protection meta regulation context. This is probably best epitomised by Art 31, which states that controllers should cooperate with regulators.

Article 30 is a good example of an internal control that can be seen both as a mandatory element of organisational design, and as a regulatory resource. On the one hand, controllers should maintain an internal record documenting their processing activities, and containing a number of information such as the controller's name and contact details; the purpose of the processing, etc (Art 30(1)). The ISO Risk Management Standard does not contain an explicit obligation to maintain a documentation of one's activities. However, such obligation underlies a number of other ones. The design of organisational accountability requires to understand the amount of risk its activities generate, which is typically done by setting up an inventory of the activities. It is also hard to conceive of efficient performance indicators without a clear view of the activities. Finally, the record appears of paramount importance with regards to review and monitoring tasks. On the other hand, and

[155] Convention 108 + Convention for the protection of individuals with regard to the processing of personal data (CETS No 223) (n 133).

[156] Art 15(a)(iv) and (vi) Revised OECD Guidelines

[157] Principle 4.1.1, Schedule 1 (Section 5) PIPEDA.

[158] See 15(a)(v) Revised OECD Guidelines, Art 7(2) Convention 108+, Principle 10.1(1), Schedule 1 (Section 5) PIPEDA. With Principle 10.1(3), Schedule 1 (Section 5) PIPEDA providing for the possible notification of the data subject.

following Art 30(4), such record should be made available to the supervisory authority upon request. As one can see, this element, which is crucial for the successful implementation of risk management, is used for the—regulatory—purpose of allowing the regulator to assess the regulatee's performance, or, as a safeguard meant to foster transparency.

The GDPR also contains a provision on data breach notification, providing both for a notification to the regulator and the data subject (Arts 33 and 34).

Data Protection Impact Assessments (DPIAs) are a risk management tool applied to data processing operations.[159] In addition to their role in the overall architecture of the GDPR, it is considered useful to dedicate a few lines to the history and emergence of DPIAs. The reason being that they can be considered the first risk management tool at the data protection level, and have often had a broader scope than what the GDPR formally assigns them.

Even though DPIAs can be traced as far back as the 1970s,[160] their emergence as an important data protection mechanism dates back to the mid-1990s, mainly in Anglo-Saxon countries (Australia, Canada, New-Zealand, and further on, the US), where they have been referred to as privacy impact assessments (PIAs).[161]

According to Tancock *et al.*, DPIAs find their origins in so-called technology assessment (TA). The latter can best be described as instruments used for the assessment of the social consequences (both benefits and harms) of technological innovation,[162] and further, EIA—Environmental Impact Assessments.[163]

Given that PIAs have emerged at the front of the scene in the mid-1990s, which is concomitant to the emergence of the risk management agenda (cf *supra*), one can therefore infer that they constitute the first application of risk management to the data protection field. That is probably the reason why they have consistently been described as an "early warning system".[164] In other words, very much in line with the risk management agenda's logic, they are the first signal of the transformation

[159] This has been confirmed by the Art 29 WP in its endorsement of the EU RFID PIA Framework, which argues that risk management is "an essential component of any Privacy and Data Protection Impact Assessment Framework". "Opinion 9/2011 on the Revised Industry Proposal for a Privacy and Data Protection Impact Assessment Framework for RFID Applications" 7, 5. See also David Wright and others, "SAPIENT, Deliverable 3.1 Privacy Impact Assessment and Smart Surveillance: A State of the Art Report" (2013) 10: "[D]PIAs developed as a risk management tool particularly targeted at information privacy."

[160] See Roger Clarke, "Privacy Impact Assessment: Its Origins and Development" (2009) 25 Computer Law & Security Review 123; Tancock, Pearson, and Charlesworth (n 117) 119.

[161] And in particular, in the aftermath of the "Privacy Issues Conference", held in Christchurch, NZ, which gave an important impetus for the worldwide adoption of DPIAs, see Nigel Waters, "Privacy Law and Policy Reporter" (1996) 3 Privacy Law and Policy Reporter 61; Blair Stewart, "PIAs—An Early Warning System" (1996) 3 Privacy Law and Policy Reporter; Elizabeth Longworth, "Notes on Privacy Impact Assessments", *Privacy Issues Forum* (1996). On the emergence of DPIAs, see also, Charles D Raab and Colin J Bennett, *The Governance of Privacy: Policy Instruments in Global Perspective* (MIT Press 2006); Bennett and others (n 67).

[162] Tancock, Pearson, and Charlesworth (n 117) 119.

[163] ibid.

[164] See Wright and others (n 159) 14.

of data controllers' activities as a matter of risk management. They are therefore to be performed at the very start of each new, planned processing operation.[165]

The EU has also adopted two DPIAs framework concerning two specific technologies: RFID (radio frequency identification),[166] and smart meters.[167] However, the adoption of these frameworks should mostly be seen as a methodological endeavour, in order to provide data controllers with a risk assessment methodology best suited to the technologies at stake.

In fact, if DPIAs can be considered the first embodiment of the risk management agenda in the data protection field, such embodiment remains partial and piecemeal, since they mostly consist in requiring data controllers to undertake a risk analysis at the start of each new processing operation. In contrast, the more recent accountability principle now features a fully-fledged risk transformation of the data controller. In this context, the role of DPIAs has somewhat shrank. Contrary to earlier experience where they entailed that a risk analysis be performed at the start of processing operations (an obligation now falling under the remit of the accountability principle), the GDPR conceives of them as a risk analysis exercise constitutive of a specific internal control. The latter is used as a regulatory resource, the goal of which is to replace the notification obligations mandated by the former EU Data Protection Directive. Recital 89 of the GDPR makes it explicit that DPIAs are meant to replace the general and indiscriminate obligation to notify the regulators, enshrined in Arts 18 and 19 of the Directive (and linked to Art 21 which provides for a publicly accessible register of such notifications). DPIAs must be performed only in cases of high risks (Art 35(1) and Art 35(3)). In place of such general notification, regulators should only be consulted (and possibly use their powers enshrined in Art 58) following a DPIA when the latter has not been able to transform the high risk into a lower one (Art 36(1)).[168,169] It follows that Art 35 on DPIAs

[165] Clarke (n 160).

[166] See European Commission, "Recommendation on the Implementation of Privacy and Data Protection Principles in Applications Supported by Radio-Frequency Identification" (2009); "Privacy and Data Protection Impact Assessment Framework for RFID Applications" (2011); Art 29 WP, "Opinion 9/2011 on the Revised Industry Proposal for a Privacy and Data Protection Impact Assessment Framework for RFID Applications" (n 159).

[167] See Smart Grid Task Force, "Data Protection Impact Assessment Template for Smart Grid and Smart Metering Systems" (2014); European Commission, Commission Recommendation of 10 October 2014 on the Data Protection Impact Assessment Template for Smart Grid and Smart Metering Systems (2014/724/EU) 2014 63; Art 29 WP, "Opinion 04/2013 on the Data Protection Impact Assessment Template for Smart Grid and Smart Metering Systems ("DPIA Template") Prepared by Expert Group 2 of the Commission's Smart Grid Task Force" (2013).

[168] For a confirmation of this interpretation of Art 36(1), see Art 29 WP, "Guidelines on Data Protection Impact Assessment (DPIA) and Determining Whether Processing Is "Likely to Result in a High Risk" for the Purposes of Regulation 2016/679" (n 89).

[169] These powers shall be discussed *infra*, but in a nutshell they include investigative powers (ie order the provision of information; carry out audits; notify controllers when they are infringing the Regulation; obtain access to relevant information, the controller's premises, and data processing equipment), corrective powers (ie warnings, reprimands, compliance orders, temporary or permanent ban, withdrawal of certification, administrative fines), and authorisation and advisory powers (ie advisory powers in the framework of Art 34, approval of codes of conduct, accredit certification bodies).

and Art 36 on prior consultation should be taken together, as constitutive of one type of formal safeguard, that overwrites not only the notification but also the prior checking mechanism (Art 20 Directive). Further collaboration and involvement of the regulators is embodied in their duty to establish a list of cases where DPIAs are required (Art 35(5)), and the faculty at their disposal to establish lists of cases where DPIAs are not required (Art 35(4)). One can also point to the existence of a non-exhaustive list of processing operations likely to present a high level of risk provided by the GDPR itself (Art 35(3)).

Articles 37 to 39 concern the Data Protection Officer (DPO). DPOs can be considered the equivalent of quality control or chief risk officers. As discussed *supra*, such officers have an essential role in the ecology of risk management as they are in charge of the whole process. Whereas the actual steps are to be performed by the concerned employees, such officers are entrusted with the task of making sure that risk management is correctly implemented and running smoothly within the organisation.[170] Article 39 concerns the DPO's tasks, and reflects the dual aspect of the DPO, both as a mechanism of organisational design and as a regulatory resource. Following Art 39(1)(b)), DPOs are responsible for monitoring compliance with the Regulation, typically a matter of internal controls, which includes the assignment of responsibilities, awareness-raising, training of staff, and the performance of internal audits. In terms of viewing DPOs as a regulatory resource, one can point to the fact that they are also entrusted with the task of acting as a contact point for the regulator, which they must consult and cooperate with (Art 39(1)(e)).

2.12.3 The risk-based approach: a piecemeal implementation of the risk management agenda?

The ISO 31000 Standard and the internal controls it features have been analysed as an embodiment of the risk management agenda. The risk-based approach, as an implementation of the latter should, at least in theory, provide for a quasi-total overlap. However, this is not universally the case. One can take the cases of PIPEDA and the GDPR.

As discussed, PIPEDA relies upon the articulation of the principle of accountability with the Privacy Management Program: a guidance document considered the official implementation of the principle. Interestingly, the PMP closely mirrors the ISO 31000 Standard, and is probably the most advanced standard for data protection risk management.[171] In a nutshell, the PMP is divided into two parts. The

[170] Art 29 GDPR. See also Art 29 WP, "Guidelines on Data Protection Officers ('DPOs')" (2016) 15: "the DPO cannot hold a position within the organisation that leads him or her to determine the purposes and the means of the processing of personal data".

[171] It is to be noted that the Office of the Privacy Commissioner for Personal Data of Hong Kong published a guidance on PMPs clearly inspired by the Canadian one "Privacy Management Programme: A Best Practice Guide" (2014). For a slightly outdated comparison of these PMPs taking into account

first part (building blocks) is about the programme itself and is also divided into two parts (one about organisational commitments, responsibilities, and ownership, the other one about the actual measures to be taken, which it refers to as "program controls"). The second part concerns the ongoing monitoring and reviewing of measures taken pursuant to the PMP.[172]

Contrary to PIPEDA's very close replication of the ISO 31000, the GDPR's take is more piecemeal. First, a number of internal controls featured in the ISO 31000 are simply absent from the GDPR. For instance, it is silent on the risk management plan, which is seen as critical in embedding risk management into the organisational structure and activities.[173] One can also mention a GDPR focus on external accountability through for instance certification (Arts 42 and 43), and possibly codes of conducts (Arts 40 and 41).[174] Yet, the focus on internal accountability is completely absent therefrom.[175] Finally one can also mention the emphasis on personnel training, which is also seen as essential by the ISO.[176] This should not be seen as redhibitory inasmuch as it is impossible for one single provision to be as complete as the whole Standard, and one could expect that this be remedied with additional guidance documents just like the Canadian PMP.[177] Second, the GDPR is also less stringent in the implementation of these controls. This is the case for instance with Art 24(2), which provides that data protection policies should be implemented only "where proportionate in relation to processing activities". However, the equivalent ISO's risk management policy is considered one of the cornerstones of organisation risk management and should always be implemented.[178] The contrast is probably most stark as far as the duties of constant monitoring and reviewing are concerned, which are essential to the ISO.[179] Taking the case of DPIAs, controllers have no obligation to document the process and keep such documentation (both are required by the ISO Standard). This also holds true for the review of the DPIA, which is left to the controller's discretion (Art 35(11)),[180]

the European Parliament's GDPR proposal, see Rolf H Weber, "Privacy Management Practices in the Proposed EU Regulation" (2014) 4 International Data Privacy Law 290.

[172] Office of the Information and Privacy Commissioner of Alberta, Office of the Privacy Commissioner of Canada and Office of the Information & Privacy Commissioner for British Columbia, "Privacy Management Program—At a Glance" (2012).

[173] ISO, "ISO: 31000 Risk Management—Principles and Guidelines" 2.

[174] The latter are indeed directly related to DPIAs, as elements to be taken into account when assessing the severity of the risk, see Art 35(8) GDPR.

[175] Contrary to the ISO, see ISO (n 173) 12.

[176] ibid 12–13.

[177] However, this has not been the case yet, and is not part of the EDPB's work programme for the period 2019/2020, see EDPB, "EDPB Work Program 2019/2020" (2019).

[178] ISO (n 173) 10–11.

[179] See ibid 12.

[180] Except in case of change to the risks created by the processing operations. Then a review is required.

and in general for the review of any measure taken pursuant to the accountability principle.[181] Another stark difference between the GDPR and the ISO 31000 is the role granted to the DPO/chief risk officer. Whereas following the ISO it is unthinkable to have proper risk management without such officers,[182] Art 37 provides for their mandatory designation only in a limited number of—risky—cases.[183] It is to be noted that earlier versions of the GDPR provided for much stringent collaboration, in particular compulsory documentation obligations for DPIAs along with review every third year.[184]

2.12.4 Enforcement: enforced self-regulation and the ladder of enforcement

As an implementation of meta regulation, the risk-based approach pertains to "enforced self-regulation" and is therefore not antithetical to enforcement. Even though it relies upon self-regulatory arrangements in the form of the risk management agenda, enforcement still has a role to play (cf ladder of enforcement). This is most clear in the GDPR for instance, where one of the objectives of the reform was clearly to improve the regulators' enforcement capabilities,[185] and which has resulted, among others, in more extensive investigative and corrective/enforcement powers (Arts 57 and 58 GDPR). Some of the other frameworks analysed in this section are also predicated upon seemingly sound enforcement competences.[186]

Pointing to the—sometimes—blurred lines between safeguards and enforcement, one can pay attention to the fact that accountable organisations must be able to demonstrate compliance. This can be taken as a means to create transparency, especially in view of documentation obligation and the disappearance of the general notification obligation,[187] or it can also be taken as a means to facilitate enforcement.[188]

The same can be said about audits or certifications schemes, which can be seen as safeguards, and in particular tokens of compliance jointly operated with regulators,[189] or as tools of delegated enforcement.[190]

[181] See Art 24(1) GDPR: "Those measures shall be reviewed and updated *where necessary*", author's emphasis.

[182] ISO (n 173) 11.

[183] eg data controller as public authority, large scale processing of sensitive data, see Art 37(1)(c).

[184] See European Commission (n 76).

[185] See eg European Commission (n 2) 18.

[186] See eg PIPEDA's Division 2; Convention 108+ Arts 12 and 15.

[187] In this sense, see Raphaël Gellert, "The Article 29 Working Party's Provisional Guidelines on Data Protection Impact Assessment" (2017) 2 European Data Protection Law Review 1.

[188] See eg Art 58(1)(a) GDPR; Art 15(b) Revised OECD Guidelines.

[189] See eg GDPR Arts 42–43.

[190] See eg PIPEDA 18(2).

2.13 Concluding thoughts on the risk-based approach

In sum, the risk-based approach to data protection consists in a "regulatory oriented" take on meta regulation, predicated upon the responsibilisation of the regulatee along the lines of the risk management agenda. This is usually done through the principle of accountability, with a few differences among statutes (eg only accountability or accountability and data protection by design as the embodiment of the alignment of goals). As has been shown, beyond this common core of regulatee responsibilisation, there are many finer grained differences and localisms pertaining to the degree of joint operationalisation of safeguards, or the extent to which such responsibilisation follows the ISO 31000 Standard, as well as the regulators' enforcement powers.

3. The standard setting oriented risk-based approach

3.1 Introduction

The previous section explored the risk-based approach, which it analysed as the implementation of meta regulation to data protection law, with a regulatory focus (ie a focus on compliance issues, on how to best implement existing standards and safeguards). The present section will discuss another strand of approaches to the risk-based approach that have put the focus on the standard setting function. Even though the regulatory dimension is not discarded—quite on the contrary—these approaches put the emphasis upon the potential of the risk-based approach as an alternative method for setting standards at the data protection level. In other words, this particular strand of the risk-based approach to data protection features a genuine change in terms of standard setting methods, shifting from command and control regulation to risk management tools. That is, shifting from a model of regulation whereby rules/standards are determined by the legislator, to one where such rules/standards are determined by regulated entities following a risk management process.

Because they put the emphasis upon the standard setting aspect of the risk management agenda, these approaches thus see it as the solution to the remaining issues associated with the "diagnosis-prescription" flaw of meta regulation. Namely, the choice of adequate standards, those that will lead to the desired behaviour, and which in turn will lead to the achievement of regulatory goals, and which are, for the most part, encapsulated in the so-called data protection "core principles". These approaches never made it past policy documents or academic publications. They all emerged around 2013/2014 at the height of the public debate on the topic. One can further distinguish between an American approach to standard setting through risk, mainly inspired by Microsoft and other similar tech companies (and endorsed in several White House official publications), and an EU approach, mainly put forth by think tanks and academics. The American approach is very much risk prone and echoes the neoliberal ethos of the risk management agenda, whereas the EU approach is less overtly risk prone. Yet its overoptimistic goal of "making things right", strongly echoes the natural compliance ideals that pervade meta regulation.

3.2 The standard setting oriented risk-based approach as a response to regulatory failures

This type of risk-based approach centred around standard setting has emerged in the wake of what its proponents see as flaws associated with standard setting in data protection as command and control. These have already been discussed in Chapter 3, but will briefly be restated here in order to provide some background to the discussion.

The first type of challenges relates to implementation shortcomings, in particular in a big data and internet of things (IoT) context. The second set of challenges is more principled insofar as the shortcomings it leads to seems to indicate that the very logic underpinning data protection standards is opposed to the logic underlying big data.

3.2.1 Implementation shortcomings

These shortcomings happen in situations where the involvement of the data subject is required, as is notably the case with consent or the data subject information rights. The proponents of this approach argue for instance that providing data subjects with adequate information and consent notices is extremely difficult given the complexity of contemporary processing operations (see also herein below). Furthermore, it is becoming increasingly difficult to trace data subjects in order to ask them for consent since in many cases data it is collected from a variety of sources not involving the data subject (eg sensors or inferred from existing data).[191]

3.2.2 Conflicting logic(s): purpose requirement vs purposeless processing, or the conflict between collection based and use based risk assessment

This category of issues is different. Whereas the previous one illustrates shortcomings in the implementation of existing standards, this category challenges the very assumptions underlying some standards. Namely, these shortcomings are based

[191] Fred H Cate and Viktor Mayer-Schönberger, "Data Use and Impact Global Workshop" (2013) 9; Centre for Information Policy Leadership, "Big Data and Analytics: Seeking Foundations for Effective Privacy Guidance" (2013) 12.

upon the trope dispelled in Chapter 3 following which big data is purposeless (cf *supra*: it doesn't collect data to answer pre-existing question, but instead collects data to find answers to question that were not yet envisaged). According to them, such logic goes counter to that of several standards, which are directly based on the logic of purpose requirement, and which should therefore be discarded.

Arguably, two types of standards require the existence of a purpose: those concerned with the legitimation of the processing—among which consent is the most prominent one,[192] and the purpose limitation and specification principle. In a nutshell, consent must be specific to each separate processing purpose (and therefore be collected at the beginning of each new processing).[193] This purpose specificity sits uneasily with the open-ended nature of big data processing operations, and results in a dilemma. Either try to accommodate such open-endedness in the information notices provided to the data subject, which is extremely complicated—if not impossible—to achieve in practice.[194] Or, ask for a renewed consent each time it is deemed necessary. However, this last option also faces a number of hurdles (consent fatigue, impossibility to retrace the original data subject in an IoT context, etc).[195] The same holds true for the principle of purpose limitation and specification, requiring that purposes be specified at the time of collection, and data should not be further processed for incompatible purposes, and which prohibit the formulation of overbroad purposes which would justify any further processing.[196]

In sum, this objection based on conflicting logics can be seen as twofold. On the one hand, it pertains to what some of the very proponents of the risk-based approach explicitly refer to as "privacy pragmatism".[197] Following this stance, standards embodying the requirement that the life cycle of processing operations be governed by a unifying purpose are simply out of touch with contemporary data processing operations and should therefore be discarded. On the other hand, one can also see a more principled objection. By requiring a link between future uses and the initial purpose, these standards do not give account of the contextuality that is necessary to the ends of determining the harmfulness/lawfulness of future

[192] In contrast, the US system for the processing of data by private parties has been entirely built around informed consent (or consent coupled to transparency obligations under the form of privacy notices), which is commonly known as "notice and choice". See Federal Trade Commission, "Privacy Online: A Report to Congress" (1998); Federal Trade Commission, "Privacy Online: Fair Information Practices in the Electronic Marketplace" (2000); Robert Gellman, "Fair Information Practices: A Basic History" (2015), http://www.bobgellman.com/rg-docs/rg-FIPShistory.pdf, last accessed 15 March 2019.

[193] See Art 29 WP, "Opinion 15/2011 on the Definition of Consent" (2011) paras 9, 17–19.

[194] Cate and Mayer-Schönberger (n 191) 7, 8–9. Therefore a consent is specific enough when it encompasses the future operations that fall within the data subject's reasonable expectations, Art 29 WP (n 193) 17.

[195] Cate and Mayer-Schönberger (n 191) 8–9.

[196] ibid 9–10.

[197] Craig Mundie, "Privacy Pragmatism" *Foreign Affairs* (2014), see <https://www.foreignaffairs.com/articles/2014-02-12/privacy-pragmatism>, last accessed 19 March 2019.

uses. In other words, the absence of a unifying purpose does not mean, *ipso facto*, that the processing operation will be harmful for the data subjects. The dual nature of these objections can be seen in discussions around the data minimisation principle. Some have argued that the requirement to minimise data is simply unworkable in a world of big data, which is predicated on an opposite principle of data "maximisation".[198] Others however, have pleaded for an adaptation of data minimisation, which should focus on the minimisation of use in each specific context (rather than *in abstracto*).[199]

3.3 The Microsoft approach

The first approach explicitly referring to itself as a risk-based approach (and conceiving of itself as concerned with standard setting) emerged in 2012 at the initiative of the Microsoft corporation (Microsoft) with the support of important data protection voices (eg Craig Mundie, Peter Cullen, Fred Cate, Viktor Mayer-Schönberger). A series of worldwide workshops were held in such places as Washington, DC, Brussels, Singapore, Sydney, or São Paulo. These workshops culminated with a final workshop at Microsoft Headquarters in Redmond, Washington (US), where the basis of the risk-based approach was laid down.[200]

Building upon the challenges described *supra*, the Microsoft approach argues that rather than telling data controllers exactly what standards they should apply, "laws should specify objectives", which controllers would achieve through the use of risk analysis, thereby leading to appropriate processing of data.[201] This is exactly the logic of meta regulation described *supra*.

3.3.1 A use-based risk-based approach

More specifically, the Microsoft approach advocates for a risk-based approach which is use-based, that is, that focuses on each operation (or use) taking place within the processing life cycle as a distinct processing, taken in isolation.

According to its proponents, this approach, which consists in discarding the requirement that there be a continuity of purpose throughout a processing operation life cycle, is called a "use-based risk-based approach",[202] and therefore seems

[198] See Centre for Information Policy Leadership (n 191) 13.

[199] Cate and Mayer-Schönberger (n 191) 16.

[200] Fred H Cate and Viktor Mayer-Schönberger, "Tomorrow's Privacy Notice and Consent in a World of Big Data" (2013) 3 International Data Privacy Law 67; Fred H Cate, Peter Cullen, and Viktor Mayer-Schönberger, "Data Protection Principles for the 21st Century: Revising the 1980 OECD Guidelines" (2014). A similar approach has also been deployed by the World Economic Forum "Rethinking Personal Data: A New Lens for Strengthening Trust" (2014). Because of their similarity, we only address the Microsoft approach.

[201] Cate and Mayer-Schönberger (n 191) v, 15.

[202] ibid iii.

to discard the collection step as the step that determines the (im)possibility of further uses. One must indeed keep in mind that the life cycle of a processing operation starts with the collection of data.[203] This means that the lawfulness of further processing operations is assessed with regards to the purpose that is determined at the collection stage. In other words, one can argue that the "use-based risk-based approach" puts an end to the continuity of purpose throughout the data processing lifecycle. In this sense, the collection step loses its status as *primus inter pares*, whereby it was the *locus* for determining the purpose of the whole processing cycle. If by forces of circumstances collection remains the first step, it nonetheless becomes unrelated to the further steps, and can simply be seen as the first use of a series of unrelated uses.[204]

3.3.2 A neoliberal take on risk analysis

However, this "use-based risk-based approach" does more than disembedding the processing life cycle from a unifying purpose. One can also argue that it embodies a good example of the neoliberal take on risk analysis in the context of risk management, which is oriented towards profitability, value creation, and the achievement of organisational goals.

As one remembers, the section dedicated to standard setting demonstrated that standard setting is actually sub-divided into two separate standard setting operations, or balancing tests. In the context of data protection, the first sub-operation falls within the remit of the data legitimacy principle, which determines whether the envisaged processing is lawful, that is, whether there is a need for a data processing at all. The second sub-operation falls within the remit of the data quality principle. It is based upon the premise that the processing can take place. Its function, then, is to spell out the modalities of the processing, and whether there is a need to process data at all to reach the goal pursued, no matter how legitimate the processing is.

The use-based risk-based approach argues that, with regard to consent, it "shift[s] the burden of protecting personal data away from individuals toward data

[203] See Art 2(b) of the EU data protection Directive: "'processing of personal data' ("processing") shall mean any operation or set of operations which is performed upon personal data, whether or not by automatic means, such as collection, recording, organization, storage, adaptation or alteration, retrieval, consultation, use, disclosure by transmission, dissemination or otherwise making available, alignment or combination, blocking, erasure or destruction".

[204] This analysis is confirmed by the fact that the criticism of the Microsoft approach is less directed to the collection stage as such than to "the terms under which the data were originally collected", Cate and Mayer-Schönberger (n 191) 8, 9, 10, 14. In this sense, we have to disagree with Hoofnagle when he says that "in a use-regulation world, companies may collect any data they wish but would be banned from certain uses of the data". Chris Jay Hoofnagle, "The Potemkinism of Privacy Pragmatism" *Slate* (2014) 1. Since collection is just another use, some collections may be barred from the outset, cf hereunder. That being said, the number of instances where the first use would be unlawful is so limited, that in practice, Hoofnagle's objection is true.

users".[205] This is so because, as explained herein above, consent is unworkable insofar as it is predicated upon an assessment of the whole processing life cycle's purpose, which is to be made by the data subject. Following this reasoning, if consent as a legitimising ground is discarded, then another ground should be chosen, and would fall within the data controller's responsibility. And given that this approach focuses on uses, we would shift from a situation whereby data subjects assess legitimacy once for the whole life cycle, towards a situation whereby the data controller assesses the legitimacy of each data use taken as such. However, when one looks at the document that can be considered as the official template operationalising the use-based risk-based approach the situation is different.[206] Whereas in the current situation, it is up to controllers to demonstrate that there is a legitimate basis to the processing by relying upon one of the legitimate grounds (cf *supra*), this approach inverts the situation: the legitimacy of the processing is presumed. As they put it, controllers "almost always have a legitimate reason for collecting or disclosing personal [data]".[207] In other words, the processing is always deemed legitimate except in a number of limited situations, such as when the law prohibits specific uses, or when the data are fraudulently collected.[208] This approach thus seems to take the advantages of focusing on uses as isolated processing operations, without the inconveniences that go along. More importantly, because it deems the processing to be always legitimate, it clearly favours the processing of data and thus, the taking of risk in the fashion described in Chapter 4. Additional evidence of this neoliberal take on risk analysis can be found in the 2014 Report of the US President's Council of Advisors on Science and Technology (PCAST)'s on big data.[209] This report is very much in line with the Microsoft approach and argues that the analysis of data should not be considered as a use/processing operation, which would therefore fall out of any regulatory framework.[210]

3.3.3 From a neoliberal take on risk analysis to a deregulatory approach?

Thus far, the Microsoft approach—which describes itself as a use-based risk-based approach—has been characterised as a neoliberal take on risk analysis, because it simultaneously discards standards requiring a unifying purpose for the complete processing life cycle and presumes each processing to have a legitimate basis.

[205] Cate and Mayer-Schönberger (n 191) 8.

[206] Cate, Cullen, and Mayer-Schönberger (n 200).

[207] ibid 16.

[208] ibid.

[209] US President's Council of Advisors on Science and Technology, "Report to the President—Big Data and Privacy: A Technological Perspective" (2014).

[210] See also Chris Jay Hoofnagle, "How the Fair Credit Reporting Act Regulates Big Data", *Future of Privacy Forum Workshop on Big Data and Privacy: Making Ends Meet* (2013) http://papers.ssrn.com/sol3/papers.cfm?abstract_id=2432955, last accessed 15 March 2019; Chris Jay Hoofnagle, "Big Brother's Little Helpers: How ChoicePoint and Other Commercial Data Brokers Collect and Package Your Data for Law Enforcement" (2004) 29 North Carolina Journal of International Law and Commercial Regulation 595.

However, it is possible to argue that it goes even further in its encouragement of risk taking (and the realisation of organisational objectives).

In order to do this, one has to remember the discussion held in Chapters 1 and 2 on safeguards. These chapters demonstrated that the provisions on standard setting could actually be boiled down to a combination of a balancing exercise (the core of the standard setting operation), and a number of safeguards (eg fairness, minimisation, etc). A standard is therefore set when both elements are combined, which allows for a determination of which type of processing operations are acceptable or not. One must also remember the criticisms addressed to—command and control—regulation: standards are "carved in stone" insofar as they apply linearly to any type of processing operation concerned. One of the appeals of meta regulation and its reliance upon risk analysis as a new method for setting standards is precisely the fact that it allows for a determination of standards on a case-by-case (ie contextual) basis, with a particular emphasis on the choice of the most adequate safeguards. Further, it has also been demonstrated that in the context of the risk management agenda, risk analysis is turned towards value creation. This, one can argue, is made possible not only because risk analysis is modelled after financial economics, which favour risk taking and financial returns (in this case the presumption of legitimacy of every use), but also because it is not predicated upon substantive safeguards, but rather, on formal safeguards. The latter, rather than focusing upon how best to address and mitigate risks, focuses upon the legitimacy of the process itself (thus arguing that risks will be adequately mitigated provided that the process is of sufficient quality and legitimacy). Accordingly, it is purported that the Microsoft approach displays a similar focus on process. It does appear that not a single substantive safeguard is featured in the document used as the official template operationalising the use-based risk-based approach. Instead, it simply requires the taking of risk mitigation measures where needed but gives no indication at all as to what these mitigation measures might consist in.[211] Further, another discussion document explicitly proves the present point. Among the possible mitigation measures to be taken, this document simply advocates for measures linked to the de-identification of personal data,[212] and for measures of organisational design such as internal oversight mechanisms, which obviously put the emphasis on the process rather than on the substance.[213] Finally, and somehow paradoxically, the Microsoft approach confirms one of the main ideas put forth in this book, namely,

[211] Cate, Cullen, and Mayer-Schönberger (n 200) 17–18.

[212] In particular so-called practical de-identification, which combines technical measures of de-identification with contractual obligations not to re-identify. On this topic see Federal Trade Commission, "Protecting Consumer Privacy in an Era of Rapid Change—A Proposed Framework For Businesses And Policymakers" (2012); FTC, "Data Brokers—A Call for Transparency and Accountability" (2014), and also Peter Leonard, "Customer Data Analytics: Privacy Settings for "Big Data" Business" (2014) 4 International Data Privacy Law 53.

[213] Cate and Mayer-Schönberger (n 191) 13–14.

that data protection law has always been about the regulation of harms stemming from data processing operations. As it puts it, the goal of this approach consists in "recaptur[ing] the early focus on data protection in Europe and the United States on risk assessment to prevent harm, rather than on protecting individual privacy rights".[214] Yet, this moment of conceptual clarity is used to further undermine data protection insofar as it is meant to limit the scope of data subject rights to situations of high risks.[215] Yet, it is doubtful that limiting such safeguards to situations of high risks would lead to an adequate level of data protection. It would most likely make processing operations even more opaque, and would leave those data subjects wishing to challenge the processing with court proceedings as their only recourse, bearing in mind the difficulties of such endeavours (cf herein below).

For all the reasons discussed herein above, it would appear that the Microsoft use-based risk analysis is geared towards allowing as much processing as possible to take place, and would offer only scant protection. In this sense, the Microsoft risk-based approach fully espouses the notion of privacy pragmatism referred to herein above. Its ambition seems less to use risk analysis as a method to find new standards that would—more—adequately address the harms entailed by big data processing operations, than to simply discard any standard that doesn't allow for big data.

On this basis, some have argued that this approach is constitutive of a deregulatory agenda.[216] The basic tenet of the argument is the following. In practice, this use-based risk-based approach allows data controllers to collect any data they wish (except rare prohibitions) and to subject them to any further use they wish. Indeed, every collection/use is presumed legitimate, and it falls within the discretion of the controllers to determine what uses are appropriate (which they will do through an assessment of the risks and benefits), knowing that the safeguards at their disposal are marginal and of limited efficiency (since they are exclusively process-based). Thus, looking at it this way, it is well a deregulatory exercise since in practice all the major safeguards are simply discarded. The only thing that stands before the processing of one's data is the result of the controller's risk analysis. In this regard, Hoofnagle gives the example of the US Fair Credit Reporting Act (FCRA), a sectorial statute that regulates the processing of data in the fields of employment, credit, and tenancy.[217] According to him, the FCRA embodies this use-based

[214] ibid 15.

[215] ie those processing "affecting the education, employment, physical or mental health, financial position, or legally protected rights" of the data subject. Cate, Cullen, and Mayer-Schönberger (n 200) 18–19.

[216] Hoofnagle (n 204); Ann Cavoukian, "Evolving FIPPs: Proactive Approaches to Privacy, Not Privacy Paternalism" in Serge Gutwirth, Ronald Leenes, and Paul De Hert (eds), *Reforming European Data Protection Law* (Springer 2015); Ann Cavoukian, Alexander Dix, and Khaled El Emam, "The Unintended Consequences of Privacy Paternalism" (2014); Hoofnagle, "How the Fair Credit Reporting Act Regulates Big Data" (n 210).

[217] Hoofnagle (n 204).

logic since it contains no meaningful safeguard, with the counterpart consisting of heightened responsibility and accountability obligations for the data controllers. This statute has been enacted since 1970, and the last forty years of experience show that it has provided no meaningful protection to data subjects. Cavoukian argues that this absence of safeguards directly affects the preventative nature of data protection, which, under such regime would become reactive/*ex post* and would simultaneously shift the burden of proof from the controllers to the data subjects, who would then have to demonstrate the existence of harm.[218] Indeed, data protection can be said to be preventative precisely because of the existence of its safeguards: it suffices that a safeguard has been violated in order to grant compensation to the data subject, irrespective of whether the latter has effectively suffered harm. However, once all the substantive safeguards (constitutive of standard setting provisions) have been removed, the only way for a data subject to contest the validity of a processing operation is to prove the existence of a harm. However, two factors stand in the way. First, since there is no commonly accepted list of harms, it is very difficult for data subjects to invoke a harm before the courts, regardless of the reality of that harm.[219] In the US context, such harms are indeed defined very narrowly, with a quasi-exclusive focus on economic injury.[220] Hoofnagle mentions the US Supreme Court case of *Robins v Spokeo*.[221] In this case, Robins sued Spokeo (an online "people search engine" that sells information about individuals based on publicly available data), for maintaining inaccurate records about him, arguing that it directly contributed to his unemployment. However, Robins has been unable to show any economic injury, and following Spokeo should therefore be barred from a legal standing. In this case, the US Supreme Court upheld Spokeo's position. Second, if a harm were proven, the data subject must still be able to show the causality link between the harm and the data use, which is notoriously difficult, in particular in the current technological context, characterised by global complex information systems the functioning of which is opaque both to the data subject and the data controller.[222]

3.3.4 Concluding remarks on the Microsoft risk-based approach

The Microsoft/use-based risk-based approach is an interesting case study because it puts the notion of a risk-based approach to data protection to the fore,

[218] Cavoukian (n 216) 301–02. On the fact that data protection core principles can be seen as putting the burden of proof onto the data controller, see Julie E Cohen, "The Regulatory State in the Information Age" (2016) 17 Theoretical Inquiries in Law 369. On the preventative nature of safeguards and of regulation more in general, see Chapter 1.

[219] Cavoukian (n 216) 301.

[220] See eg Dana Post, "Plaintiffs Alleging Only 'Future Harm' Following a Data Breach Continue to Face a High Bar" , IAPP Privacy Advisor, January 29, 2014, https://iapp.org/news/a/plaintiffs-alleging-only-future-harm-following-a-data-breach-continue-to-fa, last accessed 19 February 2019.

[221] USSC, *Spokeo Inc v Robins*, No 13–1339, 16 May 2016.

[222] Cavoukian (n 216) 301.

and because it also envisages such risk-based approach from the perspective of standard setting. Something the risk-based approach adopted in the EU context and in the other described statutes falls short of. The study of this approach also confirms the description of risk analysis tools within the risk management agenda as oriented towards risk taking, profitability, and the realisation of organisational objectives. Finally, even though this approach focuses mainly upon risk analysis, one can see that it is not possible to disentangle risk analysis from the broader risk management agenda and the latter's regulatory function. The Microsoft approach indeed argues that the shift towards use-based risk-based analysis will "shift more of the burden for being accountable for data processing activities away from both regulators and individuals".[223] In other words, adopting risk analysis entails per se to become accountable, ie to become a naturally compliant entity turned inside out through the risk management agenda. This is why the Microsoft approach argues that risk analysis should be articulated with some of the usual internal controls used as regulatory resources, such as audits or internal documentation.[224] Further evidence of this is provided by the role foreseen for regulators, which also espouses the managerialisation of regulatory activity discussed in Chapter 4. Their bureaucratic tasks should be reduced, and they should focus only on high risk cases (the famous "selective to be effective" assertion).

However, if the Microsoft approach was the first risk-based approach with a focus on the standard setting function, others have emerged in the meantime. As demonstrated, the Microsoft approach encourages risk taking to such an extent that it amounts in reality to a privacy pragmatism,[225] the goal of which is simply to discard any standard that would stand in the way of big data processing operations—and can thus be qualified as deregulatory. These other approaches are less risk prone and may be more genuine insofar as they do want to use the advantages of risk analysis and the contextuality that goes along with it as a standard setting method in order to devise new, more adequate standards. Yet, they also suffer from shortcomings pertaining to the risk management agenda logic.

3.4 A new pragmatism: less risky risk and more optimistic approaches

3.4.1 Presenting new pragmatisms

This section introduces two similar approaches insofar as even though they share the premises of the Microsoft approach,[226] the solutions they put forth are much

[223] Cate and Mayer-Schönberger (n 191) 17.
[224] ibid.
[225] Mundie (n 197).
[226] In terms of the pressures new processing practices put on the data protection principles Lokke Moerel, *Big Data Protection—How to Make the Draft EU Regulation on Data Protection Future Proof*

more balanced. One can argue that these approaches are underpinned by what one may refer to as another brand of pragmatism. Contrary to the pragmatism purported by the Microsoft approach, which consists in discarding any type of standard that would stand in the way of big data processing operation, the present kind of pragmatism aims at "making things right". In other words, its aim is to find new standards that would allow for big data analytics, whilst also ensuring an adequate level of protection. Thus, instead of arguing that any data use is legitimate per definition, they seek to find new mechanisms to ensure their legitimacy. Equally, and in addition to suggesting new safeguards, they seek to make the exercise of consent and data subject rights more practical rather than eliminating them altogether. To the knowledge of the author, one can identify the Centre for Information and Policy Leadership,[227] and Lokke Moerel,[228] as proponents of such pragmatism.

In 2015, the CIPL started a new project around big data.[229] In the white papers partaking of this project, it spells out a vision of accountability/risk management, which also includes its standard setting function through risk analysis. The CIPL reiterates that risk management is at the heart of accountability, and that the extent of accountability and the organisational design measures it leads to should follow from the latter.[230] However, it also goes further and argues that given the pressures that big data, the internet of things, etc put on "traditional privacy principles such as notice, consent, purpose specification, and collection limitation", the latter should be open to "flexible, context-specific, and creative interpretation and implementation".[231] This is clearly a call to use risk management for purposes of standard setting. The Centre argues that risk management can perform this standard setting function through a renewed focus on the principle of fair processing, which should be understood in a similar fashion as the FTC's fairness standard.[232] Further, such fairness principle should be coupled to a resorting to ethics (or data ethics), since such ethics would precisely be instrumental in determining the fairness of planned processing operations, and hence, the necessary standards and safeguards.[233] Discussing the opportunity of resorting to such fairness principle lies outside the

(Tilburg University 2014) 53, or on the need to shift the focus towards data uses in the sense of focusing on the context of each specific processing operation ibid 52–53. Identical points are made in Centre for Information Policy Leadership, "The Role of Risk Management" (2016) 4–7, 13.

[227] Centre for Information Policy Leadership, "The Role of Enhanced Accountability in Creating a Sustainable Data-Driven Economy and Information Society" (2015).

[228] Moerel (n 226).

[229] See Centre for Information Policy Leadership, "Three Solutions for Protecting Privacy in a World of Big Data" (2015).

[230] Centre for Information Policy Leadership (n 227) 4.

[231] ibid 9.

[232] Such point of view has also been made by the UK ICO in its 2014 big data report, see ICO, "Big Data and Data Protection" (2014).

[233] Centre for Information Policy Leadership (n 227) 4–5.

scope of the present book, which provides a different view as to the standard setting function in data protection.[234] What is more interesting on the other hand is the new types of standards and safeguards such an approach leads to. One example is what it refers to as a "new transparency", and which can be understood as risk-based transparency. Instead of trying to accurately and exhaustively describe all potential processing operations, such transparency would provide the data subject with an assessment of the benefits and the harms of such operation, including in cases of "unexpected, out-of-context, and non-obvious future uses". It would also explain how the controller would mitigate the potential harms stemming from such processing operations.[235]

Lokke Moerel has adopted a similar approach, putting the emphasis on the need to shift from a static and linear method of standard setting towards one that is contextual and dynamic.[236] Therefore, and similarly to the Microsoft approach, she also argues that one should not undertake a standard setting for the whole processing operation as such (which entails that there is a unifying purpose underpinning the whole processing). Instead, a standard setting operation should be performed for each stage of the processing taken individually, which allows to take the context into account,[237] and thus to show that different stages of the processing present various degrees of risk that warrant different types of safeguards.[238] Yet, she also explicitly rejects the Microsoft, use-based approach, not least on the basis that the level of protection it affords is too scant.[239] Thus, among the different solutions she puts forth, she argues—like the CIPL—that in cases where consent is not practicable, the legitimate interest of the controller appears as a useful alternative.[240] Also, the data minimisation principles might be applied more or less stringently depending upon each separate phase of the processing and its context.[241] Finally, she also introduces additional safeguards that can be used when setting standards. These include surprise minimisation, creepiness threshold, or good data stewardship.[242]

It is to be observed that these two approaches are not identical, and that overall, Moerel seems to be more risk prone than the Centre.[243] For instance, the CIPL's view of accountability related obligations is very consistent. Moerel's view instead is much more lenient insofar as she gives much more leverage to data controllers.

[234] As was described *supra*, such fairness standard amounts to a balancing test, which is already present in data protection law, and is operated through different provisions.

[235] Centre for Information Policy Leadership (n 227) 3.

[236] Moerel (n 226) 50, 52–53.

[237] ibid 58.

[238] ibid 57–58.

[239] ibid 58.

[240] ibid 58–59.

[241] ibid 57.

[242] ibid 62.

[243] Not least because the CIPL's approach is thus far more succinct.

This is epitomised by the fact that she argues in favour of the deletion of documentation obligations, which are crucial to meta regulation.[244] Further, whereas Moerel explicitly argues for a risk-based approach that is use based (even though not in the same permissive way as the Microsoft approach),[245] the CIPL's position does not seem to go that far. Finally, one can also argue that Moerel's approach is not conceptually consistent. Whereas she indeed seems to argue that in order to determine the most appropriate standards one should rely upon a balancing test—which, similarly to the present author, she locates into Art 5(1)(c) GDPR, she fails to see that standard setting involves two balancing tests (as demonstrated *supra*).[246] If this conceptual approach were to be followed, this would logically mean that Moerel considers that all processing operations are legitimate per se (since no first balancing is needed). Yet, Moerel also advocates for mechanisms to determine such legitimacy (hence the contradiction). As a matter of fact, many contributors to the debate who argue for accountability (and hence risk management)-based solutions often fail to see that a consistent approach to standard setting entails two balancing tests.[247]

3.4.2 New pragmatisms and the ideal of natural compliance at the heart of meta regulation

Finally, some remarks on the logic of such pragmatism are warranted. It has been opposed to the Microsoft pragmatism, insofar as the latter simply seems to discard standards/safeguards when they do not allow for big data processing operations, whereas the present kind of pragmatism aims at "making things right", that is, to always find the appropriate standards/safeguards so that big data processing operations can always take place. However, such kind of pragmatism is also not void of shortcomings, and one could argue that its optimism stands as the counterpart of Microsoft's cynicism.

In theory the point of the risk-based approach is to determine which standards are most efficient and most adapted to the harms at stake. From this vantage point one sees clearly that Microsoft's pragmatism certainly does not lead to this type of outcome (since it simply discards any safeguards standing in the way of processing operations). Yet, one could also argue that CIPL's and Moerel's optimistic pragmatism can be subject to the same type of criticism. It is indeed very hard to pretend that, for every single processing, one could find a safeguard that would

[244] Moerel (n 226) 61.

[245] She has developed her use-based argument more in detail in the following publication: Lokke Moerel and Corien Prins, "Privacy Voor de Homo Digitalis: Proeve van Een Nieuw Toetsingskader Voor Gegevensbescherming in Het Licht van Big Data En Internet of Things" in Nederlandse Juristen-Vereniging (ed), *Homo Digitalis* (Wolters Kluwer 2016).

[246] Moerel (n 226) 57.

[247] See eg P Balboni and others, "Legitimate Interest of the Data Controller New Data Protection Paradigm: Legitimacy Grounded on Appropriate Protection" (2013) 3 International Data Privacy Law 244.

appropriately protect data subjects whilst also allowing the processing to go on to its full extent. The idea of contextuality at the heart of the risk-based approach as a standard setting method precisely entails that one must go into the detail of each processing, and determine in each case whether there are some appropriate safeguards and, in this light, whether the processing should be pursued. In some cases, it will be possible to find adequate safeguards that will make it possible to pursue the processing with little to no changes, in other cases adopting adequate safeguards will entail to—substantially—modify the processing (possibly abandoning some operations), whereas in other cases it will not be possible to find adequate safeguards and the processing should not be further pursued.

In sum, one can argue that Microsoft's cynical pragmatism and CIPL's and Moerel's optimistic pragmatism are counterparts insofar as both reject the current method of standard setting on the ground that is not contextual enough and yet propose solutions that are... not contextual either (ie discard all safeguards, or pretend that it is always possible to authorise processing operations to their full extent and to have adequate protection).[248] This contradiction is maybe best epitomised by Moerel's arguments for adopting the risk-based approach. On the one hand, she argues that the command and control method of standard setting should be abandoned on the account that it is not contextual and that technology itself is contextual and non-deterministic.[249] Yet, on the other hand she argues that the risk-based approach should be adopted on the basis of very deterministic accounts of technology, since not doing so would be "against the technical imperative".[250]

[248] One will observe that the type of claim purported by the optimistic pragmatism is identical to the risk management agenda's claim that risks will always be fully and adequately addressed through process based measures (cf *supra*).

[249] Moerel (n 226) 1. She even includes reference to the famous Collingridge dilemma ibid, see David Collingridge, *The Social Control of Technology* (Frances Pinter 1980).

[250] Moerel (n 226) 53.

6

Risk and the risk-based approach

Between data protection risks and compliance risks

It is helpful to review suggestions that have been made to deal with the matter of protecting data subjects against harms[1]

1. Introduction: various notions of risk at play

The goal of this chapter is to understand the notion of risk at play in the risk-based approach. As was alluded in Chapter 5 already, the risk-based approach to data protection is only a piecemeal implementation of meta regulation, which focuses primarily on how to better comply with the existing data protection framework, how to better implement its provisions. This focus on compliance can be understood in two ways. From the "inner" perspective of the risk-based approach itself (be it in the General Data Protection Regulation—GDPR—or other statutes), the soundness of existing "core" data protection principles is not questioned, well on the contrary. They seem future-proof, not least because of their technological neutrality.[2] From an "external" perspective, the Article 29 Working Party (Art 29 WP) emphasised the nature of data protection as a fundamental right of the EU, and hence its rights-based nature insofar as it is meant to provide an even level of protection to all.[3]

Because meta regulation relies by definition upon risk management and ends-up nonetheless transforming the whole data protection framework as risk-based, it leads to the following question: what is the notion of risk at the heart of the risk-based approach? As already indicated, the risk-based approach is predicated upon a notion of compliance risk, which is the only one able to allow for such a piecemeal implementation of meta regulation, and in so doing, allows for a reconciliation of

[1] US Department of Health Education & Welfare, *Records, Computers, and the Rights of Citizens* (The MIT Press 1973) 2.

[2] See eg European Commission, "Communication from the Commission to the European Parliament, the Council, the Economic and Social Committee and the Committee of the Regions: A Comprehensive Approach on Personal Data Protection in the European Union" (2010) 2–3.

[3] Art 29 WP, "Statement on the Role of a Risk-Based Approach in Data Protection Legal Frameworks" (2014) 2–3.

The Risk-Based Approach to Data Protection. Raphaël Gellert, Oxford University Press (2020). © Raphaël Gellert.
DOI: 10.1093/oso/9780198837718.001.0001.

rights-based and risk-based approaches. The present chapter will therefore explore this notion of compliance risk. It will proceed in three steps.

First, it uses the technical notion of risk put forth by the International Organization for Standardization (ISO)—and discussed in Chapter 1—as a description tool in order to unfold, and show the differences between the competing understandings of risk.[4]

Second, it will define the notion that should have featured in the risk-based approach had it been a full implementation of meta regulation, ie if it relied upon risk management also for standard setting purposes (as an alternative to the core data protection principles). This notion of risk is characterised as a "data protection risk". In explaining and outlining this data protection risk, the analysis builds upon historical sources dating back to the emergence of data protection law in the 1960s and 1970s. The reason for doing so is the following. As one remembers, Chapter 1 on risk and regulation demonstrated that the object of regulation can be understood as—a series of—harms. If data protection amounts to regulation, then it follows that its object is also—a series of—harms. This is maybe best epitomised by the Ware Report according to which data protection has as its object the "serious potential for harmful consequences [stemming from automated personal data processing systems], including infringement of basic liberties".[5] Similarly, a number of data protection statutes used to conceive of their object as the avoidance of risks or harms. The first ever data protection statute was the one adopted by the German Länder of Hesse on 7 October 1970.[6] The goal of the Hesse Data Protection Act was explicitly framed as the "safeguard [of] the constitutional structure of the State (…) against all risks entailed by automatic data processing".[7] Similarly, the purpose of the German 1977 Data Protection Act was to: "(…) prevent harm to any personal interests of the person concerned that warrant protection".[8] The United States 1974 Privacy Act aims "to safeguard individual privacy from the misuse of federal records (…)".[9] One can also mention the 1980 OECD Guidelines on the Protection of Privacy and Transborder Flows of Personal Data, which apply to "personal data, which, because of the manner in which they are processed, (…) pose a danger to privacy and individual liberties" (Art 2).[10] In other words, at the

[4] ISO, "ISO: 31000 Risk Management—Principles and Guidelines".

[5] US Department of Health Education & Welfare (n 1) viii.

[6] *Hessische Datenschutzgezetz vom 7. Oktober 1970 GVBl. II 300-10*, published at Wiesbaden, 12 October 1970, in Gesetz-und Verordnungsblatt für das Land Hessen [Laws and Regulations Journal], Part I, No 41.

[7] See Lee A Bygrave, *Data Protection Law—Approaching Its Rationale, Logic, and Its Limits* (Kluwer 2002) 39.

[8] Federal Data Protection Act (*Bundesdatenschutzgesetz*) of 27 January 1977, *Federal Law Gazette* I 201, as amended by Article 1 of the Act of 25 February 2015, *Federal Law Gazette* I 162.

[9] US Privacy Act of 1974, as amended, 5 USC § 552a.

[10] Article 2 of the Explanatory Memorandum is also explicit about the risks for privacy and other fundamental freedoms that stem from modern data processing technologies.

most vernacular, a data protection risk can be defined as the chances that a data processing operation will negatively affect (ie harm) the individuals' whose data is being processed.

Third, and in contrast, a compliance risk can be defined as the chances that a processing operation does not comply with data protection requirements. It will be studied in-depth in the last part of the chapter.

2. The ISO's constitutive elements of risk

This section recalls the technical notion of risk put forth by the ISO. It will be used throughout the rest of the chapter as a tool to describe and analyse the various understandings of risk at play.[11]

- Risk source: According to the ISO, it is an "element, which, alone or in combination has the intrinsic potential to give rise to risk" (eg the computer).[12] According to the *Commission nationale de l'informatique et des libertés* (CNIL), the risk source leads to risks because it is the source of risk factors, also sometimes referred to as threats;[13]
- Risk factor/threat: According to the CNIL, a threat is what makes the occurrence of a risk possible.[14] In other words, they determine whether and how the risk will materialise (ie probability), as well as the severity of the risk (eg the amount of data processed);
- Risk is the event that may or may not happen, and which has a number of consequences both positive and negative. For this reason, the ISO prefers to talk about risk as an "event",[15] and the CNIL refers to risk as "feared event";[16] (ie certain properties or characteristics, which if displayed by processing operation, will lead to harms);
- Consequences,[17] or impacts:[18] When the impacts stemming from the feared event are negative they can be referred to as harms (ie violation of fundamental rights and ensuing harms), and when they are positive they can be referred to as benefits.

[11] ISO (n 4).
[12] ibid 4.
[13] CNIL, "Methodology For Privacy Risk Management: How to Implement the Data Protection Act" (2012) 7.
[14] ibid 6.
[15] ISO (n 4) 4.
[16] CNIL (n 13) 6.
[17] ISO (n 4) 5.
[18] CNIL (n 13) 6.

The analysis will now try to demonstrate how this technical notion of risk helps to better understand and appraise the notions of data protection risk and compliance risk.

3. Defining a data protection risk

This section will provide the author's own definition of what exactly a data protection risk is. Arguably, a data protection risk is the chance that certain processing operations' properties lead to harms to the data subjects. The demonstration is undertaken in two steps. It first takes a historical perspective, relying upon the pioneering data protection literature from the 1960s and 1970s. The point being to show that it has always been possible to think of the object of data protection as a series of harms. Second, it will confirm the historical analysis of the notion of data protection risk by showing that it is at play in the US National Institute of Standards and Technology (NIST)'s 2017 Privacy Engineering and Risk Management in Federal Systems Framework.

3.1 The computer: the risk source

The early data protection literature saw the computer as the cause for a number of societal dangers and impacts, and more in particular their harmful consequences for citizens,[19] including their fundamental rights.[20] Even though the computer had already made its appearance during the 1950s,[21] its dangers were not underlined before the mid-1960s.[22] This can be explained by the fact that up until that point it remained still an experimental and therefore "confidential" technology, limited to the use by public and private organisations for their own purposes.[23] However, at the end of this experimental period, in 1965, computer technology became an issue of increasing concern,[24] and a so-called "alarmist literature" appeared, putting the emphasis on such dangers.[25]

[19] US Department of Health Education & Welfare (n 1) viii.

[20] ibid 33.

[21] eg Alan Westin and Michael A Baker, *Databanks in a Free Society: Computers, Record Keeping and Privacy* (Quadrangle Books 1972) 12; Alan Westin, *Privacy and Freedom* (Atheneum 1967) 349.

[22] See Frits W Hondius, *Emerging Data Protection in Europe* (North-Holland; American Elsevier 1975) 3. Even though it had stirred some resistance, as was the case with discussions on the possible deployment of a universal personal identification system, Westin (n 21) 304.

[23] See also Bennett, who argues that "the advent of the computer has not been accompanied by the sort of concerns that were associated with the automobile, the airplane, or nuclear power" in the absence of "evidence equivalent to a polluted atmosphere, an air disaster, or a nuclear meltdown (...)", *Regulating Privacy* (Cornell University Press 1992) 22–23.

[24] Hondius (n 22) 4.

[25] Gloria González Fuster, *The Emergence of Personal Data Protection as a Fundamental Right of the EU* (Springer 2014) 28–29; Westin (n 21) 315. This literature started in the US, Westin (n 21); Arthur R

Computer technology was thus identified as the risk source, since "what was put forward as a threat was the automated processing of information on individuals that computers were capable of sustaining, and of trivialising".[26] The latter thus brought about "growing concern that automated personal data systems present a serious potential for harmful consequences, including infringement of basic liberties".[27]

3.2 Risk factors, risks, and harms

Assuming that the computer is indeed the risk source, one must then wonder what are the risk factors (ie the source's properties that lead to the occurrence of a risk), the risks, and the harms it generated.

On the basis of the Ware Report, one can identify three risk factors. Increased data quantity as a consequence of increased processing capacities; opaque and increased use of, and access to, data as a consequence of the interconnection of data; and the rise of a new class of bureaucrats and experts—the technicians—along with new, pre-emptive, managerial practices.[28] These risk factors directly lead to a number of risks, that is certain characteristics, or features, which data processing will (might) display, and which lead to a number of harms.

3.3 Risk factor (1): extent of the processing: increased data quantity

The increased quantity of processed data can be considered a risk factor for two reasons. On the one hand, because of computers' capacities for fast and efficient data handling, bureaucracies are incentivised to process as much data as technically possible, and to devote their resources solely to the efficiency of the system so as to offset the costs impaired by the installation of computers.[29] On the other hand, electronic files are less flexible than manual ones and are thus also more prone to errors and miscategorisations.[30]

Miller, *The Assault on Privacy: Computers, Data Banks, and Dossiers* (The University of Michigan Press 1971); Vance Packard, *The Naked Society* (Van Rees Press 1964); but similar concerns were soon voiced in all countries impacted by the development of the computer, see among many Claude Serge Aronstein, "Essai Pour Contribuer à La Survie de Notre Civilisation" (1970) 86 Journal des tribunaux 453; Claude Serge Aronstein, "De l'urgence d'ordonner Les Ordinateurs" [1971] Journal des tribunaux 161.

[26] González Fuster (n 25) 29.
[27] US Department of Health Education & Welfare (n 1) viii.
[28] ibid 12.
[29] See also Miller (n 25) 3 who refers to computers as being "data hungry".
[30] US Department of Health Education & Welfare (n 1) 13–14.

3.3.1 Risk from risk factor (1): inaccuracy

The Ware report notes that as a result of such errors, and inattentions, many processing of data were inaccurate.[31]

3.3.2 Harms stemming from inaccuracy

Typical harms following from this inaccuracy risk include receiving erroneous bills, unjustified dunning letters, and so on. These may appear more as light harms (or even barely nuisances). Yet, their importance should not be overlooked since they can lead to resentment, technophobic attitudes,[32] and ultimately lack of trust. At the level of individuals, loss of trust is not as innocuous as it may first seem, since it affects in general people's well-being, but has also insidious effects in more specific settings (eg at the workplace). Further, such discomfort may have further reaching effects, the most significant one being social unrest and violence.[33] Other harms such as "disruption of human lives" may also occur when, for instance, people are erroneously excluded from a benefit scheme.[34] Further, Packard argues that these arbitrary categorisations can also lead to labelling and stigmatisation, and their somewhat irreversible nature links these harms to infringements of due process guarantees.[35]

3.4 Risk factor (2): properties of the processing: opaque and increased access to, and use of data

This second risk factor can be sub-divided into two risk factors. Both of which concern the properties of the processing operations instead of the amount of data processed.

First, increased processing capacities have allowed for the creation of important databases containing an important number of individuals.[36] Second, these advances also allowed for the interconnection of databases. This means that a very important number of persons can now have access to the information and subsequently use it for their own purposes.[37] In turn, there is very little knowledge and control (in particular when the data are inaccurate) as to who uses the data and to what use. This is particularly severe when several users propagate these—potentially wrong—data.[38] In turn, attempts to correct the information are also doomed.

These risk factors lead to several risks.

[31] ibid.

[32] The Report refers to the Luddites movement.

[33] Miller (n 25) 52–53.

[34] US Department of Health Education & Welfare (n 1) 14. Note that the two harms are not incompatible: one can lose a benefit and also feel disrupted.

[35] Packard (n 25) 276–77.

[36] US Department of Health Education & Welfare (n 1) 15.

[37] And not only those who are at the physical location of the database.

[38] US Department of Health Education & Welfare (n 1) 17–18.

3.4.1 Risk (1) from risk factor (2): "dragnet effect"

The "dragnet effect" can be defined as "the automatic screening of all members of a population in order to discover a few members with specified characteristics".[39] It has indeed become more efficient to include all citizens in a specific database or register without differentiation whatsoever, rather than singling out the suspicious cases.[40]

3.4.2 Harms stemming from the "dragnet effect"

The "dragnet effect" descends from the first sub-factor (ie increased databases). It is said to cause serious harms. First, it is often prone to false positives. Innocent citizens are therefore put in a position whereby they have to bear the burden of proof of their innocence. In this case, the harms are not only about nuisance, but also about genuine injustice and violation of due process.[41] Packard argues that the increasing police use of surveillance methods also leads to a dragnet effect whereby everyone is a suspect, and which thus opens the door to arbitrary arrests. In addition to the violation of the presumption of innocence and other due-process related guarantees, people also bear the stigma of an arrest record.[42] This is particularly acute when specific social groups are targeted.[43]

3.4.3 Risk (2) from risk factor (2): loss of control over personal data

The loss of control over personal data descends from the second sub-factor (ie interconnection of databases). This risk can actually be seen as the bundling of three distinct risks: exposure, opacity, and impossibility to access and further rectify one's personal data. These risks have been bundled together because they are each linked to the data subject's exclusion from the processing operation.

3.4.4 Harms stemming from loss of control over personal data

A good example of data processing operations that encompasses the risk of loss of control over personal data is that of surveillance practices, which were prevalent in the US in the 1950s and 1960s, and which were gradually merged with computer technology.[44]

[39] ibid 15.
[40] The report gives the example of the National Driver register of the Department of Transport, the goal of which is to provide a list of individuals whose driving licence has been denied or withdrawn by another State, ibid.
[41] ibid 16.
[42] Packard (n 25) 257–58.
[43] ibid 260.
[44] This is why Packard refers to them as "electronic listening devices", ibid 9. See also, González Fuster (n 25) 30; Oscar M Ruebhausen, "Foreword", *Privacy and Freedom* (Atheneum 1967) xi, or Westin (n 21) 134, who describes how the computer was applied to the polygraph.

In his book *The Naked Society*, Vance Packard highlights a number of harms stemming from surveillance practices (with a focus on the United States in the 1960s), which relate to the risks of exposure and opacity. These practices were seen as particularly risky insofar as they relied upon the opaque collection of data, which in turn revealed a huge quantity of information about individuals.[45] This gave particular acuteness to a series of harms among which the chilling effect, which translated into a sense of insecurity, the infringement upon freedom of communications as well as that of "the right to live in a free society without fear".[46] Continuing his list of harms, he further argued that the right to have unfashionable opinions was infringed upon by surveillance practices, and in particular during the deleterious era of generalised suspicion, against all those who upheld subversive opinions, and which took place during the 1950s. He qualified the chilling effect that followed, as giving up "the right of moral indignation and its consequent prerogative to offend".[47] However, being characterised as subversive could also result with more tangible harms such as the loss of one's job and the ensuing extreme difficulty of getting back into work.[48]

As a matter of fact, one can observe that the "modern" right to privacy as defined by Warren and Brandeis as the right to be let alone descends from—unwanted—exposure stemming from then new technologies,[49] ie "modern devices for recording or reproducing scenes or sounds",[50] such as the photographic machine.[51] Most famously, this exposure gave rise to moral harms, which it was argued, were far greater than those resulting from bodily injuries. These included injuries to a person's esteem of herself, as well as other mental pains and distresses.[52]

However, surveillance practices could also lead to other harms, more related to the data subjects' inability to access their data and to rectify it, in particular when decisions were taken on the basis of the data collected (eventually following the interconnection of databases). As with the "dragnet effect", some decisions might be taken on the basis of false positives, thereby leading to the harm of unfair or inappropriate decision. The possibility of wrong decisions is heightened because

[45] As he puts it, "today it is increasingly assumed that the past and present of all of us—virtually every aspect of our lives—must be an open book (. . .)" Packard (n 25) 12.

[46] ibid 11–12. Packard also characterises the chilling effect in the following way: "this breeds not only sameness, but a watchfulness completely untypical of the exuberant, free-wheeling American so commonly accepted as typical of this land", ibid 11.

[47] ibid 232.

[48] ibid.

[49] Samuel D Warren and Louis D Brandeis, "The Right to Privacy" (1890) IV Harvard Law Review 193, 211.

[50] ibid 206.

[51] Godkin argued that these content reproduction technologies exalted curiosity, which he saw as the main enemy of privacy Edwin Laurence Godkin, "The Rights of the Citizen—IV: To His Reputation" (1890) 8 Scribener's 58.

[52] Warren and Brandeis (n 49) 196–97. Solove refers to "feelings of emotional distress, humiliation and outrage", *Understanding Privacy* (Harvard University Press 2008) 175. See also Danielle Keats Citron, "Mainstreaming Privacy Torts" (2010) 98 California Law Review 1805, 1819.

there is no transparency and/or control as to who accesses the data, meaning that different users might prioritise or use differently a given set of data (hence the higher chance of false positives).[53] This situation, coupled to the fact that some persons accessing the data might do so unlawfully also leads to harms linked to the infringement of other fundamental rights and constitutional principles like accountability, transparency, and the separation of powers.[54]

One can take notice that the Ware Report also tackled another processing practice that created the risk of loss of control over personal data. That of profiling, which it defined as the constitution of dossiers about citizens.[55]

3.5 Risk factor (3): type of processing: new bureaucratic and managerial practices

Finally, the third risk factor the Ware Report points to is the technocratic and instrumentalist behaviours of large organisations and institutions, which built upon the computers' increased data processing capabilities in order to transform records into "management information systems". That is, as a technological solution meant to address complex social problems.[56] More in particular, this technological fix builds upon the enhanced pre-emptive capacities of automated data processing systems, which are now capable of simultaneously processing the three types of records (ie administrative, surveillance, and statistical) and, as such, allow for pre-emptive decision-making. Such pre-emptive decision making is constitutive of the risk of social control.[57]

3.5.1 Risk from risk factor (3): social control

The risk of social control builds upon a number of data processing practices that can be characterised as risky insofar as they encompass—some of—the previously described risks. This can be illustrated by taking the example of a medical facility operating on a pre-emptive basis and therefore committed to detecting medical conditions on an as early as possible basis.

This requires the possession of as much medical information as possible, either by collecting all the already existing medical information, either by gathering additional information (cf *supra*, risk factor (1): increased data quantity). This wealth

[53] US Department of Health Education & Welfare (n 1) 19. And of course, this is even more so if the data is inaccurate.

[54] ibid 19–20.

[55] ibid 20–21. See also, Miller (n 25) 20. who talks about a "dossier society".

[56] And the report adds: "this behaviour is also fuelled by a new bureaucracy of experts, or data processing professionals, who are solely interested in exploiting the technology's capacity to its full potential, regardless of the extrinsic social consequences". US Department of Health Education & Welfare (n 1) 22.

[57] ibid 28.

of information is then used for statistical purposes, that is, the establishment of profiles of population that are more or less at risk (cf *supra*, profiling encompasses the risk of loss of control over personal data). If a patient exhibits the characteristics of a risk profile, it is assumed that they will behave accordingly, and they will automatically be eligible for a specific treatment.[58]

Social control was already considered potentially the biggest risk stemming from the computerised processing of personal data. As James B Rule argued, the biggest risk is not how private the data in an organisation's possession are, their quantity, and how much they reveal about an individual. Rather, it is the use to which they are put.[59] Data is critical for the purpose of rapid and pre-emptive decision-making, since it enables organisations to predict which individuals are at risk, and ensuingly, to discriminate and single them out.

3.5.2 Harms stemming from social control

As an increasingly prominent part of people's life is being decided on the basis of personal records, people are harmed since they start feeling that they are being stripped of their individuality, and of a meaningful existence. They suffer emotional, psychological, and moral harms such as feeling dehumanised and alienated.[60] Packard argues along similar lines.[61] The damages from technology do not only descend from their capacity to scrutinise individuals, but also from their normalising impact. The latter notably stems from the fact that record keeping technology allowed for a deeper structuration of social life through an increased number of regulatory and administrative requirements, such as the increasing number of activities for which a licence became compulsory (thereby creating a very stringent frame for individuals to live their life). As a consequence, and among the characteristically American rights Packard described as harmed, one can include the right to be different. In this respect, an interviewed person felt that citizens were robbed of eccentricity.[62] Additional rights at risk include the right to hope for tolerant forgiveness or overlooking of past foolishness, errors, humiliations, or minor sins—in short, what he refers to as the Christian notion of the possibility of redemption; and the right to make a fresh start.[63] Packard also equated

[58] ibid 26.

[59] James B Rule, *Private Lives and Public Surveillance* (The Trinity Press 1973).

[60] Miller (n 25) 49; Miller talks about "the psychosis of the Computerised Man". However, they are different than the first emotional harms, which related more to feelings of embarrassment, shame, being demeaned, see ibid 48–49.

[61] Packard (n 25) 12.

[62] As this person put it, "you are required to live just this way and no other way" ibid.

[63] Packard sees these rights as linked to the existence of America, and thus somewhat underpinning the fundamental rights legally acknowledged: "America was largely settled, and its frontiers expanded, by people seeking to get away from something unpleasant in their pasts, either oppression, painful episodes, poverty, or misdemeanours." ibid.

this new "administrative takeover" as no less than harassment.[64] From this perspective, the biggest harms stemming from automated data processing systems are not violations of privacy, which as discussed stem from loss of control over personal data, but rather, social sorting practices insofar as they are discriminating, and also infringe upon the right to due process.[65]

3.6 Concluding thoughts on the concept of a data protection risk

The previous lines have tried to flesh out the concept of data protection risk. Accordingly, a data protection risk is a property that the processing operation may have, and in that case, may lead to a number of harms (negative consequences). Several remarks are warranted at this stage.

First, a risk can only occur because of risk factors. However, there is no necessary link between the risk factors and the risk herein described. For instance, the risk factor "extent of the processing" has been associated to the risk "inaccuracy". However, it could also be associated to the risk "loss of control over personal data". The links have been made on the basis of the literature studied.

Second, the notion of what exactly is a harm is not entirely clear. One can observe that the category of harms encompasses two types of elements. It includes the violation of fundamental rights as such (ie risks lead to violation of these rights), as well as the actual harms following from such violation (eg the violation of privacy leads to moral harms, discriminatory decision-making makes it harder/impossible to find a new job—material harm). This ambivalence—also present in the GDPR—may actually allow to include a number of harms that are not always clearly linked to a fundamental right (eg the right to "moral indignation", the right to "make a fresh start").

Finally, this historical overview of the notion of data protection risk confirms the idea that, in line with regulation theory, it is possible to think of the object of data protection law as a series of harms.

[64] ibid 268. Especially taking into account the very intrusive nature of the questions part of these processes, which he refers to as "inconsiderably long, uncivilly inquisitorial, and absolutely unconstitutional" ibid 268–69. See also Ian Hacking, "Biopower and the Avalanche of Printed Numbers" (1982) 5 Humanities in Society 279, 290, who explains that the very idea of a census was already entrenched in the 1778 American Constitution. He also explains that if only four questions were asked in 1790, by 1880, his so-called "avalanche of printed numbers" had occurred since no less than 13,010 questions were being asked.

[65] See also Cynthia Dwork and Deirdre K Mulligan, "It's Not Privacy, and It's Not Fair" (2013) 66 Stanford Law Review Online 35. This is also the overarching point made in David Lyon (ed), *Surveillance as Social Sorting—Privacy, Risk, and Digital Discrimination* (Routledge 2003).

3.7 The NIST Privacy Engineering and Risk Management in Federal Systems Framework as a risk analysis methodology embodying the notion of data protection risk

The analysis of a modern framework for data protection risk management, the US National Institute of Standards and Technology (NIST)' s 2017 framework for privacy management, NISTIR 8062 (as well as its 2015 draft where relevant),[66] confirms the historical analysis of a data protection risk. To the knowledge of the author, this is the only methodology that embodies the notion of a "genuine" data protection risk, contrary to all other existing data protection risk management methodologies, which are based on the notion of compliance risk (at the heart of the GDPR).

The NIST methodology is explicitly predicated on the premise that "in practice, [data protection] impact assessments have not achieved their full potential as a process for assessing and understanding (and therefore anticipating) privacy concerns in information systems", precisely because they are used "to support regulatory compliance".[67] In sharp contrast, the goal of the NIST framework is to shift away from data protection impact assessments (DPIAs), which are "focused on compliance rather than [on] the effectiveness of achieving a positive outcome for privacy".[68] For this reason, its goal is to "assess the risk of problems for individuals arising from the operations of the system that involve the processing of their information".[69] In other words, "the underlying rationale for risk management is the achievement of mission goals while minimizing adverse outcomes or problems", these problems being constituted by "the privacy problems that [data subjects] may experience from the processing of their personal information".[70]

Tantamount to the fact that such management methodology is genuinely about data protection risk, is the fact that NIST makes it clear that its goal is not to "managing privacy risk [pertaining to] compliance with laws, regulations, and policies",[71] but rather, to "enable the setting of appropriate controls to mitigate

[66] The US subsume data protection under privacy. Note that this framework seems to be limited to Federal institutions, and that the NIST is currently working on a framework also applicable to the private sector, see National Institute of Standards and Technology, "NIST Privacy Framework Working Outline" (2019).

[67] National Institute of Standards and Technology, "NISTIR 8062 (Draft): Privacy Risk Management for Federal Information Systems" (2015) 9. See also ibid 10. where it explicitly criticises these methodologies for not proposing "a complete privacy risk model". For a similar criticism, see also World Economic Forum, "Rethinking Personal Data: A New Lens for Strenthening Trust" (2014).

[68] National Institute of Standards and Technology, "NISTIR 8062: An Introduction to Privacy Engineering and Risk Management in Federal Systems" (2017) 14.

[69] National Institute of Standards and Technology (n 67) 14.

[70] ibid 13.

[71] National Institute of Standards and Technology (n 68) 24.

potential issues",[72] that is, privacy risks, the existence of which "hinges on whether a data action becomes problematic for the individual".[73]

3.7.1 The notion of data protection risk in the NIST methodology: three feared events

As indicated, a data protection risk is a property of the processing (that may occur or not), and that will lead to harms to the data subject. The NIST methodology identifies three properties that every processing operation should possess: (un)predictability, (un)manageability, and (dis)associability.[74] Each violation of one of these properties can be considered a feared event (which is the property of the processing that will lead to harms).

Predictability is seen as essential for building trust, and upholding the data subjects' reasonable expectations with regard to the processing of their personal data.[75] It is therefore linked to the requirement that data controllers should focus on maintaining reliable assumptions about their processing operations,[76] since unpredictable processing operations (including changes thereto) are "*loci* for privacy risks".[77]

Manageability encompasses all the operations performed by the data controller upon personal data. A number of harms can indeed result when personal information is not managed properly, for instance when it is not accurate enough, stored for overly long periods, but also when unfair decisions are made on the basis of profiles, etc,[78] or when data subjects don't have adequate access to their data.[79]

Finally, disassociability refers to the requirement that the processing operation "actively protects or 'blinds' an individual's identity or associated activities from exposure".[80] Even with lawful processing operations, harm can follow from exposure, when the latter is not necessary.[81]

In other words, each of these properties can be infringed upon in a number of different ways. Each infringement will be considered a feared event/risk, bearing in mind that a single risk can infringe more than one property at the time. As a matter of fact, it is possible to map the various data protection risks uncovered (ie "inaccuracy"; "dragnet effect"; "data subjects' loss of control over their personal

72 National Institute of Standards and Technology (n 67) 12.

73 National Institute of Standards and Technology (n 68) 23; see also National Institute of Standards and Technology (n 67) 11 where it argues that such management methodology is meant to help data controllers to understand the privacy risks and to adopt the adequate mitigation measures.

74 National Institute of Standards and Technology (n 68) 3.1.

75 ibid 17.

76 ibid 18–19.

77 National Institute of Standards and Technology (n 67) 19.

78 ibid 19–20.

79 National Institute of Standards and Technology (n 68) 19.

80 ibid 20.

81 National Institute of Standards and Technology (n 67) 20.

data"; "social control") unto the NIST triad. Inaccuracy is an infringement of manageability; dragnet effect can be a violation of all: predictability, manageability, and disassociability; and the same holds true for the loss of control over personal information as well as for social control. The NIST draft of the methodology provides non-exhaustive annexes of feared events and associated harms.[82] In other words, it is impossible to exhaustively map all the processing operations that qualify as feared events. The NIST provides an illustrative list, but the point is that any processing of data can be a feared event/risk as soon as it violates one of the properties identified.

4. The notion of risk in the GDPR: compliance risk

As was argued in Chapter 5, the risk-based approach as it is embodied in the GDPR features a different conception of risk. Rather than a "genuine" data protection risk, it is predicated upon a "compliance risk". Instead of assessing how harmful the planned processing is, and determining what the most adequate safeguards are in order to reduce the level of harm to an acceptable level (data protection risk), the compliance risk asks the following question. Namely, how big the planned processing's risk of non-compliance is (ie the risk of violating compulsory safeguards enshrined into data protection statutes), and on that basis, what the most adequate safeguards are in order to reduce such risk.[83]

4.1 Better understanding compliance risk

First, it is to be noted that the notion of risk in the GDPR is an elusive one. In spite of its numerous occurrences, and just like the risk-based approach, the notion of risk is not defined in the GDPR.[84] As will now be analysed, the GDPR contains a number of constitutive elements of the notion of risk it relies upon, but it always falls short of defining what exactly the risk at stake is.

The ambiguity of this notion is probably best epitomised in Art 35 GDPR. Article 35(1) provides that: "Where a type of processing (…) is likely to result in a *high risk to the rights and freedoms* of natural persons, the controller shall, prior

[82] ibid 55–56.

[83] Some of the points developed in this section were also developed in Raphaël Gellert, "Understanding the Notion of Risk in the General Data Protection Regulation" (2018) 34 Computer Law and Security Review 279.

[84] See the discussion that took place at the Council of the EU on this issue, Council of the European Union, "Proposal for a Regulation of the European Parliament and of the Cuncil on the Protection of Individuals with Regard to the Processing of Personal Data and on the Free Movement of Such Data—Risk Based Approach" (2014).

to the processing, carry out an *assessment of the impact* (...) *on the protection of personal data*."[85]

As one can see, there seems to be a contradiction concerning what the object of impact assessment is in the first place. What should be assessed? The likely high risk to the data subject's rights and freedoms, or the impact on the protection of personal data?[86]

The only way to address this contradiction is through the notion of compliance risk. Keeping in mind the distinction between the risk as the "event" or "feared event" and its consequences discussed at the beginning of this chapter, the definition at the heart of Art 35(1) starts making much more sense since it combines the event and the harms-negative consequences. In the present interpretation, the "risks to the rights and freedoms" is the negative consequence. This interpretation is confirmed by the Art 29 WP, which has argued that they pertain to the "potential negative impact on the data subject's rights, freedoms and interests".[87] The logical corollary is that "the protection of personal data" at stake in Art 35(1) is the "event". In other words, when personal data are not adequately protected, that is, when data protection provisions and obligations are not complied with, such event leads to the potential violation of all the data subject's fundamental rights affected by said processing operation. This is why one can talk about a "compliance risk" at the heart of the GDPR.

This notion of compliance risk is instrumental to the risk-based approach in the GDPR, and can be better appraised through the latter. As discussed, one of the major goals of the risk-based approach is to allow for improved compliance and implementation of the legal framework. The very framing of this objective suggests that compliance and risk should be integrated within a single risk calculation that renders more visible the links between compliance (or the lack thereof) and the violation of the data subject's fundamental rights and freedoms. For instance, not minimising the data may result in violations of the data subject's fundamental rights. The same holds true if the data are processed for further incompatible purposes. As a matter of fact, in its opinion on the purpose limitation principle, the Art 29 WP has made the link between the violation of said principle and the harms to the data subjects this may lead to.[88] Thus, the lower the compliance, the higher the potential violations of the data subjects' fundamental rights. Inversely, just as a low level of compliance signals the likely infringement of the data subject's rights

[85] Emphasis by the author.

[86] Quelle has argued that this would suggest that compliance by data protection principles and the mitigation of the risks to the data subject's fundamental rights are two different things Claudia Quelle, "The Data Protection Impact Assessment: What Can It Contribute to Data Protection?" (2015) s 2.5, <https://arno.uvt.nl/show.cgi?fid=139503>, last accessed 20 March 2019. As will be observed, this is not so since the two are integrated into a single risk calculation.

[87] Art 29 WP (n 3) 4.

[88] Art 29 WP, "Opinion 03/2013 on Purpose Limitation" (2013).

and freedoms, ensuring in turn that the rights and freedoms are not violated by the processing operation contributes to higher levels of compliance. As a matter of fact, this is how Art 35(1) can be interpreted: a likely high risk of violation of the data subject's rights and freedoms signals a level of compliance that is too low.

4.2 Traces of the GDPR risk as compliance risk

There are numerous references to the notion of risk in the GDPR. Can they be used in order to confirm the present analysis?

First, a number of Recitals emphasise that risk-based mechanisms are first and foremost addressed towards achieving—higher—levels of compliance. This is the case with Recital 84, which provides that DPIAs are instruments designed to "enhance compliance with this Regulation". Recital 78 is maybe the most explicit as far as the articulation between the risks to the data subjects' rights and freedoms, and compliance is concerned. It provides that "the protection of the rights and freedoms of natural persons require that appropriate technical and organisational measures be taken [in order] to ensure that the requirements of this Regulation are met". This sentence perfectly espouses the logic of the argument put forth herein: addressing the risks to the data subjects' rights and freedoms directly influences the level of compliance. Similar lines of reasoning can also be found in additional Recitals (80, 81, 82).

Second, the GDPR contains many references to risk factors (ie factors that influence the probability of occurrence and severity of the risk). A number of risk factors can be found in Art 35. It should be kept in mind that Art 35 on DPIAs is only concerned with high risks, but remains a valid example. Article 35(1) contains a number of risk factors. It refers to the use of new technologies, and also to the processing operation in a general way (nature, scope, context, and purposes). The next important provision of Art 35 is Art 35(3), which, as confirmed by the Art 29 WP, contains an indicative list of risk factors.[89] Articles 35(3)(a) and (c) contain risk factors pertaining to the processing operation: a systematic and extensive evaluation of personal aspects based upon automated processing; and the systematic monitoring of a publicly accessible area on a large scale. Article 35(3)(b) contains risk factors pertaining to the type of data used, namely sensitive data such as those referred to by Art 9(1) as well as Art 10 GDPR.[90] Further, one can also mention a number of Recitals, which either reiterate (89, 90), or further specify (91) the risk factors contained in Art 35.

[89] See Art 29 WP, "Guidelines on Data Protection Impact Assessment (DPIA) and Determining Whether Processing Is 'Likely to Result in a High Risk' for the Purposes of Regulation 2016/679" (2017) 8–13.

[90] ie special categories of data, and data relating to criminal convictions and offences.

Third, as far as the harms coextensive to the violation of the data subject's rights are concerned, the main source is Recital 75.[91] It refers to "data processing which could lead to physical, material or non-material damage". These material and moral damages include discrimination, identity theft or fraud, financial loss, damage to the reputation, loss of confidentiality, unauthorised reversal of pseudonymisation, or any other significant economic or social disadvantage. As one can see, the GDPR also bundles together the violation of fundamental rights and the actual harms stemming therefrom.

Furthermore, an additional confirmation that the risk at stake is a compliance one can be found in the Art 29 WP's Guidelines on Data Protection Impact Assessments.[92] Neither the GDPR nor the Art 29 WP's guidance provides a risk management methodology. As far as the GDPR is concerned, Art 35(7) only contains rudimentary instructions to assess and mitigate risks, while Recital 76 argues that risk should be evaluated on the basis of an objective assessment, and Recital 90 argues that risks should be assessed in terms of likelihood and severity, with such assessment taking into account "the nature, scope, context and purposes of the processing and the sources of the risk". As far as the guidance of the Art 29 WP is concerned, it promotes methodological flexibility, and is therefore void of methodological considerations as such.[93] Yet, it does refer to the ISO DPIA Standard several times,[94] and therefore seems to endorse it—at least implicitly—as an adequate methodology for carrying out a DPIA (the ISO actually refers to PIA, probably given its international ambition to also apply to countries which refer to privacy rather than data protection).[95] As will be examined below, this methodology also encapsulates a notion of compliance risk, which it distinguishes from the actual harms or impacts.[96] These harms or impacts are defined in a very similar way as in the GDPR since they include physical, financial, reputational harms, embarrassment, and invasion of domestic life, etc.[97] Yet, even though, it formally distinguishes between the risk/feared event as constitutive element of a compliance risk and the harm/impact ensuing therefrom, it still links them together within a single risk calculation.[98] Finally, this can also be confirmed by the fact that the ISO based its definition of DPIA on the ISO 29100 Standard.[99] The latter is in turn very

[91] Note that this Recital concerns the principle of accountability, thus confirming our analysis.

[92] Art 29 WP (n 89).

[93] See Raphaël Gellert, "The Article 29 Working Party's Provisional Guidelines on Data Protection Impact Assessment" (2017) 2 European Data Protection Law Review 1, 215.

[94] ISO/IEC, "ISO/IEC 29134: Information Technology—Security Techniques—Guidelines for Privacy Impact Assessment" (2017).

[95] See in particular Art 29 WP (n 89) 21: "An international standard will also provide guidelines for methodologies used for carrying out a DPIA (ISO/IEC 29134)."

[96] ISO/IEC (n 94) 3.6.

[97] ibid 9.

[98] See among many examples, ibid 18: "a privacy risk map should result from an assessment of the level of *impact* and the likelihood of the assessed *risk*", emphasis by the author.

[99] ibid 3.7.

clear that DPIAs are geared towards "*ensuring compliance* with privacy and data protection legislation requirements *and assessing the privacy implications*" of processing operations.[100]

Given the scattered nature of the references to risk in the GDPR, one can try to systematise the latter through the ISO definition of risk in the following fashion.

- Risk source: According to the ISO, it is an "element, which, alone or in combination has the intrinsic potential to give rise to risk":[101]
  - The computer (this is absent from the GDPR)
- Risk factor/threat: According to the CNIL, a threat is what makes the occurrence of a risk possible.[102] In other words, they determine whether and how the risk will materialise (ie probability), as well as the severity of the risk (Arts 35(1) and (3):
- Use of new technologies
  - Systematic and extensive evaluation of personal aspects based upon automated processing;
  - Systematic monitoring of a publicly accessible area on a large scale;
  - Data such as those referred to by Art 9(1) as well as Art 10 GDPR
- Risk is the event that may or may not happen, and which has a number of consequences both positive and negative. For this reason, the ISO refers to talk about risk as an "event",[103] and the CNIL refers to risk as "feared event":[104]
  - Art 35(1): "impact . . .) on the protection of personal data" (=lack of compliance with data protection law).
- Consequences,[105] or impacts:[106] When such impacts are negative they can be referred to as harms, and when they are positive they can be referred to as benefits;
  - Violation of data subjects' fundamental rights and freedoms, which are linked to physical, material or non-material damage (Recital 75).

4.3 The risk-based approach as "data protection on the ground": doing a risk analysis with the CNIL methodology

The CNIL's 2012 Methodology for Privacy Risk Management is a good example for understanding how the GDPR compliance risk operates.[107] As was explained, risk

[100] ISO/EIC, "ISO/EIC 29100: Information Technology: Security Techniques: Privacy Framework" (2011) 10. Emphasis by the author.
[101] ISO (n 4) 4.
[102] CNIL (n 13) 6.
[103] ISO (n 4) 4.
[104] CNIL (n 13) 6.
[105] ISO (n 4) 5.
[106] CNIL (n 13) 6.
[107] ibid. It is to be noted that the CNIL methodology was updated in 2015 and 2018 "Privacy Impact Assessment (PIA): Methodology (How to Carry out a PIA)" (2015); CNIL, "Privacy Impact Assessment

management methodologies frame risk as a—feared——event of a certain likelihood and severity, and which produces a number of positive (benefits) and negative (harms) consequences.

For the CNIL a feared event is a violation of what it refers to as primary assets. Primary assets are the safeguards enshrined into data protection legislation.[108] According to the CNIL, there are different ways in which these safeguards can be violated, which means that there are different types of feared events, five in this case. Two of which concern data protection *sensu stricto* (*ss*), while the remaining three concern data security. For the purpose of the present discussion, only the data protection feared events will be listed:[109]

- Unavailability of legal processes. This feared event results from the violation of a number of safeguards, which include transparency, consent of the data subject where required, and the data subject rights.
- Change in processing. This feared event results from the violation of some data protection core principles—which as we have seen are constituted of safeguards—(eg diversion of purpose, excessive collection). The CNIL does not make it clear whether the examples it provides are exhaustive or not, but we will assume they are.

Turning to the risk factors, the CNIL determines the severity of the risk by having regard to two factors: the severity of its impacts (ie harms on data subjects), and the level of identification of personal data (ie how easy is it to identify data subjects).[110] As far as the likelihood is concerned, the CNIL frames likelihoods as a matter of threats, that is, "how can it happen?".[111] The higher the threat, the higher the likelihood.[112] A threat can be broken down into risk sources and supporting assets. A threat occurs when a risk source acts upon a supporting asset. Since a risk source may act in different ways upon a supporting asset, there are thus various types of threats. Risk sources include persons working for the data controller (eg team in charge of processing), persons not working for the data controller (eg data

(PIA): Methodology" (2018). However, the present author does not consider the latter methodology relevant insofar as it focuses exclusively upon the risks to the "security of personal data and having an impact on data subjects' privacy", "Privacy Impact Assessment (PIA): Methodology (How to Carry out a PIA)" 7; CNIL, "Privacy Impact Assessment (PIA): Methodology" 6. Arguably, such change came in the wake of the Art 29 WP statements on the risk-based approach, and its reaffirmation of the rights-based aspect of EU data protection, see Art 29 WP (n 3).

[108] The methodology was issued in 2012 and with reference to the French Data Protection Act Loi du 6 janvier 1978 relative à l'informatique, aux fichiers et aux libertés, mise à jour au 2 août 2015 1978.

[109] CNIL (n 13) 6.

[110] ibid 12–14.

[111] It is to be noted that this conceiving of likelihood as a matter of threats is directly based upon data security models, something the CNIL explicitly acknowledges (ibid 4), but which NIST has criticised, National Institute of Standards and Technology (n 67) 22.

[112] CNIL (n 13) 15.

processor), or even non-humans (eg virus). A supporting asset includes hardware (computers), software, etc.[113] The level of probability is therefore that of the threat, which is calculated as a matter of vulnerability of the supporting asset, which is added to the capabilities of the risk source.[114] The final level of risk is determined by simply adding the level of severity with the level of likelihood.[115]

Once the level of risk has been established, the CNIL provides some methodology and guidance for their management. It argues that risks should undergo risk mitigation measures.[116] Following such measures,[117] risks that are still of high severity and high likelihood should not be taken, whereas it is up to the data controller to decide if risks of lower levels should be pursued.[118]

The way risks are managed is actually a very good example of the risk-based approach's ambition to provide "protection on the ground". Following the CNIL's methodology, there are indeed various means of complying, which go beyond traditional "box-ticking compliance". The CNIL provides for four different types of mitigation measures. First, measures that will act upon primary assets (ie mandatory data protection safeguards). This is the traditional means of compliance and consists in acting directly upon the characteristics of the processing. For instance, the data controller will process less data so as to respect the data minimisation principle, will provide better transparency, etc.[119] However, the CNIL methodology also provides additional methods to lower the risk of non-compliance. Data controllers can also reduce the severity of the risk by addressing the harms stemming from it (ie impact on data subject's fundamental rights and freedoms). This can be done for instance by establishing a crisis response unit in the event of harm.[120] Data controllers can increase their level of compliance by acting upon reducing the likelihood of such risk happening. This can be done by acting both on the capabilities of the risk sources/threats (eg training of personal), and on the vulnerability of the supporting assets (eg securing access to personal data).[121] Further, and if need be, such mitigation measures can be subject to monitoring and periodical evaluation.[122]

This illustration of "data protection on the ground" is interesting because it also shows the intrinsic links between the latter and the risk transformation of the regulatee. These additional risk mitigation measures are indeed constitutive of the internal controls analysed in Chapter 4 (cf crisis response unit, training of personal,

[113] ibid 7.
[114] ibid 15–16.
[115] ibid 8.
[116] ibid 19.
[117] ibid 20–21.
[118] ibid 22.
[119] ibid 20.
[120] CNIL, "Measures For The Pirvacy Risk Treatment" (2012) 36.
[121] CNIL (n 13) 20.
[122] ibid 21. The CNIL has published an in-depth guide of risk mitigation measures, CNIL (n 120).

monitoring, etc), and which are at the heart of the risk management agenda, meta regulation, and of the whole risk-based approach. In other words, this shows that compliance becomes a matter of internal controls, which are themselves coextensive with the transformation of the data controller's structure and activities as a matter of risk taking. Thus, the same internal controls that are used by the controllers for pursuing their activities and goals are simultaneously used to the ends of compliance with data protection law in the context of risk management tools. The whole goal of improved compliance at the heart of the GDPR reform process only makes sense if compliance is integrated into a risk calculation.

An additional example of what exactly the protection "on the ground" means, pertains to the granularity of the description of the data flows upon which risk management is predicated. So instead of simply using general descriptions such as "collection", "retention", etc, data controller should go into further detail such as "collection from users at registration via mobile devices", or "storage in an internal database".[123] Such description should also extend to the type of data (eg doctor name, address, and medical diagnosis instead of simply "health information"), or to the context of the processing.[124] Such context may include the type of data processing (eg frequency of processing, the existence of transfers to third countries); the sensitivity of data; the type of data subject, their expectations with regards to the processing; the type of data controller (eg public or private, its relationship with the data subject, etc), and so on.[125] This contextuality and granularity thus enables data controllers to "pinpoint what type of [safeguard] would be most effective to mitigate a data action's privacy risk".[126] For instance, simply saying that data should be minimised "does not inherently assist an agency in determining which information should be minimised to mitigate the risk".[127] It is important to understand which exact data, processed by whom, processed through which device, for which exact processing operation, etc should be minimised.

One can observe that this analysis is confirmed in the ISO DPIA Standard. In terms of description, it advocates for the same type of granular description of data flows.[128] In terms of safeguards, it goes along the same lines as the CNIL methodology. Risks can be addressed either by acting directly on personal data (ie traditional compliance focused on the characteristics of the processing); addressing the impacts/harms; acting on the risk sources/threats and/or on the supporting assets.[129]

[123] National Institute of Standards and Technology (n 67) 25.
[124] ibid.
[125] ibid 56.
[126] ibid 26.
[127] ibid 8.
[128] ISO/IEC (n 94) 6.3.3.
[129] ibid 20–21.

4.4 Other compliance risk management methodologies

As alluded, apart from the NIST methodology, which is aimed primarily at addressing data protection [privacy] risks, all other methodologies are centred around a notion of compliance risk.

This is certainly true for the methodologies designed at the EU level.[130] Starting with the pioneer EU endorsed RFID DPIA Framework, one can see that the feared events are constitutive of the violation of standard setting provisions and other safeguards such as the processing for unspecified and unlimited purpose, the lack of transparency, or the violation of data subject rights.[131] The same holds true for the German Federal Bureau for Data Security's (BSI) Privacy Impact Assessment Guideline, very much similar to the EU Radio Frequency Identification (RFID) DPIA.[132]

In 2014, the EU endorsed another DPIA methodology, this time concerning smart metering.[133] This methodology is very much based on the CNIL 2012 methodology,[134] and therefore exhibits the same characteristics as far as the present discussion is concerned. Indeed, similarly to the CNIL, a feared event will take place when a "process" is violated,[135] with such process including data protection core principles and all the other traditional data protection safeguards (notification, transparency, data subject rights …).[136] The Spanish Data Protection Authority (DPA) issued a DPIA methodology in 2014. It too envisages feared events as the violation of data protection safeguards.[137]

As indicated *supra*, the recent ISO DPIA methodology is also based on a compliance risk. Here the risk/feared event is any problematic action on personal

[130] There are other methodologies worth mentioning in this footnote, which are the outcome of research, and are not officially endorsed by regulators, such as the MITRE methodology, or the LINDDUN, see Stuart S Shapiro, "Situating Anonymization Within a Privacy Risk Model" [2012] 2012 IEEE International Systems Conference (SysCon) 651; Kim Wuyts, "Privacy Threats in Software Architectures" (2015); Hans Lammerant and others, "Byte Deliverable D4.2: Evaluating and Addressing Positive and Negative Societal Externalities" (2015).

[131] "Privacy and Data Protection Impact Assessment Framework for RFID Applications" (2011) 13–16. See also Sarah Spiekermann, "The RFID PIA—Developed by Industry, Endorsed by Regulators" in David Wright and Paul De Hert (eds), *Privacy Impact Assessment* (Springer 2012) 336–37.

[132] Bundesamt für Sicherheit in der Informationstechnik, "Privacy Impact Assessment Guideline" (2011). This is not least because Sarah Spiekermann participated with the elaboration of both methodologies, see Spiekermann (n 131).

[133] Smart Grid Task Force, "Data Protection Impact Assessment Template for Smart Grid and Smart Metering Systems" (2014). See also European Commission, Commission Recommendation of 10 October 2014 on the Data Protection Impact Assessment Template for Smart Grid and Smart Metering Systems (2014/724/EU) 2014 63.

[134] This is quite obvious when looking at the methodology, which the latter has explicitly admitted since it acknowledges being "mainly based on ISO 31 000, EBIOS methodology and the synthesis produced by the CNIL", Smart Grid Task Force (n 133).

[135] ibid.

[136] ibid.

[137] Agencia Espanola de Proteccion de Datos, "Guía Para Una Evaluación de Impacto En La Protección de Datos Personales" (2014) 23–26.

data (primary assets), which amounts in practice to violating the data protection principles (eg excessive collection, lack of transparency, loss of right to access, etc).[138] In other words, any violation of the data protection principles is a feared event.

Another interesting methodology is that of Bieker *et al.*,[139] which under all likelihood also underpins the methodology adopted in 2016 by the German Federal and State Data Protection Commissioners.[140] Contrary for instance to methodologies which simply design the feared event as the list of all the data protection principles, this methodology is built around six data protection goals, namely, confidentiality, transparency, intervenability, availability, unlinkability, integrity.[141] The violation of any of these goals is therefore constitutive of a feared event. As one can see, these data protection goals are quite similar to those of the NIST methodology (ie predictability, manageability, disassociability). Yet, whereas the violation of the NIST properties is directly linked to the goal of preventing harm (or privacy problems), Bieker *et al.*'s methodology remains first and foremost a "methodology to ensure effective compliance with data protection obligations".[142] In other words, the violation of any of the six goals signals a compliance risk (which itself may have impacts on the data subject's fundamental rights and freedoms).

DPIA methodologies developed outside of the EU seem to be crafted along the same lines. This is notably the case in Canada. In 2009, the American Institute of Certified Public Accountants and the Canadian Institute of Chartered Accountants issued what may be considered a precursor to the DPIA methodologies that would be developed in the 2010s.[143] This methodology is also based on a notion of risk understood as the violation of the most commonly accepted data protection safeguards.[144] One can also take stock of the Chief Information Officer of British Columbia's 2014 methodology, which is predicated upon similar premises.[145]

138 ISO/IEC (n 94) 16.

139 Felix Bieker and others, "A Process for Data Protection Impact Assessment Under the European General Data Protection Regulation", *Privacy Technologies and Policy: 4th Annual Privacy Forum, APF 2016 Frankfurt/Main, Germany, September 7–8, 2016, Proceedings*, vol 3 (2016); Felix Bieker and others, "Data Protection Impact Assessment: A Hands-on Tour of the GDPR's Most Practical Tool" in Marit Hansen *et al.* (eds), *Privacy and Identity* (Springer International Publishing 2018).

140 German Federal and State Data Protection Commissioners, "The Standard Data Protection Model" (2016).

141 Bieker and others, "A Process for Data Protection Impact Assessment Under the European General Data Protection Regulation" (n 139) 30.

142 Bieker and others, "Data Protection Impact Assessment: A Hands-on Tour of the GDPR's Most Practical Tool" (n 139) 210.

143 American Institute of Certified Public Accountants and Canadian Institute of Chartered Accountants, "Generally Accepted Privacy Principles" (2009).

144 ibid 12–65.

145 Office of the Chief Information Officer of British Columbia, "Privacy Impact Assessment Guidelines" (2014) chs 8–15.

5. Conclusion: The difference between compliance and "proper" data protection risk, and the logic of meta regulation

As a reminder this chapter has framed the distinction between a data protection and a compliance risk in the following manner. "Genuine" data protection risk management methodologies aim to assess how harmful the planned processing is, and to determine what the most adequate safeguards are, in order to reduce the level of harm to an acceptable level. Risk management methodologies based on the notion of compliance risk ask the following question instead: how big is the planned processing's risk of non-compliance (ie the risk of violating compulsory safeguards enshrined into data protection statutes), and thus, what can be done in order to mitigate such risk.

Bringing back this discussion to the risk-based approach, these diverging notions of risk can also be understood from a regulatory perspective. Meta regulation theory is predicated upon the delegation of standard setting to the regulatees, which is precisely done through the "data protection" risk, since the legally enshrined standards might not always lead to satisfying regulatory outcomes. The risk-based approach on the contrary is a partial implementation of meta regulation, which discards the delegation of the standard setting function. It is predicated upon the idea that legal standards will always lead to satisfying regulatory outcomes, and its main concern consists in how to best implement them. Hence the notion of compliance risk.

Of course, one should not rule out possible overlaps between compliance and data protection risk. In some cases, a compliance risk might coincide with a data protection risk, since the goal of the data protection provisions and safeguards is precisely to avoid harms in the first place. This possible overlap between "data protection risk" and "compliance risk" can be epitomised by the large scope of the compliance risk, which indeed encompasses any violation of any fundamental right (and any harm stemming therefrom) by the processing operation. As the ISO puts it, "the impact could result from the processing of [personal data] in conformance or in violation of privacy safeguards requirements".[146] Similarly, the final, 2017, version of the NIST Privacy Framework tries to establish a clear link between its three "system objectives" (the violation of which is a feared event) and the most prevalent data protection principles (which it refers to its US version: FIPPs). Whereas the 2015 draft version of the Framework simply stated that the goal of privacy risk management was to avoid privacy risks and harms,[147] the 2017 final version makes sure to explain that upholding all three system objectives is equivalent to fully respecting the fair information practice principles (FIPPs).[148]

[146] ISO/IEC (n 94) 2.
[147] National Institute of Standards and Technology (n 67) 21.
[148] National Institute of Standards and Technology (n 68) 18.

However, potential overlaps cannot be considered the default. As the NIST argues, it is explicitly predicated on the mandate to "manag[e] privacy risk beyond compliance with laws, regulations, and policies".[149] The reason being that assessing the risks created by data processing operations as a matter of violations of safeguards can create an inaccurate assessment of these risks, since the safeguards at stake might not be the most efficient and adequate ones in the first place.[150] However, this is exactly the situation at play with the compliance risk. The ISO Standard for instance clearly refers to the compliance risk as a proxy to assess the level of impact/harm.[151] In other words, harms and violation of fundamental rights can only be addressed within the confines of the pre-existing data protection safeguards. The data protection risk precisely allows to go beyond this frame. The NIST draft methodology gives the following example in the case of big data analytics and profiling. It contemplates the possibility to restrict access to the results spawned by the analytics process, and condition their use to a further risk assessment.[152] Such risk assessment might deem the further processing of these data safe enough (eventually with resort to other mitigation measures), or it might deem it not safe enough which would require the destruction of the data. It is not entirely clear that a similar solution could be devised if one were to exclusively base it upon existing data protection safeguards and provisions (ie compliance risk).

Finally, the discussion of data protection risk and risk methodologies from a regulatory perspective can also bring some additional insights on a debate around the scope of DPIAs that took mostly place around 2012 when DPIAs (then known as PIAs—Privacy Impact Assessments) were starting to be seen as one of the most important novelties of the—then—draft GDPR. Following a certain number of scholars, mostly coming from the Anglo-Saxon tradition,[153] PIAs were to be preferred to DPIAs since the latter were only limited to compliance issues, making them not much different from existing methodologies for verifying compliance, which had been the prime target of the "box ticking" criticism.[154] Very critically, Clarke had argued that DPIAs are "at most a mere Legal Compliance Assessment, and at worst a mere Statutory Compliance Assessment".[155] A PIA, on the contrary "considers all dimensions of privacy".[156] In other words, a DPIA would not address the broader dimensions of the processing of data.

[149] ibid 24.

[150] National Institute of Standards and Technology (n 67) 33.

[151] ISO/IEC (n 94) 41.

[152] National Institute of Standards and Technology (n 67) 19.

[153] But not only, see in particular Paul De Hert, "A Human Rights Perspective on Privacy and Data Protection Impact Assessments" in David Wright and Paul De Hert (eds), *Privacy Impact Assessment* (Springer 2012).

[154] For an example of such methodology, see Office of the Privacy Commissioner of Canada, "Privacy Toolkit—A Guide for Businesses and Organizations—Canada's Personal Information Protection and Electronic Documents Act" (2015).

[155] http://www.rogerclarke.com/SOS/IA-1401.html, last accessed 9 March 2019.

[156] Roger Clarke, "An Evaluation of Privacy Impact Assessment Guidance Documents" (2011) 1 International Data Privacy Law 111, 112. In a similar sense, see David Wright and Charles Raab, "Privacy

This criticism against DPIA can be read in light of the fact that these authors have based themselves on methodologies that are mostly qualitative, and, more importantly, are little formalised. In particular, these methodologies do not make a distinction between the risk as feared event and the impact or consequence stemming therefrom. They simply employ the vernacular acceptation of risk, as a potential future danger. This is the case for the methodology issued by the Australian Information Commissioner, which clearly distinguishes between compliance and privacy risks.[157] The same used to be true with the Information Commissioner's Office (ICO)' s 2014 PIA methodology, which distinguished between compliance risks and privacy risks.[158]

However, the notion of compliance risk as embodied in the risk-based approach and all the methodologies studied is more formalised and in line with the technical notion of risk, since it distinguishes between the lack of compliance as the feared event and the broader consequences on all fundamental rights as the impact/harm/(negative) consequence. According to the ISO itself, these more formalised methodologies (including its own DPIA Standard) can be described as quantitative or semi-quantitative.[159] In this sense, the criticism of these authors appears as less warranted. The fact that the risk-based approach's compliance risk is underpinned by the technical notion of risk embodying both the feared event and its impacts has been sufficiently discussed. However, one can pay heed to the ICO's latest guidance document on DPIAs if further proof were needed.[160] Contrary to the 2014 guidance document about PIAs, the 2018 document is about DPIAs. It also makes it very clear that the goal of a DPIA is to "consider compliance risks, but also broader risks to the rights and freedoms of individuals".[161]

Yet, the more important reason why this objection does not hold can be grasped in the light of the regulatory dimension of impact assessments and risk management more generally. As has been analysed *supra*, the goal of ensuring a "protection on the ground" can only be achieved through the technical notion of risk, since the latter is coextensive with the risk transformation of the regulatees, which in turns relies upon the notion of internal controls. The latter are instrumental since they are simultaneously constitutive of organisational design,[162] and constitutive of the

Principles, Risks and Harms" (2014) 28 International Review of Law, Computers & Technology 1; David Wright, "The State of the Art in Privacy Impact Assessment" (2012) 28 Computer Law & Security Review 54; Charles D Raab and David Wright, "Surveillance: Extending the Limits of Privacy Impact Assessment" in David Wright and Paul De Hert (eds), *Privacy Impact Assessment* (Springer 2012).

[157] Office of the Australian Information Commissioner, "Guide to Undertaking Privacy Impact Assessments" (2014) ss 6–7.

[158] ICO, "Conducting Privacy Impact Assessments: Code of Practice" (2014) ch 6.

[159] ISO/IEC (n 94) 18.

[160] ICO, "Data Protection Impact Assessments (DPIAs)" (2018).

[161] ibid 4.

[162] ie the very structure and materiality of organisations and therefore the devices through which they exist and carry out their activities.

various technical and organisational measures that render such protection on the ground possible. Thus, the very regulatory logic of the risk-based approach entails per definition a technical notion of risk, whereby issues of compliance and broader impacts on the data subject's fundamental rights are integrated into a single risk calculation. In this regard it is therefore interesting to observe that even though the taking into account of the impacts on the fundamental rights can be saluted as an improvement of the type of protection afforded, it remains nonetheless an ancillary consideration, instrumental to the primary goal of compliance. In this sense, the assessment of the impact on the fundamental rights and freedoms of the data subjects is first and foremost a means to better comply.

7
The risk-based approach in practice
Caveats

> [Data protection] is constituted by what escapes institutional risk management[1]

1. Introduction

The goal of this chapter is to analyse some of the main caveats associated with the risk-based approach in practice, that is, with the use of meta regulation. As one remembers, one of the overarching points of this book is to argue that the rights-based approach can be equated to command and control regulation, whereas the risk-based approach can be equated to meta regulation. In turn, the shift towards the risk-based approach and meta regulation has been analysed as a response to some of the shortcomings associated to command and control regulation (in the context of data protection), and which were discussed in Chapter 3. Chapters 5 and 6 in particular have described and explained how such risk-based approach is deployed, at the level of statutes (including the type of regulatory collaboration they entail), and at the level of risk analysis itself. However, as alluded to in the introductory chapter, if meta regulation tries to address some of the issues plaguing command and control types of regulation, one should not see it as a silver bullet solution: in addressing these issues it also creates new issues. This is the meaning of this quote from O'Malley in the context of risk management: "risks are neither real nor unreal. Rather, they are ways in which the real is imagined to be by specific regimes of government, in order that it may be governed."[2] In other words, framing issues as risks is never neutral, and bears consequences in terms of how the protection of personal data is performed. This is exactly what Black echoes when she argues that risk and regulation models based on risk "import particular conceptions of the problem at hand, and lead to the framing of a solution in a particular

[1] Richard V Ericson and Kevin D Haggerty, *Policing the Risk Society* (University of Toronto Press 1997) 117.
[2] Pat O'Malley, *Risk, Uncertainty and Government* (Glasshouse Press 2004) 15.

The Risk-Based Approach to Data Protection. Raphaël Gellert, Oxford University Press (2020). © Raphaël Gellert.
DOI: 10.1093/oso/9780198837718.001.0001.

way".[3] The goal of the present chapter is to address these very issues. More in particular, one can distinguish between three different issues. Methodological issues concerning techniques for performing risk analysis; regulatory issues in particular as far as the collaboration between regulators and regulatees is concerned; and implementational issues, that is, concerning the way in which risk management is actually implemented in practice, "on the ground".

2. Methodological issues

Methodology is of paramount importance for the risk analysis processes. As Wynne argues, "risk is not completely determined by the evidence from nature alone, but is partly open-ended depending on what parameters are treated as the most significant".[4] However, risk analysis is presented to us as an objective, easy-to-use exercise. In doing so, risk methodologies tend to reduce "the full range of uncertainties to the more comforting illusion of controllable, probabilistic but deterministic processes".[5] This section will therefore discuss a number of caveats concerning methodological choices. In doing so, it will also act as a reminder of the fact that risk and risk analysis are "inherently judgemental processes".[6]

2.1 Risk criteria step: taking risks

As discussed before, the risk criteria step is the step containing the criteria for determining whether an event can be considered a risk, or in other words, the step that contains "the terms of reference against which the significance of a risk is evaluated".[7] These criteria can include the types of harms to be taken into account, harms to whom, how to measure the level of risk, what counts as a risk factor, etc.[8] The risk criteria step is of paramount importance since it determines the organisation's risk tolerance.[9] Indeed, the lower the threshold, the more events will be recognised as risks, and *vice versa*.

[3] Julia Black, "Risk-Based Regulation: Choices, Practices and Lessons Being Learnt" in OECD (ed), *Risk and Regulatory Policy: Improving the Governance of Risk* (OECD publishing 2010) 188.
[4] Brian Wynne, "Uncertainty and Environmental Learning—Reconceiving Science and Policy in the Preventive Paradigm" (1992) 2 Global Environmental Change 111, 122.
[5] ibid 123.
[6] Black (n 3) 205.
[7] ISO, "ISO: 31000 Risk Management—Principles and Guidelines" 5.
[8] ibid 17; ISO/IEC, "ISO/IEC 29134: Information Technology—Security Techniques—Guidelines for Privacy Impact Assessment" (2017) 8–9. See also David Wright and others, "Surveillance Impact Assessment Manual" (2014) 28; David Wright, Michael Friedewald, and Raphaël Gellert, "Developing and Testing a Surveillance Impact Assessment Methodology" (2015) 5 International Data Privacy Law 40, 50.
[9] Black (n 3) 193.

This points to a two-folded paradox associated to risk management. On the one hand, aiming for zero risks appears as an impossible objective, since there are as many risks as there are risk criteria.[10] One can always add a new harm, a new risk factor, an even more inclusive magnitude and/or risk probability, and so on, to the point where it simply becomes unmanageable to use the risk management tool, and would therefore defeat the whole purpose of resorting to risk management in the first place.[11] Thus, and on the other hand, this means that risk managers have to make choices with regards to which events (or risk) they will take into consideration.[12] In other words, they have to take risks, since there is a possibility that some of the events discarded, will actually materialise and negatively affect a number of people. Therefore, one can argue that resorting to risk-based instruments is a quasi-explicit acknowledgement that a number of issues will remain unaddressed.[13]

This issue is particularly salient as far as the scope of data protection impact assessments (DPIAs) is concerned. As discussed herein below, the Article 29 Working Party (Art 29 WP) issued a number of criteria to determine what constitutes a high risk.[14] More specifically, given the applicability of DPIAs to automated processing operations, including decision-making and profiling,[15] and given the latter's increasing prevalence, there is a real chance that DPIAs might become the rule rather than the exception.

2.2 Different possibilities to assess risks

Once a risk has been identified, the next step is to assess its level in terms of its magnitude (or severity) and probability (ie likelihood of happening). As with the previous steps, this is anything but self-evident.

2.2.1 The difference between toxicology and epidemiology

The key issue on how to assess a risk has been discussed in Chapter 1 on risk: it is the difference between toxicology and epidemiology. As a reminder, toxicology is an approach to risk management that focuses on the source of the risk (on what

[10] See also Patrick Peretti-Watel, *La Société Du Risque* (Repères, La Découverte 2010) 8.

[11] Black (n 3) 206.

[12] ibid 193.

[13] Julia Black and Robert Baldwin, "Really Responsive Risk-Based Regulation" (2010) 32 Law & Policy 181. See also Henry Rothstein and others, "The Risks of Risk-Based Regulation: Insights from the Environmental Policy Domain" (2006) 32 Environment International 1056, 1059: in devising these risk criteria it is clear that "scientific knowledge needs to be supplemented by value judgements about the relative importance of different kinds of risks".

[14] Art 29 WP, "Guidelines on Data Protection Impact Assessment (DPIA) and Determining Whether Processing Is 'Likely to Result in a High Risk' for the Purposes of Regulation 2016/679" (2017).

[15] See also Art 29 WP, "17/EN WP251rev.01— Guidelines on Automated Individual Decision-Making and Profiling for the Purposes of Regulation 2016/679—Adopted on 3 October 2017 As Last Revised and Adopted on 6 February 2018" (2018).

creates the risk). Epidemiology can be seen as the opposite since it focuses on the target of the risk (what/who will be affected by the risk).

Black indicates that some methodologies only use what she refers to as "impact measures" as proxies to determine the magnitude of the risk (both in terms of severity and likelihood), that is, without regard for the consequences of the risk.[16] In other words, these methodologies solely focus on toxicological factors. In order to better understand this, one can take the trivial example of rain as the risk/feared event. A number of factors will determine the severity and likelihood of rain. The humidity, atmospheric pressure, wind, etc will partly determine its likelihood and severity. Other factors might include the duration of the rain, its geographical scope, its density, the presence of hail as well (which might as well place it in the high-risk category, etc). As one can see, these factors are toxicological because they focus exclusively on the risk/feared event (and its sources), and do not take at all into consideration the harms in determining the severity of the risk.

Another approach is to focus on the harms following from the feared event.[17] This is the epidemiological approach. Just like the risk/feared event itself, these harms can also be measured in terms of severity and likelihood. Continuing with the example of rain, one can distinguish a number of harms. One might have their clothes wet, which is quite probable but remains of low severity. One might be late to work (this might also have consequences in terms of productivity and economic performance of the organisation they work for); some persons might get sick—eventually die—depending on the population category they belong to; others might have incidents on the—wet—roads; some areas might be more impacted than others (eg floods, houses damaged) etc.

As one can see, these are two different ways to measure the magnitude of a risk. And as indicated in Chapter 1, the modern definition of risk and risk management is an arbitrary combination of both, namely, a combination of the probability of occurrence of a feared event and the magnitude of the consequences.[18] The International Organization for Standardization (ISO) Risk Management Standard simply provides that the assessment should target both the severity of the feared event, and the severity of the consequences without any further detail.[19] The ISO 2017 DPIA methodology is also predicated upon the probability of the feared event combined to the severity of the impact.[20]

Taking the example of Art 35 General Data Protection Regulation (GDPR), one can see that it refers solely to these toxicological factors. For instance, Art 35.1 provides some risk criteria such as the type of technology used, as well as "the nature,

[16] Black (n 3) 197–98.
[17] ibid 198.
[18] Frederick Warner, "Introduction" in The Royal Society (ed), *Risk: Analysis, Perception and Management—A Report of a Royal Society Study Group* (The Royal Society 1992) 4.
[19] ISO (n 7) 18.
[20] ISO/IEC (n 8) 18.

scope, context and purposes of the processing". These are clearly toxicological criteria that say nothing about the potential harms. The same holds true as far as Art 35(3) is concerned.[21]

Such focus on toxicological factors is not benign. On the one hand, it is remarkably easier than the focus on epidemiological factors, since it entails mainly to collect data available at the data controller level (ie the properties of the processing operations as proxies for the level of harm). As discussed in Chapter 1, harms are notoriously difficult to assess not least because of their inherently subjective nature (ie not everyone perceives harms in the same way, not at the same time).[22] This is even more so of moral and psychological harms.[23,24] The DPIA context epitomises the difficulty linked to assessing harms. The literature has long established that an adequate route to determining such harms is through participatory exercises, even though these are notoriously difficult to properly conduct.[25] Article 35(9) GDPR precisely provides for such public participation. However, in addition to the fact that it is only limited to cases that are "appropriate", the Art 29 WP Guidance has given little additional clues as how to conduct these exercises in practice.[26] This shows the uneasiness of the European legislator to engage with public participation, precisely because it is poised with enormous difficulties. This focus on toxicological factors is also reminiscent of another finding from Chapter 1, namely the fact that a number of events that are, strictly speaking, uncertainties, are transformed into risks through "methodological tricks", so as to render them assessable and manageable. Clearly, the focus on toxicological factors is one of these "tricks".

On the other hand, a focus on toxicological factors makes it very difficult to adequately assess a number of risks and harms. A particularly tricky category of harms to measure are those with low probability and—very—high impact, not

[21] Art 35.3 GDPR: "a systematic and extensive evaluation of personal aspects relating to natural persons which is based on automated processing" (Art 35(3)(a)); "processing on a large scale of special categories of data referred" (Art 35(3)(b)); "a systematic monitoring of a publicly accessible area on a large scale" (Art 35(3)(c)). The only exception could be found in Art 35(3)(a), which also includes a reference to processing operations that "significantly affect the natural person".

[22] In the context of the GDPR reform, this was already acknowledged, see European Commission, "Commission Staff Working Paper: Impact Assessment Accompanying the Document Regulation of the European Parliament and of the Council on the Protection of Individuals with Regard to the Processing of Personal Data and on the Free Movement of Such Data" (2012) 29; Neil Robinson and others, "Review of the European Data Protection Directive" 1, 2–3.

[23] Such as psychological harms stemming from unwanted exposure, or the chilling effect as a result of surveillance, see Orla Lynskey, *The Foundations of EU Data Protection Law* (OUP 2015) 210–28; M Ryan Calo, "The Boundaries of Privacy Harm" (2011) 86 Indiana Law Journal 1131; Neil M Richards, "The Dangers of Surveillance" (2013) 126 Harvard Law Review 1934.

[24] In the *LabMD* case, the FTC argued that the fact that the harm had not materialised yet had no bearing, see, Federal Trade Commission, "LabMD, Inc v Federal Trade Commission (11th Cir), Response Brief of the FTC" (2017). See also *Google v Vidal-Hall and others*, 2015, EWCA Civ 311.

[25] See eg Sergio Joss and Sergio Bellucci, *Participatory Technology Assessment: European Perspectives* (Athenaeum Press 2002).

[26] Raphaël Gellert, "The Article 29 Working Party's Provisional Guidelines on Data Protection Impact Assessment" (2017) 2 European Data Protection Law Review 1, 215.

least because they require data going quite far into the future, whereas risk assessment methodologies usually assess the risks at present time, or on the short(er) term.[27] One such example has been dubbed a "World War II scenario": in case a totalitarian regime came to power, the amount and quality of data presently stored by governmental agencies would greatly facilitate the execution of their plans.[28,29] It is extremely difficult, if not impossible to determine the likelihood of such harm happening.[30] In a similar vein, big data distends the link between the risk and the ensuing harms.[31] Van Der Sloot takes the example of traditional data processing practices, such as telephone taps, which are clearly demarcated in time, place, and person. By contrast, big data analytics rely on seemingly innocuous processing operations of data contained in large data sets. Often, the harms will manifest themselves at a later stage, for instance when/if an unfavourable decision is made on the basis of patterns and profiles, or when/if the data subject becomes aware of the data processing that has taken place and which they do not agree with.[32] In other words, the differences are twofold. First, traditional processing operations can be characterised as risky because of their inherent characteristics (ie toxicology), and the link with the ensuing harms is quite close. Second, big data processing operations appear as innocuous and very much stretch the link with the ensuing harmful consequences. Thus, one might argue that one of big data analytics consequences is to render the harm assessment more difficult.[33]

Furthermore, one should add that since toxicological factors are seen as proxies for determining the level of harm, they can only lead to aggregated results.[34] The only way to have finer grained, distributed results, is to collect harm related data (given its focus on who is affected by what harm and according to which probability). This is particularly salient as far as groups or societal impacts are concerned,[35] as with the instance of medical data processing revealing a hereditary disease. In this case, all the members of the data subject's family can potentially be harmed.[36] Further, the processing of data can also affect the whole of society as such. Such an argument has been made with regards to the National Security

[27] Black (n 3) 198.

[28] Bart Van Der Sloot, "The Individual in the Big Data Era: Moving towards an Agent-Based Privacy Paradigm" in Bart Van Der Sloot, Dennis Broeders, and Erik Schrijvers (eds), *Exploring the Boundaries of Big Data* (Amsterdam University Press 2016) 190.

[29] Such harms, pervaded by total uncertainty, are also known as "unknown unknowns", see Louise Amoore, *The Politics of Possibility* (2013).

[30] See also, Rothstein and others (n 13).

[31] Van Der Sloot (n 28) 184.

[32] On the psychological harm stemming from the realisation that one's data are being/have been processed, see Calo (n 23).

[33] See also Van Der Sloot (n 28) 189.

[34] Black (n 3) 198.

[35] On theories of group and societal privacy, see also Joshua AT Fairfield and Christoph Engel, "Privacy as a Public Good" (2015) 65 Duke Law Journal 385; Priscilla M Regan, *Legislating Privacy: Technology, Social Values, and Public Policy* (The University of North Carolina Press 1995).

[36] Van Der Sloot (n 28) 187.

Agency (NSA)'s generalised surveillance practices.[37] Again, it is difficult to aggregate such harms at individual level.

These arguments tend to show that if one is to correctly assess the risks stemming from big data analytics, it is crucial to integrate the assessment of harms. Not doing so would lead to the following paradox. As has been discussed, the risk-based approach came to the fore among others as a response to the challenges of big data analytics. Yet, risk methodologies solely based upon "impact measures" would fail to correctly assess the risks stemming from such operations; hence the paradox.

Finally, this focus on harms as the consequences of the risk/feared event also brings the possibility to integrate the positive consequences (ie the benefits) into the assessment of the risk. One should not lose track of the fact that the management of risks entails a balancing between the harms and the benefits.[38] As Van Der Sloot argues, "the general interest [which justifies a processing operation] is often assessed at a general and societal level".[39] However, here too, finer grained assessments would be required.[40] One could indeed inquire as to whom exactly (individual, number of individuals, group(s)) a given measure actually benefits. A finer grained assessment of the benefits should also specify the beneficiaries. Generalised surveillance measures might indeed bring great economic benefit to those who sell them, and eventually—short term—political credit to those governments who resort to them. But what about the individuals who are subject to them? Similarly, why would anyone engage in a high-risk activity if it yields little benefits?

2.2.2 Additional caveats surrounding the assessment of risks

Another important caveat related to the assessment of risks is that of the somewhat arbitrary classification between the severity and likelihood of the feared event. Black argues that this distinction is not as crystal clear as it seems.[41] More in particular, it is not always possible to clearly distinguish whether a risk factor pertains to the severity or the likelihood of the risk. Some DPIA templates regard the transfer of data to third countries as a likelihood factor.[42] Knowing that the data collected will further be transferred increases indeed the likelihood of risk.[43] However, one could again counter argue that when the data are transferred, very risky processing operations ensue, thereby linking this factor to the magnitude of the harm. The GDPR does indeed see the transfer of data to third

[37] Richards (n 23).

[38] Reminding of the need to also assess the benefits, see Christopher Kuner and others, "Risk Management in Data Protection" (2015) 5 International Data Privacy Law 95, 3.

[39] Van Der Sloot (n 28) 187.

[40] See also ibid 185: "the social interest is increasingly difficult to specify".

[41] Black (n 3) 198.

[42] The same reasoning extends to the sharing of data between a controller and a processor.

[43] The DPIA templates referred to are internal templates used by organisations. They have been disclosed to the present author on the condition of anonymity.

countries as a severity factor.[44] Black indicates that a distinction is often made between the human and non-human factors. Non-human factors such as a site's location, capacity to pollute, quantity of emissions, etc are considered as magnitude factors. Human factors, which include the quality of the management and internal controls, compliance records, etc are linked to the likelihood of the feared event. Further, Black also notes that there is more than one way to combine probability and magnitude factors.[45] The *Commission nationale de l'informatique et des libertés* (CNIL) for instance aggregates the total number of factors.[46] The National Institute of Standards and Technology (NIST) draft Privacy Risk Management Framework used to multiply probability with magnitude.[47] One can also take note of the ISO 2017 methodology which is agnostic. It simply warns that there are varying ways of combining likelihood and severity, which will produce different outcomes.[48]

2.2.3 Examples from DPIA methodologies concerning the different possibilities of assessment

Concerning the assessment, one can contrast the CNIL methodology (and the ISO's) with that of the NIST.

The CNIL methodology previously discussed, proceeds in the following fashion. In terms of severity of the risk: it uses a single toxicological factor, namely, "the level of identification of personal data", that is, the ease with which the data processed allow for the identification of the data subject.[49] It combines this factor with an epidemiological factor: the magnitude of the harm(s) suffered by the data subject.[50] The CNIL uses likelihoods only at the toxicological level, that is, concerning the occurrence of the feared event, therefore the assessment of the likelihoods of harms is completely absent from the assessment.[51] Finally, it is not clear whether the final risk score is the result of a multiplication, addition, or aggregation between severity and likelihood.[52]

The ISO 2017 methodology similarly assesses likelihoods of the risk only from the perspective of the feared event (thus also excluding the calculation of the harms likelihood). In an ambiguous fashion, even though its notion of risk is predicated upon the severity being calculated with respect to the harm, one can see that the only epidemiological factor it uses is one that relates to the number of data subjects.

[44] See GDPR, Recital, 116: "When personal data moves across borders outside the Union it may put at increased risk the ability of natural persons to exercise data protection rights."

[45] Black (n 3) 198.

[46] eg CNIL, "Methodology For Privacy Risk Management: How to Implement the Data Protection Act" (2012).

[47] eg National Institute of Standards and Technology, "NISTIR 8062 (Draft): Privacy Risk Management for Federal Information Systems" (2015). The final, 2017 version is silent on the matter.

[48] ISO/IEC (n 8) 8, 17.

[49] CNIL (n 46) 12.

[50] ibid 13.

[51] ibid 15–16.

[52] ibid 18–19.

All the other factors are toxicological ones (eg sensitivity of data, "level of identification" of data).[53]

The NIST methodology is one of the most sophisticated attempts to assess risks given its focus on harms to data subjects (as a result of its use of a data protection risk). It therefore defines the feared events as "a problem that individuals experience as a by-product of processing of [their personal data]".[54] This entails that both the likelihood and severity of the risk be assessed from an epidemiological viewpoint (ie focus on harms). In terms of likelihood, the NIST recommends the following data subject-centred assessment methods: "using existing information on customer demographics, extrapolating from information available about privacy problems in similar scenarios, and conducting focus groups or surveys to learn more about users' privacy interests and concerns to determine whether users may consider a data action to be problematic".[55]

One would assume that similar methods would be used in order to assess the severity of the impact. Yet, and surprisingly, the NIST argues that this is particularly challenging since "it may be difficult to do with any consistency because there may be a significant divergence in the way individuals experience problems".[56] One wonders why it is easier for data subjects to assess the probability of a harm rather than its severity. Furthermore, and in the face of such difficulty, the NIST thus argues that the severity of the harms should be assessed through harms to the data controllers, and in particular, the risks to their business and organisational goals. In other words, the harms to the data subjects will be assessed through the harms to the data controllers which act as proxies. They include legal compliance risks, mission failure risks, reputational risks, and internal culture risks.[57] This case illustrates very clearly the porous and somewhat artificial distinction between the assessment of the severity and the assessment of the likelihood. Furthermore, it also illustrates the use of toxicological factors as an easier alternative to epidemiological ones, even though it renders the assessment less accurate.

2.3 Risk management *sensu stricto* (*ss*)

Finally, one can also underscore methodological issues at the level of the risk management step.

[53] ISO/IEC (n 8) 8.

[54] National Institute of Standards and Technology, "NISTIR 8062: An Introduction to Privacy Engineering and Risk Management in Federal Systems" (2017) 21. See its definition of privacy risk, putting data subjects' harms to the fore: "a measure of the extent to which an entity or individual is threatened by a potential circumstance or event", ibid 28.

[55] ibid 22.

[56] ibid.

[57] ibid.

A first caveat concerns the non-absolute nature of risk scores (ie the risk level that follows from the risk assessment).[58] For instance, a risk with low probability and high impact has the same level as a risk with high probability and low impact. Yet, they are in reality quite different. A well-known example is that of train safety, where accidents involving multiple deaths are usually rare (ie low probability, high magnitude). They attract nonetheless more attention and media coverage than more common minor accidents that involve individual fatalities and/or injuries (high probability, low magnitude), which can have the exact same risk score.[59]

Another caveat concerns risks of medium severity, and the further action to be taken concerning them.[60] As far as high risks and low risks are concerned the situation is rather clear. In case of high risks, mitigation measures will be taken, and most probably low risks will simply be taken without any mitigation measures. However, medium risks are more difficult to manage. As discussed in the section dedicated to risks, risk mitigation measures have a cost of their own. Therefore, it is not always easy to determine whether to reject medium risks, whether to simply accept them, or whether to accept them pursuant to adoption of mitigation measures. Interestingly, Black notes that some managers have shifted their focus from the level of risks (which produces a high number of risks with similar, medium levels), to an approach based on achievability (ie what are the most efficient mitigation measures to be taken given the level of resources, the number of risks, and their respective levels).[61]

Finally, one should remember—as seen in Chapter 1—that risk management does not strive to completely eliminate risks, but rather, to reduce them to an acceptable or tolerable level.[62] This is an important point on two accounts. First, it "manages expectations" as to the "end product" of the risk management exercise. Second, it acts as a powerful reminder of the important value-laden dimension of risk management. As seen in Chapter 1, to manage risks *ss*, is to take a decision as to whether or not to take a risk.[63] In other words, beyond all the subjective choices involved in the risk assessment methodologies, the exercise to manage a risk is at its core a purely subjective decision. This is crucial because different actors have different risk appetites: some will be more risk prone while others will be more risk averse. This intrinsic subjective nature of risk management is particularly important in the context of meta regulation, which relies upon the uptaking

[58] Black (n 3) 196.

[59] Rothstein and others (n 13). On this issue, see Michael Spackman, "Serving the Public Interest?" (2002) 3 Risk and Regulation: CARR Review 6.

[60] Black (n 3) 201.

[61] ibid 202.

[62] See ISO/IEC (n 8) 21, and National Institute of Standards and Technology (n 54) 22: "Risk can be managed, but it cannot be eliminated (. . .) privacy risk management should not be seen as a vehicle for creating perfect privacy-preserving systems [but rather] to achieve an acceptable degree of residual risk and avoid unacceptable consequences."

[63] Warner (n 18) 3.

of regulatory activities by regulatees because they are seen as responsible entities. As seen, this is possible because of the transformation of their activities as a matter of risk management. Crucially, this risk management was described as having a "neoliberal flavour", that is, as leading to a style of risk management which is (very) risk prone. This was clearly displayed with the Microsoft approach in Chapter 5. As a matter of fact, this is exactly what happened during the 2008 crisis in the financial sector. As will be discussed herein below, the financial sector also features a meta regulation model, and it appears that one of the decisive factors leading to the 2008 crisis was the regulates' extremely important risk appetite. Will data protection suffer a similar fate?

2.4 Risk management and data legitimacy

Another difficulty associated with risk management methodologies is specific to the data protection context and concerns the transformation of the data legitimacy requirement (ie the choice of a lawful basis according to Art 6 GDPR such as consent for instance) into a risk management exercise.

When the feared event is framed in terms of the violation of any of the data protection principles this is not so much of an issue. This is the case with the ISO 2017 methodology for instance, which, as seen, conceives of the feared event as any problematic action on personal data (primary assets),[64] so that any violation of the data protection principles is a feared event. For example, the excessive collection of personal data (ie beyond the consent of the data subject or beyond what is necessary for any of the other lawful bases) will be considered as a risk to be mitigated.[65]

The situation becomes more complex however with more sophisticated methodologies that frame the risk/feared event in terms other than the mere compliance with data protection principles. This is the case with the methodology developed by Bieker *et al.* for instance.[66] As seen before, this methodology is built around six data protection goals, namely: confidentiality, transparency, intervenability, availability, unlinkability, integrity, the violation of which constitutes a feared event.[67] Yet, the problem at hand is that none of these protection goals are linked to Art 6 GDPR, so that the choice of a legal basis is excluded from the risk management exercise. This appears very clearly from their methodology, since they explicitly argue that the

[64] ISO/IEC (n 8) 16.

[65] ibid.

[66] Felix Bieker and others, "A Process for Data Protection Impact Assessment Under the European General Data Protection Regulation", *Privacy Technologies and Policy: 4th Annual Privacy Forum, APF 2016 Frankfurt/Main, Germany, September 7–8, 2016, Proceedings*, vol 3 (2016); Felix Bieker and others, "Data Protection Impact Assessment: A Hands-on Tour of the GDPR's Most Practical Tool" in Marit Hansen *et al.* (eds), *Privacy and Identity* (Springer International Publishing 2018).

[67] Bieker and others, "A Process for Data Protection Impact Assessment Under the European General Data Protection Regulation" (n 66) 30.

determination of a legal basis belongs to the "preparation phase", and is nowhere to be found in the "execution phase", ie the phase where the risk is actually managed.[68] This is an explicit acknowledgement that the choice of a legal basis is difficult to fit in the risk management process. Their solution has been to simply exclude it therefrom. However, this is sub-optimal in view of the risk-based approach's goal of improved compliance and implementation of data protection provisions. As was seen in Chapter 3, consent is one of the prime examples of a principles the compliance with and the implementation thereof have undergone many challenges. This can be linked to the analysis in Chapter 2, according to which a number of legitimate grounds such as consent or the data subject's legitimate interests are actually also permeated by safeguards. It would therefore make more sense to try and find a way to also properly integrate the legitimate ground into the risk management exercise.

A potential solution could consist in dividing the choice of a legitimate ground into two distinct operations. The first one would consist in determining whether the processing falls within the scope of the chosen ground. The second operation concerns the implementation of safeguards (in the case of consent properly informing the data subject for instance). On this basis, one can argue that the legitimacy test should actually be spread into two different steps of risk analysis. A new preliminary step should be created and would consist in choosing the most appropriate legitimate basis.[69] However, the implementation and/or determination of safeguards taken pursuant to the chosen legitimate basis should be integrated into the risk management ss step.

3. Regulatory issues

This section addresses three regulatory issues in the context of meta regulation. The pitfalls of increased discretion to the regulatees; the extent to which the responsibilisation of regulated entities provides for a full alignment between their own goals and regulatory goals; and the possible changes regulators might undergo as a result of the use of regulation models that rely upon risk as the chief method of regulation.

3.1 Discretion and consistency: two contradictory requirements

As previously analysed, the risk-based approach has been conceived as a means for more efficient compliance. In particular, this is achieved through a shift from

[68] Bieker and others, "Data Protection Impact Assessment: A Hands-on Tour of the GDPR's Most Practical Tool" (n 66) 209.
[69] See also, CJEU, *Worten*.

the focus on the letter of the law towards the determination and implementation of appropriate safeguards,[70] which achieve the purpose of the principles.[71] In the context of the GDPR reform, it has been associated with two objectives. Namely, having more consistent rules (by enhancing the internal market dimension of the right to data protection), and increasing the effectiveness of these rules.[72]

However, such consistent and efficient implementation of the framework entails by definition a certain level of discretion and scalability.[73] The latter descends from the "on the ground" aspect, since appropriate and efficient measure "should take account of the context and the specific circumstances of the case".[74] It also descends from the responsibilisation of the regulatees. According to the Art 29 WP, "it should be left to the controller to determine which appropriate technical and organisational measures and procedures to implement to ensure compliance",[75] since the latter "can only be assessed on a case-by-case basis".[76]

One can see a clear tension underpinning the risk-based approach. One opposing the flexibility and discretion concerning the use of regulatees' resources and measures to the end of compliance, with the need to ensure a consistent framework, and thus, to potentially curb such discretion.[77] One of the most salient *loci* where the issue of discretion came to the fore are DPIAs. As discussed, DPIAs can be defined as a regulatory resource consisting of a risk management exercise that should be pursued only in case of high risk. The definition of what constitutes a high risk has crystallised many of the concerns around the discretion of the regulatees. Article 35(1) is the general provision, which refers in broad terms to the scope, which can be defined by having regard to the context, nature, purpose of the processing as well as to the use of new technologies. Given its very broad language it is complemented in a number of ways. First, Art 35(3) contains an illustrative list of three high-risk processing operations that are only illustrative.[78] Furthermore, Art 35(4) complements Art 35(1) by requiring DPAs to establish lists of high-risk processing operations.[79] Finally, the Art 29 issued a guidance document on DPIAs

[70] European Commission (n 22) 42. See also, EDPS, "Opinion of the EDPS on the Data Protection Reform Package" (2012) para 9.

[71] European Commission (n 22) 39.

[72] ibid 43.

[73] On the link between the risk-based approach and the overall consistency of the legal framework, see Art 29 WP, "Opinion 01/2012 on the Data Protection Reform Proposals" (2012) 6: "For data controllers the Regulation brings simplification and greater consistency, a strengthened focus on their accountability."

[74] EDPS (n 70) 174.

[75] Art 29 WP (n 73) 25.

[76] ibid.

[77] On the discretionary nature of the accountability principle, see also Art 29 WP, "Opinion 3/2010 on the Principle of Accountability" (2010) para 54.

[78] These are: systematic and extensive evaluation of personal aspects relating to natural persons which is based on automated processing, including profiling, and on which decisions are based that produce legal effects; processing on a large scale of special categories of data; systematic monitoring of a publicly accessible area on a large scale (Art 35(3)(a–c) GDPR). On the illustrative nature of the list, see Art 29 WP (n 14) 7.

[79] See ibid 8–9.

whereby it extracted a list of nine high risk criteria that are meant to help national supervisory authorities establish their lists,[80] and which go beyond the three criteria of Art 35(3).[81] Interestingly, the EDPB has confirmed the importance of these criteria concerning the consistency of the EU framework, and has requested national authorities to structure their own lists around these criteria.[82] The determination of what counts as a high risk can therefore be understood as based on a two-tiered system. Data controllers should look first into national lists. However, should their contemplated processing operation not be contained in the relevant national list, they should still pay heed to the criteria developed in the Art 29 WP Guidelines.[83] It is quite evident that such a system aims at curbing the discretion of the data controllers whilst still allowing for sufficient room of manoeuvre in the spirit of the risk-based approach.[84]

As far as the determination of high risk is concerned, the data controllers' discretion is quite reigned in (with among others the risk that the national lists constitute the type of administrative burdens that DPIAs were meant to avoid in the first place).[85] This can probably be explained by the DPIAs' regulatory role (as replacement for both the notification and prior checking obligations), and their resource intensive nature.[86] Yet, the GDPR also provides much more discretion as far as other elements are concerned. For instance, the obligation to review the DPIA is now very much open-ended (Art 35(11)), whereas previous drafts provided for a compulsory review every three years.[87] Similarly, the triggering of Art 36 providing for a consultation with the DPA in case the high risk was insufficiently mitigated is completely left to the discretion of the data controller. This is a very far reaching solution given that the processing operations at stake are by definition very dangerous (otherwise no need for DPIA, nor for consultation), and which would have probably required a prior checking under the system of the Directive.[88] This large discretion echoes the previous analysis of the risk-based approach in the GDPR according to which a number of internal controls, of paramount importance under the ISO 31000 Standard, were very much watered down

[80] See ibid 12: the criteria are meant to "help supervisory authorities to constitute such lists with more specific content".

[81] See ibid 9: "the criteria developed (…) go beyond a simple explanation of what should be understood by the three examples given in Article 35(3) GDPR".

[82] EDPB, "Opinion 11/2018 on the Draft List of the Competent Supervisory Authority of Ireland Regarding the Processing Operations Subject to the Requirement of a Data Protection Impact Assessment (Article 35.4 GDPR) Adopted" (2018) 5.

[83] Raphaël Gellert, "EDPB Opinion on the Draft Lists of Competent Supervisory Authorities Regarding the Processing Operations Subject to DPIAs" (2018) 4 European Data Protection Law Review 500, 502.

[84] ibid; Gellert (n 26) 213.

[85] See Gellert (n 83) 502.

[86] The European Commission estimated that a DPIA can cost up to €149,000—European Commission (n 22) 70.

[87] Gellert (n 26) 214.

[88] ibid 216.

in the GDPR. This concerned in particular the requirements of constant monitoring and reviewing, or the central place of the DPO, now limited to a rather small number of cases.

One can make a distinction between "purely internal controls" (eg employee monitoring), and those used as regulatory resources jointly operationalised by the supervisor and the regulatee (eg DPIA, data protection officer—DPO ...). In the first case, more discretion can be justified, even though a legal framework solely based on the purely discretionary regulatees' internal controls is certainly not ideal, as was discussed in the case of the Microsoft approach. In the latter case however, stricter requirements are warranted if the regulatory architecture and design is to deliver its promises. From this standpoint, the GDPR is *prima facie* built around a solid mechanism of collaboration between regulators and regulatees. On closer look, however, the quality of the protection it affords appears more dubious. Taking the case of DPIAs once more, one can observe that the record-keeping obligation pursuant to Art 30 used to contain DPIA documentation obligations, which is not the case anymore.[89] The important discretion in the undertaking of DPIAs coupled to the absolute lack of transparency (end of notification and prior checking coupled to lack of documentation obligation) bodes a regulatory architecture that is potentially much less efficient than the administrative formalities and other "red-tape" it stood against in the first place.[90]

Finally, greater discretion for regulatees also means they are exposing themselves more to so-called "interpretative risk".[91] Given that they have more responsibility for complying, they become more exposed in case their interpretations diverge from that of the regulator. Regulators can address this risk either upfront by issuing guidance documents (which can be counterproductive as seen with the DPIA lists), or downstream by adapting a so-called "responsive" enforcement strategy. That is, a mode of enforcement in which negotiation concerning the "meaning, application, and purpose of the rules plays a central role".[92] In the latter case, there is a risk that firms will try to consult regulators before they start any processing operations, thereby overburdening them and making the supervision process more resource intensive rather than less. Furthermore, such responsive enforcement only works will regulatees who "play the game", those who are well informed and intentioned.[93]

[89] See ibid.

[90] The EDPS was very much aware of the lack of transparency going along with accountability. It had therefore argued for the creation of an obligation to maintain an inventory EDPS (n 70) 190. This recommendation was not retained.

[91] Julia Black, "The Rise, Fall and Fate of Principles-Based Regulation" in Kern Alexander and Niamh Moloney (eds), *Law Reform and Financial Markets* (Edward Elgar 2011) 8.

[92] ibid 9.

[93] ibid.

3.2 Institutional or secondary risks: competing risks

The literature distinguishes between primary and secondary risks,[94] or between societal and institutional risks.[95] This distinction stems from the fact that, as seen before, risk management is more than a technical analytical practice, and it embodies ideals of accountability, legitimacy, responsibility, as well as profitability and the realisation of organisational objectives. In other words, it embodies an ideal of alignment of organisational and regulatory goals. It is this very ideal that has led to the creation of new risk categories usually known as operational or reputational risks. These risks are referred to as secondary because they are solely concerned with whether the organisation will meet its objectives. Yet, precisely in the name of this ideal of natural compliance (ie alignment of regulatory and organisational goals), all risks are recoded as a matter of secondary risks.[96]

These secondary risks may be compatible with primary risks, but they may also clash. In any case, they are integrated within risk management tools and processes. From this perspective, for instance, the fact that members of the public are harmed by a risk becomes an organisational risk that must be managed from the perspective of the organisation itself. This appeared very clearly in the UK Information Commissioner's Office (ICO)'s 2014 Code of Practice on conducting Privacy Impact Assessments. Chapter 6 entitled "identifying privacy and related risks" clearly differentiates between different risks stemming from a data processing operation: the privacy risks to the individuals whose personal data will be processed, and the compliance and any related risks to the organisations itself.[97] The latter include risks of compensation claims or business losses if individuals have been victims of privacy risks, and risks of fines and reputational damages in case of proven non-compliance with data protection statutes.[98] The NIST methodology is simply predicated upon a total adequacy between these different types of risks.[99] Yet, as seen through the analysis of the Microsoft and other standard setting risk-based approaches, the ideal of natural compliance and perfect alignment of goals remains... an ideal. Clashes between primary and secondary risks cannot be excluded. As far as public participation in risk management is concerned, the ICO's 2014 code of conduct made the difference between internal and external stakeholders and hence between internal and external participation. Whereas the first is seen as key to the success of the DPIA process, the second is portrayed as optional, and bringing only eventual added value to the process.[100] Power thus warns

[94] Michael Power, *The Risk Management of Everything—Rethinking the Politics of Uncertainty* (Demos 2004) 19.

[95] Henry Rothstein, Michael Huber, and George Gaskell, "A Theory of Risk Colonization: The Spiralling Regulatory Logics of Societal and Institutional Risk" (2006) 35 Economy and Society 91, 14.

[96] Michael Power, *Organized Uncertainty: Designing a World of Risk Management* (OUP 2007) ch 5.

[97] ICO, "Conducting Privacy Impact Assessments: Code of Practice" (2014) 23.

[98] ibid 25.

[99] National Institute of Standards and Technology (n 54).

[100] ICO (n 97) 16–19.

against the fact that the whole risk management process may be perverted into a self-legitimation exercise that serves no other purpose than that of managing operational and reputational risks, and which, ultimately, is itself a risk to the management of (primary) risks.[101] In other words, this shows that the idea of responsible entities whose goals are fully aligned with the regulatory goals (and which justifies the regulatory collaboration in the first place) might not be as solid as its proponents would like to believe. From this perspective, corporate social responsibility is a fiction.

Furthermore, these previous lines are perfectly consistent with the risk management agenda's emphasis on safeguards that are mostly process-based (eg sufficient employee-training, sufficient monitoring and feedback, etc), instead of safeguards that address the substance of the data processing operations at play (eg limits on collection and storage). In both cases, the point is to uphold the regulatee's legitimacy, and further, nurture its organisational goals.

3.3 The risk-based approach and risk-based regulation, or the risk transformation of the regulators themselves

One must make a distinction between the risk-based approach as a specific implementation of meta regulation, and risk-based regulation. Since collaborative models of regulation are predicated upon the use of risk management as a regulatory resource, one of its consequences is that regulators must managerialise their very activities in order to be able to regulate these managerialised regulatees.[102]

As internal controls permeated by risk analysis become the *locus* and focus of regulation, the supervisory activity of regulators itself becomes risk based. This is the point made by Rothstein *et al.*, who argue that the regulators' task amounts to assessing the regulatees' own risk assessment.[103] This is quite visible in the GDPR for instance with the prior consultation mechanism following which regulators must inspect the regulatees' DPIA. Similarly, the demonstration of accountability pursuant to Art 24(2) as well as the regulators' audit competence (Art 58(1)) certainly involve risk management exercises.

Because meta regulation requires regulators to engage with risk management in order to carry out their regulatory activities, one can argue that it ultimately leads to the risk transformation of regulators themselves. Therefore, in a sort of mirror effect, risk management ceases to be a mere resource for regulatory models, and becomes the regulatory model itself.[104] This is what is commonly referred to as

[101] Power (n 94) 19.
[102] Power (n 96) 41–42.
[103] Rothstein and others (n 13).
[104] Power (n 96) 87–88.

risk-based regulation.[105] The main idea of risk-based regulation is for regulators to understand their mission not anymore as a number of objectives to achieve (eg ensure the protection of personal data), but rather, as a number of risks that these objectives will not be achieved, or risks to their statutorily defined objectives.[106] Therefore, just like regulatees, they become organised along the lines of the risk management agenda, notably using risk analysis tools to determine where and how they should allocate resources and conduct enforcement actions.[107] One can thus add a third category of risks: risks to the regulators, which come in addition to, and compete with, the risks to the data subjects and to the data controllers.

It should be clear that there is no direct and logical link between meta regulation and risk-based regulation insofar as the adoption of meta regulation models doesn't lead per se to the complete risk transformation of the regulators. Indeed, risk-based regulation has its own specific origin and history, even though it shares obvious linkages with meta regulation and the risk management agenda.[108] Black locates it in what she refers to as the "new public risk management", which is the direct continuation of the UK neoliberal reform of public services undertaken in the 1980s under the name of "new public management".[109]

So, even though the risk-based transformation of regulators does not directly descend from meta regulation, the fact remains that "the two go hand in hand; each needs the other". This entails among others that risk-based regulation fuels and is fuelled by meta regulation.[110] Accordingly, regulatees are entrusted with increasing regulatory tasks, and regulators are increasingly similar to the organisations they regulate, and are increasingly regulated themselves (through the very use of the techniques and tools partaking of risk management).[111]

In sum, although data protection authorities are not risk-based, and might never fully become so, the turn to meta regulation does not go without consequences for their activities, which have great chances of becoming increasingly managerialised. In particular, this renewed focus on what Black refers to as the "technical and very dry issues of internal control"[112] is not a self-evident move for regulators, quite on

[105] See Robert Baldwin, Martin Cave, and Martin Lodge, "Risk-Based Regulation", *Understanding Regulation: Theory, Strategy, and Practice* (2nd edn, OUP 2012); Rothstein and others (n 13); Julia Black, "The Emergence of Risk-Based Regulation and the New Public Risk Management in the United Kingdom" [2005] Public Law 512; Black (n 3).

[106] Black, "The Emergence of Risk-Based Regulation and the New Public Risk Management in the United Kingdom" (n 105) 515.

[107] See ibid: risk-based regulation is "in essence, the transposition of private sector risk management methods and processes to central government".

[108] Power (n 96) 87.

[109] Black, "The Emergence of Risk-Based Regulation and the New Public Risk Management in the United Kingdom" (n 105) 513.

[110] ibid.

[111] Power (n 96) 91; Bengt Jacobsson, "Regulated Regulators: Global Trends of State Transformation" in Marie-Laure Djelic and Kerstin Sahlin-Andersson (eds), *Transnational Governance: Institutional Dynamics of Regulation* (Cambridge University Press 2006).

[112] Black, "The Emergence of Risk-Based Regulation and the New Public Risk Management in the United Kingdom" (n 105) 513.

the contrary. As she argues, this entails "a fundamental change in culture, a different analytical approach, a different understanding of the role of inspectors and supervisory staff, and a new skill set".[113]

4. Risk management on the ground

This section is concerned with a number of caveats surrounding the implementation of risk management tools.

4.1 Adequate collection and use of data

As Black puts it, "data is critical to the design and operation of risk-based frameworks, and can pose a significant problem".[114] Ericson and Haggerty make the point that risk is built upon an endless collection of knowledge.[115] Peretti-Watel confirms this by reminding us that the notion of risk removes the notion of causality by replacing it with the notion of risk factors.[116] This entails that the issue of zero risks is not only limited to the risk criteria or risk management step, but also to the risk assessment step since the advent of a risk depends on risk factors, and there are endless possibilities for a risk factor to occur, and hence of risks to assess. Importantly, the number of factors concerning a risk is infinite not least because it is directly dependent upon man's capacity to collect data: the more info about a risk one possesses, the more risk factors they will be able to untangle. In other words, risk is a knowledge-intensive concept. It always calls for more knowledge, ad infinitum.[117] For instance, the ISO 2017 methodology contains three full pages of annexes containing examples of risks, all depending upon various risk factors combinations.[118] One can therefore argue that the amount of data available has a significant bearing on which risks are selected, since organisations can only identify risks they already know about.[119]

Another issue associated with the lack of information is that collecting data is resource intensive, and can sometimes be very difficult. Therefore, some risk managements tools are built on the basis of data that is available or easy to acquire, but not on the data that is actually needed to properly assess the risks.[120]

[113] Black (n 3) 213.
[114] ibid 203.
[115] Ericson and Haggerty (n 1).
[116] Peretti-Watel (n 10) 16–17.
[117] Raphaël Gellert, "Data Protection: A Risk Regulation? Between the Risk Management of Everything and the Precautionary Alternative" (2015) 5 International Data Privacy Law 3, 15.
[118] ISO/IEC (n 8) 35–37.
[119] Black (n 3) 194, 204.
[120] ibid 203–04.

However, sometimes the issue is not only about not having enough data, but rather, about having too much data. Black confirms that sometimes risk managers have not enough of the data they need, and too much of the data they don't need.[121] It is thus quite frequent that risk managers become "swamped with data, and as a result, become locked in an endless task of processing rather than evaluating the information that comes in".[122] This issue has also been referred to as "paralysis by analysis".[123] Since analysing the collected data is also resource intensive, it is not infrequent that risk managers will fail to make full use of the data at their disposal.[124] Therefore, knowing what information to seek and managing it adequately is critical to correctly appraising the most relevant risks.[125]

Finally, this reliance upon data sheds light on another paradox: the risk-based approach to data protection actually requires the collection of even more personal data in order to protect it. This would be particularly salient in cases where data controllers would collect data relating to the potential harms to the data subjects.

4.2 Misplaced pretences at objectivity

This issue is directly linked to the subjective nature of risk management. As Black indicates, some risk managers have tried to " 'design judgment out' of their frameworks, or, if they cannot design it out, structure how it is used".[126] However, she also adds that even though such moves are intended to "ensure consistency of responses, [they do] not, of course, ensure consistency of response",[127] for the simple reason that "risk systems place heavy reliance on the exercise of discretion and judgement".[128] Rothstein *et al.* similarly argue that identical methodologies can produce different conclusions.[129] A particular situation where consistency is at jeopardy is in cases of false positives and negatives. In certain cases, risk managers will leave a blank answer simply because they are not entirely sure as to what exactly the risk level is. In most cases, a blank answer entails that the risk level is low. In order to avoid these false negatives, some systems have required that an answer be provided. However, precisely because risk managers

121 ibid 203.
122 ibid 204.
123 See Poul Harremoës and others (eds), *The Precautionary Principle in the 20th Century: Late Lessons from Early Warnings* (Earthscan 2002).
124 Black (n 3) 204.
125 ibid.
126 ibid 205. An example has been provided before, when responses to risk criteria for the identification of risks are objectively structured in terms of "yes or no".
127 ibid.
128 ibid 209.
129 Rothstein and others (n 13) 1058.

are unsure, they will score the risk as being medium, which also distorts the process. A solution envisaged to address this issue has been to require risk managers to indicate their levels of confidence. Yet, they are often reluctant to admit that they are not confident, and will thus often indicate a high level of confidence even when that is not the case.[130] This lack of consistency can be put in parallel with what Power refers to as the need for "local scripts". Risk management methodologies are ideal forms that cannot "be readily implemented without local scripts".[131] In other words, risk methodologies and guidelines are often designed in abstract, and need to continuously undergo a trial and error process of refinement.[132] This is important in order to ensure consistency between the methods on paper and the concrete, material, cases to which the latter apply. This means that every data controller will adapt the templates to the local reality they face, thereby producing a potentially very different type of data protection than the one foreseen in the templates and methodologies. Black refers to a number of experiences that have been carried out in order to ensure such consistency, such as internal panels that would validate the manner in which the risk management tool is implemented, or the constitution of specific departments that deal with specific aspects of the risk management process. However, these solutions are all very cumbersome and resource intensive.[133]

This lack of consistency at the level of regulatees is not without consequences as far as regulators' supervisory duty is concerned. Because every regulatee can potentially use different methodologies that produce different results, the regulator's supervisory task requires high levels of expertise and of resources. This is paradoxical insofar as one of the purported benefits of the risk-based approach and meta regulation is precisely to rely upon the regulatees' expertise and resources in order to ease the pressure on the regulator. Yet, from this perspective, the risk-based approach might require even more expertise and resources from the regulator.[134] In order to remedy these issues some regulators have adopted templates or methodologies.[135] Yet, because—as shown herein above—identical methodologies will nonetheless yield diverging results, some regulators have included mandatory values for risk criteria or risk tolerance thresholds. This is also a paradox since the whole purpose of the risk-based approach is precisely to avoid situations where regulators set the standards.[136]

[130] Black (n 3) 214.
[131] Power (n 96) 95.
[132] Black (n 3) 221.
[133] ibid 208–09.
[134] Rothstein and others (n 13) 1059.
[135] In the data protection field, one can think of the smart meters and RFID methodologies, cf Chapter 5.
[136] Rothstein and others (n 13) 1058.

4.3 Complexity and lack of adequate expertise

Another hurdle with the use of risk management tools resides in their complexity. Indeed, risk management can deliver its promises only provided that it is accurate enough and correctly assesses the risks at stake. However, as discussed, fine grained risk assessment requires more data, more expertise, and more resources. Such needs will drive regulatees to go for methodologies that are more practical and easier to implement in practice. Thereby creating tensions between the need for practical, easy-to-use solutions, and the need for assessments that are robust and of high quality.[137] Thus, one of the challenges of the risk-based approach is to combine simplicity with complexity, to produce assessment methodologies that are both accurate and practical.[138]

Another aspect of risk management's complexity concerns the consequences it bears on their quantitative nature. Many of risk management promises are predicated upon their formalised, (semi) quantitative nature, insofar as it is thanks to this property that they are seen as objective and defensible frameworks for decision making, which can be used all across, and thus provide for a harmonised level of protection. However, some risk assessments are very complex (for instance because of the amount of data, number of risk criteria, risk factors, etc) so that it is extremely difficult to proceed to a quantitative assessment. In such cases, risk managers simply undertake subjective, "rule-of-thumb" assessments, while pretending to undertake quantitative assessments.[139] Rothstein *et al.* also note that some organisations use formalised assessments only for a specific number of risks, where it is most needed.[140] As a matter of fact, this is exactly what the ISO 2017 DPIA Standard argues for.[141]

The complexity of risk management in practice also points to a fundamental criticism against one of the two key reasons for adopting a meta regulation model. Namely, the regulatees' superior expertise. However, the previous lines tend to show that the regulatees' expertise is not as adequate as meta regulation theory would have it. As Black puts it, "no single actor has all the knowledge required to solve complex, diverse, and dynamic problems".[142]

[137] ibid 1059.

[138] Black (n 3) 219. Power goes along the same lines arguing that in practice, within organisations, technical risk assessment is actually undertaken by a handful of experts, and risk managers focus on the management *ss*. Power (n 96) 83–85. As he puts it, "agents of governance cannot be embroiled in risk analytics" ibid 84.

[139] Rothstein and others (n 13) 1059.

[140] ibid 1060.

[141] See ISO/IEC (n 8) 18: "in practice, qualitative analysis is often used first to obtain a general indication of the level of risk and to reveal the major risks. When possible and appropriate, one should also undertake more specific and quantitative analysis of the risks."

[142] Julia Black, "Decentring Regulation: Understanding the Role of Self-Regulation in a 'Post-Regulatory' World" (2001) 54 Current Legal Problems 103, 107.

4.4 The risk-based approach and resource efficiency: a zero-sum game?

One of the arguments in favour of the risk-based approach pertained to its resource efficient nature, and in particular the shift from the use of resources from inefficient "red tape" obligations towards accountability-based measures that provide effective protection.[143] Risk management however, might not be as resource efficient as originally thought. For instance, the literature has shown that risk management might amount to simply shifting the use of resources. Risk management is predicated upon the collection of large troves of data, which itself can be resource intensive. In other words, this is a zero-sum game whereby the resources saved through the implementation of adequate safeguards are simply reinvested in the undertaking of adequate risk management exercises.[144] Similarly, it is not so easy to allocate resources on the basis of risks. If distinguishing between low risks and high risks appears quite self-intuitive, how to divide resources among a pool of high risks is much less clear.[145]

These considerations were echoed in the course of the GPDR overhaul, where the Dutch government commissioned a report on the costs of the reform. The report found that if administrative burdens would slightly lower (from €1.7mln/year to €1.5 mln/year), compliance costs pertaining to accountability-related obligations would significantly rise (from €70 mln/year to €1.1 bln/year—€1.4bln/year).[146] These increasing compliance costs can also be linked to the uneven resources at the disposal of data controllers. The Commission's draft GDPR provided exceptions to certain accountability obligations for SME's (fewer than 250 employees), apparently taking the number of employees as risk factor (ie the size of the organisation as a proxy for the level of risk it creates).[147] One can argue that such differential treatment relied upon pragmatic considerations linked to the lack of available resources for smaller organisations. In a sense, the risk-based approach is mainly targeted at very large organisations.[148]

These caveats stand as an explicit rebuttal at another foundational rationale of meta regulation. Namely, that regulatees have more appropriate resources than regulators and know better how to use them.

[143] See eg European Commission (n 22) 41–43.

[144] Rothstein and others (n 13) 1059.

[145] Black (n 3) 210.

[146] Council of the European Union, "Proposal for a Regulation of the European Parliament and of the Cuncil on the Protection of Individuals with Regard to the Processing of Personal Data and on the Free Movement of Such Data—Risk Based Approach" (2014) 97. See SIRA Consulting, "Toetsing Europese Dataprotectieverordening" (2013).

[147] Art 29 WP (n 73) 16.

[148] This is a sense one can get from the study of Bamberger and Mulligan, which only focuses on multinational organisations Kenneth A Bamberger and Deirdre K Mulligan, *Privacy on the Ground: Driving Corporate Behavior in the United States and Europe* (The MIT Press 2015).

4.5 Evaluation of efficiency

The argument in favour of the risk-based approach as a more efficient implementation of the legal framework have been made multiple times. Yet, it is not always easy to evaluate the effectiveness of risk management tools, since what is to be evaluated is sometimes invisible, ie what would have happened had that risk not been mitigated, or had it been taken? In some cases, it is easier to assess risk management tools, as is the case with the environmental field, where it is possible to measure levels of pollution.[149] However, the highly personal and subjective dimension of data protection harms renders these types of exercises difficult.

4.6 A new organisational mindset

Power argues that discourses around risk management embody an overly simplistic understanding of organisations.[150] Black concurs by emphasising that the training of staff is an essential element that has often been overlooked. As she argues, "training has to be not just in the mechanics of the assessment, but in the whole philosophy of risk-based regulation".[151] She continues by explaining that one of the most common mistakes is to assume that staff "would know what a risk assessment was, and that therefore they simply needed to be trained on how to fill in the assessment spread sheets, etc.".[152] Experience revealed instead that staff were not really aware of the distinction between "a compliance-based approach and a risk-based approach".[153] In other words, what is required is "a training in the whole philosophy of risk-based regulation".[154] Yet, such training is lengthy, as it can go up to two years,[155] and even then, some staff will still retain the "tick-box mind-set" associated to compliance.[156] This leads Power to argue that "implementation deficits will be the norm",[157] and there is certainly a need to ensure that risk tools are effectively applied in practice at internal level.[158]

149 Black (n 3) 218.
150 Power (n 96) 79: Risk management's "underlying cybernetic form may not be suitably descriptive of organizational realities".
151 Black (n 3) 207. See also ibid 214: "Many (…) admit that in hindsight they spent too little time on training, and/or that the training they did was focused on the wrong things."
152 ibid.
153 ibid.
154 ibid 214.
155 See also ibid 220.
156 ibid 214.
157 Power (n 96) 79.
158 Black (n 3) 220.

5. Conclusions: meta regulation and utopia

One of the reasons for such implementation deficits, may be linked to the fact that in conveying overly simplistic conceptions of organisational life, risk management overlooks its—sometimes—conflictual dimension.[159] It has indeed been found that staff may be reluctant to risk-based change. Risk tools modify the content of staff's job. In particular, because of their quantitative dimension they curtail the staff's discretion, and some resist this.[160] Equally, some staff may view risk tools as a sort of "mandatory cosmetic change" bearing no real consequences on the content of their activity.[161] This has led some organisations to argue that in order to effectively shift to a risk culture, it is necessary to replace existing staff by new people, who would be less likely to resist the risk culture and the organisational changes it brings along.[162] In other words, risk analysis and risk management "project an image of design clarity and order which has little or no relationship to existing academic scholarship on organizations".[163]

As a matter of fact, the whole of meta regulation can be said to suffer from the same flaw. As Black argues, the vision underpinning meta regulation (and more generally, principles-based types of regulation) is a utopian one. "In this regulatory Utopia, regulation is targeted and focused, and preferably harmonised across jurisdictions, regulated firms are given the flexibility they need to get on with running their businesses, and consequently regulatory outcomes are achieved with no undue cost to business".[164] She further argues that this is a powerful vision with a strong appeal both to politicians, regulators, and regulated organisations.[165] The other side of the coin, however, is a regulatory context where meta regulation is simply "a license for 'backsliding', that is, for allowing regulatees to do what they want in practice".[166] Black suggests that the financial sector, which has been one of the pioneering adopters of meta regulation, experienced its utopic nature in the aftermath of the 2008 financial crisis. Prior to the crisis the UK Financial Service Authority (FSA)'s regulatory style could be characterised as "light touch". It was a combination of a high level of trust

[159] See Christopher Hood, "Where Extremes Meet: 'SPRAT' versus 'SHARK' in Public Risk Management" in Christopher Hood and David KC Jones (eds), *Accident and Design: Contemporary Debates in Risk Management* (UCL Press 1996).

[160] (n 3) 214.

[161] ibid 220.

[162] ibid 214.

[163] Power (n 96) 79.

[164] Black, "The Rise, Fall and Fate of Principles-Based Regulation" (n 91) 14.

[165] ibid.

[166] As a matter of fact, one can also argue that it also works in favour of regulators insofar as the focus on the firms' internal controls and management system opens the door to more arbitrary enforcement practices, ibid.

that regulated entities did their share of the regulatory tasks, therefore coupled with low enforcement actions. As a result of this trust, the regulator's approach was characterised by a focus on the firms' internal controls, that is, their structure, processes, systems, and whether reporting lines were correct. Yet, it left all hard, sensitive, judgments and decisions to the senior staff, without interfering or trying to inspect them.[167] After the financial crisis, the regulator became much less trustful, and started making judgements over the judgments of the regulated firms' senior managers, and/or stopped taking the results of firms' risk management exercises at face value. It also ratcheted up its enforcement actions in order to achieve so-called "credible deterrence".[168]

It is quite remarkable to observe that meta regulation's utopian vision has fully pervaded the risk-based approach. This was clearly visible during the GDPR adoption process. In particular, the influence of the Rand Corporation's review of the DPD (subcontracted thereto by the ICO) is clearly palatable in the various reform documents put forward by the EU legislator,[169] and by other EU independent bodies such as the Art 29 WP or the European Data Protection Supervisor (EDPS).[170] All these various documents seem to simply repeat the "mantras" of the Rand Corporation about accountability being a means for better compliance, and more in particular for "making the implementation of existing principles more effective and their application more cost efficient",[171] that is, for "implement[ing] appropriate measures to achieve the purpose of the instruments".[172] The lack of critical distance with which the European legislator was eager to embrace this regulatory vision precisely illustrates the power of such visions. It also tells us something about the vision of the European legislator itself, since it has also been promoting its own agenda of "better regulation", which relies upon the same utopic visions.[173]

Yet, and contrary to the FSA's light touch regulation, the GDPR embodies credible deterrence from the start given the impressive sanction powers now endowed

[167] ibid.
[168] ibid 15–17.
[169] European Commission (n 22); eg European Commission, "Communication from the Commission to the European Parliament, the Council, the Economic and Social Committee and the Committee of the Regions: A Comprehensive Approach on Personal Data Protection in the European Union" (2010).
[170] Art 29 WP and Working Party on Police and Justice, "The Future of Privacy: Joint Contribution to the Consultation of the European Commission on the Legal Framework for the Fundamental Right to the Protection of Personal Data" (2009); Art 29 WP (n 73); eg EDPS (n 70).
[171] European Commission (n 22) 38.
[172] ibid 39.
[173] See https://ec.europa.eu/info/law/law-making-process/planning-and-proposing-law/better-regulation-why-and-how_en, last accessed 27 March 2019.

to the regulatory authorities, or its efforts to coordinate cross-border enforcement activities. Enforcement practice remains nonetheless the prerogative of national authorities, so it remains to be seen concretely what type of enforcement practice it will lead to. Early experience, suggest, however, a tendency towards credible deterrence.[174]

[174] See eg the €50 mln fine that the CNIL imposed against Google in January 2019, https://www.cnil.fr/en/cnils-restricted-committee-imposes-financial-penalty-50-million-euros-against-google-llc, last accessed 12 March 2019.

Conclusions

Back to the rights/risk-based approaches, and the future of data protection

1. Summary of the findings: approaching the debate on rights/risk-based approaches from a different perspective

The present book has attempted to explain and describe the risk-based approach to data protection. In a nutshell, such approach consists in the implementation at the data protection level of a collaborative model of regulation known as meta regulation. This model of regulation is said to be collaborative because it relies upon the delegation of regulatory activities typically falling within the remit of the regulator's competences to the regulatee, ie data controllers (and/or processors in some statutes). More in particular these competences concern the regulatory activities of standard setting, and those of monitoring and behaviour control (the last two can be understood as the operationalisation of safeguards). In order to be endowed with these activities, regulatees must be made responsible in the first place. Such responsibilisation occurs through the risk management agenda and the ensuing transformation of the latter's activities as a matter of risk taking. The regulator is left with an ancillary role of enforcement following which it must assess the regulatees' performance. It was shown that in the case of data protection, all the statutes that implement meta regulation do so only in a piecemeal way. This includes not only the General Data Protection Regulation (GDPR), but also many if not all of the other modern statutes that rely upon an accountability provision. Data controllers are being turned inside out through the risk management agenda, which is actualised through the principle of accountability. Yet, they are only entrusted with the operationalisation of safeguards, that is, with the task to better implement existing data protection principles and to render the whole framework more efficient. This is what the core of the risk-based approach to data protection is about. Among the various statutes implementing this risk-based approach there are differences. For instance, the GDPR provides for the most comprehensive framework of collaboration between regulators (data protection authorities—DPAs) and regulatees (data controllers). Finally, this approach relies upon a debasement of the notion of data protection risk, in order to reconcile the absence of delegation of the standard setting function to the regulatees, with the risk transformation of their activities, which meta regulation entails. Instead of relying upon the classical notion of data

The Risk-Based Approach to Data Protection. Raphaël Gellert, Oxford University Press (2020). © Raphaël Gellert.
DOI: 10.1093/oso/9780198837718.001.0001.

protection risk understood as the chances that the properties of a processing operation lead to a number of harms to the data subject, it relies upon a notion of compliance risk understood as the chances that the processing operation at stake does not comply with data protection requirements.

The risk-based approach as the effectuation of data protection through risk management tools is a good opportunity to come back to the debate between rights-based and risk-based approaches to data protection, as a way to end this contribution.

This debate, which has set the stage for the whole book, was mainly discussed in the introductory chapter. More particularly, it was addressed from a regulatory perspective. As one remembers, it was shown that data protection can be assimilated to regulation on the account of the overlap existing between law and regulation. It was subsequently shown that regulation and risk have a common root, the proportionality principle.[1] The debate between rights-based and risk-based approaches could then be reframed as a competition between two models of regulation. Namely, between the traditional model known as command and control regulation, and a newer model known as meta regulation, which is itself part of a broader family of regulatory models known as principles-based regulation (which rely on risk management tools as the main method of regulation).

The present conclusion wishes to come back to this debate, but instead of addressing it from the perspective of regulation, it wishes to do so from the perspective of risk management. Such an endeavour is rendered possible—again—by the close links observed between regulation and risk, namely, that managing risks amounts to regulating them, and that regulating an event or activity amounts to managing the risks stemming therefrom (cf Introduction). Keeping in mind that this symmetry between risk and regulation was uncovered following the finding that the proportionality principle is a common core/root between risk and regulation, one can make the following points.

Rules, which are the defining feature of command and control regulation,[2] can be said to embody the regulatory standard setting function (in other words, a rule amounts to the setting of a standard). As Black puts it, "rules perform social management and instrumental functions. Rules are embodiments of policy decisions."[3] In conformity with the findings mentioned herein above, this can be taken to mean that rules embody a proportionality test, or at the very least one of its elements (ie a balancing exercise and/or a safeguard).[4] However, precisely because risk

[1] Which itself can be boiled down into a matter of two balancing tests associated with safeguards.

[2] See Julia Black, *Rules and Regulators* (OUP 1997) 5.

[3] ibid 9. See also ibid 7: it is thus the overall regulatory goal underpinning the rule, which determines its formulation.

[4] As seen in the chapter on data protection as regulation, even a traditional command of behaving in a certain way can be reframed as a safeguard pertaining to the scope of the activity at stake (in this case, reduction of the scope for instance).

management is also constitutive of a proportionality test, one can argue that rules are an exercise in risk management by definition. Turning to data protection, this means that the provisions of data protection law are of course to be complied with, but in being complied with they also amount to the managing of data processing risks. This re-understanding of rules, and hence of the whole of command and control regulation as risk management allows to approach the rights-based *vs* risk-based approaches debate from a fresh perspective.

As one remembers, one of the key criticisms against the risk-based approach is that it leads to a level of data protection that depends on the level of risk at stake, and which is therefore uneven. This criticism actually encapsulates a key distinction in the way that risk and regulation manage risks. Command and control regulation manages risks from the outset, since it enshrines the safeguards it deems adequate in its legal provisions and rules. In other words, regulatees have no choice but to implement a risk management exercise that has already been performed for them in advance. In stark contrast, the chapter on risk showed that the main question of risk reduction measures (ie safeguards)[5] in the field of risk management is that of "what actions make what difference to risk outcomes".[6] This means that risk management adopts a case-by-case, tailor-made approach. For each specific risk, it will try to determine what the most adequate safeguards/risk reduction measures are. In this sense, one can reframe the debate between rights-based and risk-based approaches as competing approaches to proportionality: one centred around universal or linear and pre-determined balancing tests with associated safeguards, and another one centred around a contextual balancing test.

Taking the example of data protection, this entails that one applies always the same safeguards/risk reduction measures (such as those contained in the data quality provision—Art 5 GDPR) in a linear and universal manner no matter the type and level of risk addressed. In this sense, the balancing test embodied in the requirement that the data processed should be adequate, relevant, and not excessive in relation to the purpose pursued, amounts to a balancing of the benefits and the harms associated to the—legitimate enough—processing operation. However, and paradoxically, the result of such balancing exercise is not taken into account given that exactly the same safeguards apply all the time, regardless of the level of harm. That is not to say of course that regulatees have no discretion at all. As seen throughout the present book, risk management has an inherent subjective dimension, which in the context of risk reduction measures has been captured by the expression of "risk tolerance".[7] There are indeed always some subjective choices to be made concerning the acceptable level of risk, and therefore, the extent to which

[5] The introduction has demonstrated that safeguards and risk reduction measures are essentially equivalent terms.
[6] David KC Jones and Christopher Hood, "Introduction" in Christopher Hood and David KC Jones (eds), *Accident and Design: Contemporary Debates in Risk Management* (UCL Press 1996) 6.
[7] See ibid 7.

the risk should be reduced (hence the tolerance to risks). For instance, how much minimisation is sufficient minimisation?[8] However, what is beyond discussion is the choice of safeguards to be implemented in the first place. Taking the example of data minimisation again, data controllers have no choice but to implement this safeguard. This is also what the Article 29 Working Party (Art 29 WP) had in mind when it argued that the data protection principles are inherently scalable.[9]

Given their pre-existing and linear nature, one can argue that the data protection safeguards (such as the data quality principles) operate as a presumption. When they are applied they offer an adequate protection and the processing operation is considered safe enough to be pursued, with this being valid for every single processing operation. Some have argued that such a stance is aligned with the logic of the precautionary principle,[10] which, as briefly discussed in Chapter 1, consists in taking risk reduction measures even in the absence of a clearly assessed risk due to insufficient knowledge. This is not void of sense insofar as these safeguards have been deemed adequate in advance, without any knowledge with regards to the harms created by each specific situation. As a matter of fact, this debate is well-known in the regulation literature, where it is referred to as the choice between Type I and Type II errors.[11] Type I errors err on the side of caution (ie assume something is risky when it is not); whereas Type II errors err on the side of risk (ie assume something is safe when it is not). Such debate takes place at the moment of setting standards. As Black puts it, "in writing rules or setting standards, should regulators err on the side of protecting consumers (making Type I errors) or favouring producers (making Type II errors)?"[12] In the case of command and control regulation, this issue is of particular salience since the debate on standard setting takes place only once, that is, when the regulation is being devised. This debate between Type I and II errors also reminds us of another feature of risk management, namely, that achieving a zero-risk situation is impossible. Rather, risks can only be reduced to a certain level, and it is a matter of subjective decision to decide when the level of risk is sufficiently low. In this sense, the whole "Type I *vs* Type II errors" debate embodies this impossibility to achieve zero risk, and the ensuing focus on the determination of what level of risk is tolerable. Taking the

8 As a matter of fact, the subjectivity inherent in the proportionality principles has also been underscored by the Art 29 WP in its analysis of the proportionality test by the ECtHR, where it emphasises that such test is subjective and context-dependent, as well as the need for providing relevant and sufficient justification of the balance achieved Art 29 WP, "Opinion 01/2014 on the Application of Necessity and Proportionality Concepts and Data Protection within the Law Enforcement Sector" (2014) 8, 11.

9 Art 29 WP, "Statement on the Role of a Risk-Based Approach in Data Protection Legal Frameworks" (2014) 2–3.

10 Julie E Cohen, "The Regulatory State in the Information Age" (2016) 17 Theoretical Inquiries in Law 369.

11 Kristin Shrader-Frechette, *Risk and Rationality: Philosophical Foundations for Populist Reforms* (University of California Press 1991).

12 Julia Black, "Risk-Based Regulation: Choices, Practices and Lessons Being Learnt" in OECD (ed), *Risk and Regulatory Policy: Improving the Governance of Risk* (OECD Publishing 2010) ch 188.

argument further, if risk management is inherently unable to eliminate all the risks, it should follow that the protection afforded by data protection suffers from the same caveat. As a matter of fact, this has been underscored numerous times. The Art 29 WP's understanding of compliance is perfectly in line with this perspective. According to the Working Group, full compliance (ie respect with all data protection provisions) does "not prevent any negative impact on the data subject. Rather, its purpose is to prevent disproportionate impacts."[13] Similarly, this vision of data protection as unable to protect against all risks was already present since its inception. As Sieghart put it, there is no—completely—harmless processing of data.[14] The Ware Report was quite explicit that the protection afforded by the then contemplated "Fair Information Principles" constituted what was deemed an appropriate balance between the interests of the data controller and those of the data subject.[15] This is why Hondius argued that full compliance with data protection provided "a tolerable minimum of privacy against adverse factors of modern life".[16]

In any case, this difference (ie contextual risk *vs* universal regulation) echoes Hayek's seminal criticism that was analysed in the chapter dedicated to the shortcomings of command and control models of regulation.[17] As one remembers, Hayek criticised the "diagnosis-prescription" aspect of the standard setting function of command and control regulation. This aspect is predicated upon the assumption that it is possible to know what is good and what is bad behaviour, and how to address the latter, precisely through standards which, when applied, will thus "automatically" lead to the achievement of regulatory goals (ie when the data protection core principles are applied, the data protection operation is considered safe enough to be pursued). In theory, standards can therefore be applied linearly to all the activities falling within the scope of a given regulation and always lead to satisfying outcomes. However, Hayek precisely criticises this assumption. According to him, it is simply impossible to know of a standard that would satisfactorily address all existing and potential processing situations.[18] From the perspective of risk management, this criticism appears very sensible. For indeed, it appears highly unlikely that the balancing of harms and benefits will always result with identical decisions and that exactly the same mitigation measures should be warranted for every situation. A clear illustration of this issue is embodied in this

[13] Art 29 WP, "Opinion 06/2014 on the Notion of Legitimate Interests of the Data Controller under Article 7 of Directive 95/46/EC" (2014) 41.

[14] Paul Sieghart, "Information Privacy and the Data Protection Bill" in Colin Bourn and John Benyon (eds), *Data Protection: Perspectives on Information Privacy* (University of Leicester 1984).

[15] US Department of Health Education & Welfare, *Records, Computers, and the Rights of Citizens* (The MIT Press 1973) 52.

[16] Frits W Hondius, *Emerging Data Protection in Europe* (North-Holland; American Elsevier 1975) 6–7.

[17] Friedrich A Hayek, *Law, Legislation and Liberty: A New Statement of the Liberal Principles of Justice and Political Economy* (Routledge 1982).

[18] For a similar criticism, see Frederik Schauer, *Playing by the Rules: A Philosophical Examination of Rule-Based Decision-Making in Law and Life* (OUP 1991) 35.

quote from Cavoukian. According to her, "consumers, increasingly, are experiencing what they consider to be 'privacy harms' even where there has been no technical violation of a privacy statute".[19] As one can see, compliance with safeguards does not mean *ipso facto* that these safeguards have adequately addressed the risks at stake. This is exactly the reason why the key question of risk mitigation is: "what actions make what difference to risk outcomes". Such key question is predicated upon the assumption that for each specific situation one should determine what the most appropriate mitigation measures are.

Seen from this perspective, the major objection against the risk-based approach loses some of its edge. Yes, it might lead to an uneven level of protection, but such protection is in any case already uneven (to the extent that the data protection principles are inherently scalable). Furthermore, it might also address some of the issues that descend precisely from the "minimum and non-negotiable level of protection" that the rights-based approach affords to all individuals,[20] since the latter is linear and fixed once and for all. One can argue that each approach has the drawbacks of its advantages. The rights-based approach provides a—more or less—even level of protection to all, but this protection might simply be inadequate in a number of cases. The risk-based approach on the contrary might provide a type of protection that is tailor-made to each specific processing operation, but this leads to a style of data protection that is individualised and uneven.

The scepticism with which a "full" risk-based approach (ie not limited to compliance risk) has been accompanied is not unwarranted. In addition to the many caveats discussed, the way it has been operationalised in the Microsoft approach for instance confirms that it can serve as a blank cheque for data controllers and is reminiscent of the neoliberal dimension of risk underpinning meta- and principles-based regulation. Yet, if one is to take the risk-based approach seriously it might be helpful in achieving a stronger level of protection. As demonstrated, the straightforward application of even some of the more fundamental data protection principles such as data minimisation or data accuracy can lead to contradictory and unsatisfactory solutions. This finding has been confirmed by a recent study, which demonstrated that the full application of data protection by design and by default leads to clashes between a number of data protection principles, with particularly nefarious consequences for the exercise of data subject rights.[21] Similarly, in the contemporary technological context characterised by machine learning, many actors, in particular institutional ones,[22] have hailed risk management

[19] Ann Cavoukian, "Privacy by Design in Law, Policy and Practice: A White Paper for Regulators, Decision-Makers and Policy-Makers" (2011) 24.

[20] Art 29 WP, "Opinion 1/98 Platform for Privacy Preferences (P3P) and the Open Profiling Standard (OPS)" (1998) 2.

[21] Michael Veale, Reuben Binns, and Jef Ausloos, "When Data Protection by Design and Data Subject Rights Clash" (2018) 8 International Data Privacy Law 105.

[22] Council of Europe, Guidelines on the Protection of Individuals with Regard to the Processing of Personal Data in a World of Big Data 2017 6; see eg Art 29 WP, "17/EN WP251rev.01—Guidelines

(oftentimes in the form of data protection impact assessments—DPIAs) as a solution at a time where the quality of the protection afforded by data protection in the face of these new technological challenges remains uncertain to say the least.[23]

These potentially promising aspects of the risk-based approach echo a number of positive elements associated with risk-based models of regulation. Among these advantages, one can point to the fact that it contributes to regulatory efficiency and effectiveness insofar as it enables to target efforts where they are proportionate to the risks, that is, to use resources more efficiently.[24] In this sense, it has the potential for easing the burdens of data controllers, who know better where to target their regulatory resources, to scale them, and to choose the most adapted ones. Linked to the latter, another advantage of the risk-based approach is that it renders explicit a number of standard setting choices that had always been made, albeit implicitly. As discussed, traditional standard setting sets standards from the outset. How exactly these standards are set is not always clear and explicit. The risk-based approach on the contrary offers an explicit and defensible framework for setting such standards.[25] Further, the assessment of risks (which is absent from the traditional standard setting method) can generate new insights about the risks and thus lead to better decisions and standard setting.[26] Similarly, the better understanding of risks also provides for much needed flexibility in the face of different and ever evolving situations.[27] Finally, the risk-based approach can also provide for a common language between regulators and regulatees.[28]

The potential for improved dialogue between regulators and regulated entities seems crucial as far as the articulation of the rights-based and risk-based approach is concerned. A possible solution to the conundrum of the rights-based/risk-based distinction (ie ensuring safeguards that are most adequate or ensuring an equal level of protection for all) might call for an increased dialogue between regulatees and regulators, and in particular courts. For instance, in the *Google Spain* case, the Court of Justice of the European Union (CJEU) provided some indications on how

on Automated Individual Decision-Making and Profiling for the Purposes of Regulation 2016/679—Adopted on 3 October 2017 As Last Revised and Adopted on 6 February 2018" (2018).

[23] See eg Lee A Bygrave, "EU Data Protection Law Falls Short as Desirable Model for Algorithmic Regulation" (2017) 85; Seda Gürses and Joris van Hoboken, "Privacy After the Agile Turn", *Cambridge Handbook of Consumer Privacy* (2017); Katja de Vries, "Machine Learning/Informational Fundamental Rights: Makings of Sameness and Difference" (2016); Isak Mendoza and Lee A Bygrave, "The Right Not to Be Subject to Automated Decisions Based on Profiling" in Tatiana Eleni Synodinou and others (eds), *EU Internet Law: Regulation and Enforcement* (Springer 2017); Christopher Kuner and others, "Expanding the Artificial Intelligence-Data Protection Debate" (2018) 8 International Data Privacy Law 289.

[24] Henry Rothstein and others, "The Risks of Risk-Based Regulation: Insights from the Environmental Policy Domain" (2006) 32 Environment International 1056, 1061.

[25] ibid; Black (n 12) 193.

[26] Rothstein and others (n 24) 1061.

[27] Black (n 12) 222.

[28] ibid.

to manage risks. More in particular, it argued that in case of high risk to the data subject, the processing of the latter's data could not be "justified by merely the economic interest which the operator of such an engine has in that processing".[29] One can also mention the *Digital Rights Ireland* case,[30] where the court found that if the initial balance undertaken by the then data retention Directive (2006/24/EU) between the harms and benefits associated to its data retention system might be legitimate. But, the fact that the balance may tilt in favour of the retention of data does not suffice to make it lawful,[31] and therefore any system of retention of personal data should feature a minimum number of safeguards ("governing the scope and application of the measures in question").[32] The Court even went on to suggest what these safeguards should consist of.[33]

Regulators and courts might thus help data controllers conduct their risk management exercises, but resorting to them in such a potentially extensive manner is no panacea either. As a matter of fact, this is one of the contradictions at the heart of meta regulation. To what extent can guidance be provided without unduly constraining the discretion of the regulatees?[34] This problematic role for the regulators taps right into the difficulties associated with the responsibilisation of regulatees. The increased discretion afforded to the regulatees does indeed allow for "local customisation", which can help regulators make the shift from the general and aggregate level of rules to the local and the particular where these rules are meant to be applied.[35] In this sense it addresses some of the command and control issues pertaining to the difficulty of complying with, and implementing regulatory rules and standards. Yet, such discretion even if beneficial for all the reasons mentioned herein above also creates the need for regulated organisations to concretely work out what they must do. In this sense, the balance that should be struck between the regulatees' discretion and the guidance from the regulator is an essentially contested one. Regulatees want very specific guidance, whilst regulators do not want to become "unpaid consultants".[36]

These are just but a few of the contradictions at the heart of meta regulation. What remains probably its chief contradiction, however, is that it might defeat some of the very things it promises. For instance, it promises more simplicity and

[29] CJEU, Case C-131/12 *Google Spain SL and Google Inc v Agencia Espanola de Proteccion de Datos (AEPD) and Mario Costeja Gonzalez* [2014] ECLI:EU:C:2014:317 para 81 (hereafter *Google Spain*).

[30] Joined Cases C-293/12 and C-594/12 *Digital Rights Ireland Ltd v Minister for Communications, Marine and Natural Resources and Others* and *Kärtner Landesregierung and Others* [2014] ECLI:EU:C:2014:238 (hereafter *Digital Rights Ireland*).

[31] ibid, para 51

[32] ibid, para 54.

[33] They include storage duration, initial limitation of collection scope, prior authorisation by a judicial or independent administrative body, see ibid, paras 51–71.

[34] See Rothstein and others (n 24) 1058.

[35] Julia Black, "The Rise, Fall and Fate of Principles-Based Regulation" in Kern Alexander and Niamh Moloney (eds), *Law Reform and Financial Markets* (Edward Elgar 2011) 13.

[36] ibid 10.

to reduce the use of resource going into inefficient "red-tape" style bureaucratic measures. But in practice it appears as very complex, and eventually requiring even more resources. It promises objective and harmonised solutions, yet it relies on localism and "local scripts", making it anything but objective and harmonised. It promises to go beyond creative compliance and box ticking, but in many situations, and owing to a number of different factors (lack of training, resentment towards new methods, lack of clear response) it also becomes an automatic and somewhat random exercise of box-ticking. It promises improved compliance, but its managerial dimension runs the real risk of leading to a new style of risk management (and hence of compliance), which is foremost concerned with blame avoidance and the achievement of the regulatees' business goals, and "which at worst imprisons risk management in a pretence of control rather than enabling [it] to become a mechanism for encountering issues".[37]

Thus, Black warns that one should not adopt the risk-based approach for "the wrong reasons", that is, hoping it will miraculously work.[38] Those adopting a risk-based approach should therefore recognise its limitations and caveats, and make sure that once adopted it actually works for them, ie lead to better regulatory outcomes.[39] Yet, the possibility that the risk-based approach leads to dubious results should not be taken as such as an argument in favour of conservatism ("data protection was better before"—when exactly?). The challenges data protection faces are real. In particular those pertaining to command and control have been abundantly commented in the literature,[40] and there aren't many people in the data protection community who would argue that no update of the 1995 Directive (DPD) was necessary. As a matter of fact, the whole history of data protection has been permeated by evolutions, what Mayer-Schönberger has famously referred to as "the generations of data protection".[41] Licensing mechanisms that were so prevalent in the early days have now disappeared, data subject rights have become "mainstream" only in the second generation of statutes in the 1980s, and consent still had a very marginal role in the first Commission proposals for the EU Data Protection Directive.[42] If anything, then, the GDPR and with it the risk-based approach are a—more or less—honest attempt at tackling some of the issues stemming from contemporary processing operations.[43] For better or worse, the GDPR

[37] Michael Power, *The Risk Management of Everything—Rethinking the Politics of Uncertainty* (Demos 2004) 49.

[38] Black (n 12) 222. In other words, one should not take the risk-based approach for what it is not: it can achieve a number of results, but it also comes along with a number of challenges to be addressed.

[39] ibid.

[40] For another overview, see also Christine Parker, *The Open Corporation: Effective Self-Regulation and Democracy* (Cambridge University Press 2002) 8–12.

[41] Viktor Mayer-Schönberger, "Generational Development of Data Protection in Europe" in Philip E Agre and Marc Rotenberg (eds), *Technology and Privacy: The New Landscape* (MIT Press 1997).

[42] Eleni Kosta, *Consent in European Data Protection Law* (Martinus Nijhoff 2013).

[43] For a slightly hagiographical account of the GDPR adoption process, which nonetheless renders well the difficulties faced by the EU legislator, see, David Bernet's 2015 movie "Democracy", which

and the risk-based approach have now entered into force: can we expect them to deliver on their promises?

2. The risk-based approach and the future of data protection

It is useful to remember that regulation models are only analytical constructs.[44] In practice, however, they depend upon an important number of practical and contingent factors that have a great influence on the type of regulatory outcomes they lead to. Because of its collaborative nature, meta regulation relies upon a so-called responsive strategy of enforcement.[45] Such responsive enforcement is based on a collaboration and negotiation between regulators and regulatees as to the meaning and implementation of the rules at stake. Thus, contrary to regimes characterised by tough and punitive approaches, regulators adopt a more purposive approach, and are ready to overlook potential instances of ill-compliance provided that it is part of a regulatory conversation aimed *in fine* at achieving the regulatory goals.[46] However, such a model depends in practice on the attitude of the regulatees. Some regulatees are well informed and well intentioned. Others however, are ill-intentioned and ill-informed, have no real intention of actually performing the regulatory tasks that befall upon them,[47] and responsive enforcement will in practice never work with them. In her study of the way in which regulated organisations integrate their new regulatory roles and duties, Parker has analysed and reviewed some of the various elements that influence the success of principles-based regulation, such as the existence of sufficient resources, the quality of the personal, or the actual willingness of senior management.[48] In any case, it reminds us that the ideal of "natural compliance", whereby the objectives of data controllers and data protection authorities are perfectly aligned, and further, where the two work seamlessly hand in hand, remains what it is, ie an ideal, which is often contradicted in practice.

At the time of writing, the GDPR is into force for less than a year, but some relevant observations can already be made. It would seem that in many cases data controllers are quite reluctant to transform their operations in order to make room

documented the adoption of the GDPR within the EU institutions, http://www.democracy-film.de, last accessed 13 March 2019.

[44] See Julia Black, "Decentring Regulation: Understanding the Role Self-Regulation in a 'Post-Regulatory' World" (2001) 54 Current Legal Problems 103.

[45] See Ian Ayres and John Braithwaite, *Responsive Regulation: Transcending the Deregulation Debate* (OUP 1992).

[46] See Robert Baldwin and Julia Black, "Really Responsive Regulation" (2008) 2003 Modern Law Review 59.

[47] See Eugene Bardach and Robert Kagan, *Going by the Book: The Problem of Regulatory Unreasonableness* (Temple University Press 1982).

[48] Parker (n 40) 43 ff.

for the GDPR-based changes.[49] A number of them have had risk management programs for a number of years but are afraid that the risk-based provisions of the GDPR, as a specific instantiation of the risk management agenda in the data protection field, do not totally match their existing risk management programs. It is therefore not rare to hear data controllers adopt an overly legalistic position, trying to find loopholes in the GDPR in order not to have to invest additional resources in these new risk-based obligations.[50] A case in point seems to be the Data Protection Officer (DPO). As seen, the number of cases where it is mandatory has been diminished to only a handful of cases in the adopted version of the GDPR. Yet, some data controllers seem to be resisting this obligation.[51] This might seem strange given that a number of them were at the forefront to support the adoption of the principle of accountability and similar risk management-style measures, which, supposedly, would give them the freedom and discretion to comply efficiently.[52] Yet, it is to be noted that other corporate actors were also opposed to any additional compliance-related obligations, however possibly aligned with their pre-existing internal risk management programs.[53] Parker suggests that one way of addressing regulated organisations' willingness and attitude is through "external regulatory pressure", that is, the type of enforcement practice and attitude of the regulator.[54] In this sense there is reason for cautious optimism, since early GDPR implementation reports suggest a somewhat "serious" enforcement practice.[55]

Another caveat that points to the "analytical constructs" dimension of regulatory models is the gap that exists between regulation models "in the books" and "on the ground". Black distinguishes between substantial and formal principles-based regulation. Meta regulation can be adopted and implemented in practice, irrespective of what is in "the rulebook". As she puts it, "regulatory practice can be quite divorced from the nature of the rule being implemented".[56] This can work both ways. That is, meta regulation can occur in practice in a regulatory environment formally characterised as command and control. Symmetrically, a command and control style of regulatory practice can take place in spite of the rulebook being

[49] See Ryan Chiavetta, "Privacy Professionals Begin to Look Back at Year One of the GDPR" (*The Privacy Advisor*, 2019) <https://iapp.org/news/a/privacy-professionals-begin-to-look-back-at-year-one-of-the-gdpr/> accessed 26 March 2019.

[50] See eg Maria Eduarda Gonçalves, "The Risk-Based Approach under the New EU Data Protection Regulation: A Critical Perspective" (2019) 23 Journal of Risk Research 139, 148.

[51] Chiavetta (n 49). This point is confirmed by the author's personal knowledge, stemming from anonymous informal discussions with stakeholders.

[52] See among many, Vodafone, "A Comprehensive Approach on Personal Data Protection in the European Union: Vodafone's Response" (2010) http://ec.europa.eu/justice/news/consulting_public/news_consulting_0006_en.htm, last accessed 06 February 2019.

[53] See for instance EUROFINAS, "Response to the European Commission's Consultation on the Commission's Comprehensive Approach on Personal Data Protection in the European Union" (2011).

[54] Parker (n 40) 53.

[55] See EDPB, "First Overview on the Implementation of the GDPR and the Roles and Means of the National Supervisory Authorities" (2019).

[56] Black (n 35) 7.

grounded in meta regulation.[57] This fluidity between formal model of regulation and the reality of regulatory practice can also be observed in the data protection context. For a start, one can argue that the risk-based approach did not come out of vacuum. It has been shown that there have existed a number of risk-based tools prior to the adoption of the risk-based approach (be it in the GDPR or in other statutes). This includes audits, certification schemes, DPIAs, etc, which have been used for a number of years. In this respect, the work of Bamberger and Mulligan is of great interest.[58] Their study of data protection "on the ground" has shown that in the US, and increasingly in the EU, data controllers have been resorting to risk management independently of what statutes require them to do. This observation is coherent with some of the findings on the emergence of corporate governance and of the risk management agenda. The latter emerged in the 1990s and all organisations have been exposed to it. There is indeed no reason why data controllers would be an exception to this global trend. In this sense, one can argue that the risk-based approach is a mere attempt of catching up with the organisational reality and the practices of data controllers,[59] of equating regulation "in the books" and "on the ground".

This "fluidity" and lack of analytical clarity that characterises regulation in practice can also be observed at the level of the risk management tools used. This contribution has studied in-depth the notion of data protection risk, as well as the various associated risk management methodologies. On the one hand, one can argue that these—sometimes—very arid and technical discussions can be helpful in order to better understand the risk-based approach, what to expect from it, and how to operationalise it. On the other hand, one can argue these very findings are actually useless. As has been seen, the risk-based approach requires a high level of technical knowledge which is not to be found often, and employees in organisations often rely upon the ancestral "rule of thumb" when implementing said risk-based approach. This is particularly the case when they rely upon technical and semi-quantitative templates for risk management, which, it is helpful to remind, is the path that seems to have been chosen at EU level given for instance the Art 29 WP's quasi-explicit endorsement of the International Organization for Standardization (ISO) DPIA Standard.[60] However, it is interesting to observe that a number of countries who have been at the forefront of the use of risk management tools in the

[57] ibid 7–8.

[58] Kenneth A Bamberger and Deirdre K Mulligan, *Privacy on the Ground: Driving Corporate Behavior in the United States and Europe* (The MIT Press 2015).

[59] This was actually explicitly recognised by the European Commission during the reform process, see European Commission, "Commission Staff Working Paper: Impact Assessment Accompanying the Document Regulation of the European Parliament and of the Council on the Protection of Individuals with Regard to the Processing of Personal Data and on the Free Movement of Such Data" (2012) 35–36.

[60] See Art 29 WP, "Guidelines on Data Protection Impact Assessment (DPIA) and Determining Whether Processing Is 'Likely to Result in a High Risk' for the Purposes of Regulation 2016/679" (2017).

data protection field, such as the US,[61] or Australia,[62] or until recently the UK,[63] officially rely upon guidance documents and templates that are much less technically sophisticated than the DPIA methodologies reviewed. Instead, they often consist of simple qualitative, semi-structured guidelines (ie a list of questions), which are very far from some of the technical sophistication that traditionally characterises risk management. From this perspective one can wonder whether the risk-based approach will make any real change in practice. It might be likely that data controllers will implement it in their own pragmatic way, and that the situation will actually not change much from the present one.

These indistinctions in practice between command and control and meta regulation echo Black's seminal analysis of regulation as being "decentred".[64] Black's analysis is an attempt to shift the study of regulation away from ideal analytical and monolithic concepts such as "the state", "the market", etc.[65] As she argues, it makes little sense to conceive of meta- and principles-based regulation as the exact counterpart of command and control. On the contrary, and following Offe, "regulation is co-produced".[66] In this sense, just as the shortcomings of command and control regulation reveal some of the illusions it is predicated upon (ie the state provides for rules that adequately apply to all situations not least because it has sufficient knowledge; implementing rules is self-evident, etc), some of the solutions put forth by principles-based regulation can be said to suffer from the "reversed illusions" (ie regulated organisations have sufficient resources as well as all the information necessary; interactions between regulators and regulatees is seamless, etc).[67] From this vantage point, the change of regulatory model can be assimilated to the replacement of one "diagnosis-prescription" issue (ie "rules always work") by another one (ie "risk management always works").[68] In practice, things are more complicated. Concepts such as the state, or regulated organisations, do not exist in isolation, in the vacuum. Rather, and just like regulation, they are also "co-produced",[69] thereby

[61] Even though the situation might now be changing in the US with the advent of the various NIST methodologies, National Institute of Standards and Technology, "Risk Management Framework for Information Systems and Organizations A System Life Cycle Approach for Security and Privacy" (2018); National Institute of Standards and Technology, "NISTIR 8062: An Introduction to Privacy Engineering and Risk Management in Federal Systems" (2017). Yet, official templates and actual performed DPIA continue to remain qualitative, semi-structured decision-making tools, see eg the DPIA templates for the US Department of Justice, https://www.justice.gov/opcl/doj-privacy-impact-assessments, last accessed 12 March 2019.

[62] See, Office of the Australian Information Commissioner, "Guide to Undertaking Privacy Impact Assessments" (2014).

[63] ICO, "Conducting Privacy Impact Assessments: Code of Practice" (2014).

[64] Black (n 44).

[65] ibid 105.

[66] ibid 109; Claus Offe, *Contradictions of the Welfare State* (John Keane ed, Hutchinson & Co 1984).

[67] Black (n 44) 106–09.

[68] On "diagnosis-prescription" and its link with the analytical nature of regulation, see Chapter 3, and in particular Julia Black, "The Role of Risk in Regulatory Processes" in Robert Baldwin, Martin Cave, and Martin Lodge (eds), *The Oxford Handbook of Regulation* (OUP 2010).

[69] For the seminal argument on this matter, see Sheila Jasanoff, "The Idiom of Co-Production" in Sheila Jasanoff (ed), *States of Knowledge: The Co-production of Science and Social Order* (Routledge 2004).

pointing to a complexity of things that analytical models are unable to capture. This is why Black's decentred analysis argues that regulation, and society (within which regulation operates) are characterised by "complexity, fragmentation of knowledge, fragmentation of the exercise of power and control, autonomy, interactions and interdependencies, and the collapse of the public/private distinction".[70] From a decentred point of view, the distinction between command and control and newer, risk-inspired, models of regulation becomes much subtler, if not sometimes blurred.[71] Further, this inherent complexity of social life, which the decentred analysis reveals, also points to the "inherent ungovernability of social actors, systems, and networks".[72] And as a consequence, to the inherent complexity and difficulty of regulatory activity, irrespective of the type of regulatory model at stake.

This indistinction between command and control and meta regulation—and therefore between rights-based and risk-based approaches to data protection—might point to some intractable difficulties associated to regulatory activity. Yet, it also points to the common root observed between risk and regulation, between rights-based and risk-based approaches. Namely, the proportionality principle. Given this common root, this indistinction acquires a novel meaning. Notably, it mitigates some claims following which the rights-based approach is "morally superior", or that the risk-based approach is a denaturation of the fundamental right to personal data protection. Rather, this signals at most the shift from one way of doing a proportionality test to another. Yet, this cannot be taken to mean that risk-based and rights-based iterations of data protection are identical either. As Power insightfully argues, both risk and regulation are "always a practice under some description or other, a description which embodies ideas about purpose and which embeds practices in larger systems of value and belief. Very similar material routines can be mobilised by actors around different ideas and descriptions, [effectively transforming them into] distinct practices".[73] Maybe then the difference between rights-based and risk-based approaches to data protection is to be found not in the properties and the tools of the risk-based approach such as risk analysis tools, their technicalities, the renewed role for regulators and regulatees, etc, but simply in the ideals that underpin it (such as natural compliance, responsibilisation, the production of self-legitimation, the neoliberal focus on the achievement of organisational objectives, etc), and which may at the end of the day shape the manner in which the protection of personal data is effectuated.

[70] Black (n 44) 111.

[71] See ibid 123: "There is a danger, however, that despite the warnings for contextual analysis and that despite the great claims made for it as an innovative policy form, collective self-regulation or intra-firm regulation may well be simply the displacement of command and control regulation to another level, be it the association or the individual firm."

[72] ibid 111.

[73] Michael Power, *Organized Uncertainty: Designing a World of Risk Management* (OUP 2007) 25.

Bibliography

35th International Conference of Data Protection and Privacy Commissioners, "Warsaw Declaration on the 'Appification' of Society" (2013)

Agencia Espanola de Proteccion de Datos, "Guía Para Una Evaluación de Impacto En La Protección de Datos Personales" (2014)

Alexy R, *A Theory of Constitutional Rights* (English edn, OUP 2010)

Alhadeff J, Van Alsenoy B, and Dumortier J, "The Accountability Principle in Data Protection Regulation: Origin, Development and Future Directions" in Daniel Guagnin and others (eds), *Managing Privacy Through Accountability* (Palgrave Macmillan 2012)

American Institute of Certified Public Accountants and Canadian Institute of Chartered Accountants, "Generally Accepted Privacy Principles" (2009)

Amoore L, *The Politics of Possibility* (2013)

Aronstein CS, "Essai Pour Contribuer à La Survie de Notre Civilisation" (1970) 86 Journal des tribunaux 453

——, "De l'urgence d'ordonner Les Ordinateurs" [1971] Journal des tribunaux 161

Art 29 WP, "Opinion 1/98 Platform for Privacy Preferences (P3P) and the Open Profiling Standard (OPS)" (1998)

——, "Working Document Privacy on the Internet—An Integrated EU Approach to On-Line Data Protection" (2000)

——, "Opinion 4/2007 on the Concept of Personal Data" (2007)

——, "Opinion 3/2010 on the Principle of Accountability" (2010)

——, "Advice Paper on Notification" (2011)

——, "Opinion 15/2011 on the Definition of Consent" (2011)

——, "Opinion 9/2011 on the Revised Industry Proposal for a Privacy and Data Protection Impact Assessment Framework for RFID Applications" (2011)

——, "Privacy and Data Protection Impact Assessment Framework for RFID Applications" (2011)

——, "Opinion 01/2012 on the Data Protection Reform Proposals" (2012)

——, "Opinion 03/2013 on Purpose Limitation" (2013)

——, "Opinion 04/2013 on the Data Protection Impact Assessment Template for Smart Grid and Smart Metering Systems ('DPIA Template') Prepared by Expert Group 2 of the Commission's Smart Grid Task Force" (2013)

——, "Opinion 01/2014 on the Application of Necessity and Proportionality Concepts and Data Protection within the Law Enforcement Sector" (2014)

——, "Opinion 06/2014 on the Notion of Legitimate Interests of the Data Controller under Article 7 of Directive 95/46/EC" (2014)

——, "Opinion 8/2014 on the Recent Developments on the Internet of Things" (2014)

——, "Statement on the Role of a Risk-Based Approach in Data Protection Legal Frameworks" (2014)

——, "Guidelines on Data Protection Officers ('DPOs')" (2016)

——, "Guidelines on Data Protection Impact Assessment (DPIA) and Determining Whether Processing Is 'Likely to Result in a High Risk' for the Purposes of Regulation 2016/679" (2017)

——, "17/EN WP251rev.01—Guidelines on Automated Individual Decision-Making and Profiling for the Purposes of Regulation 2016/679—Adopted on 3 October 2017 As Last Revised and Adopted on 6 February 2018" (2018)

——, "Article 29 Working Party Guidelines on Consent under Regulation 2016/679" (2018)

Art 29 WP and Working Party on Police and Justice, "The Future of Privacy: Joint Contribution to the Consultation of the European Commission on the Legal Framework for the Fundamental Right to the Protection of Personal Data" (2009)

Ayres I and Braithwaite J, *Responsive Regulation: Transcending the Deregulation Debate* (OUP 1992)

Baker T and Simon J (eds), *Embracing Risk: The Changing Culture of Insurance and Responsibility* (The University of Chicago Press 2002)

——, "Embracing Risk" in Tom Baker and Jonathan Simon (eds), *Embracing Risk: The Changing Culture of Insurance and Responsibility* (The University of Chicago Press 2002)

Balboni P and others, "Legitimate Interest of the Data Controller New Data Protection Paradigm: Legitimacy Grounded on Appropriate Protection" (2013) 3 International Data Privacy Law 244

Baldwin R, "Why Rules Don't Work" (1990) 53 The Modern Law Review 321

——, *Rules and Government* (OUP 1995)

—— and Black J, "Really Responsive Regulation" (2008) 2003 Modern Law Review 59

——, Cave M, and Lodge M, "Risk-Based Regulation", *Understanding Regulation: Theory, Strategy, and Practice* (2nd edn, OUP 2012)

——, *Understanding Regulation: Theory, Strategy, and Practice* (2nd edn, OUP 2012)

——, Scott C, and Hood C (eds), *A Reader on Regulation* (OUP 1998)

Bamberger KA, "Regulation as Delegation: Private Firms, Decisionmaking, and Accountability in the Administrative State" (2006) 56 Duke Law Journal 377

——and Mulligan DK, "Privacy in Europe : Initial Data on Governance Choices and Corporate Practices" (2013) 81 The George Washington Law Review 1529

——, *Privacy on the Ground: Driving Corporate Behavior in the United States and Europe* (The MIT Press 2015)

Barak A, *Proportionality: Constitutional Rights and Their Limitations* (Cambridge University Press 2012)

Bardach E and Kagan R, *Going by the Book: The Problem of Regulatory Unreasonableness* (Temple University Press 1982)

Barocas S and Nissenbaum H, "On Notice : The Trouble with Notice and Consent", *Proceedings of the Engaging Data Forum: The First International Forum on the Application and Management of Personal Electronic Information* (Cambridge, Massachusetts 2009)

——, "Big Data's End Run around Anonymity and Consent" in Julia Lane and others (eds), *Privacy, Big Data, and the Public Good* (Cambridge University Press 2014)

Barth A and others, "Privacy and Utility in Business Processes" [2007] Proceedings—IEEE Computer Security Foundations Symposium 279

Bendor AL and Sela T, "How Proportional Is Proportionality?" (2015) 13 International Journal of Constitutional Law 530

Bennett CJ, *Regulating Privacy* (Cornell University Press 1992)

——, "Convergence Revisited: Toward a Global Policy for the Protection of Personal Data" in Philip E Agre and Marc Rotenberg (eds), *Technology and Privacy: The New Landscape* (The MIT Press 1997)

——, *The Privacy Advocates: Resisting the Spread of Surveillance* (The MIT Press 2008)

——, "Privacy Impact Assessments: International Study of Their Application and Effects" (2007)

Bernstein PL, *Against The Gods—The Remarkable Story of Risk* (John Wiley & Sons, Inc 1996)
BEUC, "Response to the European Commission's Consultation on the Commission's Comprehensive Approach on Personal Data Protection in the European Union" (2011)
Bieker F and others, "A Process for Data Protection Impact Assessment Under the European General Data Protection Regulation", *Privacy Technologies and Policy: 4th Annual Privacy Forum, APF 2016 Frankfurt/Main, Germany, September 7–8, 2016, Proceedings*, vol 3 (2016)
——, "Data Protection Impact Assessment: A Hands-on Tour of the GDPR's Most Practical Tool" in Marit Hansen and *et al.* (eds), *Privacy and Identity* (Springer International Publishing 2018)
Bijker WE, Bal R, and Hendriks R, *The Paradox of Scientific Authority: The Role of Scientific Advice in Democracies* (The MIT Press 2009)
Black J, *Rules and Regulators* (OUP 1997)
——, "Decentring Regulation: Understanding the Role Self-Regulation in a "Post-Regulatory" World" (2001) 54 Current Legal Problems 103
——, "Critical Reflections on Regulation" (2002) 27 Australian Journal of Legal Philosophy 1
——, "The Emergence of Risk-Based Regulation and the New Public Risk Management in the United Kingdom" [2005] Public Law 512
——, "Risk-Based Regulation: Choices, Practices and Lessons Being Learnt" in OECD (ed), *Risk and Regulatory Policy: Improving the Governance of Risk* (OECD Publishing 2010)
——, "The Role of Risk in Regulatory Processes" in Robert Baldwin, Martin Cave, and Martin Lodge (eds), *The Oxford Handbook of Regulation* (OUP 2010)
——, "The Rise, Fall and Fate of Principles-Based Regulation" in Kern Alexander and Niamh Moloney (eds), *Law Reform and Financial Markets* (Edward Elgar 2011)
——, "Learning from Failures: 'New Governance' Techniques and the Financial Crisis" (2012) 75 Modern Law Review 1037
——, and Baldwin R, "Really Responsive Risk-Based Regulation" (2010) 32 Law & Policy 181
Boli J, "The Rationalization of Virtue and Virtuosity in World Society" in Marie-Laure Djelic and Kerstin Sahlin-Andersson (eds), *Transnational Governance: Institutional Dynamics of Regulation* (Cambridge University Press 2006)
Braithwaite J, "Enforced Self-Regulation: A New Strategy for Corporate Crime Control" (1982) 80 Michigan Law Review 1466
—— and Drahos P, *Global Business Regulation* (Cambridge University Press 2008)
Brkan M, "The Concept of Essence of Fundamental Rights in the EU Legal Order: Peeling the Onion to Its Core" (2018) 14 European Constitutional Law Review 332
Brownsword R, *Rights, Regulation and the Technological Revolution* (OUP 2008)
—— and Yeung K (eds), *Regulating Technologies: Legal Futures, Regulatory Frames and Technological Fixes* (Hart Publishing 2008)
Bruening PJ, "Data Privacy Day 2014: Today Has Been a Day to Rethink Privacy" (2014) <http://blogs.intel.com/policy/2014/01/28/today-day-rethink-privacy)/> accessed 29 January 2019
Brunton F and Nissenbaum H, *Obfuscation: A User's Guide for Privacy and Protest* (The MIT Press 2015)
Buitelaar JC, "Privacy: Back to the Roots" (2012) 13 German Law Journal 171
Bundesamt für Sicherheit in der Informationstechnik, "Privacy Impact Assessment Guideline" (2011)
Burkert H, "Institutions of Data Protection—An Attempt at a Functional Explanation of European National Data" (1981) 3 Computer Law Journal 167

——, "Data-Protection Legislation and the Modernization of Public Administration" (1996) 62 International Review of Administrative Sciences 557
——, "Privacy-Enhancing Technologies: Typology, Critique, Vision" in Philip E Agre and Marc Rotenberg (eds), *Technology and Privacy: The New Landscape* (The MIT Press 1997)
——, "Privacy—Data Protection: A German/European Perspective", *2nd Symposium of the Max Planck Project Group on the Law of Common Goods and the Computer Science and Telecommunications Board of the National Research Council* (1999)
Bygrave LA, "Where Have All the Judges Gone? Reflections on Judicial Involvement in Developing Data Protection Law Judicial Involvement" in P Wahlgren (ed), *IT och juristutbildning. Nordisk årsbok i rättsinformatik*, vol 7 (Jure AB 2000)
——, *Data Protection Law—Approaching Its Rationale, Logic, and Its Limits* (Kluwer 2002)
——, "Data Protection by Design and by Default: Deciphering the EU's Legislative Requirements" (2017) 4 Oslo Law Review 105
——, "EU Data Protection Law Falls Short as Desirable Model for Algorithmic Regulation" (2017) 85
—— and Schartum DW, "Consent, Proportionality and Collective Power" in Serge Gutwirth and others (eds), *Reinventing Data Protection?* (Springer 2009)
Calo MR, "The Boundaries of Privacy Harm" (2011) 86 Indiana Law Journal 1131
Cate FH and Mayer-Schönberger V, "Data Use and Impact Global Workshop" (2013)
—— and Mayer-Schönberger V, "Tomorrow's Privacy Notice and Consent in a World of Big Data" (2013) 3 International Data Privacy Law 67
——, Cullen P, and Mayer-Schönberger V, "Data Protection Principles for the 21st Century Revising the 1980 OECD Guidelines" (2014)
Cavoukian A, "Privacy by Design: The 7 Foundation Principles" (2009)
——, "Privacy by Design in Law, Policy and Practice: A White Paper for Regulators, Decision-Makers and Policy-Makers" (2011)
——, "Evolving FIPPs: Proactive Approaches to Privacy, Not Privacy Paternalism" in Serge Gutwirth, Ronald Leenes, and Paul De Hert (eds), *Reforming European Data Protection Law* (Springer 2015)
——, Dix A, and El Emam K, "The Unintended Consequences of Privacy Paternalism" (2014)
Centre for Information Policy Leadership, "Big Data and Analytics: Seeking Foundations for Effective Privacy Guidance" (2013)
——, "'A Risk-Based Approach to Privacy?' An Initial Issues Paper for Privacy Risk Framework and Risk-Based Approach to Privacy Project" (2014)
——, "A Risk-Based Approach to Privacy: Improving Effectiveness in Practice" (2014)
——, "The Role of Risk Management in Data Protection" (2014)
——, "The Role of Enhanced Accountability in Creating a Sustainable Data-Driven Economy and Information Society" (2015)
——, "Three Solutions for Protecting Privacy in a World of Big Data" (2015)
——, "The Role of Risk Management" (2016)
Chiavetta R, "Privacy Professionals Begin to Look Back at Year One of the GDPR" (*The Privacy Advisor*, 2019) <https://iapp.org/news/a/privacy-professionals-begin-to-look-back-at-year-one-of-the-gdpr/> accessed 26 March 2019
Clarke L, *Using Fantasy Documents to Tame Disaster* (University of Chicago Press 2001)
Clarke R, "Privacy Impact Assessment: Its Origins and Development" (2009) 25 Computer Law & Security Review 123
——, "An Evaluation of Privacy Impact Assessment Guidance Documents" (2011) 1 International Data Privacy Law 111

Clifford D and Ausloos J, "Data Protection and the Role of Fairness" (2018) 37 Yearbook of European Law 130
CNIL, "Measures For The Privacy Risk Treatment" (2012)
——, "Methodology For Privacy Risk Management: How to Implement the Data Protection Act" (2012)
——, "Privacy Impact Assessment (PIA): Methodology (How to Carry out a PIA)" (2015)
——, "Privacy Impact Assessment (PIA): Methodology" (2018)
Coglianese G and Mendelson E, "Meta-Regulation and Self-Regulation" in Robert Baldwin, Martin Cave, and Martin Lodge (eds), *The Oxford Handbook of Regulation* (OUP 2010)
Cohen-Eliya M and Porat I, "American Balancing and German Proportionality: The Historical Origins" (2010) 8 International Journal of Constitutional Law 263
Cohen JE, "The Regulatory State in the Information Age" (2016) 17 Theoretical Inquiries in Law 369
Collingridge D, *The Social Control of Technology* (Frances Pinter 1980)
Costa L and Poullet Y, "Privacy and the Regulation of 2012" (2012) 28 Computer Law & Security Review 254
Council of Europe, Guidelines on the Protection of Individuals With Regard to the Processing of Personal Data in a World of Big Data 2017 6
——, Explanatory Report—Modernised Convention for the Protection of Individuals with Regard to the Processing of Personal Data 2018
Council of the European Union, "Proposal for a Regulation of the European Parliament and of the Council on the Protection of Individuals with Regard to the Processing of Personal Data and on the Free Movement of Such Data (General Data Protection Regulation)—Key Issues of Chapters I–IV" (2013)
——, "Proposal for a Regulation of the European Parliament and of the Council on the Protection of Individuals with Regard to the Processing of Personal Data and on the Free Movement of Such Data—Risk Based Approach" (2014)
Cranston R, *Regulating Business: Law and Consumer Agencies*, vol 53 (Macmillan 1979)
Custers B and others, "Informed Consent in Social Media Use—The Gap between User Expectations and EU Personal Data Protection Law" (2013) 10 SCRIPTed 435
—— and Uršič H, "Big Data and Data Reuse: A Taxonomy of Data Reuse for Balancing Big Data Benefits and Personal Data Protection" (2016) 6 International Data Privacy Law 4
De Hert P, "A Human Rights Perspective on Privacy and Data Protection Impact Assessments" in David Wright and Paul De Hert (eds), *Privacy Impact Assessment* (Springer 2012)
—— and Gutwirth S, "Data Protection in the Case Law of Strasbourg and Luxemburg: C onstitutionalisation in Action" in Serge Gutwirth and others (eds), *Reinventing Data Protection?* (Springer 2009)
de Sadeleer N, "The Precautionary Principle in European Community Health and Environment Law: Sword or Shield for the Nordic Countries?" in Nicolas de Sadeleer (ed), *Implementing the Precautionary Principle: Approaches from the Nordic Countries, EU and USA* (Earthscan 2007)
——, *EU Environmental Law and the Internal Market* (OUP 2014)
de Vries K, "Machine Learning/Informational Fundamental Rights: Makings of Sameness and Difference" (2016)
Dean M, *Governmentality—Power and Rule in Modern Society* (Sage 2010)
Demortain D, *Scientists and the Regulation of Risk—Standardising Control* (Edward Elgar Publishing 2011)

Desrosières A, *La Politique Des Grands Nombres: Histoire de La Raison Statistique* (Editions La Découverte 1993)

Determann L, "Social Media Privacy: A Dozen Myths and Facts" (2012) 7 Stanford Technology Law Review 1

DigitalEurope, "Consultation on the Legal Framework for the Fundamental Right to Protection of Personal Data" (2009)

——, "DIGITALEUROPE Comments on the Risk-Based Approach" (2013) 1

Diver CS, "The Optimal Precision of Administrative Rules" in Robert Baldwin, Collin Scott, and Christopher Hood (eds), *A Reader on Regulation* (OUP 1998)

Douglas M, "Risk as a Forensic Resource" in Edward J Burger (ed), *Risk* (University of Michigan 1990)

—— (ed), *Risk and Blame: Essays in Cultural Theory*, vol 22 (Routledge 1993)

Drori GS, "Governed by Governance: The New Prism for Organizational Change" in Gili S Drori, John M Meyer, and Hyoku Hwang (eds), *Globalization and Organization: World Society and Organizational Change* (OUP 2006)

Duggal P, *Appification of Society and the Law* (Saakshar Law Publications 2013)

Dumortier J and Goemans C, "Data Privacy and Standardization: Discussion Paper Prepared for the CEN/ISSS Open Seminar on Data Protection" (2000)

Dwork C and others, "Fairness Through Awareness", *Proceedings of the third ICTS* (ACM 2012)

—— and Mulligan DK, "It's Not Privacy, and It's Not Fair" (2013) 66 Stanford Law Review Online 35

Dworkin R, "The Model of Rules" (1967) 35 The University of Chicago Law Review 14

EDPB, "Endorsement 1/2018" (2018)

——, "Opinion 11/2018 on the Draft List of the Competent Supervisory Authority of Ireland Regarding the Processing Operations Subject to the Requirement of a Data Protection Impact Assessment (Article 35.4 GDPR) Adopted" (2018)

——, "EDPB Work Program 2019/2020" (2019)

——, "First Overview on the Implementation of the GDPR and the Roles and Means of the National Supervisory Authorities" (2019)

EDPS, "Opinion of the EDPS on the Data Protection Reform Package" (2012)

——, "Guidelines on the Rights of Individuals with Regard to the Processing of Personal Data" (2014)

——, "Opinion 7/2015: Meeting the Challenges of Big Data: A Call for Transparency, User Control, Data Protection by Design and Accountability" (2015)

——, "Assessing the Necessity of Measures That Limit the Fundamental Right to the Protection of Personal Data: A Toolkit" (2017)

Ericson RV and Haggerty KD, *Policing the Risk Society* (University of Toronto Press 1997)

EU Fundamental Rights Agency, "Data Protection in the European Union : The Role of National Data Protection Authorities Strengthening the Fundamental Rights Architecture in the EU II" (2010)

EUROFINAS, "Response to the European Commission's Consultation on the Commission's Comprehensive Approach on Personal Data Protection in the European Union" (2011)

European Commission, "Recommendation on the Implementation of Privacy and Data Protection Principles in Applications Supported by Radio-Frequency Identification" (2009)

——, "Communication from the Commission to the European Parliament, the Council, the Economic and Social Committee and the Committee of the Regions: A Comprehensive Approach on Personal Data Protection in the European Union" (2010)

——, "Commission Staff Working Paper: Impact Assessment Accompanying the Document Regulation of the European Parliament and of the Council on the Protection of Individuals with Regard to the Processing of Personal Data and on the Free Movement of Such Data" (2012)

——, "Proposal for a Regulation of the European Parliament and of the Council on the Protection of Individuals with Regard to the Processing of Personal Data and on the Free Movement of Such Data (General Data Protection Regulation)", vol COM(2012) (2012)

European Commission, Commission Recommendation of 10 October 2014 on the Data Protection Impact Assessment Template for Smart Grid and Smart Metering Systems (2014/724/EU) 2014 63

European Parliament, Legislative Resolution of 12 March 2014 on the proposal for a regulation of the European Parliament and of the Council on the protection of individuals with regard to the processing of their personal data and on the free movement of such data 2014

Ewald F, "La Société Assurancielle" (1990) 1 Les cahiers de l'assurance 5

——, "Insurance and Risk" in Graham Burchell, Colin Gordon, and Peter Miller (eds), *The Foucault Effect—Studies in Governmentality* (The University of Chicago Press 1991)

Fairfield JAT and Engel C, "Privacy as a Public Good" (2015) 65 Duke Law Journal 385

Federal Trade Commission, "Privacy Online: A Report to Congress" (1998)

——, "Privacy Online: Fair Information Practices in the Electronic Marketplace" (2000)

——, "Protecting Consumer Privacy in an Era of Rapid Change—A Proposed Framework For Businesses And Policymakers" (2012)

——, "LabMD, Inc v Federal Trade Commission (11th Cir), Response Brief of the FTC" (2017)

Fisher E, "Risk and Environmental Law: A Beginner's Guide" in Benjamin J Richardson and Stephan Wood (eds), *Environmental Law for Sustainability* (Hart Publishing 2006)

Flaherty DH, *Protecting Privacy in Surveillance Societies—The Federal Republic of Germany, Sweden, France, Canada, and the United States* (The University of North Carolina Press 1989)

Foucault M, "Governmentality" in James D Faubion (ed), *Power: Essential Work of Michel Foucault* (Penguin 2001)

——, *Sécurité, Territoire, Population* (Gallimard, Seuil 2004)

——, *The Birth of Biopolitics: Lectures at the Collège de France, 1978–1979* (Michel Senellart ed, Palgrave Macmillan 2008)

Freedman J, "Defining Taxpayer Responsibility: In Support of a General Anti-Avoidance Principle" (2004) 4 British Tax Review 332

Freund E, *Legislative Regulation: A Study of the Ways and Means of Written Law* (The Commonwealth Fund 1932)

FTC, "Data Brokers—A Call for Transparency and Accountability" (2014)

Funtowicz S and Ravetz J, "Three Types of Risk Assessment and the Emergence of Post-Normal Science" in Sheldon Krimsky and Dominique Golding (eds), *Social Theories of Risk* (Praeger Publishers 1992)

Galetta A and De Hert P, "The Proceduralisation of Data Protection Remedies under EU Data Protection Law: Towards a More Effective and Data Subject-Oriented System?" (2015) 8 Review of European Administrative Law 123

Garante per la Protezioni dei Dati Personali, "Video Surveillance The General Provision Adopted by the Garante—Doc Web n 1003482" (2004)

Gellert R, "Data Protection: A Risk Regulation? Between the Risk Management of Everything and the Precautionary Alternative" (2015) 5 International Data Privacy Law 3

——, "We Have Always Managed Risks in Data Protection Law: Understanding the Similarities and Differences Between the Rights-Based and Risk-Based Approaches to Data Protection" (2016) 4 European Data Protection Law Review 481

——, "Discussion · On Risk, Balancing, and Data Protection: A Response to van Der Sloot" (2017) 3 European Data Protection Law Review 180

——, "The Article 29 Working Party's Provisional Guidelines on Data Protection Impact Assessment" (2017) 2 European Data Protection Law Review 1

——, "EDPB Opinion on the Draft Lists of Competent Supervisory Authorities Regarding the Processing Operations Subject to DPIAs" (2018) 4 European Data Protection Law Review 500

——, "Understanding the Notion of Risk in the General Data Protection Regulation" (2018) 34 Computer Law and Security Review 279

Gellman R, "Fair Information Practices: A Basic History" (2015) <http://www.bobgellman.com/rg-docs/rg-FIPShistory.pdf> last accessed 15 March 2019

Gerards J, "How to Improve the Necessity Test of the European Court of Human Rights" (2013) 11 International Journal of Constitutional Law 466

——, "Margin of Appreciation and Incrementalism in the Case Law of the European Court of Human Rights" (2018) 18 Human Rights Law Review 495

German Federal and State Data Protection Commissioners, "The Standard Data Protection Model" (2016)

Godard O and others, *Traité Des Nouveaux Risques* (Gallimard 2002)

Godkin EL, "The Rights of the Citizen—IV: To His Reputation" (1890) 8 Scribener's 58

Gonçalves ME, "The Risk-Based Approach under the New EU Data Protection Regulation: A Critical Perspective" (2019) 23 Journal of Risk Research 139

González Fuster G, "Inaccuracy as a Privacy-Enhancing Tool" (2010) 12 Ethics and Information Technology 87

——, "Fighting For Your Right to What Exactly? The Convoluted Case Law of the EU Court of Justice on Privacy and/or Personal Data Protection" (2014) 2 Birkbeck Law Review 263

——, *The Emergence of Personal Data Protection as a Fundamental Right of the EU* (Springer 2014)

—— and Gutwirth S, "Opening up Personal Data Protection: A Conceptual Controversy" (2013) 29 Computer Law & Security Review 531

Goodrich P, *Languages of Law: From Logics of Memory to Nomadic Masks* (Butterworths 1990)

Graham JD and Wiener JB (eds), *Risk vs Risk—Tradeoffs in Protecting Health and the Environment* (Harvard University Press 1997)

Gray J and Hamilton J, *Implementing Financial Regulation: Theory and Practice* (John Wiley & Sons, Ltd 2006)

Greenleaf G, "APEC's Privacy Framework Sets a New Low Standard for the Asia-Pacific" in Andrew T Kenyon and Megan Richardson (eds), *New Dimensions in Privacy Law: International and Comparative Perspectives* (Cambridge University Press 2006)

——, "Five Years of the APEC Privacy Framework: Failure or Promise?" (2009) 25 Computer Law & Security Review 28

Gunningham N, "Enforcement and Compliance Strategies" in Robert Baldwin, Martin Cave and Martin Lodge (eds), *The Oxford Handbook of Regulation* (OUP 2010)

—— and Grabosky P (eds), *Smart Regulation: Designing Environmental Policy* (OUP 1998)

Gürses S, Troncoso C, and Diaz C, "Engineering. Privacy by Design", *Computers, Privacy and Data Protection Conference (CPDP)* (2011) <http://www.ncbi.nlm.nih.gov/pubmed/17761870> last accessed 22 February 2019

—— and van Hoboken J, "Privacy After the Agile Turn", *Cambridge Handbook of Consumer Privacy* (2017)
Gutwirth S, *Privacy and the Information Age* (Rowman & Littlefield 2002)
——, "Providing the Missing Link: Law after Latour's Passage" in Kyle McGee (ed), *Latour and the Passage of Law* (Edinburgh University Press 2015)
——, De Hert P, and de Sutter L, "The Trouble with Technology Regulation: Why Lessig's 'Optimal Mix' Will Not Work" in Roger Brownsword and Karen Yeung (eds), *Regulating Technologies: Legal Futures, Regulatory Frames and Technological Fixes* (Hart Publishing 2008)
Hacking I, "Biopower and the Avalanche of Printed Numbers" (1982) 5 Humanities in Society 279
Haines F, "Regulation and Risk" in Peter Drahos (ed), *Regulatory Theory: Foundations and Applications* (Australian National University Press 2017)
Hancher L and Moran M, "Organizing Regulatory Space" in Leigh Hancher and Michael Moran (eds), *Capitalism, Culture and Economic Regulation* (OUP 1989)
Harremoës P and others (eds), *The Precautionary Principle in the 20th Century: Late Lessons from Early Warnings* (Earthscan 2002)
Hart HLA, *The Concept of Law* (2nd edn, Clarendon Press 1994)
Hawkins K, *Law as Last Resort: Prosecution Decision-Making in a Regulatory Agency* (OUP 2003)
—— and Hutter BM, "The Response of Business to Social Regulation in England and Wales: An Enforcement Perspective" (1993) 15 Law and Policy 199
Hayek FA, *Law, Legislation and Liberty: A New Statement of the Liberal Principles of Justice and Political Economy* (Routledge 1982)
Hildebrandt M, "A Vision of Ambient Law" in Roger Brownsword and Karen Yeung (eds), *Regulating Technologies: Legal Futures, Regulatory Frames and Technological Fixes* (Hart Publishing 2008)
——, *Smart Technologies and the End(s) of Law* (Edward Elgar Publishing 2015)
——, "Privacy As Protection of the Incomputable Self: From Agnostic to Agonistic Machine Learning" (2019) 20 Theoretical Inquiries in Law 83
—— and Gutwirth S (eds), *Profiling the European Citizen: Cross-Disciplinary Perspectives* (Springer 2008)
Hilgartner S, "The Social Construction of Risk Objects: Or, How to Pry Open Networks of Risk" in James F Short Jr and Lee Clarke (eds), *Organizations, Uncertainties, and Risk* (Westview Press 1992)
Hintze M, "Viewing the GDPR Through a De-Identification Lens: A Tool for Clarification and Compliance" 1 <https://fpf.org/wp-content/uploads/2016/11/M-Hintze-GDPR-Through-the-De-Identification-Lens-31-Oct-2016-002.pdf> last accessed 14 March 2019
Hondius FW, *Emerging Data Protection in Europe* (North-Holland; American Elsevier 1975)
——, "Data Law in Europe" (1980) 16 Stanford Journal of International Law 87
Hood C, "Control Over Bureaucracy: Cultural Theory and Institutional Variety" (1995) 15 Journal of Public Policy 207
——, "Where Extremes Meet: 'SPRAT' versus 'SHARK' in Public Risk Management" in Christopher Hood and David KC Jones (eds), *Accident and Design: Contemporary Debates in Risk Management* (UCL Press 1996)
——, "Risk Management" in The Royal Society (ed), *Risk: Analysis, Perception and Management—A Report of a Royal Society Study Group* (The Royal Society 1992)

—— and Jones DKC, "Anticipationism versus Resilience" in Christopher Hood and David KC Jones (eds), *Accident and Design: Contemporary Debates in Risk Management* (UCL Press 1996)

——, "Should Regulation Be Targeted on Physical Products or Institutional Processes?" in Christopher Hood and David KC Jones (eds), *Accident and Design: Contemporary Debates in Risk Management* (UCL Press 1996)

——, Rothstein H, and Baldwin R, *The Government of Risk—Understanding Risk Regulation Regimes* (OUP 2001)

Hoofnagle CJ, "Big Brother's Little Helpers: How ChoicePoint and Other Commercial Data Brokers Collect and Package Your Data for Law Enforcement" (2004) 29 North Carolina Journal of International Law and Commercial Regulation 595

——, "How the Fair Credit Reporting Act Regulates Big Data", *Future of Privacy Forum Workshop on Big Data and Privacy: Making Ends Meet* (2013) <http://papers.ssrn.com/sol3/papers.cfm?abstract_id=2432955> last accessed 15 March 2019

——, "The Potemkinism of Privacy Pragmatism", *Slate* (2014) 1

Huber M, "Colonised by Risk—The Emergence of Academic Risks in British Higher Education" in Bridget M Hutter (ed), *Anticipating Risks and Organising Risk Regulation* (Cambridge University Press 2010)

Hustinx PJ, "EU Data Protection Law: The Review of Directive 95/46/EC and the Proposed General Data Protection Regulation" (2014)

Hutter BM, *Compliance: Regulation and Environment* (OUP 1997)

——, "Risk, Regulation, and Management" in Peter Taylor-Gooby and Jens Zinn (eds), *Risk in Social Science* (OUP 2006)

ICO, "The Privacy Dividend: The Business Case for Investing in Proactive Privacy Protection. Volume 1—The Business Case" (2010)

——, "The Privacy Dividend: The Business Case for Investing in Proactive Privacy Protection. Volume 2—Supporting Material" (2010)

——, "Big Data and Data Protection" (2014)

——, "Conducting Privacy Impact Assessments: Code of Practice" (2014)

——, "Data Protection Impact Assessments (DPIAs)" (2018)

Information and Privacy Commissioner Ontario Canada, "Privacy Risk Management: Building Privacy Protection into a Risk Management Framework to Ensure That Privacy Risks Are Managed, by Default" (2010)

International Conference of Data Protection and Privacy Commissioners, "Resolution on the Urgent Need for Protecting Privacy in a Borderless World, and for Reaching a Joint Proposal for Setting International Standards on Privacy and Personal Data Protection" (2008)

——, "International Standards on the Protection of Personal Data and Privacy: The Madrid Resolution" (2009)

ISO/EIC, "ISO/EIC 29100: Information Technology: Security Techniques: Privacy Framework" (2011)

——, "ISO/IEC 29134: Information Technology—Security Techniques—Guidelines for Privacy Impact Assessment" (2017)

ISO, "IEC 31010:2009: Risk Management—Risk Assessment Techniques" (2009)

——, "ISO: 31000 Risk Management—Principles and Guidelines"

——, "ISO 31000:2018-02 Risk Management—Guidelines" (2018)

Jacobsson B, "Regulated Regulators: Global Trends of State Transformation" in Marie-Laure Djelic and Kerstin Sahlin-Andersson (eds), *Transnational Governance: Institutional Dynamics of Regulation* (Cambridge University Press 2006)

Jasanoff S, *The Fifth Branch: Science Advisers as Policymakers* (Harvard University Press 1990)
——, "Technologies of Humility: Citizen Participation in Governing Science" (2003) 41 223
——, "The Idiom of Co-Production" in Sheila Jasanoff (ed), *States of Knowledge: The Co-production of Science and Social Order* (Routledge 2004)
——, "Beni Incalcolabili. Reimmaginare Il Nostro Futuro Technologico" in Sheila Jasanoff, Alice Benessia, and Silvio Funtowicz (eds), *L'innovazione tra utopia e storia* (Codice edizioni 2013)
Jay R, *Data Protection Law and Practice* (Sweet & Maxwell 2007)
Jones DKC and Hood C, "Introduction" in Christopher Hood and David KC Jones (eds), *Accident and Design: Contemporary Debates in Risk Management* (UCL Press 1996)
Joss S and Bellucci S, *Participatory Technology Assessment: European Perspectives* (The Athenaeum Press 2002)
Kahneman D and Tversky A, "Prospect Theory: An Analysis of Decision under Risk" (1979) 47 Econometrica: Journal of the Econometric Society 263
Keats Citron D, "Mainstreaming Privacy Torts" (2010) 98 California Law Review 1805
Kelleher JD and Tierney B, *Data Science* (The MIT Press 2018)
Keynes JM, *A Treatise on Probability* (Macmillan 1921)
Klatt M and Meister M, *The Constitutional Structure of Proportionality* (OUP 2012)
Knight FH, *Risk, Uncertainty And Profit* (Century Press 1921)
Koops B-J, "The (In)Flexibility of Techno-Regulation and the Case of Purpose-Binding" (2011) 5 Legisprudence 171
——, "The Trouble with European Data Protection Law" (2014) 4 International Data Privacy Law 250
Korff D, "EC Study on Implementation of Data Protection Directive: Comparative Summary of National Laws" (2002)
——, "EC Study on Implementation of Data Protection Directive—Annex 3: Report on the Findings of the Study" (2002)
Kosta E, *Consent in European Data Protection Law* (Martinus Nijhoff 2013)
Kuner C, "Proportionality in European Data Protection Law And Its Importance for Data Processing Companies" (2008) 7 Privacy & Security Law Report 1615
——, "The "Internal Morality" of European Data Protection Law" (2008)
——, *Transborder Data Flows and Data Privacy Law* (OUP 2013)
——, "Risk Management in Data Protection" (2015) 5 International Data Privacy Law 95
——, "Expanding the Artificial Intelligence-Data Protection Debate" (2018) 8 International Data Privacy Law 289
L'Hoiry XD and Norris C, "The Honest Data Protection Officer's Guide to Enable Citizens to Exercise Their Subject Access Rights: Lessons from a Ten-Country European Study" (2015) 5 International Data Privacy Law 190
Lammerant H and others, "Byte Deliverable D4.2: Evaluating and Addressing Positive and Negative Societal Externalities" (2015)
Laügt O, *Discours d'expert et Democratie* (L'Harmattan 2000)
Leenes R and others (eds), *Data Protection and Privacy: The Internet of Bodies* (Hart Publishing 2018)
Lemon WM, Tatum KW, and Turley S, *Developments in the Audit Methodologies of Large Accounting Firms* (Auditing Practices Board 2000)
Leonard P, "Customer Data Analytics: Privacy Settings for 'Big Data' Business" (2014) 4 International Data Privacy Law 53
Lessig L, *Code 2.0* (Basic Books 2006)

Levi-Faur D, "From 'Big Government' to 'Big Governance'?" in David Levi-Faur (ed), *The Oxford Handbook of Governance* (OUP 2012)
Llewellyn KN, "The Normative, the Legal, and the Law-Jobs: The Problem of Juristic Method" (1940) 49 The Yale Law Journal 1355
Longworth E, "Notes on Privacy Impact Assessments", *Privacy Issues Forum* (1996)
Lynskey O, *The Foundations of EU Data Protection Law* (OUP 2015)
Lyon D (ed), *Surveillance as Social Sorting—Privacy, Risk, and Digital Discrimination* (Routledge 2003)
MacCormick N, *Institutions of Law: An Essay in Legal Theory* (OUP 2007)
Macenaite M, "The "Riskification" of European Data Protection Law through a Two-Fold Shift" (2017) 8 European Journal of Risk Regulation 506
Macrae C, "Regulating Resilience? Regulatory Work in High-Risk Arenas" in Bridget M Hutter (ed), *Anticipating Risks and Organising Risk Regulation* (Cambridge University Press 2010)
Mahieu RLP, Asghari H, and Van Eeten M, "Collectively Exercising the Right of Access: Individual Effort, Societal Effect" (2018) 7 Internet Policy Review 1
Majone G, "Introduction" in Giandomenico Majone (ed), *Deregulation or Re-regulation? Regulatory Reform in Europe and the United States* (Palgrave Macmillan 1990)
——, "Regulation and Its Modes" in Giandomenico Majone (ed), *Regulating Europe* (Routledge 1996)
——, "From the Positive to the Regulatory State: Causes and Consequences of Changes in the Mode of Governance" (1997) 17 Journal of Public Policy 139
Marcus AA, "Implementing Externally Induced Innovations: A Comparison of Rule-Bound and Autonomous Approaches." (1988) 31 Academy of Management Journal 235
Mayer-Schönberger V, "Generational Development of Data Protection in Europe" in Philip E Agre and Marc Rotenberg (eds), *Technology and Privacy: The New Landscape* (MIT Press 1997)
McBarnet D and Whelan C, "The Elusive Spirit of the Law: Formalism and the Struggle for Legal Control" (1991) 54 The Modern Law Review 848
Mendoza I and Bygrave LA, "The Right Not to Be Subject to Automated Decisions Based on Profiling" in Tatiana Eleni Synodinou and others (eds), *EU Internet Law: Regulation and Enforcement* (Springer 2017)
Merton RK, *Social Theory and Social Structure* (The Free Press 1968)
Meyer J, "Globalization and the Expansion and Standardization of Management" in Kerstin Sahlin-Andersson and Lars Engwall (eds), *The Expansion of Management Knowledge: Carriers, Flows and Sources* (Stanford University Press 2002)
Meyer JW and Rowan B, "Institutionalized Organizations : Formal Structure as Myth and Ceremony" (1977) 83 American Journal of Sociology 340
Millard C (ed), *Cloud Computing Law* (OUP 2013)
Miller AR, *The Assault on Privacy: Computers, Data Banks, and Dossiers* (The University of Michigan Press 1971)
Mitchell JK, "Human Dimensions of Environmental Hazards" in Andrew Kirby (ed), *Nothing to Fear: Risks and Hazards in American Society* (University of Arizona Press 1990)
Moerel L, *Big Data Protection—How to Make the Draft EU Regulation on Data Protection Future Proof* (Tilburg University 2014)
—— and Prins C, "Privacy Voor de Homo Digitalis: Proeve van Een Nieuw Toetsingskader Voor Gegevensbescherming in Het Licht van Big Data En Internet of Things" in Nederlandse Juristen-Vereniging (ed), *Homo Digitalis* (Wolters Kluwer 2016)
Monahan T, *Surveillance in the Time of Insecurity* (Rutgers University Press 2010)

Morgan B and Yeung K, *An Introduction to Law and Regulation: Text and Materials* (Cambridge University Press 2007)
Moses LB, "How to Think about Law, Regulation and Technology: Problems with "Technology" as a Regulatory Target" (2013) 1 Law Innovation and Technology 1
Mowbray A, "A Study of the Principle of Fair Balance in the Jurisprudence of the European Court of Human Rights" (2010) 10 Human Rights Law Review 289
Mundie C, "Privacy Pragmatism" *Foreign Affairs* (2014) <https://www.foreignaffairs.com/articles/2014-02-12/privacy-pragmatism> last accessed 19 March 2019
National Institute of Standards and Technology, "NISTIR 8062 (Draft): Privacy Risk Management for Federal Information Systems" (2015)
——, "NISTIR 8062: An Introduction to Privacy Engineering and Risk Management in Federal Systems" (2017)
——, "Risk Management Framework for Information Systems and Organizations A System Life Cycle Approach for Security and Privacy" (2018)
——, "NIST Privacy Framework Working Outline" (2019)
Nissenbaum H, *Privacy in Context: Technology, Policy, and the Integrity of Social Life* (Stanford University Press 2010)
O'Malley P, *Risk, Uncertainty and Government* (Glasshouse Press 2004)
OECD, "Cybersecurity Policy Making at a Turning Point: Analysing a New Generation of National Cybersecurity Strategies for the Internet Economy" (2012)
OECD, Supplementary explanatory memorandum to the revised recommendation of the council concerning guidelines governing the protection of privacy and transborder flows of personal data 2013 19
Offe C, *Contradictions of the Welfare State* (John Keane ed, Hutchinson & Co 1984)
Office of the Australian Information Commissioner, "Guide to Undertaking Privacy Impact Assessments" (2014)
Office of the Chief Information Officer of British Columbia, "Privacy Impact Assessment Guidelines" (2014)
Office of the Information and Privacy Commissioner of Alberta, Office of the Privacy Commissioner of Canada and Office of the Information & Privacy Commissioner for British Columbia, "Getting Accountability Right with a Privacy Management Program" (2012)
——, "Privacy Management Program—At a Glance" (2012)
Office of the Privacy Commissioner for Personal Data of Hong Kong, "Privacy Management Programme: A Best Practice Guide" (2014)
Office of the Privacy Commissioner of Canada, "Privacy Toolkit—A Guide for Businesses and Organizations—Canada's Personal Information Protection and Electronic Documents Act" (2015)
——, *A Guide for Businesses and Organisations: Privacy Toolkit* (2014)
Ogus AI, *Regulation: Legal Form and Economic Theory* (Hart Publishing 2004)
Ohm P, "Broken Promises of Privacy: Responding to the Surprising Failure of Anonymization" (2010) 57 UCLA Law Review 1701
Packard V, *The Naked Society* (Van Rees Press 1964)
Parker C, "Compliance-Oriented Regulatory Innovation" (2000) 32 Administration and Society 529
——, *The Open Corporation: Effective Self-Regulation and Democracy* (Cambridge University Press 2002)
——, "Introduction", *Regulating Law* (OUP 2004)
—— and Evans A, *Inside Lawyers' Ethics* (Cambridge University Press 2006)

Peretti-Watel P, *La Société Du Risque* (Repères, La Découverte 2010)
Perrow C, *Normal Accidents: Living With High-Risk Technologies*" (Basic Books 1984)
Pocs M, "Will the European Commission Be Able to Standardise Legal Technology Design without a Legal Method?" (2012) 28 Computer Law & Security Review 641
Popelier P and Heyning C Van De, "Procedural Rationality: Giving Teeth to the Proportionality Analysis" (2014) 9 European Constitutional Law Review 230
Porcedda MG, "On Boundaries—Finding the Essence of the Right to the Protection of Personal Data" in Ronald Leenes and others (eds), *Data Protection and Privacy: The Internet of Bodies* (Hart Publishing 2018)
Porter TM, *Trust in Numbers: The Pursuit of Objectivity in Science and Public Life* (Princeton University Press 1995)
Poullet Y, "EU Data Protection Policy. The Directive 95/46/EC: Ten Years After" (2006) 22 Computer Law & Security Review 206
Pound R, "Law in Books and Law in Action" (1910) 44 American Law Review 12
Power M, *The Audit Society: Rituals of Verification* (OUP 1997)
——, "The Audit Implosion: Regulating Risk from the Inside" (1999)
——, "Auditing and the Production of Legitimacy" (2003) 28 Accounting, Organizations and Society 379
——, "Risk Management and the Responsible Organisation" in Richard V Ericson and Aaron Doyle (eds), *Risk and Morality* (University of Toronto Press 2003)
——, *The Risk Management of Everything—Rethinking the Politics of Uncertainty* (Demos 2004)
——, *Organized Uncertainty: Designing a World of Risk Management* (OUP 2007)
Prins JEJ *et al.*, *In Het Licht van de Wet Persoonsregistraties: Zon, Maan of Ster?* (Samsom 1995)
Prosser T, *Nationalised Industries and Public Control: Legal, Constitutional, and Political Issues* (Willey Blackwell 1986)
Quelle C, "The Data Protection Impact Assessment: What Can It Contribute to Data Protection?" (2015) <https://arno.uvt.nl/show.cgi?fid=139503> last accessed 20 March 2019
——, "The "Risk Revolution" in EU Data Protection Law: We Can't Have Our Cake and Eat It, Too" in Ronald Leenes and others (eds), *Data Protection and Privacy: The Age of Intelligent Machines* (Hart Publishing 2017)
Raab CD and Bennett CJ, *The Governance of Privacy: Policy Instruments in Global Perspective* (MIT Press 2006)
—— and Wright D, "Surveillance: Extending the Limits of Privacy Impact Assessment" in David Wright and Paul De Hert (eds), *Privacy Impact Assessment* (Springer 2012)
Regan PM, *Legislating Privacy: Technology, Social Values, and Public Policy* (The University of North Carolina Press 1995)
Richards NM, "The Dangers of Surveillance" (2013) 126 Harvard Law Review 1934
Robinson N and others, "Review of the European Data Protection Directive" 1
Ross J, "Legally Binding Prior Informed Consent" (1999) 10 Colorado Journal of International Law and Policy 499
Rostain T, "Self-Regulatory Authority, Markets, and the Ideology of Professionalism" in Robert Baldwin, Martin Cave, and Martin Lodge (eds), *The Oxford Handbook of Regulation* (OUP 2010)
Rothstein H and others, "The Risks of Risk-Based Regulation: Insights from the Environmental Policy Domain" (2006) 32 Environment International 1056
——, Huber M, and Gaskell G, "A Theory of Risk Colonization: The Spiralling Regulatory Logics of Societal and Institutional Risk" (2006) 35 Economy and Society 91

Ruebhausen OM, "Foreword", *Privacy and Freedom* (Atheneum 1967)
Rule JB, *Private Lives and Public Surveillance* (The Trinity Press 1973)
——, *Privacy in Peril: How We Are Sacrificing a Fundamental Right in Exchange for Security and Convenience* (OUP 2007)
——, *The Politics of Privacy: Planning for Personal Data Systems as Powerful Technologies* (Elsevier 1980)
Schauer F, *Playing by the Rules: A Philosophical Examination of Rule-Based Decision-Making in Law and Life* (OUP 1991)
Schwartz PM, "Privacy, Participation, and Cyberspace: An American Perspective" in Bruno Baeriswyl and Beat Rudin (eds), *Perspektive Datenschutz: Praxis und Entwicklungen in Recht und Technik* (Schutless Juristiche Medien AG 2002)
Selznick P, "Focusing Organizational Research on Regulation" in Roger G Noll (ed), *Regulatory Policy and the Social Sciences* (The University of California Press 1985)
Shapiro SS, "Situating Anonymization Within a Privacy Risk Model" [2012] 2012 IEEE International Systems Conference (SysCon) 651
Shrader-Frechette K, *Risk and Rationality: Philosophical Foundations for Populist Reforms* (University of California Press 1991)
Sieghart P, *Privacy and Computers* (Latimer 1976)
——, "Information Privacy and the Data Protection Bill" in Colin Bourn and John Benyon (eds), *Data Protection: Perspectives on Information Privacy* (University of Leicester 1984)
SIRA Consulting, "Toetsing Europese Dataprotectieverordening" (2013)
Smart Grid Task Force, "Data Protection Impact Assessment Template for Smart Grid and Smart Metering Systems" (2014)
Solove DJ, *Understanding Privacy* (Harvard University Press 2008)
——, "Privacy Self-Management and the Consent Dilemma" (2013) 126 Harvard Law Review 1880
Spackman M, "Serving the Public Interest?" (2002) 3 Risk and Regulation: CARR Review 6
Speer L, "Variable Funding of EU Privacy Law Means Uneven Enforcement Across European Union" (2007) 7 Privacy & Security Law Report 49
Spiekermann S, "The RFID PIA—Developed by Industry, Endorsed by Regulators" in David Wright and Paul De Hert (eds), *Privacy Impact Assessment* (Springer 2012)
Spina A, "A Regulatory Mariage de Figaro: Risk Regulation, Data Protection, and Data Ethics" (2017) 8 European Journal of Risk Regulation 88
Starr C, "Social Benefit versus Technological Risk" (1969) 165 Science 1232
Steele J, *Risks and Legal Theory* (Hart Publishing 2004)
Steger MB and Roy RK, *Neoliberalism: A Very Short Introduction* (OUP 2010)
Stewart B, "PIAs—An Early Warning System" (1996) 3 Privacy Law and Policy Reporter 134
Stirling A, "Risk at a Turning Point ?" [1999] Journal of Environmental Medicine 119
Sturm S, "Second Generation Employment Discrimination: A Structural Approach" (2001) 101 Columbia Law Review 458
Tadros V, "Between Governance and Discipline: The Law and Michel Foucault" (1998) 18 Oxford Journal of Legal Studies 75
Tancock D, Pearson S, and Charlesworth A, "Analysis of Privacy Impact Assessments within Major Jurisdictions" [2010] 8th International Conference on Privacy, Security and Trust 118
Taylor-Gooby P and Zinn J (eds), *Risk in Social Science* (OUP 2006)
Teubner G, *Dilemmas of Law in the Welfare State* (De Gruyter 1986)
The Centre for Information Policy Leadership, "Data Protection Accountability: The Essential Elements" (2009)

——, "Demonstrating and Measuring Accountability: A Discussion Document Accountability Phase II—The Paris Project October 2010" (2010)

——, "Implementing Accountability in the Marketplace: A Discussion Document Accountability Phase III—The Madrid Project November 2011" (2011)

Torfing C and Ansell J (eds), *Handbook on Theories of Governance* (Edward Elgar 2016)

Tranberg CB, "Proportionality and Data Protection in the Case Law of the European Court of Justice" (2011) 1 International Data Privacy Law 239

Twining W, *Globalisation & Legal Theory* (Butterworths 2000)

US Department of Health Education & Welfare, *Records, Computers, and the Rights of Citizens* (The MIT Press 1973)

US President's Council of Advisors on Science and Technology, "Report to the President—Big Data and Privacy: A Technological Perspective" (2014)

Van Der Sloot B, "From Data Minimization to Data Minimummization" in Bart Custers and others (eds), *Discrimination and Privacy in the Information Society: Data Mining and Profiling in Large Databases* (Springer-Verlag 2013)

——, "The Individual in the Big Data Era: Moving towards an Agent-Based Privacy Paradigm" in Bart Van Der Sloot, Dennis Broeders, and Erik Schrijvers (eds), *Exploring the Boundaries of Big Data* (Amsterdam University Press 2016)

van Dijk N, Gellert R, and Rommetveit K, "A Risk to a Right? Beyond Data Protection Risk Assessments" (2016) 32 Computer Law & Security Review 286

Van Gerven W, "Principe de Proportionnalité, Abus de Droit et Droits Fondamentaux" [1992] Journal des Tribunaux 305

Van Hoboken J, "From Collection to Use in Privacy Regulation? A Forward-Looking Comparison of European and US Frameworks for Personal Data Processing" in Bart Van Der Sloot, Dennis Broeders, and Erik Schrijvers (eds), *Exploring the Boundaries of Big Data* (Amsterdam University Press 2016)

Veale M, Binns R, and Ausloos J, "When Data Protection by Design and Data Subject Rights Clash" (2018) 8 International Data Privacy Law 105

Veljanovski CG, "Regulatory Enforcement: An Economic Study of the British Factory Inspectorate" (1983) 5 Law and Policy Quarterly 75

Vodafone, "A Comprehensive Approach on Personal Data Protection in the European Union: Vodafone's Response" (2010) <http://ec.europa.eu/justice/news/consulting_public/news_consulting_0006_en.htm> last accessed 06 February 2019

Voltaire, *Candide* (Millenium Publications 2014)

Warner F, "Introduction" in The Royal Society (ed), *Risk: Analysis, Perception and Management—A Report of a Royal Society Study Group* (The Royal Society 1992)

Warren SD and Brandeis LD, "The Right to Privacy" (1890) IV Harvard Law Review 193

Waters N, "Privacy Law and Policy Reporter" (1996) 3 Privacy Law and Policy Reporter 61

Weber RH, "Privacy Management Practices in the Proposed EU Regulation" (2014) 4 International Data Privacy Law 290

Weinberg AM, "Science and Trans-Science" (1972) 10 Minerva 209

Westin A, *Privacy and Freedom* (Atheneum 1967)

——, "Entering the Era of Databank Regulation and How We Got There" in OECD (ed), *Policy Issues in Data Protection and Privacy—Principles and Perspectives* (OECD 1976)

—— and Baker MA, *Databanks in a Free Society: Computers, Record Keeping and Privacy* (Quadrangle Books 1972)

William B and Chiasson M, "If Fair Information Principles Are the Answer, What Was the Question? An Actor-Network Theory Investigation of the Modern Constitution of Privacy" (2005) 15 Information and Organization 267

Wilson GK, "Social Regulation and Explanations of Regulatory Failure" (1984) 32 Political Studies 203
World Economic Forum, "Rethinking Personal Data: A New Lens for Strengthening Trust" (2014)
Wright D, "The State of the Art in Privacy Impact Assessment" (2012) 28 Computer Law & Security Review 54
——, "SAPIENT, Deliverable 3.1 Privacy Impact Assessment and Smart Surveillance: A State of the Art Report" (2013)
——, "Surveillance Impact Assessment Manual" (2014)
—— and De Hert P (eds), *Privacy Impact Assessment* (Springer 2012)
—— (eds), *Enforcing Privacy: Regulatory, Legal and Technological Approaches* (Springer 2016)
——, Friedewald M, and Gellert R, "Developing and Testing a Surveillance Impact Assessment Methodology" (2015) 5 International Data Privacy Law 40
—— and Raab C, "Privacy Principles, Risks and Harms" (2014) 28 International Review of Law, Computers & Technology 1
Wuyts K, "Privacy Threats in Software Architectures" (2015)
Wynne B, "Uncertainty and Environmental Learning—Reconceiving Science and Policy in the Preventive Paradigm" (1992) 2 Global Environmental Change 111
Yeung K, *Securing Compliance: A Principled Approach* (Hart Publishing 2004)
Younger K, *Report of the Committee on Privacy* (Stationery Office Books 1972)
Zanfir G, "Forgetting About Consent. Why The Focus Should Be On 'Suitable Safeguards" in Data Protection Law' in Serge Gutwirth, Ronald Leenes, and Paul De Hert (eds), *Reloading Data Protection—Multidisciplinary Insights and Contemporary Challenges* (Springer 2014)

Index

For the benefit of digital users, indexed terms that span two pages (e.g., 52–53) may, on occasion, appear on only one of those pages.